Instructor's Manual and Test Bank

The Leadership Experience

THIRD EDITION

Richard L. Daft
Vanderbilt University

Prepared by

Susan M. Leshnower
Midland College

Australia · Canada · Mexico · Singapore · Spain · United Kingdom · United States

THOMSON

SOUTH-WESTERN

Instructor's Manual with Test Bank

to accompany

The Leadership Experience, Third Edition

Richard L. Daft

Prepared by Susan M. Leshnower

VP/Editorial Director:
Jack W. Calhoun

VP/Editor-in-Chief:
Mike Roche

Acquisitions Editor:
Joe Sabatino

Developmental Editor:
Emma Guttler

Marketing Manager:
Jacquelyn Carrillo

Production Editor:
Cliff Kallemeyn

Technology Project Editor:
Kristen Meere

Media Editor:
Karen Schaffer

Designer:
Michelle Kunkler

Manufacturing Coordinator:
Rhonda Utley

Printer:
Globus Printing, Minster OH

Printed in the United States of America
1 2 3 4 5 07 06 05 04

ISBN: 0-324-23637-9

For more information
contact South-Western,
5191 Natorp Boulevard,
Mason, Ohio 45040.
Or you can visit our Internet site at:
http://www.swlearning.com

TABLE OF CONTENTS

TABLE OF CONTENTS

PART I: INTRODUCTION TO LEADERSHIP

PART II: RESEARCH PERSPECTIVES ON LEADERSHIP

PART III: THE PERSONAL SIDE OF LEADERSHIP

PART IV: THE LEADER AS A RELATIONSHIP BUILDER

PART V: THE LEADER AS SOCIAL ARCHITECT

CHAPTER ONE
WHAT DOES IT MEAN TO BE A LEADER?

CHAPTER SUMMARY

This chapter introduces the concept of leadership and explains how individuals grow as leaders. Leadership is defined as an influence relationships among leaders and followers who intend real changes and outcomes that reflect their shared purposes. Concepts of leadership have evolved over time. Major research approaches include Great Man theories, behavior theories, situational theories, influence theories, and relational theories.

The biggest challenge facing leaders today is the changing world that wants a new paradigm of leadership. The new reality involves the shift from stability to change and crisis management, from control to empowerment, from competition to collaboration from uniformity to diversity, and from a self-centered focus to a higher purpose. The challenge for leaders is to evolve a new mindset that relies on human skills, integrity, and teamwork.

Although leadership is often equated with good management, leadership and management are different processes. Management strives to maintain stability and improve efficiency. Leadership, on the other hand, is about creating a vision for the future, designing social architecture that shapes culture and values, inspiring and motivating followers, developing personal qualities, and creating change, to improve organizational effectiveness. Most people are not born with natural leadership skills and qualities, but leadership can be learned and developed.

CHAPTER OPENER

Leadership at MTV

You may have never heard of Tom Freston, but almost everyone in the United States—and many other parts of the world---has watched on of the successful cable television channels built on the strength of his leadership. What does it mean to be a leader? For Tom Freston, it means loving what you do and infusing others with energy and enthusiasm. It means creating an inspiring vision and building an environment where people have the ability, the freedom, and the will to accomplish amazing results.

LECTURE/OUTLINE

---

1. To understand the full meaning of leadership and see the leadership potential in yourself and others.

The Nature of Leadership *Exhibit 1.1*

➢ *What does leadership mean?*

Leadership has been a topic of interest to historians and philosophers since ancient times, but scientific studies began only in the twentieth century.

Defining leadership has been a complex and elusive problem because the nature of leadership is complex.

Some have suggested that leadership is nothing more than a romantic myth.

In recent years, however, much progress has been made in understanding the essential nature of leadership as a real and powerful influence in organizations and societies.

Definition of Leadership

Leadership is an influence relationship among leaders and followers who intend real changes that reflect their shared purposes.

Leadership involves influence, it occurs among people, those people intentionally desire significant changes, and the changes reflect purposes shared by leaders and followers.

Influence means that the relationship among people is not passive; it is multidirectional and non-coercive.

Leadership is reciprocal. Superiors influence subordinates, but subordinates also influence superiors.

Leadership involves creating changes which reflects purposes leaders and followers share.

Leadership is a people activity and is distinct from administrative paperwork or planning.

It occurs *among* people; it is not something done to people. Since leadership involves people, there must be followers.

Good leaders know how to follow, and they set an example for others.

Leadership is shared among leaders and followers, with everyone fully engaged and accepting higher levels of responsibility.

➢ *Is a musician or athlete who is an expert considered a leader?* (Only if followers are involved.)

The qualities for effective leaders are the same as those needed for an effective follower.

Effective followers think for themselves and carry out assignments with energy and enthusiasm.

Discussion Question #1: *What do you consider your own strengths and weaknesses for leadership? Discuss your answer with another student.*

Notes____

Leadership and the Business of Living

By not equating leadership with "greatness" and public visibility, it becomes easier to see our own opportunities for leadership and recognize the leadership of people we interact with every day.

Leadership that has big outcomes often starts small.

There are opportunities for leadership all around us that involve influence and change toward a desired goal or outcome.

Leadership is an everyday way of acting and thinking that has little to do with a niche or formal position in an organization.

➢ *What opportunities for leadership do you recognize at hand?*

Discussion Question #3: *Of the elements in the leadership definition in Exhibit 1.1, which is the easiest for you? Which is hardest? Explain.*

Notes____

---

2. To recognize and facilitate the six fundamental transformations in today's organizations and leaders.

The New Reality for Today's Organization *Exhibit 1.2*

The world of organizations is changing rapidly through---globalization, deregulation, e-commerce, telecommuting, virtual teams, and. outsourcing.

People feel the impact of these trends and must adapt to new ways of working

Economic uncertainty, wide-spread ethical scandals, war, and terrorism make leaders face a tough job in keeping people grounded, focused, and motivated.

Rapid environmental changes are causing fundamental shifts from a traditional to a new paradigm.

A *paradigm* is a shared mindset that represents a fundamental way of thinking about, perceiving, and understanding the world.

Although many leaders are still operating from an old-paradigm mind-set, they are increasingly ineffective.

Successful leaders will respond to the new reality.

From Cherishing Stability to Valuing Change

Today's world is in constant motion and nothing seems certain anymore.

➢ *What events have shattered the illusion of stability?*

Most leaders realize that trying to maintain stability is a losing battle.

The new paradigm acknowledges, as suggested by the science of chaos theory, that we live in a complex world characterized by randomness and uncertainty and small events have far-reaching consequences.

The pervasiveness of change has taught leaders to actively embrace and create changes within the organization to develop workers and move the organization forward.

Discussion Question #2: *How do you feel about changing yourself in order to become a leader who can change an organization?*

Notes____

____

____

From Control to Empowerment

Traditionally, leaders thought workers should be told what to do, how to do it, and when to do it, and with whom to do it.; they believed in strict control.

Today's leaders need to share power rather than hoard it and find ways to increase an organization's brain power by getting everyone in the organization involved and committed.

One reason is that the financial basis of today's economy is rapidly becoming *information* rather than the tangible assets of land, buildings, and machines.

The primary factor of production is human knowledge which increases the power of employees.

➢ *Do today's highly-educated workers want only good salaries or do they insist upon interesting and challenging jobs?*

Today, one of the leader's most challenging jobs is to guide workers in using their own power effectively and responsibly by creating and developing a climate of respect and development.

Discussion Question #4: *What does the paradigm shift from control to empowerment mean for you? Discuss.*

Notes____

____

____

From Competition to Collaboration

Although some companies encourage competition and aggressiveness, today's organization's are stressing teamwork and cooperation.

Self-directed teams and other forms of horizontal collaboration are breaking down boundaries between departments and helping to spread knowledge and information throughout the organization.

The concept of *knowledge management,* which relies on a culture of sharing rather than hoarding information, has firmly taken hold in many companies.

There is a growing trend toward reducing boundaries and increasing collaboration as many companies think of themselves as teams that value creativity jointly rather than as autonomous entities in competition with all others.

A new form of global business is composed of networks of independent companies that share financial risks and leadership talents and provide access to one another's technologies and markets.

Within the organization, leaders will need to create an environment of teamwork and community that fosters collaboration and mutual support.

Use Discussion Question #5: *Describe the best leader you have known. How did this leader acquire his or her capability?*

Notes____

____

____

From Uniformity to Diversity

Many of today's organizations were built on assumptions of uniformity, separation, and specialization.

People who think alike, act alike, and have similar jobs skills are grouped into a homogeneous department (e.g., accounting) separate from the remainder of the organization.

The uniform thinking that arises can be a disaster in a world becoming more multi-national and diverse.

The world is rapidly moving towards diversity at both the national and international levels.

In the United States, roughly 40 percent of all additions to the labor force will be non-white—half will be first-generation immigrants, mostly from Asia and Latin countries.

Almost two-thirds will be female.

Diversity is the way to attract the best talent and to develop a broad organizational mind-set.

From Self-Centered to Higher Purpose

The old-paradigm emphasis on individual ability, success, and prosperity sometimes pushed leaders to cross the line, culminating in organizational corruption on a broad scale (e.g., Enron).

New-paradigm leaders emphasize accountability, integrity, and responsibility to something larger than self-interest, including employees, customers, the firm, and all stakeholders.

From Hero to Humble

There is a shift from the celebrity "leader-as-hero" to the hard-working behind-the-scenes leader who builds a strong enduring company by supporting and developing others.

The new-paradigm leader is characterized by an almost complete lack of ego. Author Jim Collins calls this new breed Level 5 leaders, those who often seem shy and unpretentious.

➢ *Despite personal humility, how do ambitious new-paradigm leaders produce great and lasting results for their organizations?*

Discussion Question #7: *Discuss some recent events and societal changes that might have contributed to a shift "from hero to humble." Do you agree or disagree that humility is important for good leadership?*

Notes____

***In the Lead*:** Reuben Mark, Colgate-Palmolive.

The CEO of Colgate-Palmolive since 1984, Reuben Mark consistently shuns publicity and turns down requests for media profiles about him. Mark's brand of leadership ardently emphasizes teamwork over individual accomplishment. Mark wants his company to be a superstar, not him. Since Mark took over, profit margins have risen from 39 to 54 percent and earnings have grown at an annual rate of 12.8 percent. Mark is known for being indifferent to privilege. He answers his own phone frequently and travels overseas on a regular flight not a corporate jet. One analyst who follows Colgate for USB Warburg says many of Mark's employees "would take a bullet for him."

Q: *Describe Reuben Mark as a new-paradigm leader.*

A: Reuben Mark has built a strong organization by creating an open, nonhierarchical culture emphasizing continuous improvement and steady growth, suppressing his own ego and sharing credit with his employees, and staying focused on long-term success rather than short-term profits.

---

3. To recognize the traditional functions of management and the fundamental differences between leadership and management.

Comparing Management to Leadership *Exhibit 1.3*

The new paradigm reflects a shift from a traditional, rational management approach that emphasizes stability and control to a leadership approach that values change, empowerment, and relationships.

The study of leadership begins by considering what distinguishes the process of leadership from management.

Management can be defined as the attainment of organizational goals in an effective and efficient manner through planning organizing, staffing, directing, and controlling organizational resources.

With current emphasis of leadership, managers have gotten a bad name. Many managers possess abilities and qualities to be effective leaders.

Leadership cannot replace management; it should be in addition to management.

Notes____

4. To appreciate the crucial importance of providing direction, alignment, relationships, personal qualities, and outcomes.

Providing Direction

Both leadership and management provide direction for the organization.

Management focuses on establishing detailed plans and schedules for achieving specific results, then allocating resources to accomplish the plan.

Leadership calls for creating a compelling vision of the future and developing farsighted strategies for producing the changes needed to achieve that vision.

A *vision* is a picture of an ambitious, desirable future for the organization or team. To be compelling for followers, the vision has to be one that they can relate to and share.

➢ *Ask students to cite examples of a vision.* (IKEA: to provide affordable furniture for people with limited budgets)

Aligning Followers

Management entails organizing a structure to accomplish the plan; staffing the structure with employees; and developing policies, procedures, and systems to direct employees and monitor implementation of the plan.

Managers are thinkers and workers are doers.

Leadership is concerned with communicating the vision and developing a shared culture and set of core values that can lead to the desired future state.

This involves others as thinkers, doers, and leaders themselves.

Leaders encourage people to expand their minds and abilities and to assume responsibility for their own actions.

Notes____

____

____

Building Relationships

Management focuses on objects such as machines and reports, on taking the steps needed to produce the organization's goods and services.

Leadership focuses on motivating and inspiring people.

Management relationship is based on formal authority.

Formal *position power* means that there is a written, spoken, or implied, contract wherein people accept a superior or subordinate role and see the use of coercive and noncoercive behavior as acceptable to achieve results.

Leadership relies on influence, which is less likely to use coercion

Leadership power comes from the personal character of the leader.

➢ *Cite examples showing that leadership depends on who you are rather than on your position or title.*

Notes____

- ❑ *Living Leadership: A Lesson for Leaders*

General Colin Power: *"The day soldiers stop bringing you their problems is the day you stop leading them."*

➢ According to Powell, real leaders make themselves available. Do you agree?

Developing Personal Leadership Qualities

Leadership is more than a set of skills, it relies on subtle personal qualities that are hard to see but are very powerful.

Good leadership springs from passion for the work and a genuine concern for other people; management encourages emotional distance.

Where there is leadership, people become part of a community and feel they are contributing to something worthwhile.

True leaders tend to have an open mind, care about others, and build personal connections.

Leaders listen and are willing to say no.

They step outside the traditional boundary and comfort zone. Leaders are honest with themselves and others to the point of developing trust.

True leaders draw on a number of subtle but powerful forces within themselves.

They set high moral standards by doing the right thing, rather than just going along with standards set by others.

Notes

In the Lead: Frances Hesselbein and the Girl Scout Way

Frances Hesselbein began her career more than 40 years ago as a volunteer Scout leader and rose to CEO of the Girl Scouts, a troubled organization of 680,000 people of whom 1 percent were paid. When she retired in 1990, Hesselbein had turned around declining membership, dramatically increased participation by minorities, and replaced a brittle hierarchy with a vibrant organization. Hesselbein would listen carefully and link people in such a way that their personal needs were met at the same time they were serving the needs of the organization.

Q: *How was Frances Hesselbein a new-paradigm leader?*

A: Hesselbein realized that the only way to achieve high performance is through the work of others, and she consistently treats people with respect. She feels that taking people for granted is contrary to the definition of what makes a leader.

Creating Outcomes

The differences between management and leadership create two different outcomes.

Management produces a degree of stability, predictability, and order through a *culture of efficiency.* This helps the organization achieve short-term results.

Leadership creates change within a *culture of integrity* that helps the organization thrive over the long haul by promoting openness and honesty, positive relationships, and a long-term focus.

Leadership means questioning and challenging the status quo so that outdated or unproductive norms can be replaced to meet new challenges.

Good leadership can lead to valuable change such as new products or services that gain new customers or expand markets.

Discussion Question #6: *Why do you think there are so few people who succeed at both management and leadership? Is it reasonable to believe someone can be good at both?*

Notes

---

5. To realize how historical leadership approaches apply to the practice of leadership today.

Evolving Theories of Leadership

- ➢ *To understand leadership as it viewed today, why is it important to recognize how leadership has evolved over time?* (Leadership reflects the larger society that has changed.)

Historical Overview of Major Approaches

The various leadership theories can be categorized into six basic approaches, many of which are applicable to leadership studies today.

Great Man Theories

The earliest studies of leadership adopted the belief that leaders were born with certain heroic leadership traits and natural abilities of power and influence.

Leadership was conceptualized s a single "Great Man" who put everything together and influenced others to follow along based on inherited traits, qualities, and abilities.

Trait Theories

Beginning in the 1920s, researchers looked to see if leaders had particular traits or characteristics, such as intelligence height, or energy that distinguished them from nonleaders.

Although research failed to produce a list of traits, the interest in leadership characteristics has continued to the present day.

Behavior Theories

In the 1950s, researchers began looking at what a leader does, rather than who he or she is.

Researchers looked at how a leader behaved toward followers—whether autocratic or democratic and how this correlated with leadership effectiveness.

Situational Theories

Researchers next began to consider the contextual and situational variables that influence what leadership behaviors will be effective.

Situational theories emphasize that leadership cannot be understood in a vacuum separate from various elements of the group or organizational situation.

Influence Theories

These theories examine influence processes between leaders and followers.
One primary topic of study is *charismatic leadership.*

Theories of charismatic leadership attempt to identify how charismatic leaders behave, how they differ from other people, and the conditions that give rise to charismatic leadership.

Relational Theories

Since the late 1970s, many ideas of leadership have focused on the relational aspect---how leaders and followers interact and influence one another.

Leadership is viewed as a relational process that meaningfully engages all participants and enables each person to contribute to achieving the vision.

Emerging Leadership Theories

The understanding of the world as "turbulent, ever-changing, risky, and always challenging" is being translated into new concepts of what it means to be a leader.

In this view, *facilitating change* is the key aspect to be a leader.

Discussion Question #8: *"Leadership is more concerned with people than is management." Do you agree? Discuss.*

Notes____

____

____

---

6. To identify the primary reasons for leadership derailment and the new paradigm skills that can help you avoid it.

Leadership is Not Automatic

Exhibit 1.4

Many leaders are caught in the transition between the practices and principles that defined the industrial era and the new reality of the twenty-first century.

Attempts to achieve collaboration, empowerment, and diversity may fail because leaders and employees have beliefs and though processes stuck in the old paradigm that values control, stability, and homogeneity.

One of the most important aspects of the new paradigm of leadership is the ability to use human skills to build a culture of performance, trust, and integrity.

A study compared 21 derailed executives with 20 executives who successfully arrived at the top of the company.

The derailed managers had reached a plateau, were fired, or were forced to retire early.

The successful executives had good people skills; the best leaders are deeply interested in others.

➢ *What is your experience with CEOs who have good or bad people skills?*

In the Lead: David Pottruck, Charles Schwab & Co.

David Pottruck, now co-CEO of Charles Schwab & Co., spent years thinking he was a great leader, even as people around him cowered in fear. His strict, demanding, ego-centric approach left hard feelings and damaged self-esteem almost everywhere he went. Pottruck's boss told him that people didn't like working with him and didn't trust him. Pottruck hired an executive coach to help him transform his approach to one that valued the ideas and input of others. He says his new leadership approach centers on authenticity---constantly communicating with employees and being honest with them about the company's current problems and painful restructuring and layoffs.

Q: *How did Pottruck become a new-paradigm leader?*

A: The new paradigm reflects a shift from a rational management approach that emphasizes control to a leadership approach that values change, empowerment, and relationships. As financial and ethical scandals have rocked the corporate world, Pottruck believes leaders more than even need to be self-aware and able to manage their own emotions so they treat people well and do the right thing.

Discussion Question #9: *What personal capacities should a person develop to be a good leaders versus those developed to be a good manager?*

Notes____

____

____

Learning the Art and Science of Leadership

- *How can a book on leadership help you to become a better leader?*

Leadership is both an art and a science.

It is an art because many leadership skills and qualities cannot be learned from a textbook.

Leadership takes practice and hands-on experience.

Learning about leadership research helps people analyze situations from a variety of perspectives and learn how to be effective as leaders.

Leadership is a science because a growing body of knowledge and objective facts describe the leadership process and how to use leadership skills to attain organizational goals.

Studying leadership provides skills that help in the practice of leadership in everyday life.

This book is designed to help students gain a firm knowledge of what leadership means and some of the skills and qualities that make a good leader.

Discussion Question #10: *Why is leadership considered both an art and a science?*

Notes____

Organization of the Rest of the Book *Exhibit 1.5*

The plan for this book reflects the shift to the new paradigm and the discussion of management versus leadership.

Part 1 introduces leadership, its importance, and the transition to the new leadership paradigm.

Part 2 explores research perspectives that evolved during a more stable time to include: the Great Man and trait theories, behavior theories, and contingency theories.

Parts 3, 4, and 5 switch to leadership perspectives that reflect the paradigm shift to the chaotic, unpredictable nature of the environment and the need for fresh leader approaches.

Part 3 focuses on the personal side of leadership and looks at the qualities and forces required to be effective in the new reality.

Part 4 is about building effective relationships, including motivating and empowering others, communicating as a leader, leading teams, embracing diversity, and using power and influence.

Part 5 brings together all of these ideas to examine the leader as builder of a social architecture that can help create a brighter future.

Notes____

DISCUSSION QUESTIONS

1. *What do you consider your own strengths and weaknesses for leadership? Discuss your answer with another student.*

Leadership involves the following elements: influence, intention, personal, responsibility, change, shared purpose, and followers. Leadership is a people activity, which occurs among people so it is helpful to have strong people skills. Since leadership involves people, there must be followers. Good followers know how to follow and set an example for others. Intention means that people are actively involved in the pursuit of change. Each person takes personal responsibility to achieve the desired future. Leadership is shared among leaders and followers, with everyone fully engaged.

2. *How do you feel about changing yourself in order to become a leader who can change an organization?*

If we stop equating leadership with "greatness" and public visibility, it becomes easier to see our own opportunities for leadership and recognize the leadership of people with whom we interact every day. Leaders come in all shapes and sizes, and many true leaders are working behind the scenes. There are opportunities for leadership all around us that involve influence and change toward a desired future.

3. *Of the elements in the leadership definition in Exhibit 1.1, which is the easiest for you? Which is hardest? Explain.*

The leaders of tomorrow's organization will come from anywhere and everywhere. You can start now, wherever you are, to practice leadership in your own life. Leadership is an everyday way of acting and thinking that has little to do with a title or formal position.

4. *What does the paradigm shift from control to empowerment mean for you? Discuss.*

Today, one of the leader's most challenging jobs is to guide workers in using their own power effectively and responsibly by creating and developing a climate of respect and development. Power lies more in the strength and quality of relationships rather than in titles, policies, and procedures. Empowerment is an entirely new way of looking at organizational behavior. It takes much more skill to delegate and make employees participate in decision-making than to follow strict policies and procedures.

5. *Describe the best leader you have known. How did this leader acquire his or her capability?*

Students will give examples such as the following: As president of the Midland-Odessa Symphony & Chorale, Ingrid Zeeck had a vision for the organization and the ability to inspire other volunteers to carry out the vision. She selected good volunteers who had the appropriate skills for each committee and worked with the volunteers using a team approach. She always listened to their ideas and incorporated them into the project. She made both volunteers and staff members feel important and always recognized their efforts.

6. *Why do you think there are so few people who succeed at both management and leadership? Is it reasonable to believe someone can be good at both? Discuss.*

Management and leadership are both important, but it is often difficult for CEOs to focus on both dimensions of their job. Traditional management is needed to meet current obligations to customers, stockholders, employees, and others. The problem is that too many people are doing management, two few providing leadership, and fewer still who have integrated the skills and qualities needed for meeting both leadership and management challenges.

Organizations need leaders to visualize the future, motivate and inspire employees, and adapt to changing needs. Jack Welsh of General Electric is one of the best-known examples of a business executive who combines good management and effective leadership. He understands and practices good management such as cost control but is a master leader, actively promoting change and communicating a vision.

7. *Discuss some recent events and societal changes that might have contributed to a shift "from hero to humble." Do you agree or disagree that humility is important for good leadership?*

The events of September 11th showed the world how the firefighters of New York were humble leaders, dedicated to the greater good rather than their own personal advancement. They ran into the twin towers to save others. Humility is important for good leadership because it places the focus is on getting the job done rather than self-aggrandizement.

8. "*Leadership is more concerned with people than is management." Do you agree? Discuss.*

Human skills are increasingly important for leaders in today's economy. Leadership means being emotionally connected to others. Where there is leadership, people become part of a community and feel that they are contributing to something worthwhile. Unfortunately, attempts to achieve collaboration, empowerment, and diversity may fail because leaders and employees have beliefs and though processes stuck in the old paradigm that values control, stability, and homogeneity---rather than people.

9. *What personal capacities should a person develop to be a good leaders versus those developed to be a good manager?*

One of the most important aspects of the new paradigm of leadership is the ability to use human skills to build a culture of performance, trust, and integrity. A study compared 21 derailed executives with 20 executives who successfully arrived at the top of the company. The successful executives had good people skills; the best leaders are deeply interested in others.

10. *Why is leadership considered both an art and a science?*

It is an art because many leadership skills and qualities cannot be learned from a textbook. Leadership takes practice and hands-on experience. Learning about leadership research helps people analyze situations from a variety of perspectives and learn how to be effective as leaders. Leadership is a science because a growing body of knowledge and objective facts describe the leadership process and how to use leadership skills to attain organizational goals.

TEACHING TOOLS AND EXERCISES

1. Assign the book *Good to Great: Why Some Companies Make the Leap...and Others Don't* by Jim Collins. Students will describe in writing the strengths and weaknesses of Level 5 leaders.

2. *Leader's Bookshelf: Leadership* by Rudolph Giuliani. What are Rudy Giuliani's leadership principles? Giuliani makes the point that leadership does not just happen. It can be learned and developed. Comment on this idea in a discussion or in writing.

3. *Leadership Self-Insight:* Students will evaluate their own leadership potential by completing the quiz in Leader Self- Insight 1.1. Students will share their findings with the class.

4. *Debate* the following: Management is an art and a science.

   Divide the class into two teams.
   - Team I: Management is an art.
   - Team II: Management is a science.

   Allow 25 minutes for this exercise.

5. *On the Web:* Go to the website for The John Ben Shepperd Public Leadership Institute at The University of Texas Permian Basin *www.utpb.edu/JBS/leadership.htm* and click on the Leadership Resources and Links and then click on Leadership Quotes. Which quotations best describe your view of leadership?

LEADERSHIP DEVELOPMENT: CASES FOR ANALYSIS

I. Synopsis: Sales Engineering Division

When DGL International, a manufacturer of refinery equipment, brought in John Terrill to manage its Sales Engineering division, company executives informed him of the urgent situation. Sales Engineered had the highest-paid, best-educated, and least-productive division in the company. Terrill was to turn it around! Terrill showed concern for the personal welfare of the engineers. Terrill envisioned a future in which engineers were free to work with customers and join self-directed teams for product improvement. Terrill collected the engineers reports and showed the stacks of paper to the president. He explained that the lack of productivity was a result of excessive paperwork and reporting.

Case questions and answers:

1. *Does John Terrill's leadership style fit the definition of leadership in Exhibit 1.1. Explain.*

Yes, Terrill is trying to influence top managers by showing them that the reports are a waste of time. By allying himself with the engineers and bringing about a change in reporting procedures, Terrill is building a better relationship with them and establishing trust. Together, Terrill, and the engineers can focus on the shared purpose of increasing the productivity of the sales engineering division. He is using empowerment to turn the division around.

2. *With respect to Exhibit 1.2, in what paradigm is Terrill? In what paradigm is headquarters?*

Terrill is in the NEW Paradigm because he wishes to empower the employees and build relationships with them. He is open to change because he listens to the engineers and respects their desire to work with customers. Headquarters is in the OLD Paradigm because the triplicate reports for top management represent a control mechanism to assure stability and uniformity.

3. *What approach would you have taken in this situation?*

A less confrontational approach with the president would have been more appropriate and helped Terrill build a good relationship with both the engineers and top management. Human skills are increasingly important for leaders in today's economy. In the new paradigm, leaders put people first and build relationships with all members of the organization.

II. Synopsis: Airstar, Inc.

Airstar, Inc. manufactures, repairs, and overhauls pistons and jet engines for smaller, often privately owned aircraft. The company has a solid niche, and most managers have been with the founder for over 20 years. With the founder's death five years ago, Roy Morgan became president. Mr. Morgan has called you in as a consultant. Your research indicates that this industry is changing rapidly. Airstar is feeling encroachment from large conglomerates and its backlog of orders is the lowest in several years. Senior managers are not sure what direction to take. Morgan confides that organizing should be as easy as dividing the work into simple, logical, routine tasks. Tasks are assigned superficially in an informal manner. Communications are atrocious. Responsibilities overlap.

1. *What is your reaction to this conversation? What would you say to Morgan to help him lead the organization?*

Morgan has an outdated view. He is managing under the assumptions of a stable, predicable environment. Explaining that today's environment is changing and chaotic would help him rethink his position as leader of the organization.

Morgan needs both leadership and management skills to provide direction for Airstar. Management focuses on establishing detailed plans and schedules for achieving specific results, then allocating resources to accomplish the plan. Leadership calls for creating a compelling vision of the future for Airstar and developing farsighted strategies for producing the changes needed to achieve that vision. A *vision* is a picture of an ambitious, desirable future for the organization or team. To be compelling for followers, the vision has to be one that Airstar employees can relate to and share. Morgan needs to develop his leadership skills.

2. *Describe Morgan's management style in terms of alignment.*

In terms of alignment, Morgan's management style entails organizing a structure to accomplish the plan; staffing the structure with employees; and developing policies, procedures, and systems to direct employees and monitor implementation of the plan. Morgan feels that managers are thinkers and workers are doers.

Alignment has a different meaning for leaders and Morgan needs to learn it. Leadership is concerned with communicating the vision and developing a shared culture and set of core values that can lead to the desired future state. Morgan needs to involve others as thinkers, doers, and leaders themselves. Morgan needs to encourage the senior management to expand their minds and abilities and to assume responsibility for filling the backlog of orders.

3. *If you were to take over as president of Airstar, what would you do first? Second? Third?*

First, the president should make sure that Morgan gains some leadership skills. Leadership takes practice and hands-on experience. Knowing about leadership research would help Morgan analyze situations from a variety of perspectives and learn how to be a more effective leader. Morgan should study leadership training and develop a vision for the future of Airstar in a changing environment. Second, Morgan should align employees to carry out the vision for Airstar. Third, Morgan must develop personal relationships to motivate and energize others and to unlock the personal qualities of Airstar's employees so they can work toward the fulfillment of Airstar's vision.

CHAPTER TWO
TRAITS, BEHAVIORS, AND RELATIONSHIPS

CHAPTER SUMMARY

The point of this chapter is to understand the importance of traits and behaviors in the development of leadership theory and research. Traits include self-confidence, honesty and drive. A large number of personal traits and abilities distinguish successful leaders from non-leaders, but traits themselves are not sufficient to guarantee effective leadership. The behavior approach explores autocratic versus democratic leadership, consideration versus initiating structure, employee-centered versus job- centered leadership, and concern for people versus concern for production. The theme of people versus tasks runs through this research, suggesting these are fundamental behaviors through which leaders meet followers' needs. There has been some disagreement in the research about whether a specific leader is either people- or task-oriented or whether they can be both. Today consensus is that leaders can achieve a "high-high" leadership style.

Another approach is the dyad between a leader and each follower. Followers have different relationships with the leader, and the ability of the leader to develop a positive relationship with each subordinate contributes to team performance. The leader-member exchange theory says that high quality relationships have a positive outcome for leaders, followers, work units, and the organization. Leaders can attempt to build individualized relationships with each subordinate as a way to meet needs for both consideration and structure.

The historical development of leadership theory introduces some important ideas about leadership. While certain personal traits and abilities constitute a greater likelihood for success in a leadership role, they are not in themselves sufficient to guarantee effective leadership. Rather, behaviors are equally significant, as outlined by the research at several universities. Therefore, the style of leadership demonstrated by an individual greatly determines the outcome of the leadership endeavor. Often, a combination of styles is most effective. To understand the effects of leadership upon outcomes, the specific relationship behavior between a leader and each follower is also an important consideration.

CHAPTER OPENER

Swan's Personal Attributes of Leadership

Robert Swan led a team to the North Pole and ice cap began to melt beneath their feet. Swan's carefully-planned expedition, made up of eight people from seven countries, became a nightmare when the ice cap began to melt in April-four months earlier than usual. The group survived barely because of teamwork and Swan's extraordinary leadership. Swan's honesty, as well as his ability to maintain his poise, self-confidence, and sense of purpose amid life-threatening and constantly changing conditions, helped to nourish the spirit and motivation of the team. With the completion of the journey, Swan became the first person ever to walk to both the North and South Poles. Today, he recounts his adventures to the world, including business people hungry to learn what it means to be a leader in a dangerous and hostile world.

LECTURE/OUTLINE

---

1. To identify personal traits and characteristics that are associated with effective leaders.

The Trait Approach *Exhibit 2.1*

➢ *Do you think some people are born with traits that make them natural leaders?*

Early efforts understand leadership success focused on the leader's personal traits.

Traits are the distinguishing personal characteristics of a leader, such as intelligence, values, self-confidence, and appearance.

The *Great Man approach* sought to identify the traits leaders possessed that distinguished them from people who were not leaders.

Research found only a weak relationship between personal traits and leader success.

During the 1940s and 1950s, researchers examined personality traits---creativity and self confidence, physical traits--- age and energy-level, abilities---knowledge and fluency of speech, social characteristics---popularity and sociability, and work-related characteristics---the desire to excel and persistence against obstacles.

In 1948, Stogdill examined over 100 studies based on the trait approach.

He uncovered traits that appeared consistent with effective leadership---general intelligence, initiative, interpersonal skills, self-confidence, drive for responsibility, and personal integrity.

Stogdill's cautioned that the value of a particular trait varies with the organizational situation.

Discussion Question #1: *Is the "Great Man" perspective on leadership still alive today? Think about some recent popular movies. Do they stress a lone individual as hero or savior? Discuss*

Notes____

There has been recent interest in examining leadership traits. A 1991 review identified personal traits that distinguish leaders from non-leaders.

Studies measuring followers' perceptions indicate that certain traits are associated with perceptions about leadership.

One study found that the traits of intelligence, masculinity, and dominance strongly related to how individuals perceived leaders.

A concern with traits relates to the recent interest in *emotional intelligence,* which includes self-awareness, the ability to manage emotions, the capacity to be hopeful and optimistic, empathy, and social and interpersonal skills.

Over time, trait research has considered certain traits essential---self-confidence, honesty and integrity, and drive.

Self-confidence

➢ *Why do active leaders need self-confidence to initiate change?*

Self- confidence is assurance in one's own judgments, decision making, ideas, and capabilities.

Leaders need self-confidence to make decisions fast and inspire others to support them.

Leaders need self-confidence to gain trust and commitment.

Leaders initiate take risks.

Self-confidence is the one trait that helps a leaders face all these challenges.

Honesty/Integrity.

➢ *Explain how the virtues of honest and integrity create the foundation of trust between leaders and followers?*

Honesty refers to truthfulness and non-deception and implies an openness that subordinates welcome.

Integrity means that one is whole, that actions match words. Successful leaders seem to be highly consistent, doing exactly what they say.

Successful leaders have been found to be highly consistent, doing exactly what they say they will do when they say they will do it; successful leaders are easy to trust.

Drive

➢ *Why is drive considered essential for effective leadership?*

Drive refers to the high motivation that creates a high effort level by a leader.

A strong drive is associated with high energy; leaders rise to the top often because they actively pursue goals.

Ambition enables them to set challenging goals and take initiative to achieve those goals.

Discussion Question #2: *Suggest some personal traits of leaders you have known. Which traits do you believe are most valuable? Why?*

Notes

___

___

However, traits alone cannot define effective leadership.

***In the Lead*:** Kenneth Lay, Enron Corporation

Kenneth Lay, former CEO of Enron, was considered by many to be a decent, hard-working man who got caught in a situation out of his control. Lay says that he always wanted Enron to be a highly moral and ethical company. Yet, Lay will be remembered as the leader of an organization whose demise, fueled by vast deception, wiped out billions of investor dollars and cost thousands of jobs. Some employees feel that Lay's boundless optimism and easy trust in others led him to believe the company was in good shape and the complex accounting machinations were acceptable. Despite the Enron scandal, Lay still has the self-confidence and optimism that he will get through this ordeal.

Q: *How did the same traits that led to success also lead to Ken Lay's downfall?*

A: Lay clearly had self-confidence, a strong ambition and a drive for achievement and success. However, his ambition outweighed his ethics, causing him to turn a blind eye to the situation at Enron.

Notes___

___

___

- *Living Leadership: Leader Qualities*

  Deng Ming-Dao, "*When all other factors are equal, it is the character of the leader that determines the outcome.*"

➢ Give an example of this idea from history or from your personal experience.

---

2. To recognize autocratic versus democratic leadership behavior and the impact of each.

Behavior Approaches

Exhibit 2.2

The inability to define effective leadership based solely on traits led to looking at the behavior of leaders.

The behavior approach says that anyone who adopts the appropriate behavior can be a good leader.

Behaviors are learned more readily than traits, making leadership accessible to all.

Autocratic versus Democratic Leadership

One study that served as a precursor to the behavior approach recognized autocratic and democratic leadership styles.

An *autocratic leader* tends to centralize authority and derive power from position, control of rewards, and coercion.

A *democratic* leader delegates authority to others, encourages participation, relies on subordinates' knowledge for completion of tasks, and depends on subordinate respect for influence.

Discussion Question #3: *What is the difference between trait theories and behavioral theories of leadership?*

Notes____

____

____

Kurt Lewin at the University of Iowa showed that the groups with autocratic leaders performed well as long as the leader was present to supervise them.

However, group members were displeased with the close, autocratic style of leadership, and feelings of hostility arose.

Groups assigned to democratic leaders and performed well when the leader was absent.

These characteristics of democratic leadership may explain why empowerment of employees is a popular trend in companies today.

Further work by Tannenbaum and Schmidt indicated that leadership behavior could exist on a continuum reflecting different amounts of employee participation.

One leader might be autocratic (boss-centered) another democratic (subordinate-centered), and a third a mix of the two styles.

The extent to which leaders should be boss-centered or subordinate-centered depended on organizational circumstance; leaders might adjust their behavior to fit the circumstance.

➢ *When does a more autocratic the leader approach work better? When can a participative style be used?*

The University of Iowa studies found that leadership behavior had a definite effect on outcomes such as follower performance and satisfaction.

Discussion question #7: *Why would subordinates under a democratic leader perform better in the leader's absence than would subordinates under an autocratic leader?*

Notes____

---

3. To know the distinction between people-oriented and task-oriented leadership behavior and when each should be used.

Ohio State Studies.

Based on extensive survey research at Ohio State University, two wide-ranging categories of leader behavior types emerged: consideration and initiating structure.

Consideration describes the extent to which a leader is sensitive to subordinates, respects their ideas and feelings, and establishes mutual trust (e.g., listening, seeking input, and showing).

Initiating structure describes the extent to which a leader is task oriented and directs subordinates' work activities toward goal achievement (e.g., directing tasks, planning, and ruling with an iron hand).

A leader can display a high degree of both types, a low degree of both types, high consideration and low initiating structure, or low consideration and high initiating structure behavior.

Research indicates that all four types of leader style combinations can be effective.

Discussion Question #4: *Would you prefer working for a leader who has a "consideration" or an "initiating leadership" style? Discuss the reasons for you answer.*

Notes____

In the Lead: John Fryer, Duval County Schools

As a major general in the U.S. Air Force, John Fryer learned about setting goals and establishing high performance standards. He is trying to turn Duval County's schools around. Students score well below the state average on standardized tests, and five schools got Fs from the Florida Department of Education. When Fryer became superintendent, he behaved like a general, setting a strategic plan that included rigorous goals for academics and discipline in every class in every school. He set high performance standards for teachers and students. Students are challenged to read 25 books each. Fryer provides teacher training. There is greater motivation and commitment even if it is too early to tell if Fryer can completely change the county schools.

Q: *Describe Fryer's leadership behavior?*

A: Fryer used initiating structure behavior to clarify goals and set performance standards to be achieved. The high degree of initiating structure behavior was necessary to get everyone focused in the same direction moving Duval County towards higher standards. He also demonstrated consideration by involving the teachers in the change process through dinners and training.

Additional studies showed that "considerate" supervisors has a more positive impact on subordinate satisfaction than "structuring" supervisors.

Yet, research using performance criteria such as output showed that initiating structure was more effective.

Other studies revealed that leaders rated effective by subordinates exhibited a high level of both consideration and initiating structure behaviors.

Less effective leaders were rated low in both behavior styles.

Notes____

The University of Michigan Studies

Studies at the University of Michigan compared the behavior of effective and ineffective supervisors.

The effectiveness of leaders was determined by productivity of the subordinate group.

Over time, two types of leadership behavior were established, each consisting of two dimensions.

Employee-centered leaders display a focus on the human needs of their subordinates, as expressed through the dimensions of leader support and facilitating positive interaction among followers.

Because relationships are so important in today's work environment, many organizations are looking for leaders who can facilitate positive interaction among others.

Job-centered leaders direct activities towards efficiency, cost cutting, and scheduling, as expressed through the dimensions of goal emphasis and work facilitation

A leader is identifiable by behavior characteristics of one or the other style, not both.

Another hallmark of the studies is the acknowledgement that the behaviors of goal emphasis, work facilitation, support, and interaction facilitation can be meaningfully performed by a subordinate's peers, not only the designated leader.

Leadership behavior was found to affect the performance and satisfaction of subordinates; however, performance was also affected by situational factors.

Notes____

____

____

The Leadership Grid

Exhibit 2.3

The Leadership Grid builds on the work of the Ohio State and Michigan studies.

It is a two dimensional leadership theory that describes major leadership styles based on measuring both concern for people and concern for production..

Researchers rated leaders on a scale of one to nine according to these two criteria:

- *Team Management* (9,9) often is considered the most effective style and is recommended because members work together to accomplish tasks.

- *Country club management* (1,9) occurs when emphasis is given to people rather than to work output.

- *Authority-compliance management (9,* 1) occurs when efficiency in operation is the dominant orientation.

- *Middle-of-the-road management* (5,5) reflects concern for both people and production.

- *Impoverished management (1. 1)* means the absence of a leadership philosophy.

***In the Lead*:** TruServ and North Jackson Elementary School

Pamela Forbes Lieberman makes no apologies for her hard-driving management style. Here emphasis on tough goals and bottom-line results is helping to restore the health of hardware cooperative TruServ. Despite her hard-nosed approach, Lieberman also believes in the importance of keeping morale high.

Joyce Pully, the new principal at Jackson Elementary School in Jackson, Mississippi, had a vision of transforming North Jackson into a model of creative learning. However, she didn't may any changes at all during the first year, working instead to build trust with the teachers, staff, and students.

Q: *Place these two leaders on the Leadership Grid.*

A: The leadership of Lieberman is characterized by high concern for tasks and low-to-moderate concern for people. Joyce Pully, is high on concern for people and moderate on concern for production. Both concerns shown in the Leadership Grid are present, but they are integrated at different levels.

Notes____

____

____

Theories of a "High-High " Leader *Exhibit 2.4*

The research into the behavior approach culminated in two predominant types of leadership behaviors --- people-oriented and task-oriented.

The findings raised four questions:

- whether these two dimensions are the most important behaviors of leadership

One recent review of 50 years of leadership research identifies task-oriented behavior and people-oriented behavior as primary categories related to effective leadership.

- whether people orientation and task orientation exist together in the same leader, and how

The Grid theory argues that yes, both are present when people work with or through others to accomplish an activity.

There is considerable belief that the best leaders are high on both behaviors.

- whether a "high- high" leadership style is universal or situational

Research has indicated some universality: people-oriented behavior is related to higher employee satisfaction and fewer personnel problems; task-oriented behavior is associated with higher productivity.

- whether people can actually change themselves into leaders high on people and/or task-orientation.

Researchers found that behaviors of effective leaders could be emulated by anyone who wished to become an effective leader..

There is a general belief that "high-high" leadership is a desirable quality, because the leader will meet both needs simultaneously.

Discussion question #8: *Which type of leader---task-oriented or people-oriented---do you think would have an easier time becoming a "high-high" leader. Why?*

Notes____

---

4. To understand how dyadic theories of leadership have broadened the understanding of relationships between leaders and followers and recognize how to build partnerships for greater effectiveness.

Individualized Approaches *Exhibit 2.5*

Traditional trait and behavior theories assume that a leader adopts a general leadership style that is used with all group members.

A more recent approach to leadership, *individualized leadership,* is based on the idea that a leader develops a unique relationship with each subordinate or group member which determines how the leader behaves toward the member and how the member responds to the leader.

Leadership is a series of *dyads,* two-person interactions.

Dyadic theory examines why leaders have more influence over and greater impact on some followers than on others.

The dyadic view focuses on the concept of *exchange;* leaders can meet followers needs and offer a sense of support; followers can provide commitment and high performance.

Some dyads may be "rich" with a high level of giving and receiving by both partners while some may be "poor" with little giving and receiving by both dyadic partners.

This viewpoint includes four stages

- the awareness of a relationship between a leader and each individual
- the specific attributes of the exchange relationship
- the ability of the leader to develop partnerships intentionally with each group member
- the inclusion of larger systems and networks

The Vertical Dyad Linkage Model *Exhibit 2.6*

➢ *Why do some subordinates get their needs met while others do not?*

The Vertical Dyad Linkage Model (VDL) argues for the importance of the dyad formed by a leader with each member of the group.

Initial findings indicated that subordinates provided different descriptions of the same leader (i.e., high on people and tasks or low on leadership behaviors).

Based on these two exchange patterns, subordinates were found to exist in either an in-group or out-group in relation to the leader.

The model delineates the differences in leader behavior toward in-group versus out-group members.

In the terminology of the VDL model, the insiders, who are highly trusted and enjoyed special privileges, participated in an *in-group exchange* relationship.

Others who did not experience a sense of trust and extra consideration participate in an *out-group exchange.*

In-group members had higher job satisfaction and performance while out-group subordinates had a low-quality relationship with the same leader, such as a low degree of trust, respect, and obligation.

Discussion question #5: *The Vertical Dyad Linkage model suggests that followers respond individually to the leader. If this were so, what advice would you give leaders about displaying people-oriented versus task-oriented behavior?*

Notes____

____

____

Leader-Member Exchange

Leader-Member Exchange (LMX) is stage two in the individualized leadership model, exploring how leader-member relationships develop over time and how the quality of exchange relationships impacts outcomes.

Studies evaluating characteristics of the LMX relationship explored communication frequency, value agreement, characteristics of followers, job satisfaction, job climate, and commitment.

Overall, the research found that the quality of the leader-member exchange relationship is substantially higher for in-group members.

➢ *Why do leaders benefit from the increased initiative effort of in-group participants?*

A higher-quality LMX relationship leads to higher performance.

For followers, a high-quality relationship leads to more interesting assignments, greater responsibility, and rewards such as pay increases and bonuses.

Theorists identified three stages for dyad members in their working relationship

- testing each other to find comfortable behavior
- shaping and refining their roles
- attaining a steady behavior pattern.

At stage three, leader-member exchanges were difficult to change, and in-group/out-group status was determined.

Notes____

____

____

5. To recognize how to build partnerships for greater effectiveness.

Partnership Building

In this third phase of research, the focus was on whether leaders could develop positive relationships with a large number of subordinates.

If leaders are perceived as granting benefits and advantages to in-group members, members of the out-group may rebel, which can damage the entire organization.

The research focused on whether leaders could develop positive relationships with each individual and provide all employees access to high-quality leader-member exchanges.

This, in turn, would lead to a more equitable environment and greater benefits to leaders, followers, and to the organization.

When leaders were trained to offer the opportunity for a high-quality relationship to all group members, the followers who responded to the offer improved their performance dramatically.

This implication of this finding is that true performance and productivity gains can be achieved by having the leader develop positive relationships one-on-one with each subordinate.

Discussion Question #6: *Does it make sense to you that a leader should develop an individualized relationship with each follower? Explain advantages and disadvantages to this approach.*

Notes____

Systems and Networks

The final stage of this work suggests that leader dyads can be expanded to larger systems.

Rather than focusing on leaders and subordinates, a systems-level perspective examines how dyadic relationships can be created across traditional boundaries to embrace a larger system.

Leader relationships are not limited to subordinates, but include peers, teammates, and other stakeholders relevant to the work unit.

The theory suggests the need for leaders to build networks on one-to-one relationships and to use their traits and behaviors selectively to create positive relationships with as many people as possible.

A larger number of people can be influenced by the leader, and these stakeholders will contribute to the success of the work unit.

In the Lead: University Public Schools

The University Public Schools (UPS) of Stockton, California at San Joaquin is a model of partnership. Teachers are expected to develop partnerships with students, each other, parents, and other community members. They are given an unprecedented amount of freedom to set their own goals and develop their own curriculum. Teacher's pay raises are based on merit and tied to meeting both individual and team goals. Teachers sign one-year contracts and there is no notion of tenure.

Q: *How does partnership building integrate the students, teachers, and parents?*

A: Teachers feel they are involved in a genuine partnership with the school system, one another, and the community. UPS is trying to build a system that empowers everyone to shape a new vision of learning and make a real difference in the lives of students and the larger world.

Notes____

____

____

DISCUSSION QUESTIONS

1. *Is the "Great Man" perspective on leadership still alive today? Think about some popular movies. Do they stress a lone individual as hero or savior? Discuss*

Yes. There are many movies that show that hope and optimism can be driving forces for success. The movie *Seabiscuit,* set in the era of the Great Depression, is the true story of a man who inspired a small group of people to form a team and race a lame horse and its disabled jockey to victory against all odds.

2. *Suggest some personal traits of leaders you have known. Which traits do you believe are most valuable? Why?*

Qualities like courage, self-confidence, good communication skills, dedication come to mind. Leaders like Martin Luther King, Winston Churchill, John F. Kennedy, Rosa Parks, and others are a few suggestions.

3. *What is the difference between trait theories and behavioral theories of leadership?*

The Trait Approach, an early effort to understand leadership success, focused on the leader's personal traits which are distinguishing personal characteristics such as intelligence, values, self confidence, and appearance. Fundamental to this theory was the idea that some people are born with traits that make them natural leaders. The behavior approach says that anyone who adopts the appropriate behavior can be a good leader. Behaviors can be learned more readily than traits, making leadership accessible to all.

4. *Would you prefer working for a leader who has a "consideration" or an "initiating-structure" leadership style? Discuss the reasons for your answer.*

Answers will vary. It depends on the project. I would prefer a leader who has both styles, a "high-high" leader. This is particularly important if tasks are interdependent and require coordination. In preparing this instructor's manual, I need input from the editor and other members of the textbook team. I need positive feedback and suggestions presented in a non-judgmental manner. However, I also need materials delivered on time so that I can finish the job and meet my deadline.

5. *The Vertical Dyad Linkage model suggests that followers respond individually to the leader. If this is so, what advise would you give leaders about displaying people-oriented versus task oriented behavior?*

The subordinates who rated the leader highly had developed close relationships with the leader and often became assistants who played key roles in the functioning of the work unit. Out-group members were not key players in the work unit. The key to developing in-group members was to form one-on-one relationships, which also resulted in higher job satisfaction and performance.

6. *Does it make sense to you that a leader should develop an individualized relationship with each follower? Explain advantages and disadvantages to this approach.*

Yes.

Advantages: Higher performance and improved job satisfaction which allowed leaders to rely on followers for assistance and followers to participate in decision making

Disadvantages: Following stage three of the leader-member relationship, it was difficult to change the pattern. The leader-member exchange determined in-group and out-group status.

7. *Why would subordinates under a democratic leader perform better in the leader's absence than would subordinates under an autocratic leader?*

The democratic leader shares in decision making and values the opinions of subordinates. Therefore, in his absence, the subordinates have already engaged in decision-making and are able to carry on. The autocratic leader does not allow subordinate decision making, and subordinates would be afraid to change their behavior in the absence of the leader. In addition, autocratic leadership is used when there is a great difference in skill level and the subordinates cannot function independently.

8. *Which type of leader ---- task-oriented or people-oriented --- do you think would have an easier time becoming a "high-high" leader? Why?*

A people-oriented leader. It is far easier to learn task-oriented (i.e., organizational) skills and become a "high-high" leader than it is to change character traits and develop empathy and consideration for others.

TEACHING TOOLS AND EXERCISES

1. *Leadership Bookshelf: Lessons from the Top: The Search for American's Best Business Leaders* by Thomas J. Neff and James. What are the six core principles used by successful leaders? How can the experiences of real-life leaders help readers apply these lessons to their own lives? What did you find most helpful for yourself? Discuss.

2. *On the Web*: Leadership.com is revolutionizing business by helping leaders take full advantage of the most valuable assets of any company: its people and their knowledge. Leadership.com provides the tools every leader needs to create successful organizations:

   Inspire more creatively **Build** more effectively **Deliver** more successfully

. Go to <u>*www.leadership.com*</u> and find out what information and services are available.

3. *Discuss the following leader*: **Napoleon Bonaparte**

   His brain is among the most perfect that have ever been. His ever ready attention seizes indefatigably upon facts and ideas, which his memory registers and classifies. His imagination plays with them freely, and a state of incessant secret tension enables it tirelessly to produce those political and strategic theses which reveal themselves to him as sudden intuitions comparable to of the mathematician and the poet. This happens especially at night when he wakes up suddenly. He himself speaks of "the moral spark" and "the after-midnight presence of mind."

   Out of this physical and intellectual disposition arose that irresistible impulse towards action and domination, which is called his ambition. He saw clearly into himself, "It is said that I am ambitious, but this is an error, or at least my ambition is so intimately allied to my whole being that it cannot be separated from it." It cannot be better expressed. Napoleon is before all else a temperament.

   Source: Pieter Geyl, *Napoleon For and Against* (New Haven: Yale University Press, 1968), 422-423.

- Using Exhibit 2.1, *Personal Characteristics of Leaders*, identify the leadership characteristics of Napoleon.

- Napoleon had the ability to rally the French army. Researchers have shown that effective leaders were often identified with exceptional follower performance. What traits made Napoleon's followers support him?

- Could Napoleon be considered a people-oriented, task-oriented leader, or a "high-high"? Explain. This question could be used as an out-of-class library assignment.

4. *Out-of-class reading*: Jay A. Conger and Robert M. Fulmer, " Developing Your Leadership Pipeline," *Harvard Business Review* (December 2003): 76-84.

5. *Leadership Styles in Action*

Divide the class into two groups. One group works for a leader who has a "consideration" leadership style while the other works for a leader who has an "initiating-structure" style. Each group has ten minutes to defend its leader, giving reasons and examples.

- Group I: *Consideration* describes the extent to which a leader is sensitive to subordinates, respects their ideas and feelings, and establishes mutual trust (e.g., listening, seeking input, and showing).

- Group II: *Initiating structure* describes the extent to which a leader is task oriented and directs subordinates' work activities toward goal achievement (e.g., directing tasks, planning, and ruling with an iron hand).

LEADERSHIP DEVELOPMENT: CASES FOR ANALYSIS

I. Synopsis: Consolidated Products

Consolidated Products is a medium-sized manufacturer of consumer products. Ben Samuels was a plant manager who was well liked by employees. They were grateful for the fitness center, picnics, and holiday parties. Ben believed it was important to treat employees properly so they would have a sense of loyalty. Under Ben, the plant had the lowest turnover but the second worst record for costs and production levels. He was asked to take early retirement and Phil Jones replaced him. Phil had a reputation as a manager who could get things done. Supervisors were instructed to establish high-performance standards. Costs were cut by trimming the fitness center, picnics and parties, and training. Phil believed that if workers did not want to work, the company should get rid of them.

Case questions and answers

1. *Compare the leadership traits and behaviors of Ben Samuels and Phil Jones.*

   Ben Samuels is an employee-centered or people-oriented boss. Ben shows more interest in people. Employee-centered leaders display a focus on the human needs of their subordinates, as expressed through the dimensions of leader support and facilitating positive interaction among followers.

   Phil Jones is a job or task- oriented boss who shows more interest in productivity. Job-centered leaders direct activities towards efficiency, cost cutting, and scheduling, as expressed through the dimensions of goal emphasis and work facilitation

2. *Which leader do you think is more effective? Why? Which leader would you prefer to work for?*

   Ben is more democratic, and Phil is more autocratic. An autocratic leader achieves high productivity, but the workers feel hostile and when the boss is absent, they produce less. A work environment that leads to job satisfaction is more democratic than Phil's. In the short run, Phil is more effective in terms of reducing costs and increasing productivity, but in the long term, the high employee turnover will increase company costs. I would rather work for Ben.

3. *If you were Phil Jones' boss, what would you do now?*

   Phil should be encouraged to change his leadership behavior and become a "high-high" leader. A 9,9 Team Management style shows the same level of concern for people, but it takes on completely different characteristics as it joins with a high level of concern for results. There is a general belief that "high-high" leadership is a desirable quality, because the leader meets both needs simultaneously.

II. Synopsis: D.L.Woodside, Sunshine Snacks

D.L. Woodside had become research and development director for Sunshine Snacks, a snack food company. Woodside had been the research director at Skid's, a competitor. Despite his ambition, hard work, and excellent technical knowledge, Woodside was considered an easy-going fellow. He listened to his assistant's problems and covered the mistakes of an employee with a drinking problem. At Sunshine, Woodside sensed a loyalty to his assistant Harmon Davis who lacked technical knowledge and had been passed over for the job. Woodside knows he needs to build good relationships with the team, but he was selected because of his record of accomplishment with new product development.

Case questions and answers

1. *What traits does Woodside possess that might be helpful to him as he assumes his new position? What traits might be detrimental?*

Woodside has self-confidence, the degree to which one is self-assured in judgments, decision making, ideas, and capabilities. Woodside will need self-confidence to gain trust and commitment from Davis and the other employees at Sunshine. Woodside will need to initiate change and take risks. Self-confidence will help him face these challenges. He also has drive, high motivation that creates a high effort level by a leader.

The people-pleasing trait might be detrimental to Woodside because he has to get the job done. He was hired to bring new products to market.

2. *Would you consider Woodside a people-oriented or a task-oriented leader? Discuss which you think would be best for the new research director at Sunshine?*

   Woodside is a people-oriented leader, which may lead him ignore tasks. A 1,9 Country Club style shows a leader who puts people first even at the expense of achieving results. When a team member was abusing policies and drinking on the job, Woodside ignored the problem and covered for him.

   At Sunshine, a "high-high" leader is needed to build relationships and develop new products. A 9,9 Team Management style shows the same level of concern for people, but it takes on different characteristics when joined with a high concern for results.

3. *Do you believe an understanding of the dyadic theory might be useful to Woodside in this circumstance? Discuss.*

   Yes. Woodside realizes that he must form a good relationship with the research team to develop the new products and with the top managers at Sunshine. Woodside could look at the systems perspective of dyad theory. Rather than focusing on leaders and subordinates, a systems-level perspective examines how dyadic relationships can embrace a larger system. Relationships include peers, teammates, and other stakeholders. The theory suggests the need for leaders to build networks on one-to-one relationships to create positive relationships.

CHAPTER THREE
CONTINGENCY APPROACHES

CHAPTER SUMMARY

This chapter centers on the idea that situational variables affect leadership outcomes. The contingency approaches were developed to systematically address the relationship between a leader and the organization. The contingency approaches focus on how the components of leadership style, subordinate characteristics, and situational elements impact one another. Fiedler's contingency model, Hersey and Blanchard's situational theory, the path-goal theory, and substitutes for leadership examine how different situations call for different styles of leadership behavior.

According to Fiedler, leaders can determine if the situation is favorable to their leadership style. Task-oriented leaders perform better in very easy or very difficult situations, while person-oriented leaders perform best in situations of intermediate favorability. Hersey and Blanchard contend that leaders can adjust their task or relationship style to accommodate the readiness level of their subordinates.

The path-goal theory states that leaders can use a style based on contingencies such as quality requirement, commitment requirement, or leader's information. Concern for time (the need for a fast decision) versus concern for follower development come into play. Leaders can analyze each situation and answer a series of questions that determine the appropriate level of follower participation. Substitutes-for-leadership allow leaders to adjust their style to provide resources not otherwise provided in the organizational situation. Effective leadership is about developing diagnostic skills and being flexible in leadership behavior.

CHAPTER OPENER

Leadership Changes at PeopleSoft

David A. Duffield, founder, chairman, and former CEO of software company PeopleSoft, emphasized treating people well and letting them be "whole people" who felt free to bring their emotions and outside concerns to work with them. Duffield built PeopleSoft into and early enterprise software giant, and his leadership approach was successful. However, as the environment and competitive conditions changed, the strong laid-back style became a liability. In 1999, Duffield brought in a different kind of leader to pull PeopleSoft out of a sharp decline. The new leader installed clear-cut rules and standard procedures for everything. The new mission statement included—competitiveness, intensity, and accountability. Duffield believes that the new style of leader is just what was needed. PeopleSoft showed impressive sales results and a return to profitability. Both leaders were running the same company in very different situations.

LECTURE/OUTLINE

1. To understand how leadership is often contingent on people and situations.

The Contingency Approach *Exhibit 3.1*

The failure to find universal traits or behaviors that would determine effective leadership led researchers to focus on the situation in which leadership occurred.

The basic tenet was that behavior effective in some circumstances may be ineffective in others.

Effectiveness of leader behavior is *contingent* upon organizational situations.

Contingency means that one thing depends on other things, and for a leader to be effective, there must be an appropriate fit between the leader's behavior and style and the conditions of the situation.

Research implies that situational variables such as task, structure, and environment are important to leadership style.

The *contingency approaches* seek to delineate the characteristics of situations and followers and examine the leadership styles that can be used effectively.

If a leader can diagnose a situation and behave according to the appropriate style, successful outcomes are likely.

Discussion Question #2: *Do you think leadership style is fixed and unchangeable or flexible and adaptable? Why?*

Notes____

2. To apply Fiedler's contingency model to key relationships among leader style, situational favorability, and group task performance.

Fiedler's Contingency Model *Exhibit 3.2*

Research has identified two metacategories---task behavior and relationship behavior---as applicable to leadership in a variety of situations or time periods.

A leader can adapt his style to be high or low on both task and relationship behavior.

The model illustrates the four possible behavior approaches---high task-low relationship, high task-high relationship, high relationship-low task, and low task-low relationship.

Fiedler's idea was to match the leader's style with the situation most favorable for success.

Fiedler's model was designed to diagnose both leadership style and the organizational situation.

Leadership Style

The cornerstone of Fiedler's theory is the extent to which the leader's style is relationship-oriented or task-oriented.

A relationship-oriented leader is concerned with people, establishing trust, respect, and listening to employee needs.

A task-oriented leader is motivated by task accomplishment, providing clear direction and sets performance standards.

Leadership was measured with a questionnaire called the least preferred coworker (LPC) scale.

The LPC scale has a set of 16 bipolar adjectives along an 8-point scale:
(open_ _ _ _ _ _ _ _ _ _ _ _ _ _guarded)

If the leader describes the least preferred co-worker using positive concepts, he is considered relationship-oriented; if a leader uses negative concepts, he is task-oriented.

Situation *Exhibit 3.3*

Fiedler's model presents the leadership situation in terms of three key elements that can be favorable or unfavorable to a leader:

- *Leader-member relations*--- the quality of the group atmosphere and members' attitude toward and acceptance of the leader

- *Task structure*---- the extent to which tasks are defined, involve procedures, and have goals

- *Position power*--- the extent to which the leader has formal authority over subordinates

Combining the three situational characteristics yields eight leadership situations.

Situation I is the most favorable to the leader because all three characteristics are high and Situation VIII is the least favorable because all three are low.

Contingency Theory

Results show the following:

- Task-oriented leaders excel in favorable situations because everyone gets along, and the leader has all the power.

- Task oriented leaders excel if the situation is highly unfavorable to the leader, because structure and task direction are needed.

- Relationship-oriented leaders are more effective in situations of moderate favorability because human relations skills are important in achieving high group performance.

To use Fiedler's contingency theory, a leader must define his personal style as relationship- or task-oriented.

Then, a leader diagnoses the situation and determines whether leader-member relations, task structure, and position power are favorable or unfavorable.

In the Lead: Stanley O'Neal, Merrill Lynch

A lot of employees at Merrill Lynch grudgingly admit Stan O'Neal, the new CEO might be just what the company needs since profits, revenue, and reputation have been fallen. The loss of public trust plus economic uncertainty and a decline in the stock market have been a heavy blow. O'Neal has cut jobs, sold or closed underperforming field offices, and slashed costs. He's revising management processes, implementing strict performance standards, and changing policies to improve accountability. Under O'Neal profits have improved. The former CEO, David Komanski, was warm-hearted and friendly and beloved by everyone.

Q: *Using Fiedler's contingency theory, compare the two leaders at Merrill Lynch.*

A: O'Neal is a task-oriented leader who excels in a highly unfavorable situation because structure and task direction are crucial for the survival of Merrill Lynch. Komanski is a relationship-oriented leader with excellent human relations skills, a quality needed in a situation that is moderately favorable when high group performance is important. Komanski led Merrill when economic conditions were far better.

Discussion Question #1: *Consider Fiedler's theory as illustrated in Exhibit 3.3. How often do you think favorable, intermediate, or very unfavorable situations occur to leaders in real life? Discuss.*

Notes____

An important aspect of Fiedler's research is that it shows how leader styles fit the situation.

Many studies have tested Fiedler's research and provided some support for the model.

However, the model has been criticized as too simplistic, too arbitrary in determining the favorability of a situation, with unclear results long-term.

For example, if a task-oriented leader in an unfavorable situation is successful, then the situation improves and becomes more appropriate for a relationship-oriented leader.

The model fails to consider medium LPC leaders.

New research has improved Fiedler's model, and it is still considered important to leadership studies, although its major impact may have been to consider situational factors more seriously.

- ❑ *Living Leadership: Polarities*

  Any over-determined behavior produces its opposite. Knowing how polarities work, the wise leader does not push to make things happen, but allows process to unfold on its own.

- ➢ How can overbearing leadership behavior be a disadvantage?

Notes____

---

3. To apply Hersey and Blanchard situational theory of leader style to the level of follower readiness.

Hersey and Blanchard's Situational Theory *Exhibit 3.4*

Situational theory focuses on the characteristics of followers as an important element of the situation and of determining effective leader behavior.

The point of the theory is that subordinates vary in readiness level.

People low in task readiness, because of little ability or training, or insecurity, need a different leadership style that those high in readiness with good ability, skills, confidence, and willingness to work.

The leader can adopt one of four leadership styles based on a combination of relationship and task behavior.

The four styles include:

- *telling,* a high concern for tasks and a low concern for people----very directive with the leader giving explicit directions for tasks.

- *selling*, a high concern for both relationships and tasks---explaining decisions but giving followers a chance to ask questions

- *participating,* a high relationship and low task behavior----sharing ideas and encouraging participation and decision making

- *delegating*, a low concern for both tasks and relationships---providing little direction or support because responsibility for decisions rests with followers

The appropriate style depends on the readiness of the followers, such as their degree of education and skills, experience, self-confidence, and work attitudes.

Low Readiness Level

Telling is for low-readiness because people are unable or unwilling to be responsible for their task behavior.

➢ *Why does the owner of two McDonald's franchises use the telling style?*

Moderate Readiness Level

The selling style works for followers with moderate readiness.

Followers might lack some education and experience on the job but demonstrate high confidence and interest.

➢ *Why does a small corporate relocation company find a selling style fitting?*

High Readiness Level

When followers are at a high level of readiness, a participating style can be very effective.

Followers might have the necessary education but need guidance from the leader.

- *Why is this style effective for the owner of a visual effects company that employs artists and animators?*

Very High Readiness Level

The delegating style of leadership can be effective when followers have very high levels of education, experience and readiness to accept responsibility for their task behavior.

- *Why is this style effective for lawyers, college professors, and social workers?*

This contingency model is easier to understand than Fiedler's model, because it focuses only on the characteristics of followers, not those of the situation.

In the Lead **:** Carole McGraw, Detroit Public Schools

When Carole McGraw walks into a classroom, she diagnoses what teenagers have in common to find the best way to help students of such varying degrees of readiness to learn. She realizes that all teenagers are exposed to countless hours of MTV, television programs, and disc jockeys. McGraw developed her teaching method focused on three concepts: painless, interesting, and enjoyable. Student in biology do their work in labs or teams. The method combines telling and participating. Students are provided with direction. McGraw provides the structure and discipline some of her readiness level students need to succeed. Most of McGraw's leadership focuses on supporting students as they learn

Q: *How can situational theory apply to classroom teaching?*

A: Classroom teachers face one of the toughest leadership challenges because they usually deal with students at widely different levels of readiness. Situational theory focuses on the characteristics of followers as an important element of the situation and of determining effective leader behavior. McGraw's students who are low in task readiness need a different leadership style that those who are high in readiness and have good ability, skills, confidence, and willingness to work.

Discussion Question #5: *Think of a situation in which you have worked. At what level of readiness (R1 to R4) would you rate yourself and coworkers? Did your leader use the correct style according to the Hersey and Blanchard models?*

Notes____

4. To explain the path-goal theory of leadership.

Path-Goal Theory

Exhibit 3.5

Path-goal theory is a contingency theory to leadership in which the leader's responsibility is to increase subordinates' motivation to attain personal and organizational goals.

The leader increases follower motivation by:

- clarifying the follower's path to available rewards
- increasing the rewards that the follower values and desires.

Path clarification means that the leader works with subordinates to help them identify and learn the behaviors that lead to successful task accomplishment and rewards.

Increasing rewards means that the leader talks with subordinates to learn which rewards are important to them---whether they desire intrinsic rewards from the work itself or extrinsic rewards such as raises or promotions.

This model has three contingencies --- leader style, followers and situation, and the rewards to meet followers' needs.

Whereas Fiedler assumed that new leaders could take over as situations change, the path-goal theory proposes that leaders change their behaviors to match the situation.

Leader Behavior

Exhibit 3.6

Path-goal theory suggests four leader behavior classifications:

- *Supportive leadership*---concern for subordinates' well-being and personal needs
- *Directive leadership*---task-oriented, telling subordinates what to do
- *Participative leadership*---consults with subordinates about decisions
- *Achievement-oriented leadership*---sets challenging goals for subordinates.

In the Lead: Alan Robbins, Plastic Lumber Company

Alan Robbins vowed to be both a boss and friend to his employees at Plastic Lumber Company, which converts plastic bottles into fake lumber. Robbins wanted to give everyone a chance to participate and he stressed teamwork. However, his low-skilled workers didn't care about participating and simply wanted clear direction and consistent standards. Robbins shifted to a directive leadership style

Q: *Apply Robbins shift to a directive leadership styles in terms of the path-goal theory.*

A: Path-goal theory suggests leader behavior classifications. The directive leadership style is appropriate when the subordinates have little education and experience. Leadership behavior must be tailored to the situation. Robbins realized that with low-skilled workers, the participative style led to serious problems such as absenteeism and drug use. The workers wanted clear directives with rules and guidelines.

Situational Contingencies

Situational contingencies include:

- the personal characteristics of group members --- a self-centered employee may require the leader to use monetary rewards for motivation.

- the work environment---contingencies include the degree of task structure, the nature of the formal authority system, and the work group characteristics such as educational level of subordinates and the quality of relationships among them.

Use of rewards

The leader's responsibility is to clarify the path to rewards or increases the amount of rewards to enhance satisfaction and job performance.

The leader works with subordinates to help them acquire the skills and confidence need to perform tasks.

A leader may develop new rewards to meet the specific needs of a subordinate.

Leadership behavior is tailored to the situation

Discussion Question #4: *Compare Fiedler's contingency model with the path-goal theory. What are the similarities and differences? Which do you prefer?*

Notes____

In the Lead: Pat Kelly, PSS World Medical

PSS World Medical strives to hire enterprising and hard-working professionals who thrive on challenge, responsibility, and recognition. Then, Pat Kelly keeps them performing at high levels by consistently setting high financial and sales targets. Kelly realizes that employees have a need to win and receive high rewards for their performance. PSS spends 5 percent on its payroll on training, emphasizes promotion from within, and moves people to different divisions to give them opportunities.

Q: *Why is achievement-oriented leadership suited to PSS World Medical?*

A: By setting ambitious goals, Kelly keeps talented, ambitious workers challenged and motivated. Using the path-goal model to specify relationships and make predictions about employee outcomes provides a useful way for leaders to think about motivating subordinates.

Discussion Question #6: *Think back to teachers you have had, and identify one each who fits a supportive style, directive style, participative style, and achievement-oriented style according to the path-goal theory. Which style did you find most effective? Why?*

Notes____

5. To use the Vroom-Jago model to identify the correct amount of follower participation in specific decision situations.

The Vroom-Jago Contingency Model *Exhibit 3.7*

The Vroom-Jago model focuses on varying degrees of participative leadership, and how each level of participation influences quality and accountability of decisions.

The model tells the leader the correct amount of participation by subordinates to use in making a decision.

This helps the leader gauge the appropriate amount of participation for subordinates.

The model has three components: leader participation styles, diagnostic questions to analyze a situation, and a series of decision rules.

Leader Participation Styles

The model employs five levels of subordinate participation in decision making, ranging from highly autocratic (leader decides alone) to highly democratic (leader delegates to group).

The five styles fall along a continuum:

- *Decide*---the leader decides alone
- *Consult individually*---presenting the problem to subordinates for suggestions and then deciding alone
- *Consult group*---presenting the problem to subordinates as a group, collectively obtaining their ideas and then making the decision alone
- *Facilitate*---sharing the problem with subordinates as a group and acting as a facilitator to help the group arrive at a decision
- *Delegate*---delegating the problem and permitting the group to make the decision within prescribed limits.

Diagnostic Questions

➢ *How does a leader decide which of the five decision styles to use?*

The appropriate degree of decision participation depends on situational factors.

Leaders can analyze the appropriate degree of participation by answering seven diagnostic questions:

- How significant is this decision?
- How important is subordinate commitment to carrying out the decision?
- What is the level of leader's expertise in relation to the problem?
- If the leader made the decision alone, would subordinates have a high or low level of commitment?
- What degree of subordinate support for the objectives rests in the decision?
- What is the level of the group's knowledge in relation to the problem?

- How skilled and committed are group members to working together to solve the problem?

Notes____

____

____

Selecting a Decision Style *Exhibits 3.8 & 3.9*

Development of the model added concern for time constraints and concern for follower development as criteria for determining the level of participation.

This led to two decision matrixes, *a time-based model,* if time is critical and a *development-based model*, if developing follower decision-making is critical.

The leader enters the matrix at Problem Statement, and considers the seven situational questions in sequence from left to right, answering high (H) or low (L) to each one and avoiding crossing any horizontal lines.

The time-driven model leads to the first decision style that preserves decision quality and follower acceptance, whereas the development-driven model takes other considerations into account.

Leaders can quickly learn to use the basic model to adapt their styles to fit the situation.

However, researchers developed a computer-based program that allows for greater complexity and precision and incorporates time and follower development as situational factors rather than using separate decision trees.

In the Lead: Dave Robbins, Whitlock Manufacturing

When Whitlock Manufacturing won a contract from a large auto manufacturer to produce an engine to power their flagship sports car, Dave Robbins was thrilled to be selected as project manager. Robbins and his team of engineers serious engine problems and manufacturers suspended sales and halted production. Unless the engine problem was solved quickly, Whitlock faced litigation. Robbins consults with team members before making his final decisions.

Q: *How can Robbins use Vroom-Jago model for decision-making?*

A: In moving through the decision tree, the answers to the first five questions is high. This leads to the question: *What is the level of group members knowledge in relation to the problem?* The answer is low, which leads Robbins to Consult Group decision style.

Discussion Question #7: *Do you think leaders should decide on a participative style based on the most "efficient" way to reach the decision? Should leaders let people participate for other reasons?*

Notes____

---

6. To know how to use the power of situational variables to substitute for or neutralize the need for leadership.

Substitutes for Leadership

Exhibit 3.10

This contingency approach suggests that situational variables can be so powerful as to substitute or neutralize the need for leadership.

This approach outlines those organizational settings in which task-oriented and people-oriented leadership styles are unimportant.

Substitutes for leadership are situational variables make style unnecessary or redundant.

Highly educated, professional subordinates such as research scientists know how to do their tasks and do not need a leader to initiate structure and tell them what to do.

Long-term education often develops autonomous, self-motivated individuals.

Task- oriented and people-oriented leadership is substituted by professional education and socialization.

Discussion Question #3: *Consider the leadership position of the managing partner in a law firm. What task, subordinate, and organizational factors might serve as substitutes for leadership in this situation?*

Notes____

A *neutralizer* counteracts leadership style and prevents the leader from displaying certain behaviors.

If a leader is physically removed from subordinates, the leader's ability to give directions to subordinates is greatly reduced.

Situational variables include characteristics of the followers, the task, and the organization itself.

Highly structured tasks substitute for a task-oriented style, and satisfying tasks substitute for a people-oriented style.

With respect to the organization itself, group cohesiveness substitutes for both leader and styles.

Leaders should adopt a style to complement the organizational situation.

Recent research has examined how to design substitutes to have more impact than leader behaviors on outcomes such as subordinate satisfaction

The ability to use substitutes to fill leadership "gaps" is advantageous to organizations.

Substitutes-for-leadership researchers define effective leadership as the ability to recognize and provide the support and direction not provided by task, group, and organization.

Discussion Question #8: *Consider the situational characteristics of group cohesiveness, organizational formalization, and physical separation. How might each of these substitute for or neutralize task-oriented or people-oriented leadership? Explain.*

Notes____

DISCUSSION QUESTIONS

1. *Consider Fiedler's theory as illustrated in Exhibit 3.3. How often do you think very favorable, intermediate, or very unfavorable situations occur to leaders in real life? Discuss.*

Highly favorable and highly unfavorable situations are more rare than intermediate situations. Highly unfavorable refers to a situation that requires a turnaround, and most situations are not that critical. Highly favorable situations last only a short time in a fast changing world. For most situations, people-oriented leadership is appropriate. Most of the world revolves around the mean (average) of leader-member relations, task structure, and position power.

Relationship-oriented leaders are more effective in situations of moderate favorability because human relations skills are important in achieving high group performance. Task-oriented leaders excel in favorable situations because everyone gets along, and the leader has all the power. If the situation is highly unfavorable to the leader, structure and task direction are needed.

2. *Do you think leadership style is fixed and unchangeable or flexible and adaptable? Why?*

Trait theories assume that leadership style is fixed: people with the correct traits make good leaders. Fiedler assumes that the situation rather than the leader must be changed to suit the leader's style. According to Hersey and Blanchard's Situational Theory, the characteristics of followers determine effective leader behavior. Subordinates low in task readiness need a different leadership style that those high in readiness. The path-goal theory and Vroom-Jago model assume that leaders can tailor behavior to situation. The weight of the evidence is that leadership style can be flexible.

3. *Consider the leadership position of the managing partner in a law firm. What task, subordinate, and organizational factors might serve as substitutes for leadership in this situation?*

Variables such as formalization, inflexibility, and physical separation would not be typical of a law firm. Task characteristics are not highly structure, but subordinates get automatic feedback on performance, such as winning or losing a case, a substitute for task-oriented leadership. A law practice is intrinsically satisfying, a substitute for people-oriented leadership. The group characteristics of professionalism and experience substitute for task-oriented leadership and to some extent people-oriented leadership. Professions like law police themselves through peer review to assure that professional and ethical standards are met. The senior partner needs to provide only nominal leadership and concentrate on personal clients.

4. *Compare Fiedler's contingency model with the path-goal theory. What are similarities and differences? Which do you prefer?*

Both consider the situation. Whereas Fiedler assumes that task-oriented or relationship-oriented leaders should match the favorability of the situations, the path-goal theory proposes that leaders change their behaviors to match the situation. The path-goal is easier to follow because there are four types of leader behavior, not personality traits, which every leader can adopt, depending on the situation: supportive leadership, directive leadership, participative leadership, and achievement-oriented leadership. I prefer the path-goal theory because I believe a leader can use different styles as needed.

5. *Think of a situation in which you worked. At what level of readiness (R I to R4) would you rate yourself and coworkers? Did your leader use the correct style according to the Hersey and Blanchard model?*

In a foreign language class, the students are at different readiness levels to communicate in the language. They have varied backgrounds in language learning and different abilities and skills in vocabulary development, grammar, and pronunciation. They are at different readiness levels. For students, a teacher must use a more directive style and for others the teacher can allow small conversation groups to function autonomously. The teacher can adopt a more participative style.

6. *Think back to the teachers you have had, and identify one each who fits a supportive style, directive style, participative style, and achievement-oriented style according to the path-goal theory. Which style did you find most effective?*

Supportive (i.e., people-oriented) Prof. Spector taught medieval literature and based the classes on discussion and teacher-student interaction.

Directive, (i.e., task-oriented); My high school Latin teacher gave long, translation assignments every night.

Participative (i.e., group decisions) Prof. Lukens taught management at the University of Texas-Permian Basin and regularly used small groups to present the material in the chapters.

Achievement-oriented (i.e., setting challenging goals) Prof. Weinberg at the University of Chicago challenged the students to write very challenging assignments using his critical methods techniques.

7. *Do you think leaders should decide on a participative style based on the most "efficient" way to reach a decision? Should leaders sometimes let people participate for other reasons?*

It depends on whether there is a need for a quick decision or whether follower development is a priority. An autocratic style saves time without reducing decision quality or acceptance. In today's organizations, where knowledge sharing and participation are critical to success, leaders are placing emphasis on follower development. Researchers have developed a computer-based program that allows for greater complexity and precision in the Vroom-Jago model and incorporates the value of time and follower development as situational factors rather than portraying them in separate decision trees.

8. *Consider the situational characteristics of group cohesiveness, organizational formalization, and physical separation. How might each of these substitute for or neutralize task-oriented or people- oriented leadership? Explain.*

If group cohesiveness meets employee social needs, people-oriented leadership is not needed. Group members behave alike according to social and group norms. For example, a dress code is understood (e.g., wearing jeans on Friday or wearing a suit and tie) and no one needs to remind employees. The leader is then free to concentrate on task-oriented behavior. If organizational formalization is in place, task-oriented leadership is substituted. Employees are well aware of the policies and rules and do not need to be told. The leader is free to concentrate on people-oriented behavior. If the leader is physically separated from subordinates, his ability to support and direct is neutralized.

TEACHING TOOLS AND EXERCISES

1. Invite a leader of a group in the community to speak to the class about leadership style. Leaders might come from local organizations, student clubs, from the military, or from a corporation.

2. *On the Web:* Watch the video about Leadership at Sunshine Cleaning Systems.

   Click on ***www.swlearning.com/management*** Scroll down to video library and click on the icon. You will see the Video Clip Index. Scroll down to Leadership: Sunshine Cleaning Systems (11:51) . You will have to download Quicktime Plugin play the video.

3. *Leader's Self-Insight*

   T-P Leadership Questionnaire: An Assessment of Style

   Some leaders deal with people needs, leaving tasks details to subordinates. Other leaders focus on specific details with the expectation that subordinates will carry out orders The important issue is the ability to identify relevant dimensions of the situation and behave accordingly.

   After completing and scoring the questionnaire, students can identify their leadership orientation. Ask them what would be considered an ideal leader situation for their leadership style.

4. *Leader Behaviors: small group exercise*

   In small groups, think of a group or team to which you currently belong or of which you have been a member. What type of leadership style did the leader of this group appear to exhibit?

   Give some specific examples of the type of leadership behavior used. Evaluate the leadership style. Was it appropriate for the group? Why or why not? What would you have done differently? Why?

5. *Out-of-class reading:* Ian Mount, "Underlings: That's *Mister* Conway to You. And I Am *Not* a PeoplePerson," *Business 2.0* (February 2002): 53-58.

LEADERSHIP DEVELOPMENT: CASES FOR ANALYSIS

I. Synopsis: Alvis Corporation

Kevin McCarthy is the manager of a production department in Alvis Corporation, a firm that manufactures office equipment. After reading an article that stressed the benefit of participative management, Kevin believes that these benefits could be realized in his department if the workers participated in decision making. The first decision involved vacation schedules. On the vacation issue the group was deadlocked and Kevin would have to resolve the dispute himself. The second decision involved production standards. New equipment made it possible for workers to earn more with working more. The savings from higher productivity would pay for the new equipment. The workers recommended keeping production standards the same. The spokesman explained that their base pay had not kept up with inflation and the pay incentive simply restored their base pay to its prior level.

Case questions and answers

1. *Analyze this situation using the Hersey-Blanchard model and the Vroom-Jago model. What do these models suggest as the appropriate leadership or decision style. Explain.*

According to Hersey-Blanchard, the performance of the employees determines the leadership style. Kevin wants to use a participative style (S3) and give support to employee ideas. When employees develop a higher level of readiness, they benefit from support, not directives. These employees have a lower level of readiness and quality control issues in their jobs. So, Kevin must return to a telling style (S I) because the workers need direction.

Vroom and Jago note that the autocratic style saves time without reducing decision quality or acceptance. The workers prefer to have Kevin make the decisions.

2. *Evaluate Kevin McCarthy's leadership style before and during his experiment in participative management.*

In the past Kevin had a telling style (S 1), directing employees and making all decisions for them. Then Kevin gave rewards based on productivity. During the experiment, he used a participative style (S3), allowing them to make some decisions about their vacations and the production standards of their work, but the workers were not ready. They were not used to making decisions and could not reach consensus. They preferred to have Kevin direct them.

3. *If you were Kevin McCarthy, what would you do now? Why?*

Kevin should use a more directive style. The workers are far more comfortable with a task-oriented leadership style. He could develop the workers abilities and skills through training and then increase their readiness for a more participative style.

II. Synopsis: Finance Department

Ken Osborne, head of the finance department of a government agency, inherited a group of highly trained professionals who pursued their jobs with energy and enthusiasm. The department practically ran itself until Larry Gibson, one of the department's best employees, took a professional development seminar. Larry was spending more time on outside professional activities than he was on the job. The new accounting system is floundering because Gibson is not spending time to train people in its effective use, so Ken is getting complaints. Ken also noticed that other people are starting to come in late.

Case questions and answers

1. *Why has Osborne's department been so successful even though he has provided littler leadership over the past two years?*

The group characteristics of professionalism and experience substitute for task-oriented leadership and to some extent people-oriented leadership. The highly trained professionals in the finance department pursued their jobs with energy and enthusiasm and did not require a leader. Osborne was essentially free to pursue other activities because the department had high standards and functioned autonomously.

2. *Based on Hersey and Blanchard's situational theory, which style best describes Osborne's current leadership? Which style do you think Osborne might most effectively use to turn things around with Larry Gibson?*

Currently Osborne is using the leadership style of delegating (S4) which provides little direction and little support. Employees assume responsibility for their work and for the organization. The professionals in the finance department are high in readiness with good ability, skills, confidence, and willingness to work (R4). Larry Gibson now has moderate readiness (R3), able but an unwilling degree of readiness, so Osborne needs to adopt a different leadership style. He can try the participating style (S3), sharing ideas and facilitating decision making while providing guidance. This is appropriate because Gibson is a very highly skilled employee with the ability to perform the job. If this fails, Osborne will have to become more task-oriented and directive.

3. *Do you see ways in which Osborne might apply the path-goal theory to improve Gibson's performance.*

Yes. It is Osborne's responsibility to clarify the *path to rewards* for Gibson or to increase the *amount of rewards* to enhance satisfaction and job performance. Since Gibson does have the skills, Osborne should develop new rewards to meet the specific needs of Gibson. Maybe the reward could be another seminar if Gibson performs well on the job instead of leaving for other meetings and shirking responsibilities.

4. *If you were in Osborne's position, describe how you would evaluate the changed situation and handle the problem with Larry Gibson.*

Gibson had negatively affected the professionalism and morale of the entire department. Other people no longer abide by norms based on group cohesiveness. The substitutes for leadership ---both task-oriented substitutes and people-oriented substitutes—are no longer in place. Gibson needs participative leadership as described in the path-goal theory to clarify followers needs and rewards. According to the theory, the outcome should be more effort in the finance department plus improved satisfaction (less complaining) and better performance.

CHAPTER FOUR
THE LEADER AS AN INDIVIDUAL

CHAPTER SUMMARY

This chapter explores some of the individual differences that affect leaders and the leadership process. Individuals differ in many ways, including personality, values and attitudes, and styles of thinking and decision making. One model personality, the Big Five personality dimensions, examines whether individuals score high or low on the dimensions of extroversion, agreeableness, conscientiousness, emotional stability, and openness to experience. Although there is some indication that a high degree of each of the personality dimensions is associated with successful leadership, individuals who score low on various dimensions may also be effective leaders. Two specific personality traits that have a significant impact on leader behavior are locus of control and authoritarianism.

Values are fundamental beliefs that cause a person to prefer that things be done one way rather than another. One way to think about values is in terms of instrumental and end values. End values are beliefs about the kinds of goals that are worth pursuing while instrumental values are beliefs about the types of behavior that are appropriate for reaching goals. Values also affect an individual's attitudes. A leader's attitudes about self and others influence how the leader behaves toward and interacts with followers. Two sets of assumptions called Theory X and Theory Y represent two very different sets of attitudes leaders may hold about people in general.

Another area of individual differences is cognitive style. The whole brain concept explores a person's preferences for right-brained versus left-brained thinking and for conceptual versus experiential thinking. The model provides a powerful metaphor for understanding differences in thinking styles. Individuals can learn to use their "whole brain" rather than relying on one thinking style. Another way of looking at cognitive difference is the Myers-Briggs Type Indicator, which measures an individual's preferences for introversion versus extroversion, sensing versus intuition, thinking versus feeling, and judging versus perceiving.

Two leadership styles that rely strongly on the individual leader's personal characteristics are charismatic leadership and transformational leadership. Charismatic leaders have an emotional impact on people by appealing to both the heart and mind. They create an atmosphere of change, articulate an idealized vision of the future, communicate clearly, inspire faith and hope, and incur personal risks to influence followers. Charisma can be used to benefit organizations and society, but it can also be dangerous. Transformational leaders also create an atmosphere of change, and they inspire followers not just to follow them personally but to believe in the vision of organizational transformation. Transformational leaders inspire followers to go beyond their own self-interest for the good of the whole.

CHAPTER OPENER

Personality Profiling at Transocean

Thom Keaton, an off-shore oil rig manager for Transocean Sedco Forex, keeps a color chart under the glass at his desk. When a crew member comes in, Keeton checks the color of the dot on his hard hat to help him know how to relate to the worker. The colored dots are a shorthand way to help people understand one another' s personality styles. Reds tend to be strong-willed and decisive, whereas Greens are cautious and serious. Blues are sensitive and dislike change and sunny Yellows are emotional and talkative. If Keeton as a red-green leaders sees that a worker is a blue-yellow, he knows to tone down his blunt, to-the-point style to enhance communication and understanding. The color-coded system grew out of a training program that profiled employees' personalities to help managers better communicate with employees, but now it's standard or Transocean's 8,300 workers. Transocean leaders are convinced the training has helped people get along better and relieve tensions.

LECTURE/OUTLINE

To identify major personality dimensions and understand how personality influences leadership and relationships within organizations.

Personality and Leadership *Exhibit 4.1*

Personality is the set of unseen characteristics and processes that underlie a relatively stable pattern of behavior in response to ideas, objects, or people in the environment.

Leaders who understand how personalities differ can improve leadership effectiveness.

A Model of Personality

Researchers have examined thousands of traits and their findings have been distilled into five general dimensions that describe personality, the *Big Five personality dimensions:*. extroversion, agreeableness, conscientiousness, emotional stability, and openness to experiences.

A person may have a low, moderate, or high degree of each of these dimensions.

Exhibit 4.2

- *Extroversion* refers to the degree to which a person is outgoing, sociable, talkative, and comfortable meeting and talking to people.

  This dimension also includes the characteristic of *dominance.*

These people are self-confident, seek out positions of authority and are competitive and assertive.

Both dominance and extroversion could be valuable for a leader, but not all effective leaders have a high degree of these characteristics.

Discussion Question #1: *Extroversion is often considered a "good" quality for a leader to have. Why might introversion be considered an equally positive quality?*

Notes____

- *Agreeableness* is the degree to which a person is able to get along with others by being good natured, cooperative, forgiving, compassionate, understanding, and trusting.

  A leader who scores high on agreeableness seems warm and approachable, whereas one who is low may seem cold, distant, and insensitive.

- *Conscientiousness* refers to the degree to which a person is responsible, dependable, persistent, and achievement-oriented.

  A conscientious person is focused on a few goals, pursued in a purposeful way, whereas a less conscientious person is easily distracted and impulsive.

  This dimension relates to the work itself, not to relationships.

- *Emotional stability* refers to the degree to which a person is well-adjusted, calm, and secure.

  A leader who is emotionally stable handles stress well, is able to handle criticism, and generally doesn't take mistakes and failures personally.

  Leaders, low in emotional stability, are likely to become tense, anxious, or depressed.

- *Openness to experience* is the degree to which a person has a broad range of interests and is imaginative, creative, and willing to consider new ideas.

  These people are intellectually curious, and seek out new experiences.

  People lower in this dimension have narrower interests and stick to the tried-and-true ways of doing things.

Open-mindedness is important to leaders because leadership is about change rather than stability.

Discussion Question #2: *What might be some reasons the dimension of "openness to experience" correlates so strongly with historians' ratings of the greatest U.S. presidents but has been less strongly associated with business leaders? Do you think this personality dimension might be more important for business leaders of today than it was in the past?*

Notes____

Researchers have found considerable evidence that people who score high on the dimensions of extroversion, agreeableness, conscientiousness, and emotional stability are more successful leaders.

Recent studies of the personality traits of the greatest U.S. presidents showed that openness to experience produced the highest correlation with ratings of greatness.

Few leaders consistently score high across all of the Big Five dimensions, yet there are many successful leaders.

The value of the Big Five for leaders is to help them understand their personality dimensions and emphasize the positive and mitigate the negative aspects of their style.

***In the Lead*:** Vinita Gupta, Quick Eagle Networks

Vinita Gupta, the founding CEO of Quick Eagle Networks, saw that sales and profits were going up, but employee morale kept going down. Employees were quitting, with annual turnover hitting 30 percent. Gupta realized that her own personality was part of the problem. Introverted, soft-spoken, and highly focused on work, Gupta had always depended on managers to be the cheerleaders of the company. She heard that people found her aloof and unapproachable and the stiff, serious atmosphere she created made employees miserable. Gupta worked to develop empathy and improve her social skills, using humor to create a lighter atmosphere.

Q: *How did Gupta learn to manage her behaviors at Quick Eagle?*

A: The value of the Big Five for leaders is to help them understand their personality dimensions and emphasize the positive and mitigate the negative aspects of their style. Gupta will never score high on extroversion, but she is more open and less defensive. She makes a point of greeting people upon arrival, introducing herself to employees she's never met, and having lunch with colleagues.

Notes____

____

____

Personality Traits and Leader Behavior

Two personality attributes affect behavior: locus of control and authoritarianism.

Locus of control

Locus of control refers to whether a person places the primary responsibility within himself or on outside forces.

People who believe their actions determine what happens to them have a high *internal* locus of control (internals), while those who believe outside forces determine what happens to them have a high *external* locus of control (externals).

Research on locus of control shows real differences:

- *Internals* are more self-motivated, participate more in social and political activities, and seek information actively.

  Internals are better able to handle complex information and problem solving and are more achievement-oriented.

  They are more likely to influence others and seek leadership opportunities.

- *Externals* prefer a structured, directed work situation.

  Externals are better able to handle work that requires compliance and conformity.

  They do best in situations where success depends on complying with the direction of others and are less likely to enjoy or succeed in leadership positions.

Authoritarianism

Authoritarianism is the belief that power and status differences *should* exist in an organization.

Individuals who have a high degree of this trait adhere to conventional rules and values, obey established authority, respect power and toughness, critically judge others, and disapprove of the expression of personal feelings.

A leader's degree of authoritarianism affects wielding and sharing power.

A closely related trait is *dogmatism*, which refers to a person's receptiveness to new ideas.

In a leadership position, dogmatic leaders make decisions based on limited information and are unreceptive to ideas that conflict with their opinions.

Effective leaders are open-minded.

Understanding how personality traits and dimensions affect behavior can be a valuable ability for leaders.

Knowledge of individual differences gives leaders valuable insights into their own behaviors as well as that of followers.

It offers a framework to diagnose situations and make beneficial changes.

Discussion Question #3: *In which of the Big Five personality dimensions would you place the traits of locus of control and authoritarianism?*

Notes____

To clarify your instrumental and end values, and recognize how value guide thoughts and behavior.

Values and Attitudes

Leader's Self-Insight 4.2

People differ in the values and attitudes they hold, and these differences affect the behavior of leaders and followers.

Instrumental and End Values

Values are fundamental beliefs that an individual considers to be important, that are relatively stable over time, and that have an impact on attitudes and behavior.

Social scientist Milton Rokeach developed a list of 18 instrumental and 18 end values to be found across cultures.

End values, also called terminal values, are beliefs about the kinds of goals or outcomes worth pursuing (e.g., security, a comfortable life, good health).

Instrumental values are beliefs about the types of behavior that are appropriate for reaching goals (e.g., being helpful, honest, or courageous.)

Individuals differ in how they order the values into priorities, which accounts for tremendous variation among people.

Part of this difference relates to culture---(e.g., In the U.S., independence is highly valued whereas other cultures place more value on being part of a tight-knit community).

A person's family background influences values because they are learned, not inherited.

Some values become incorporated into a person's thinking very early in life; however, some values can change.

- *Living Leadership: Developing Character*

  Ronald Reagan: *" The character that takes command in moments of critical choices has already been determined...by a thousand other choices made earlier... "*

- What day-to-day decisions have you made that have developed your character?

A leader's personal values affect the perception of a situation or problem.

Perception is the process people use to make sense out of the environment by selecting, organizing, and interpreting information.

Values affect how leaders relate to others; a leader who values obedience, conformity, and politeness may not understand a follower who is self-reliant and a bit rebellious.

Values guide a leader's choices and actions; a leader who values courage and standing up for personal beliefs is more likely to make decisions which are right, even if unpopular.

In the Lead: Jeffrey S. Potter, Frontier Airlines

Frontier Airlines, a small airline in Denver, Colorado, has a growing reputation for doing the right thing and caring about employees and customers. As large airlines face huge losses, small carriers have an opportunity to grow by keeping costs low, offering low fares, and winning customers with a fair approach to business. Whereas most airlines charge a stiff penalty for switching a return flight, Frontier eliminated this practice. Potter regularly listens to the ideas, complaints, and suggestions of flight attendants and mechanics.

Q: *How do values guide Jeffrey Potter's choices and actions?*

A: Values guide a leader's choices and actions. Potter's values of openness, honesty, fairness, and cooperation are part of the culture at Frontier. Potter's values have helped to build a family atmosphere among employees, who, in turn, spread that feeling to customers.

Discussion Question #4: *From Exhibit 4.3, identify 4 or 5 values (either instrumental or end values) that could be a source of conflict between leaders and followers. Explain.*

Notes____

To define attitudes and explain their relationship to leader behavior.

How Attitudes Affect Leadership

Values help determine the attitudes leaders have about themselves and about their followers.

An *attitude* is an evaluation—either positive or negative---about people, events, or things.

Behavioral scientists consider attitudes to have three components: cognitions (thoughts), affect (feelings), and behavior.

- The *cognitive* component includes ideas and knowledge about the object of an attitude--- a leader's ideas about an employee's performance.
- The *affective* component concerns feelings about the object---a leader resents helping the employee perform tasks.
- The *behavioral* component predisposes a person to act a certain way---a leader avoids an employee.

One consideration is a leader's attitudes about himself.

Self-concept refers to the collection of attitudes people have about themselves, including the element of self-esteem, whether a person has positive or negative feelings about himself.

A person with a positive self-concept has high self-esteem, whereas a person with a negative self-concept has low self-esteem.

➢ *Why are leaders with positive self-concepts are more effective?.*

Leaders with negative self-concepts, who are insecure and have low self-esteem, create environments that limit other people's growth and development?

Discussion Question #5: *How do a person's attitudes and assumptions about human nature in general affect his or her leadership approach? How might a leader's attitudes about him or herself alter or reinforce this approach?*

Notes____

A leader's style is based on attitudes about human nature in general---ideas and feelings about what motivates people, whether people are honest trustworthy, and can grown and change.

Exhibit 4.3

Douglas McGregor identified two sets of assumptions about human nature, *Theory X and Theory Y.*

- Theory X reflects the assumption that people are lazy, not motivated to work, and have a natural tendency to avoid responsibility.

  A Theory X leader believes that people must be coerced, controlled, directed, or threatened to get their best effort.

- Theory Y is based on the assumption that people seek out greater responsibility and will exercise imagination and creativity to solve organizational problems.

  A Theory Y leader is more people-oriented and concerned with relationships and doesn't believe people need to be controlled or coerced to perform.

➢ *Give an example from your own experience of Theory X and Theory Y.*

In the Lead: Mark Schmink, Dana Corp.

Dana Corp.'s plant makes truck chassis for Toyota, a contract the company won by promising to decrease prices by 2 percent within two years. Mark Schmink, the founding plant manager, knew that meant finding production efficiencies and providing good wages and benefits for employees. Schmink wanted to create a "culture of inventiveness" in which employees were constantly developing new and better ways of working. He hired welders with no experience and training to perform every job in the plant. He opened a library in the plant and offered tuition reimbursement, signaling that mental work was valued. He required that employees submit two ideas a month and provided continuous feedback by displaying productivity figures on electronic signs. Every success was celebrated with a special lunch, free sodas, or a barbecue.

Q: *Is Mark Schmink a Theory X or Theory Y leader? Explain.*

A: Mark is a Theory Y leader because he feels that the welders will seek out greater responsibility and will exercise imagination and creativity to cut costs and keep the Toyota contract. Mark is concerned with relationships and doesn't coerce workers. As workers saw their ideas implemented, they became more excited about proposing new ways to do things, questioning every procedure.

McGregor believed Theory Y to be more realistic and productive for viewing subordinates and shaping leader attitudes.

Studies exploring the relationship between leader attitudes and leadership success in general support McGregor's idea.

Notes____

To recognize individual differences in cognitive style and broaden your own thinking style to expand leadership potential.

Cognitive Differences

Exhibit 4.4

Cognitive style refers to how a person perceives, processes, interprets, and uses information.

Cognitive differences refer to approaches to perceiving and assimilating data, making decisions, and solving problems.

Cognitive approaches are *preferences* that are not rigid, but most people have preferred habits of thought.

One cognitive difference is between left-brained versus right-brained thinking.

Patterns of Thinking and Brain Dominance

The left hemisphere of the brain controls movement on the body's right side and is associated with logical, analytical thinking.

The right hemisphere of the brain controls movement on the body's left side and is associated with creative, intuitive, values-based thought processes.

This concept provides a powerful metaphor for two different way of thinking and decision-making.

Everyone uses both left- and right-brained thinking, but to varying degrees.

The whole brain concept, developed by Ned Hermann, considers not only a right- or left-brained thinking preference , but also a conceptual versus experiential thinking.

Herman's whole brain model identifies four quadrants of the brain related to different thinking styles.

An individual's preference for each of the four styles is determined through a survey called *The Hermann Dominance Instrument (HBDI).*

The model provides an overview of an individual's mental preferences, which in turn affect patterns of communication, behavior, and leadership.

- *Quadrant A* is associated with logical thinking; this leader focuses on tasks and activities and likes to deal with concrete information and facts.

- *Quadrant B* is associated with planning, organizing facts, and careful, detailed review; this leader is typically conservative and highly traditional.

- *Quadrant C* is associated with interpersonal relationships and affects intuitive and emotional thought processes; leaders are friendly, trusting, and empathetic.

- *Quadrant D* is associated with conceptualizing, synthesizing, and integrating facts and patterns; this leader is imaginative, adventurous, and enjoys change.

Every individual has a coalition of preferences of each of the four quadrants.

Hermann believes that people can learn to use their "whole brain," rather that relying on one or two quadrants.

Leaders who reach the top of organizations often have well-balanced brains.

Discussion Question #6: *Do you believe understanding your preferences according to the whole brain model can help you be a better leader? Discuss.*

Notes____

Understanding that individuals have different thinking styles helps leaders be more effective in interacting with followers.

Some leaders act as if everyone responds to the same material and behavior in the same way, but this isn't true.

Some prefer facts and figures while others prefer to know about relationships and patterns; some followers prefer freedom and flexibility while others crave structure.

Discussion Question #7: *How can leader use an understanding of brain dominance to improve the functioning of the organization?*

Notes____

***In the Lead*:** Jerry Hirshberg, Nissan Design International

Jerry Hirshberg is a predominantly D-quadrant leader. He likes thinking broadly and dreaming big, deriving ideas intuitively—and he abhors tight structure and control. He wanted his designers to be creative and was surprised to leader that a few of his followers actually wanted and needed more structure. Hirshberg realized that some designers wanted and needed time to "process" information and develop logical approaches to Hirshberg's intuitively-derived ideas. He now hires designers in *divergent pairs* with different cognitive styles.

Q: *How does Hirshberg create a "whole brain" company at Nissan Design?*

A: Hirshberg now hires designers in *divergent pairs* with different cognitive styles. By putting together two gifted people who have different cognitive styles and see the world in different ways, he builds a creative tension that keeps the organization energized and provides unlimited potential for innovation.

Problem Solving Styles: The Myers-Briggs Type Indicator

Carl Jung believed that behavioral differences resulted from preferences in gathering and evaluating information for solving problems and making decisions,

Based on his work is a widely-used personality test, the *Myers-Briggs Type Indicator (MBTI)*, which measures how individuals differ in these areas.

The MBTI uses four different pairs of attributes to classify people in one of 16 different personality types:

- *Introversion versus Extroversion*: This dimension focuses on where people gain interpersonal strength and mental energy. Extroverts (E) gain energy from others while Introverts (I) gain energy from personal thoughts and feelings.

- *Sensing versus Intuition*: This identifies how a person absorbs information. Those with a sensing preference (S) gather and absorb information through the five senses, whereas intuitive people (N) rely on less direct perceptions and more on patterns and relationships.

- *Thinking versus Feeling*: This dimension relates to how much consideration a person gives to emotions in making a decision. Feeling types (F) rely on morals and values, whereas thinking types (T) rely on logic and objectivity.

- *Judging versus Perceiving*: This dimension concerns an individual's attitudes toward ambiguity and how quickly a person makes a decision. People with a judging preference (J) like certainty and closure. Perceiving people (P) enjoy ambiguity, dislike deadlines, and change their minds.

The various combinations of preferences result in 16 unique personality types.

Each person has developed unique strengths and weaknesses because of their preferences.

➢ *Do you think the MBTI indicators should be considered unalterable?*

People's awareness of their preferences, training, and life experiences can cause them to change their preferences over time.

Research reveals some interesting, although tentative, findings:

- Leaders in the real world are equally divided between introverts and extroverts.

- Sensing types are in the majority in fields where the focus is on the immediate and tangible (e.g., banking, manufacturing.)

- In long-range planning, intuitive leaders are in the majority.
- Thinking types are more common in business, industry, and science.
- Judging types are in the majority among leaders.

In the Lead: John Bearden, GMAC Home Services

John Bearden hired a personal coach to help him learn why he behaved the way he did---passionate, driven, nonempathetic, and inclined to make hasty decisions. The MBTI indicated that Bearden was an ENTJ (extroverted, intuitive, thinking, and judging). ENTJ types can be dynamic but also overbearing, insensitive, and hasty in their judgments.

Q: *How did Bearden use Myers-Brigs indicators to add to his understanding of his strengths and weaknesses?*

A: Bearden began consciously revising his leadership style. As CEO of GMAC Home Services, he made a determined effort to give consideration to hard data and listen more carefully to colleagues instead of interjecting his own position early on and biasing the process.

One area in which research may offer insight is the relationship between cognitive styles and two types of leadership that rely on the leaders personal characteristics: charismatic leadership and transformational leadership.

Discussion Question #8: *Why do you think thinking and judging are the two characteristics from the Myers Briggs Type Indicator that are most strongly associated with effective leadership?*

Notes____

To practice aspects of charismatic leadership by pursuing a vision or idea that you care deeply about and want to share with others.

Personality and Leadership Style: The Role of Charisma *Exhibit 4.5*

➢ *Why had charismatic Leadership has been called "a fire that ignites followers" ?*

Charismatic leaders have the ability to inspire and motivate people to do more than they would normally do, despite obstacles and personal sacrifice.

Charismatic leaders have an emotional impact on people because they appeal to both the heart and the mind.

They often emerge in troubled times because a strong, inspiring personality can help reduce stress and anxiety among followers.

Used wisely and ethically, charisma can lift the entire organization's level of performance.

Charismatic leaders can raise people's consciousness about new possibilities and motivate them to transcend their own interests for the sake of the team, department, or organization.

What Makes a Charismatic Leader

Studies have identified the unique qualities of charismatic leaders, documented the impact on followers, and described the behaviors that help them achieve remarkable results.

Charismatic leaders create an atmosphere of change and articulate an idealized vision of a future that is significantly better in some way than the present.

They have the ability to communicate complex ideas and goals in clear, compelling ways, so that everyone can understand and identify with the message and the leader.

Charismatic leaders inspire followers with an abiding faith, even if the faith cannot be stated in specific goals that are easily attained. (e.g., Martin Luther King.)

Charismatic leaders earn trust by incurring great personal risk.

- *Why is Michael Jordan a charismatic leader?*

The source of influence of a charismatic leader comes from personal power as opposed to the power and authority granted by the organization.

Notes____

____

____

The Black Hat of Charisma

- *Give an example of how charisma is not always used to benefit the group, organization or society.*

It can also be used for self-serving purposes, which leads to deception, manipulation, and exploitation (e.g., Saddam Hussein).

One explanation is the difference between *personalized* and *socialized* leaders.

Personalized, charismatic leaders are self-aggrandizing, nonegalitarian, and exploitative whereas socialized charismatic leaders are empowering, egalitarian, and supportive.

Personalized behavior is based on caring about self; socialized behavior is based on valuing others.

Discussion Question #9: *What do you consider the essential traits of a charismatic leader? Why is charismatic leadership considered potentially dangerous?*

Notes____

To apply the concepts that distinguish transformational from transactional leadership.

Transactional versus Transformational Leadership

Transactional leadership

The basis of *transactional leadership* is a transaction or exchange between leaders and followers.

The leader recognizes specific follower desires and provides goods that meet those desires in exchange for followers meeting specified objectives or performing certain duties.

Followers receive rewards and leaders benefit from task completion.

Transactional leaders focus on the present and excel at keeping an organization running smoothly and efficiently.

Because transactional leadership involves a commitment to "follow the rules," transactional leaders maintain stability rather than change.

Transactional skills are important for all leaders.

Transformational leadership

Transformational leadership is characterized by the ability to bring about significant changes in vision, strategy, culture, products and technologies.

Leaders focus on intangible qualities such as shared values to enlist followers in the change process.

Transformational and transactional leadership differ in four areas:

- *Transformational leadership develops followers into leaders.* Followers are given freedom to control their own behavior.

- *Transformational leadership elevates followers' concerns from lower-level needs (e.g., safety and security) to higher-level needs (e.g., self-esteem and self-actualization).* The leader pays attention to individual needs for growth and development.

- *Transformational leadership inspires followers to go from self-interest to group welfare.* Leaders motivate people to do more than originally expected.

- *Transformational leadership envisions a desired future state and communicates it in a way that makes the pain of change worth the effort.* The most significant role of the leader is to find a vision and enlist others in sharing the dream.

Discussion Question #10: *What are the primary differences between transactional and transformational leadership?*

Notes____

____

____

Transactional leaders promote stability and transformational leaders promotes significant change.

Leaders can learn to be transformational as well as transactional.

Effective leaders exhibit both leadership patterns.

They accentuate not only their abilities to build a vision and empower and energize others, but also the transactional skills of designing structures, control systems, and reward systems that can help people achieve the vision.

In the Lead: Richard Kovacevich, Wells Fargo

Richard Kovacevich has been called one of the best bankers in America because of his careful attention to the structures and systems that keep banks stable and profitable. However, he's also a transformational leader who has steered the mid-sized Norwest Corp. through numerous acquisitions, such as Wells Fargo, to become the fourth-largest U.S. banking company. Kovacevich inspires followers with a vision of transformation --- of turning Wells Fargo's nationwide network of offices into a Wal-Mart style retailing powerhouse.

Q: *How does Richard Kovacevich reflect a balance of transactional and transformational leadership.*

A: Kovacevich motivates with slogans such as "Mind share plus heart share equals market share." It's the substance behind the slogan that matters. Employees are rewarded for putting their hears and minds into their work. Kovacevich spends a lot of time in the field , meeting with team members (employees) and customers, patting backs and giving pep talks.

Discussion Question #11: *What personality dimensions, values, and attitudes might be particularly useful to an individual who wants to act as a transformational leader? Do you believe anyone can develop them? Discuss.*

Notes____

____

____

DISCUSSION QUESTIONS

1. *Extroversion is often considered a "good" quality for a leader to have. Why might introversion be considered an equally positive quality?*

   Not all effective leaders have a high degree of extroversion. A high degree of dominance, associated with extroversion, could even be detrimental to effective leadership if not tempered by other qualities, such as agreeableness or emotional stability. A person may have be introverted, that is, quiet, withdrawn, and unassertive, and be an effective leader as long as some of the other Big Five dimensions are present.

   A person may have a low, moderate, or high degree of each of these general dimension. An introverted leader, high in agreeableness, openness to experience, and conscientiousness could be very effective. Situational factors play a role in determining which traits are the most important. A leader's intelligence, knowledge of the business, values and attitudes, and problem-solving styles, which are not measured by the Big Five, also play a role in leadership effectiveness.

2. *What might be some reasons the dimension of "openness to experience" correlates so strongly with historians' ratings of the greatest U.S. presidents but has been less strongly associated with business leaders? Do you think this personality dimension might be more important for business leaders of today than it was in the past? Discuss.*

   Open-mindedness is important for a president because leadership is about change. Thomas Jefferson needed open-mindedness when wrote the Declaration of Independence because the colonies were severing ties with England, changing their form of government, and building a new country. Business leaders who promote stability and maintaining the status quo can be effective without being open-minded---if they are working in a stable business environment (e.g., producing cowboy boots). However, since the global environment is changing rapidly, business leaders need open-mindedness to manage change.

3. *In which of the Big Five personality dimensions would you place the traits of locus of control and authoritarianism?*

   Locus of control would fit with extroversion, which is associated with self-confidence. Internals believe they are responsible for their fate and believe they can bring about positive outcomes through their efforts. Authoritarianism would fit with conscientiousness, the degree to which a person is responsible, dependable, persistent, and achievement-oriented. Individuals with a high degree of authoritarianism adhere to conventional rules and values and obey established authority.

4. *From Leader Self-Insight 4.2, identify four or five values (either instrumental or end values) that could be a source of conflict between leaders and followers. Explain.*

   Values affect how leaders relate to others. A leader who values obedience, conformity, and politeness may have a difficult time understanding and appreciated a follower who is self-reliant, independent, creative, and a bit rebellious. However, understanding these value differences can help leaders better understand and work with varied followers.

5. *How do a person's attitudes and assumptions about human nature in general affect his or her leadership approach? How might a leader's attitudes about him or herself alter or reinforce this approach?*

   Attitudes reflect a person's fundamental values as well as a person's background and life experiences. A leader who values forgiveness, compassion, and helping others would have different attitudes and behave differently toward a subordinate that a leader who values personal ambition and capability.

Leaders with positive self-concepts are more effective. Leaders who have a negative self-concept, who are insecure and have low self-esteem, often create environments that limit their subordinates' growth and development.

6. *Do you believe understanding your preferences according to the whole brain model can help you be a better leader? Discuss.*

   Yes, first a person can assess personal preferences and determine the dominant quadrants. Each quadrant is associated with specific leader behavior. However, Hermann suggests that people can learn to use the "whole brain" rather than relying on one or two quadrants. This gives an individual the opportunity to develop weaker quadrants and gain more balance. In today's changing, global environment, leaders need the skills associated with Quadrant D, conceptualizing, synthesizing, and integrating facts, and seeing the big picture. Knowing this, a leader can make an effort to become more imaginative, adventurous, and enjoy change.

7. *How can leader use an understanding of brain dominance to improve the functioning of the organization?*

   Understanding that individuals have different thinking styles helps leaders be more effective in interacting with followers. Some leaders act as if everyone responds to the same material and behavior in the same way. Some people prefer facts and figures while others prefer to know about relationships and patterns. This can help a leader work with subordinates more effectively and improve the functioning of the organization.

8. *Why do you think thinking and judging are the two characteristics from the Myers Briggs Type Indicator that are most strongly associated with effective leadership?*

   Thinking types rely on logic and tend to be very objective in decision making. This is important for a leader who must treat all subordinates fairly and not show favoritism based on personal feelings. People with a judging preference like certainty and closure. They enjoy having goals and deadlines and tend to make decisions quickly based on available data. In the fast-paced global economy, leaders must make decisions quickly and then move on to the next decision.

9. *What do you consider the essential traits of a charismatic leader? Why is charismatic leadership considered potentially dangerous?*

   Charismatic leaders have a vision for the future about which they are passionate and willing to take personal risk. They use unconventional means to communicate the vision clearly and inspire followers. Their power transcends their formal position and results from expertise, admiration, and respect in followers.

   Charisma is potentially dangerous because it is not always used to benefit the group, organization or society. It can also be used for personalized, self-serving purposes, which leads to deception, manipulation, and exploitation. Personalized, charismatic leaders are self-aggrandizing, nonegalitarian, and exploitative.

10. *What are the primary differences between transactional and transformational leadership?*

    Transactional leadership is a transaction or exchange between leaders and followers. The leader recognizes specific follower desires and provides goods that meet those desires in exchange for followers meeting specified objectives or performing certain duties. Transactional leaders focus on the present and excel at keeping an organization running smoothly and efficiently. Transactional leaders maintain stability rather than change.

    Transformational leadership is characterized by the ability to bring about significant changes in vision, strategy, culture, products and technologies. Leaders focus on intangible qualities such as shared values to enlist followers in the change process.

11. *What personality dimensions, values, and attitudes might be particularly useful to an individual who wants to act as a transformational leader? Do you believe anyone can develop them? Discuss.*

    Transactional leaders have charisma, energy, self-confidence, and a positive view for their organization. The view is social not personal. Leaders can learn to be transformational as well as transactional. Effective leaders exhibit both leadership patterns. They accentuate not only their abilities to build a vision and empower and energize others, but also the transactional skills of designing structures, control systems, and reward systems that can help people achieve the vision.

TEACHING TOOLS AND EXERCISES

1. *Leader's Bookshelf: Maximum Success: Changing the 12 Behavior Patterns That Keep You From Getting Ahead* by James Waldroop and Timothy Butler.

   By understanding their individual "Achilles' heels," leaders can learn to change their behaviors and improve leader effectiveness. A few weaknesses include: never feeling quite "good enough; pushing too hard; being emotionally tone-deaf.

   Do you recognize any of these in your own attitudes and behaviors? Give examples. Work in pairs or small groups.

2. *Debate:* Personality and ability have major implications for how people feel, think, and behave in organizations. Now that you have a good understanding of these individual differences, debate the following issues.

- *Team A.* Organizations should hire prospective employees on the basis of their personality traits.

- *Team B.* Organizations should *not* select or hire prospective employees on the basis of their personality traits.

3. *On the Web:* Visit the website of HR Solutions at *www.hrsolutions.com* and click on PCRecruiterHR Software. This company offers software for staffing professionals, executive search software, and online recruiting. Determine how this company matches a candidates interests and abilities to the job? Prepare a short report based on your answers and bring them to class to share for discussion.

4. *Out-of-class reading*: Matt Doherty, "What is Leadership: Observation from a Basketball Coach," *Leadership Digest* (December 2003) *www.leadership.wharton.upenn.edu*

5. *Leader's Self-Insight*

   Personality Assessment: Jung's Typology and the Myers-Briggs Type Indicator

   After filling out the personality assessment, answer the following questions:

   - Were you surprised by the results?
   - What have you learned from this exercise?
   - How can this assessment help you in your career choice?

LEADERSHIP DEVELOPMENT: CASES FOR ANALYSIS

I. **Synopsis** **International Bank**

Top executives and board members of a large international bank in New York are meeting to consider three finalists for a new position. The winning candidate will be in a high-profile job, taking charge of a group of top loan officers who have recently gotten the bank into some risky financial arrangements in Latin America. The bank had taken a financial bath when the Mexican peso collapsed, and the board voted to hire someone to oversee this group of loan officers and make sure the necessary due diligence is done on major loans before further commitments are made. Three candidates seem to have the intellect and experience to handle the job. The three have taken personality tests.

Case questions and answers

1. *Based only on the consultant's summary, which of the three candidates would you select as a leader for the group of loan officers? Discuss and defend your decision.*

I would select F.C. because this candidate is an extrovert, which implies people skills, plus self-confidence and high self-esteem, but F.C does not have a strong desire for dominance, so that other loan officers, who are skilled professionals could be left alone to do their jobs. F.C. is highly conscientious and goal-oriented and will address the serious financial problem at the bank and communicate the importance of the task at hand to subordinates. F.C.'s avoiding of close relationships is acceptable because of a positive attitude and the situation. F.C. is leading a group of professionals who have standards dictated by their education and professional groups who do not need a close personal friendship with their supervisor.

2. *The selection committee is more divided than before on who would be best for the job. What additional information do you think you would need to help you select the best candidate?*

   I would add that J.T should not be considered for the position because this candidate has a Theory X view of employees, believing that the average person has a dislike for work and will avoid responsibility when possible. This attitude fosters a work environment characterized by close monitoring which would not be satisfactory in a loan department working with highly skilled professionals who require freedom.

3. *How much weight do you think should be given to the personality assessment? Do you believe personality tests can be useful in predicting the best person for a job? Discuss.*

   I would give little weight to the personality test and rely more on a candidate's education, work and personal experience, and personal references. People can change and do change on the job. If certain leadership qualities need to emerge for greater effectiveness, this is possible.

II. Synopsis: The Deadlocked Committee

Ned Norman tried to reconstruct the series of events that had culminated in this morning's deadlocked committee meeting. Each of the members had suddenly seemed to resist any suggestions that did not exactly coincide with their own ideas for implementing the program under consideration. Ned stated that the committee had discussed several factors connected with the proposed expanded services program and now it seemed time to make a decision. Robert Romany protested that they had barely scratched the surface of the possibilities of implementing the program. Hilary Thomas and David Huntington had sided with Romany. Walther Weston stated that the decision was uncalled for, since the program had been implemented in district offices in the past.

Case questions and answers

1. *Based on the Whole Brain concept, what different thinking styles are represented by the committee members and division directors? Do you believe they can ever be brought together?*

- Ned represents Quadrant A, associated with logical thinking and analysis of facts. He is directive and authoritative.
- Walter Weston represents Quadrant B, highly conservative and traditional. Leaders tend to avoid risks and prefer to stay with what is reliable.
- Robert Romany, Hillary Thomas, and David Huntington represent Quadrant D, associated with conceptualizing, synthesizing, and integrating facts. This leader enjoys change and adventure.

They cannot be brought together as long as their thinking styles are so different. However, according to the "whole brain" theory, people can learn to use all four quadrants for balanced decision making and problem solving over time. Here, the committee must make a decision in a short period of time.

2. *Do you see ways in which Norman might use the ideas of transformational leadership to help resolve this dilemma and break the impasse?*

   Yes, transformational leadership is characterized by the ability to bring about significant changes in vision, strategy, culture, products and technologies. Ned could focus on intangible qualities such as shared values to enlist the other members of the committee in the change process. Ned could inspire the committee members to go from self-interest to group welfare. He could motivate the members to be open to opposing ideas.

3. If you were the chairman of the committee, what would you do? Discuss.

   I would use the computerized decision-tree in the Path-Goal Theory. All the questions about subordinate approval and knowledge would take into consideration the divergent views of the committee members. The computer model also considers the importance of the speed of the decision and the importance of follower development.

CHAPTER FIVE
LEADERSHIP MIND AND HEART

CHAPTER SUMMARY

Leaders use intellectual as well as emotional capabilities and understandings to guide organizations through today's turbulent environment and help employees feel energized, motivated, and cared for in the face of rapid change, confusion, and job insecurity. Leaders can expand the capacities of their minds and hearts through conscious development and practice.

Leaders should be aware of how their mental models affect their thinking and may cause "blind spots" that limit understanding. Two components of mental models are assumptions and perceptions. Becoming aware of mental models is a first step toward being able to see the world in new and different ways. Four key issues important to expanding and developing a leader's mind are independent thinking, open mindedness, systems thinking, mental models, and personal mastery.

Leaders should understand the importance of emotional intelligence. Four basic components of emotional intelligence are self-awareness, self- management, social awareness, and relationship management. Emotionally intelligent leaders can have a positive impact on organizations by helping employees grow, learn, and develop; creating a sense of purpose and meaning; instilling unity and team spirit; and basing relationships on trust and respect, which allows employees to take risks and fully contribute to the organization.

Most work in organizations is done in teams, and emotional intelligence applies to teams as well as to individuals. Leaders develop a team's emotional intelligence by creating norms that foster a strong group identity, build trust among members, and instill a belief among members that they can be effective and succeed as a team.

Traditional organizations have relied on fear as a motivator. While fear does motivate people, it prevents people from feeling good about their work and often causes avoidance behavior. Fear can reduce trust and communication so that important problems and issues are hidden or suppressed. Leaders can choose to lead with love instead of fear. Love can be thought of as a motivational force that enables people to feel alive, connected, and energized; as feelings of liking, caring, and bliss; and as actions of helping, listening, and cooperating.

Each of these aspects of live has relevance for organizational relationships. People respond to love because it meets unspoken needs for respect and affirmation. Rational thinking is important to leadership, but it takes love to build trust, creativity, and enthusiasm.

CHAPTER OPENER

Rear Admiral Albert H. Konetzni, U.S. Navy

When Rear Admiral Albert H. Konetzni took command of the U.S. Navy's Pacific submarine fleet, the Navy was facing a serious personnel crisis. Despite the largest pay raise in history, recruitment was dismal, and sailors were jumping ship as soon as possible. Konetzni thought the problem was based on the assumptions, perceptions, and mindsets of top officers who created an environment that ran people off. Adm. Konetzni wanted to try a new approach. He concluded that to keep sailors, he had to make sure they had time off for a life outside the Navy between their grueling six-month long deployments. The old mental model was that submarine commanders expected hard work, long hours, and near-perfection. Konetzni ordered that crews should work from 8 a.m. to 4 p.m. in port. He has struggled to save sailors who would have been discharged from the Navy for psychological or disciplinary problems. Despite criticisms, there's no doubt that Konetzni's approach that considers the needs and feelings of sailors had positive results. Within two years, the percentage of Pacific fleet sailors who signed up for a second tour of duty doubled, morale dramatically improved, and there has been no indication that the fleet's ability to execute its military mission has been diminished.

LECTURE/OUTLINE

Leadership Capacity versus Competence

Traditionally, effective leadership, like good management, has been thought of as competence in a set of skills; once these skills are acquired, all one has to do is put them into action.

Still, it is clear that good leadership requires more than practical skills; it requires drawing on our thoughts, beliefs, or feelings—and appealing to those aspects in others.

➢ *In today's organizations, why is competence important, but it is not enough?*

Organizations face key issues:

- how to give people a sense of meaning and purpose when major shifts occur almost daily
- how to make employees feel valued and respected in an age of downsizing and job uncertainty
- how to keep morale and motivation high in the face of rapid changes and the stress it creates.

Rather than discussing competence, this chapter focuses on a person's *capacity* for mind and heart.

Capacity is the potential of each person to do more and be more.

Leadership involves something deeper and subtler than leadership traits and styles.

Living, working, and leading based on capacity means using the whole self, including intellectual, emotional, and spiritual abilities and understandings.

A broad literature has emphasized that being a whole person means operating from the mind, heart, spirit, and body.

This chapter builds on ideas of how individuals think, make decisions, and solve problems based on values, attitudes, and patterns of thinking to provide a broader view of the leadership capacities of mind and heart.

Discussion Question #2: *Do you agree that people have a capacity for developing their minds and hearts beyond current competency? Can you give an example? Discuss.*

Notes____

____

____

____

To recognize how mental models that guide your behavior and relationships.

Mental Models *Exhibit 5.1*

Mental models are theories people hold about specific systems in the world and their expected behavior.

- *An organization is a system, as is a football team, a marriage, a university. What are the mental models that govern how a leader interprets experience and responds?*
  (the coach controls the information; wives should do housework; students should attend class)

Leaders should be aware of how these elements affect their thinking and cause "blind spots" that limit understanding.

The greatest factor determining the success of leaders may be the ability to shift one's mental model and align it with organizational needs, goals, and values.

Two important components of mental models are assumptions and perceptions.

Assumptions

Theory X and Theory Y are assumptions about subordinates, which affect leader behavior.

A leader who assumes that people cannot be trusted (Theory X)will act differently than one who thinks people are trustworthy (Theory Y).

A leader's assumptions are part of a mental model; leaders have assumptions about events, situations, and circumstances.

In the Lead: Charles F. Feeney, Atlantic Philanthropist

Charles Feeney convinced that board of his Atlantic Philanthropies foundation to do what some once considered unthinkable: *Give it all away.* The foundation adopted a plan to exhaust its $4 billion endowment over a period of about 15 years. Charitable foundations have long functioned on the assumption that they should sustain their endowments and their grant making forever, but Feeney began acting on a different idea---that urgent problems need solving right now and long-term economic growth will take care of the future. Many long-established foundations continue to manage their assets for perpetuity, but a few agree with Feeney that new assumptions are needed to enable foundations to focus on bold problem solving.

Q: *What are the new assumptions that Feeney is suggesting for charitable foundations?*

A: Under the new assumptions, delaying social investment through conservative granting policies to perpetuate the foundation helps no one and harms society. It also means that these foundations have a new goal, essentially to put themselves out of business by granting large amounts of money targeted toward major social problems.

Leaders can become prisoners of their own assumptions; they find themselves simply going along with the traditional way of doing things without ever realizing they are acting within the limited frame of their own mind-sets.

➢ *How have successful global managers learned to expand their mind-sets by questions assumptions about the right way to do business?*

The leader can question whether long-held assumptions fit the reality of the situation.

Discussion Question #3: *What are some specific reasons leaders need to be aware of these mental models?*

Notes____

To break out of categorized thinking patterns and open your mind to new ideas and multiple perspectives.

Perceptions: How Leaders Interpret Experience *Exhibit 5.2*

Perception is the process people use to make sense out of the environment by selecting, organizing, and interpreting information from the environment.

Perception can be broken down into a step-by-step process:

- First, we observe information (sensory data) from the environment through our senses.
- Second, our mind screens the data and selects certain items to process.

- Third, we organize selected data into meaningful patterns for interpretation and response.

We are aware of the environment, but not everything is of equal importance to our perception; a leader's values, attitudes, personality, and past experiences affect the selection of sensory data.

Also, characteristics of the data affect selection; something different gets more notice, and this perception leads to either a positive or negative impression.

By being aware of the factors that affect perception, leaders can avoid perceptual distortions such as stereo typing.

Stereotyping is the tendency to assign a person to a group or broad category and then attribute widely held generalizations about the group to an individual.

Stereotyping prevents leaders from getting to know people as individuals and prevent the individual from contributing fully to the organization.

Becoming aware of assumptions and perceptions and understanding how they influence emotions and actions is the first step toward being able to shift mental models.

Leaders can learn to question their own beliefs, assumptions, and perceptions and see things in unconventional ways.

Notes____

To engage in independent thinking by staying mentally alert, thinking critically, and being mindful rather than mindless.

Developing a Leader's Mind

The leader's mind can be developed beyond the non-leader's in five critical areas: independent thinking, open mindedness, systems thinking, mental models, and personal mastery.

These four disciplines provide a foundation that can help leaders examine their mental models a and overcome blind spots that may limit their leadership effectiveness and the success of their organizations.

Independent Thinking

Independent thinking means questioning assumptions and interpreting data and events according to one's own beliefs, ideas, and thinking, not according to pre-established rules, routines, or categories defined by others.

It means being mindful not mindless.

Mindfulness is the process of continuously reevaluating previously learned ways of doing things in the context of evolving information and shifting circumstances.

It is the opposite of *mindlessness*, which means blindly accepting rules and labels created by others---letting other people do the thinking.

When leaders think critically, they question all assumptions, vigorously seek divergent opinions, and try to give balanced consideration to all alternatives.

Leaders can also encourage others to be mindful rather than mindless; Bernard Bass talks about the value of intellectual stimulation—arousing followers' thoughts and imaginations.

Open Mindedness

One approach is to break out of the mental boxes, the categorized thinking patterns people have been conditioned to accept as correct.

The power of conditioning that guides our thinking is called the *Pike Syndrome*:.

- A hungry pike in an aquarium with a glass divider makes repeated attempts to attack minnows but only hits the glass. The divider is removed, but the pike makes no attempt to attack the minnows because conditioning has made the task seem futile.

When people assume they have complete knowledge of a situation because of past experiences, they exhibit the Pike Syndrome---a rigid commitment to what was true in the past.

Leaders have to forget many conditioned ideas to be open to new ones.

This openness—putting aside preconceptions--- is referred to as the "beginner's mind."

Whereas the expert's mind rejects new ideas based on past experience and knowledge, the beginner's mind reflects the openness and innocence of a young child.

❑ *Living Leadership: An Empty Sort of Mind*

Benjamin Hoff, *"An empty sort of mind is valuable for finding pearls ands tails and things Because it can see what's in front of it."*

➢ How does this wisdom from Winnie the Pooh speak to the value of keeping an open mind?

Effective leaders strive to keep open minds and cultivate an organizational environment that encourages curiosity.

Discussion Question #4: *Discuss the similarity and differences between mental models and open mindedness.*

Notes____

To begin to apply systems thinking, and personal mastery to your activities at school or work.

Systems Thinking *Exhibit 5.3*

Systems thinking means seeing patterns in the organizational whole instead of just the parts, and learning to reinforce or change system-patterns.

Traditional managers solve problems by breaking things down into discrete pieces and working to make each part perform as well as possible.

However, the success of each piece does not add up to the success of the whole; it is the *relationship* among parts that form the whole system.

Systems thinking is a mental discipline and framework for seeing patterns and interrelationships.

It is important to see organizational systems as a whole because of their complexity.

When leaders can see the structures that underlie complex situations, they can facilitate improvement; however, it requires a focus on the big picture.

An important element is to discern circles of causality. Peter Senge, author of *The Fifth Discipline,* argues that reality is made up of circles rather than straight lines.

- There are circles of influence for producing new products. In the circle on the left, a high-tech firm grows rapidly by pumping out new products.
- New products increase revenues, which enable further increases in the R&D budget for adding more new products.
- Another circle of causality is influenced. As R&D grows, the engineering and research staff increases and is hard to manage.
- Senior engineers are managers who now have less time to develop new products, which reduces development time and has a negative impact.

Understanding the circle of causality (i.e., the system) enables leaders to allocate resources to training as well as to new products.

The other element of systems thinking is learning to influence the system with reinforcing feedback as an engine for growth or decline.

Without an understanding of systems thinking, managers will face limits to growth and resistance to change because the large complex system will appear impossible to manage.

Discussion question #10: *Think about the class for which you are reading this text as a system. How might making changes without whole-systems thinking cause problems for students.*

Notes____

Personal Mastery

Personal Mastery, introduced by Peter Senge, is the discipline of personal growth and learning and of mastering yourself. It embodies personal visions, facing reality, and holding creative tension.

It embodies three qualities --- personal vision, facing reality, and holding creative tension.

- Leaders know and clarify what is important to them and focus on the end result.
- Facing reality means a commitment to the truth; leaders are relentless in uncovering the mental models that limit and deceive them.
- A gap exists between the current situation and the vision, but it is a source of creative energy; the creative leader reorganizes current activities to work toward the vision.

Leaders with personal mastery learn to accept both the dream and the reality simultaneously, and to close the gap by moving the organization toward the dream.

All five elements of mind are interrelated.

Independent thinking and open-mindedness improve systems thinking helping leaders shift and expand their mental models.

Discussion Question #5: *What is the concept of personal mastery? How important is it to a leader?*

Notes____

To exercise emotional intelligence, including being self-aware, managing your emotions, motivating yourself, displaying empathy, and managing relationships.

Emotional Intelligence---- Leading with Heart and Mind *Exhibit 5.4*

➢ *Do you think that emotion, more than intellectual ability, drives our thinking and decision making, as well as our relationships? Explain.*

Emotional intelligence refers to a person's abilities to perceive, identify, understand, and successfully manage emotions in self and others.

Emotional understanding and skills affect our success and happiness in our work as well as in our personal lives.

Leaders can harness, and direct the power of emotions to improve employee satisfaction, morale, and motivation, as well as to enhance organizational effectiveness.

What Are Emotions? *Exhibit 5.5*

One important ability for leaders is to understand the range of emotions and how they manifest themselves.

Some researchers accept eight "families" of emotions: anger, sadness, fear, enjoyment, love, surprise, disgust, and shame.

People in cultures around the world have been found to recognize these same basic emotions when shown photographs of facial expressions.

Leaders, attuned to their own feelings and the feelings of others, can use this understanding to enhance the organization.

Discussion Question #1: *How do you feel about the emotional qualities of yourself and other people in the organization as a way to be an effective leader? Discuss.*

Notes____

The Components of Emotional Intelligence *Exhibit 5.6*

The competencies and abilities of emotional intelligence are grouped into four fundamental categories:

- *Self-awareness* is the ability to recognize and understand your own emotions and how they affect your life and work.

People who are in touch with their emotions are better able to guide their own lives.

Leaders with a high level of self-awareness learn to trust their "gut feelings" for decision making.

This component includes the ability to assess one's own strengths and limitations, with a healthy sense of self-confidence.

- *Self-management* includes the ability to control disruptive or harmful emotions.

  Leaders learn to balance their own emotions so that worry, anxiety, or anger do not get in the way, enabling them to think clearly and effectively.

  Managing emotions means understanding them and using that understanding to deal with situations productively.

  Other characteristics in this category include trustworthiness, conscientiousness, and adaptability.

- *Social awareness* refers to one's ability to understand and empathize with others.

  Socially aware leaders practice *empathy,* the ability to put yourself in some else's shoes, sense their emotions, and understand their perspective.

  These leaders are capable of understanding divergent points of view and interacting effectively with many different types of people and emotions.

  The characteristic of *organizational awareness* is the ability to get along in organizational life, build networks, and use political behavior to accomplish positive results.

- *Relationship management* is the ability to connect to others, build positive relationships.

  Leaders with high emotional intelligence treat others with compassion, sensitivity, and kindness.

  Leaders use their understanding of emotions to inspire change and lead people toward something better, to build teamwork and collaboration, and to resolve conflicts as they arise.

In the Lead: Joe Torre, New York Yankees

For Joe Torre, coach of the New York Yankees, a leader's job is to help people fulfill their potential as individuals and as members of a team---an approach that requires putting the needs and feelings of followers first. Torre's leadership is based on knowing his team members as individuals and treating everyone with fairness, trust, and respect. Torre doesn't give a lot of big, motivational speeches. He watches, listens, and tries to understand the needs, motivations, and problems of each player, recognizing that what's going on in a player's personal life affects his performance on the field.

Q: *How did Joe Torre use emotional intelligence?*

A: For Torre, emotions are channeled toward creating a positive rather than a negative impact. He makes his goals and standards clear and lets everyone know of their contribution to the team. He has created the kind of workplace where relationships with employees are more important than technology and material resources.

Discussion Question #6: *Which of the four elements of emotional intelligence do you consider most essential to an effective leader? Why?*

Notes____

Implications for Leadership

- *How is emotional intelligence related to effective leadership?*

A leader's emotional abilities play a key role in charismatic leadership behavior.

Charismatic leaders hold strong emotional convictions and to followers on an emotional basis.

Transformational leaders project an inspiring vision for change and motivate followers to achieve it, which requires all the components of emotional intelligence.

A high level of self-awareness, plus the ability to manage one's emotions, enables a leader to display self-confidence and earn the respect and trust of followers.

The emotional state of the leader affects the entire group, department, or organization.

This *emotional contagion* means that leaders who maintain balance and keep themselves motivated are positive role models to help motivate and inspire others.

Emotionally intelligent leaders help followers grow and develop, see and enhance their self-worth , and help meet their needs and achieve their personal goals.

Notes____

The Emotional Intelligence of Teams

Research is beginning to emerge concerning how emotional intelligence relates to teams.

One study found that untrained teams with members with high emotional intelligence performed as well as trained teams with members who rated low on emotional intelligence.

The high emotional intelligence of the untrained team enabled them to assess and adapt to the requirements of teamwork and the task at hand.

Research suggests that emotional intelligence can be developed as a *team* competency; teams -------not just individuals---can become emotionally intelligent.

Leaders can build the emotional intelligence of teams by creating norms that support emotional development and influence emotions in constructive ways.

Emotionally intelligent team norms :

- Create a group identity
- Build trust among members
- Instill a belief among members that they can be effective and succeed as a team.

Leaders "tune in" to the team's emotional state and look for unhealthy or unproductive norms that inhibit cooperation and harmony.

Building the emotional intelligence of the team means exploring unhealthy norms, deliberately bringing emotions to the surface, and understanding how they affect the team's work.

Only by getting emotions into the open can the team build new norms and move to a higher level of group satisfaction.

Discussion Question #9: *Do you think it is appropriate for a leader to spend time developing a team's emotional intelligence? Why or why not?*

Notes____

To apply the difference between motivating others based on fear and motivating others based on love.

Leading with Love versus Leading with Fear

➢ *Do you think that traditionally, organizations have been based on fear?*

An unspoken notion among many senior-level executives is that fear benefits the organization.

Fear does motivate people.

When organizational success depended primarily on people mindlessly following orders, leading with fear met organizational needs.

The drawback is that fear creates avoidance behavior because no one wants to make a mistake, and this inhibits growth and change.

Today, organizational success depends on the knowledge, mind power, commitment, and enthusiasm of everyone in the organization.

Leaders can learn to bind together for a shared purpose through more positive forces such as caring and compassion, listening, and relating to others on a personal level.

Showing respect and trust not only enable people to perform better, it allows them to feel emotionally connected with their work so that their lives are richer and more balanced.

Fear in Organizations

The workplace hold many kinds of fear--- fear of failure, fear of change, fear of personal loss, and fear of the boss.

Fear can prevent employees from doing their best, from taking risks, from challenging and changing the status quo.

It creates an atmosphere in which people feel powerless, so that their confidence, commitment, enthusiasm, imagination, and motivation are diminished.

Aspects of Fear

Fear in the workplace can diminish trust and communication; employees feel threatened by repercussions if they speak up about work-related concerns.

A survey of employees showed:

- Fears center around lack of career advancement, damaged relations with the supervisor, or job loss.
- Employees are afraid to talk about a wide range of issues, but mainly the interpersonal and relationship skills of executives.
- When fear is high, managers destroy the opportunity for feedback, blinding them to reality and denying them the chance to alter their decisions and behaviors.

Relationship with Leaders

➢ *Do you think leaders control the fear level in the organization?*

The legacy of fear and mistrust in the traditional hierarchy, in which bosses gave orders and employees jumped to obey, still colors organizational life.

Leaders are responsible for creating an environment that allows a person to speak up and still feel safe.

Leaders can act from love rather than fear to free employees and the organization from the chains of the past.

Bringing Love to Work

When leaders act from their own fear, they create fear in others.

A leader's fear can manifest itself in arrogance, selfishness, deception, unfairness, and disrespect for others.

Leaders can learn to develop their capacity for the positive emotions of love and caring.

In the Lead: Andy Pearson, Tricon Global Restaurants

When he was CEO of PepsiCo, Inc., Andy Pearson was named one of the ten toughest bosses in the U.S. by *Fortune* magazine. He was notorious for his brutal management style and the extreme, relentless demands he put on subordinates. Now, at Tricon Global Restaurants, Pearson leads not with fear, surprise, and intimidation but with humility, respect, and genuine caring. Pearson saw that tapping into positive human emotions was the key driver of success.

Q: *Describe Andy Pearson's new approach to leadership.*

A: Pearson does not issue orders but seeks answers from others. He talks and listens to people throughout the company and makes an enormous effort to let people know their individual contribution is vital to the organization's success. Pearson considers caring about others a sign of leadership.

There are a number of aspects of love that are directly relevant to work relationships and organizational performance:

- *Love as motivation* is the force within that allows a person to feel alive, connected, energized, and "in love" with life and work.

  Western cultures place emphasis on the mind and the rational approach. Yet, it is the heart rather than the mind that powers people forward.

The best leaders are those who love what they do, because they infect others with their enthusiasm and passion.

- *Love as feelings* involves attraction, fascination, and caring for people, work, or other things.

  Feelings of compassion and caring for others are a manifestation of love, as are forgiveness, sincerity, respect, and loyalty, all of which are important for healthy working relationships.

  This type of feeling and caring about work is a major source of charisma.

- *Love as action* means more than feelings; it is translated into behavior.

  Love is something a person does, the sacrifices made, and giving of oneself.

  Feelings of unity and cooperation by leaders or followers translate into acts of helping, cooperation, sharing, and understanding.

  Sentiments emerge as action

Discussion Question #7: *Consider fear and love as potential motivators. Which is the best source of motivation for soldiers during a war? For members of a new product development team? For top executives at a media conglomerate? Why?*

Notes____
____
____

Why Followers Respond to Love

Leaders who lead with love have extraordinary influence because they meet five unspoken employee needs:

- Hear and understand me.
- Even if you disagree with me, please do not make me wrong.
- Acknowledge the greatness within me.
- Remember to look for my loving intentions.
- Tell me the truth with compassion.

When leaders address emotional needs, people respond by loving their work and becoming emotionally engaged in solving problems and serving customers.

Enthusiasm for work and the organization increases.

People want to believe that their leaders genuinely care about them.

From the followers' point of view, love versus fear has different motivational potential.

- *Fear-based motivation*: I need a job to pay for my basic needs. You give me a job, and I will give you enough to keep my job.

- *Love-based motivation:* If the job and leader make me feel valued and provide meaning and contribution to the community at large, then I will give you all I have to offer.

Rational thinking is important, but leading with love can build trust, stimulate creativity, inspire commitment, and create boundless energy.

Discussion Question #8: *Have you ever experienced love and/or fear from leaders at work? How did you respond?*

Notes____

DISCUSSION QUESTIONS

1. *How do you feel about the emotional qualities of yourself and other people in the organization as a way to be an effective leader? Discuss.*

Emotional understanding and skills affect our success and happiness in our work as well as in our personal lives. Leaders can harness, and direct the power of emotions to improve employee satisfaction, morale, and motivation, as well as to enhance organizational effectiveness. Leaders who are attuned to their own feelings and the feelings of others can use their understanding to enhance the organization's effectiveness. Developing self-awareness, managing emotions, motivating oneself, empathy, and social skills are emotional qualities that help a person at work and in personal relationships.

2. *Do you agree that people have a capacity for developing their minds and hearts beyond current competency? Can you give an example? Discuss.*

According to the "whole brain" concept, people who rely on one or two quadrants of the brain as a thinking style can learn to use all four quadrants. They have the ability to develop their minds beyond current competency. Many people can develop their minds and hearts as a result of personal experience. Lance Armstrong, a cyclist who won the prestigious Tour de France bicycling competition, personally faced cancer. Having successfully experienced medical treatment, he became a spokesperson for this deadly disease. By reaching millions of cancer patients and giving them hope, he has personally developed his mind and heart beyond his former role of simply being a top-notch athlete. Personal goals have been extended to social goals.

3. *What are some specific reasons leaders need to be aware of these mental models?*

A leader's assumptions are part of a mental model. Mental models govern how leaders interpret their experiences and the actions they take in response to people and situations. For example, many organizations whose leaders operated on those traditional assumptions are now hurting as Internet-based competitors steal market share. Leaders can learn to regard their assumptions as temporary ideas rather than fixed truths. The leader can question whether long-held assumptions fit the reality of the situation.

4. *Discuss the similarity and differences between mental models and open mindedness.*

Open mindedness means breaking out of the categorized thinking patterns people have been conditioned to accept as correct. Mind potential is released when opened up to new ideas and multiple perspectives. By contrast, mental models are deep-seated assumptions, beliefs, blind spots, biases, and prejudices that determine how leaders make sense of the world. Mental models govern the actions leaders take in response to situation.

5. *What is the concept of personal mastery? How important is it to a leader?*

Personal mastery refers to three qualities --- personal vision, facing reality, and holding creative tension. Leaders know and clarify what is important to them and focus on the end result. Leaders are committed to the truth and are relentless in uncovering mental models that limit and deceive. Leaders resolve the gap between the current situation and the vision by reorganizing current activities to work towards the vision.

6. *Which of the five elements of emotional intelligence do you consider most essential to an effective leader? Why?*

Answers will vary. Managing emotions is essential to effective leadership. A leader who makes decisions based on anger, for example, can be dangerous to the firm. Leaders, who can manage their emotions can perform better because they are able to think clearly. Managing emotions does not mean suppressing them or denying them but understanding them and using that understanding to deal with situations productively. Leaders can recognize a mood or feeling, think about its effect, and choose how to act.

7. *Consider fear and love as potential motivators. Which is the best source of motivation for soldiers during a war? For members of a new product development team? For top executives at a media conglomerate? Why?*

The best source of motivation for soldiers during war is love of country and fear of losing the freedoms that would come with defeat. For members of a new product development team, it is the love of science and innovation to put together a new product. It is the love of teamwork and feelings of affiliation for team members and the love of competition with other businesses. It is also the fear of not bringing a product to market in advance of the competition. For top executives at a media conglomerate, the fear of the competition is a motivator and love as action. Feelings of teamwork, cooperation, unity, and sharing drive executives. These sentiments emerge as actions.

8. *Have you ever experienced love and/or fear from leaders at work? How did you respond?*

Answers will vary. When leaders address emotional needs, people respond by loving their work and becoming emotionally engaged in solving problems and serving customers. Enthusiasm for work and the organization increases. People want to believe that their leaders genuinely care about them. I worked as the marketing director to build a centennial park in an area of Texas that has few parks, little greenery, and almost no rain. All the members of the team realized what an important contribution we were making. Despite long hours, we realized it was a labor of love.

Fear in the workplace is real. Employees feel threatened by repercussions if they speak up about work-related concerns. Employees are afraid to talk about a wide range of issues, but mainly the interpersonal skills of executives. One extreme example of fear in the work place is the true story of a group of deaf immigrants in New York who sold key chains in the subway and were held captive.

9. *Do you think it is appropriate for a leader to spend time developing a team's emotional intelligence? Why or why not?*

Yes, research showed that untrained emotionally intelligent teams perform as well on the job as trained teams with low ratings in emotional intelligence. Emotionally intelligent teams can assess the situation. Emotionally intelligent team norms create a group identity, build trust among members, and instill a belief among members that they can be effective and succeed as a team.

10. *Think about the class for which you are reading this text as a system. How might making changes without whole-systems thinking cause problems for students.*

If the format of the class were changed from a classroom setting to a distance learning setting, the system would be affected. First of all, the facility would be different. This class would be have to be held in a room with special equipment to allow students from other campuses to see the instructor and ask questions. This would mean that the university would have to provide an employee with sufficient skills to run the equipment and be a trouble-shooter. Problems with the equipment would affect a student's ability to participate in the class. If the class were offered as a webclass, this would also affect the system. The information technology department and the webmaster would be involved setting up an educational server such as Blackboard, and the students would have to learn enough computer skills to log into Blackboard to find out class information and scheduling.

TEACHING TOOLS AND EXERCISES

1. *Leader's Bookshelf: Geeks and Geezer: How Era, Values and Defining Moments Shape Leaders* by Warren G. Bennis and Robert J. Thomas. The authors discovered that, in both generations, successful leaders possess certain attributes that contribute to success: adaptive capacity, the ability to engage others in sharing meaning, character and a distinctive voice, and integrity and small values. Do you agree that while we come of age in a particular environment, the core essentials of leadership remain constant? Discuss in small groups.

2. *Small group discussion:* Think of a group or team to which you currently belong or of which you have been a part. What type of leadership style did the leaders of their appear to exhibit? Give some specific examples of the types of leadership behaviors he or she used. Evaluate the leadership style. Was it appropriate for the group? Why or why not? What would you have done differently? Why?

3. *On the Web:* Go to `www.swlearning.com/management/` Click on Topic Index and then click on Leadership, then click on the article "*Do You Have the Will to Lead?* Briefly summarize the author's view of leadership.

4. *Activity*: **Developing Trust**

   Trust plans an important role in a leader's relationship with employees. Given the importance of trust, today's leaders should actively seek to develop it within their work group. The following activity reinforces the behaviors associated with developing trust.

   Keep a one-week log describing ways that your daily decisions and actions encouraged people to trust you and not to trust you. What things did you do that led to trust? What things did you do that may have led to distrust? How could you have changed your behavior so that situations of potential distrust could have been situations of trust. Share your answers with the class.

5. *Out-of-class reading*:

   P. J. Jordan, N.M. Ashkanasy, C.E.J. Hartel, and G. S. Hooper, " Workgroup Emotional Intelligence Scale Development and Relationship to Team Process Effectiveness and Goal Focus," *Human Resource Management Review* 12, no. 2 (Summer 2002): 195-214.

6. *Leader's Self-Insight: Emotional Intelligence*

   The questionnaire on p. 197 provides some indication of your emotional intelligence. If you received a total score of 80 or more, you are considered a person with a high level of emotional intelligence. A score below 50 indicates that your are below average in emotional intelligence. Review the discussion of the four components of emotional intelligence and think about how you cant develop the areas in which you scored low. Compare your scores to those of other students. What will you do to improve your scores?

LEADERSHIP DEVELOPMENT: CASES FOR ANALYSIS

I. Synopsis: The New Boss

Sam Nolan was Chief Information Officer at Century Medical, a large medical products company. He had joined the company four years ago and Century had made great progress integrating technology into its systems and processes. Nolan had developed trust with people throughout the company and showed them how technology could not only save money, but also support team-based work, encourage information sharing, and give people more control over their own jobs. A new boss, Tom Carr, arrived at Century and considered Nolan's project, a

Web-based job posting program, a waste of time and money. Carr had no understanding of why and how technology was being used. The vibrant and innovative human resources department Nolan's team had imagined now seemed like nothing more than a pipe dream.

Case questions and answers

1. *Describe the two different mental models represented in this story.*

Mental models are deep-seated assumptions, beliefs, blind spots, biases, and prejudices that determine how leaders make sense of the world. They govern how leaders interpret their experiences and the actions they take.

Nolan is open to experience and believes in the power of technology in the systems and processes at Century, including the Human Resources function. He believes that the Web-based job posting program is an innovative use of technology for selection, recruiting, and hiring of new employees who will take the company to new heights.

Carr thinks that human resources implies the old personnel department, a person to person activity with no need of computers. He thinks the old filing cabinet system of the past is just fine. Past experience is the key to Carr's decision making for the future.

2. *What are some of the assumptions and perceptions that shape the mind-set of Sam Nolan? Of Tom Carr?*

Both Carr and Nolan have assumptions about events, situations, and circumstances. Perceptions are part of both Carr and Nolan's mental models, determining how they views people, situations, and events. Nolan is operating on Theory Y assumptions, that workers are trustworthy and like their jobs. He believes in the capabilities of the team at Century. He believes in empowering the team members and in sharing information. He realizes that posting jobs on the Internet will attract good candidates, which will make Century even better.

Carr is operating on traditional assumptions---the Internet is a fad and human resources is just about talking to people in the organization---and these assumptions will harm Century Medical as Internet-based competitors steal market share. He has a narrow view of the work place and believes that the way business operated in the past is fine for the future. He thinks that people, situations, and events are unchanged. Carr refuses to be open-mined about technology.

3. *Do you think it is possible for Carr to shift to a new mental model? If you were Sam Nolan, what would you do?*

Carr can learn to regard his assumptions as temporary ideas rather than fixed truths. The more aware he is of personal assumptions, the more he can understands how his outdated assumptions guide his behavior. He can question whether long-held assumptions fit today's reality at Century. Carr could shift to a new mental model through education and training. He does not understand what technology can do and needs to be shown. Sam Nolan should use benchmarking to prove his point. He should find a company that has used a Web-based job posting system successfully and show it to Carr to convince him of the power of technology to remain competitive and profitable in the 21st century.

II. Synopsis: The USS Florida

The atmosphere in a Trident nuclear submarine is generally calm and quiet. The Trident ranks among the world's most dangerous weapons. When Michael Alfonso took charge of the USS Florida, the crew welcomed his arrival, but Commander Alfonso swiftly admonished his sailors that he would push them hard. He loudly and publicly reprimanded those whose performance he considered lacking. The crew, accustomed to Navy's adage of "praise in public, penalize in private," were shocked when Alfonso publicly relieved Chief Petty Officer MacArthur of his diving duty. The captain's outbursts were not always connected with job performance. He exploded when he arrived at a late-night meal and found that his fork was missing. When the Trident reached home port, the sailors slumped ashore. "Physically and mentally, we were just beat into the ground," recalls one sailor. Alfonso was surprised when Admiral Sullivan eventually relieved him of his command because the USS Florida had posted "the best-ever grades assigned for certifications and inspections."

Case questions and answers

1. *Analyze Alfonso's impact on the crew in terms of love versus fear. What might account for the fact that he behaved so strongly as captain of the USS Florida?*

Traditionally, organizations have often been based on fear. An unspoken notion among many senior-level executives is that fear benefits the organization. Fear does motivate people. The military is a traditional organization and has long used fear to assure discipline. Alfonso was behaving as a traditional military leader. He believed he was leading correctly from a command control perspective.

2. *Which do you think a leader should be more concerned about aboard a nuclear submarine high certification grades or high-quality interpersonal relationships? Do you agree with Admiral Sullivan's decision to fire Alfonso? Discuss.*

The two are interrelated. A ship cannot function in a state of preparedness without the commitment of the crew. For organizations where employees do mindlessly as they are told, leading with fear has worked to meet the organization's needs. The Trident crews are the "cream of the crop," highly trained professionals whose opinions, ideas, and energy are needed. They should not be managed by fear. Alfonso should not have been fired; he should have be reassigned following leadership training.

3. *Discuss Commander Alfonso's level of emotional intelligence in terms of the five components listed in the chapter. What advice would you give him?*

He lacked self-awareness and did not manage his emotions because he lost his temper at MacArthur. He lacked empathy by criticizing MacArthur in public. He did not motivate himself because he was negative and demanding. He lacked social skills and had a history of being a loner. He did not build positive relationships, respond to the emotions of others or influence others. He could develop leadership skills by changing his attitude and studying effective leadership behavior.

CHAPTER SIX
COURAGE AND MORAL LEADERSHIP

CHAPTER SUMMARY

The chapter explores several ideas concerning moral leadership and leadership courage. People want honest and trustworthy leaders. However, the ethical climate in many organizations is at a low point. Leaders face pressures that challenge their ability to do the right thing---pressures to cut costs, increase profits, meet the demands of various stakeholders, and look successful. Creating an ethical organization requires that leaders act based on moral principles. Leaders cause things to go wrong in the organization when they excessively promote self-interest, practice deception and breach agreements, and lack the courage to confront unjust acts. Ethical leaders are humble, honest, and straightforward. They maintain a concern for the greater good, strive for fairness, and demonstrate the courage to stand up for what is right. Acting s a moral leader means demonstrating the importance of serving people and society as well as increasing profits or personal gain.

One personal consideration for leaders is the level of moral development. Leaders use an understanding of the stages of moral development to enhance their own as well as followers' personal moral growth. Leaders who operate at higher stages of moral focus on the needs of followers and universal moral principles.

Ideas about control versus service between leaders and followers are changing and expanding, reflected in a continuum of leader-follower relationships. The continuum varies from authoritarian managers to participative managers to stewardship to servant leadership. Leaders who operate from the principles of stewardship and servant leadership can help build ethical organizations.

The final section of the chapter discusses leadership courage and how leaders can fmd their own courage. Courage means the ability to step forward through fear, to accept responsibility, to take risks and make changes, to speak your mind, and to fight for what you believe. Two expressions of courage in organizations are moral leadership and ethical whistleblowing. Sources of courage include belief in a higher purpose, connection with others, experience with failure, and harnessing anger.

CHAPTER OPENER

Raoul Wallenberg, a Righteous Man

Virtually alone in Hungary, one of the most perilous places in Europe in 1944 during the waning months of World War II, Raoul Wallenberg worked miracles on a daily basis, using courage, self-confidence, and a deep, unwavering belief in the rightness of his mission---to save Jews headed for the death camps. Wallenberg became a symbol of good in a world dominated by evil, and a reminder of the hidden strength of the human spirit.

He was 32 years old in 1944, a wealthy, politically-connected, upper-class Swede from a prominent, well-respected family. When asked by the U.S., War Refugee Board to enter Hungary and help stop Hitler's slaughter of the innocent civilians, Wallenberg had everything to lose and nothing to gain. He plunged into the struggle to free Jews.
One of the lessons from Wallenberg's life is that being a real leader means learning who you are and what you stand for, and then having the courage to act.

LECTURE/OUTLINE

To combine a rational approach to leadership with a concern for people and ethics.

Moral Leadership Today *Exhibit 6.1*

➢ *What are some of the ethical scandals in the corporate world?*

The corporate world has reeled from scandals---the names of once-revered companies have become synonymous with greed, deceit, and financial improprieties. (Enron, Martha Stewart, HealthSouth)

A CBS poll taken in 2002 found that 79 percent of respondents believed questionable business practices are widespread; fewer than one-third think CEO's are honest.

The Ethical Climate in U.S. Business

Ethical lapses occur at all levels of organizations, but top leaders have recently been spotlighted for their unethical and illegal actions.

What's going on at the top trickles down through organizations and society.

When leaders fail to set and live up to high ethical standards, organizations, employees, shareholders, and the general public suffer.

Unethical behavior can lead to serious consequences for organizations because they have a difficulty attracting good employees, customers leave, and investors withdraw support.

Leaders at all levels carry responsibility for setting the ethical climate.

At the same time, leaders face pressures that challenge their ability to do the right thing---pressures to cut costs, increase profits, meet the demands of vendors, and look successful.

Leaders sometimes do the wrong thing just to they will look good to others.

The question for leaders is whether they can summon the fortitude to do the right thing despite outside pressures.

Discussion Question #1: *If you were in a position similar to Raoul Wallenberg, what do you think you would do? Why?*

Notes____

What Leaders Do to Make Things Go Wrong

➢ *What actions of leaders contribute to a lack of integrity within an organization?*

Exhibit 6.1 compares unethical and ethical leadership by looking at 10 things leaders do to that make things go wrong for the organization from a moral standpoint.

The behaviors listed in column 1 contribute to an organizational climate ripe for ethical and legal abuses. Column 2 lists the opposite behaviors which lead to trust and fairness.

The leader as a hero is an outdated notion, but some executives are preoccupied with their own importance, feed their greed, and nourish their own egos.

These leaders pay more attention to getting benefits for themselves than for the organization or for larger society.

Unethical leaders frequently treat people unfairly, perhaps giving special favors to followers who flatter their egos or promoting people based on favoritism.

Unethical leaders take credit for successes, but blame others when things go wrong.

By taking credit for followers' accomplishments, failing to allow others participation in decision making, and treating people with dishonesty, they diminish the dignity of others.

Leaders also contribute to an unethical and potentially corrupt organization is by failing to speak up against acts they believe are wrong.

Discussion Question #2: *What are some pressures you face as a student that challenge your ability to do the right thing? Do you expect to face more or fewer pressures as a leader?*

Notes____

To recognize your own stage of moral development and ways to accelerate your moral maturation.

Acting Like a Moral Leader

Exhibit 6.2

➢ *Do you think that many leaders forget that business is about values, not just economic performance?*

Despite the corporate realities of greed, competition, and the drive to achieve goals and profits, leaders can act from moral values and encourage moral values in the workplace.

Employees learn which values are important by watching the organization's leaders.

In the Lead: Alfred P. West, SEI Investments Co.

"The CEO sets the tone for an organization's [values]," says Alfred P. West, the founder and CEO of SEI Investments. West is careful to espouse and model values that build integrity, accountability, and trustworthiness into the organization's culture. West doesn't have a spacious office; he answers his own phone, doesn't take stock options, and pays himself $660,000 , compared to the $2 million earned by the CEO at Tyco in 2002.

Q: *How does West teach his employees about the values that are important to SEI?*

B: West believes that if you separate yourself from your employees with perks, it sends the wrong message. He believes that an open culture not only improves performance, but makes it easier for employees to report ethical lapses or unfair practices. Leaders like West put values into action.

Exhibit 6.3

Leaders articulate and uphold moral standards and serve as a model for the organization.

Exhibit 6.3 shows the clear concise, personal honor code used by NASA's Jet Propulsion Laboratory.

A visible leadership position entails the responsibility for conducting one's personal and professional life in an ethical manner.

Leaders build ethical organizations by demonstrating the importance of serving people and society.

Discussion Question #9: *Do you agree that it is important for leaders to do the right thing even if no one will ever know about it? Why or why not?*

Notes____

To know and use mechanisms that enhance an ethical organizational culture.

Becoming a Moral Leader

Exhibit 6.4

All leadership practices can be used for good or evil and thus have a moral dimension.

Leaders choose whether to diminish others or inspire and motivate others to develop their full potential as employees and human beings.

Moral leadership is about distinguishing right from wrong and doing right; seeking the just, honest, and good in the practice of leadership.

Leaders have great influence over others, and moral leadership enhances the lives of others whereas immoral leadership takes away from others in order to enhance oneself.

Specific personality characteristics such as ego strength, self-confidence, and a sense of independence may enable leaders to behave morally in the face of opposition.

Leaders can develop these characteristics; the capacity to make moral choices is related to a leader's level of moral development.

A model of personal moral development shows three stages:

- *Preconventional level:* individuals are concerned with receiving external rewards and avoiding punishments.

  They obey authority to avoid detrimental consequences.

  The leadership position is autocratic and aims for personal advancement.

- *Conventional leve:* people conform to the expectations of good behavior as defined by colleagues, family, friends, and society.

  They follow the rules, norms, and values of the corporate culture---if honesty is the rule, honesty is followed. If dishonesty is the rule, people will go along.

- *Postconventional level:* leaders are guided by an internalized set of principles universally recognized as right or wrong.

  People disobey rules or laws that violate these principles.

  Internalized values become more important than the expectations of others.

In the Lead: Roy Vagelos, Merck & Co.

"We are in the business of preserving and improving human life," Merck's mission statement reads. However, in the late 1970s Roy Vagelos, VP of research, and his colleagues found a potential cure for river blindness, they faced a dilemma. The drug would cost more than $200 million to develop, and it was needed only by people who couldn't afford to pay for it---poor villagers in West Africa and other developing countries. Vagelos became CEO and decided to authorize a drug that would never make money and cost more than $3 a tablet to produce and distribute. Merck announced that it would give the drug away.

Q: *Why did Vagelos develop the drug and give it away?*

A: He felt that focusing on the company's guiding mission was the best way to create shareholder value in the long run, and he stuck by these principles. This drug is considered a medical triumph and has nearly eradicated river blindness as a public health threat in many areas. Vagelos broke the unspoken corporate rule by putting the lives of poor children in developing countries above the short-term interests of share holders.

Most adults operate at level two.

Research has consistently found a direct relationship between higher levels of moral development and more ethical behavior on the job.

Leaders can use an understanding of these stages to enhance their own and their followers moral development and to initiate ethics training programs to move people to higher levels of moral reasoning.

When leaders operate at level three, they focus on higher principles and encourage others to think for themselves and expand their understanding of moral issues.

Discussion Question #3 here: *If most adults are at a conventional level of moral development, what does this mean for their potential for moral leadership?*

Notes____

The thinking about leadership today implies that moral leadership encourages change toward developing followers into leaders, thereby developing their potential.

A continuum of leadership thinking and practice:

- *Stage 1*: subordinates are passive and expected to do as they are told.
- *Stage 2*: subordinates are involved more actively in their work.
- *Stage 3* : stewardship moves responsibility from leaders to followers.

Servant leadership represents a stage beyond stewardship, whereby leaders give up control and make a choice to serve employees.

Authoritarian Management

The traditional understanding of leadership is that leaders are good managers who direct and controls their people.

Followers are obedient subordinates who follow orders.

Power, purpose, and privilege reside with the top management.

Organizational stability and efficiency are paramount, and followers are routinized and controlled along with machines and raw materials.

The leadership mindset emphasizes top-down control, standardization and specialization, and management by impersonal measurement and analysis.

Notes____

____

____

Participation Management

Leaders have increased employee participation through employee suggestion programs, participation groups, and quality circles.

Teamwork as an importan part of how work is done in many organizations.

The success of Japanese firms that emphasize employee involvement encouraged U.S. firms to try participatory management in response to increased global competition.

Yet, the mind-set is still paternalistic in that top leaders determine purpose and goals, make final decisions, and decide rewards.

Employees make suggestions for quality improvements, act as team players, and enjoy greater responsibility, but they are not true partners in the enterprise.

Leaders are responsible for outcomes, but act as coaches and mentors.

Notes____

To apply the principles of stewardship and servant leadership.

Stewardship

Stewardship is a pivotal shift in leadership thinking.

Stewardship supports the belief that leaders are accountable to others and to the organization, without trying to control others, define meaning and purpose for others, or take care of others.

Four principles provide the framework for stewardship:

- *Reorient toward a partnership assumption.* Partnership happens only when power and control shift away from formal leaders to core workers.

  Leaders and followers are jointly responsible for defining vision and purpose.

- *Localize decisions and power to those closest to the work and the customer.* Decision–making power and authority to act should reside right at the point where the work is done.

  Everyone is doing the core work part of the time; no one gets paid to plan.

- *Recognize and reward the value of labor.* The reward systems tie everyone's fortunes to the success of the enterprise.

  Stewardship involves redistributing wealth by designing compensation so that core workers make significant gains when they make exceptional contributions.

- *Expect core work teams to build the organization.* Teams of workers who make up the core of the organization or division define goals, maintain controls, create a nurturing environment and the marketplace they serve.

Steward leaders guide the organization without dominating it and facilitate followers without controlling them.

Stewardship leaders can help organizations thrive in today's complex environment because they tap into the energy of and commitment of followers.

Discussion Question #4: *Do you feel that the difference between authoritarian leadership and stewardship should be interpreted as a moral difference? Discuss.*

Notes____

Servant Leadership

➢ *How does servant leadership takes stewardship one step further?*

In *servant leadership,* the leader transcends self-interest to serve the needs of others, helps others grow and develop, and provides opportunity for others to gain materially and emotionally.

There has been an explosion of interest in servant leadership because of the emphasis in organizations on empowerment, participation, shared authority, and building a community of trust.

According to Robert Greenleaf, author of *Servant Leaders,* servant leaders:

- *Put service before self-interest.* Servant leaders make a conscious choice to use their gifts in the cause of change and growth for other individuals and for the organization.

  The desire to help others takes precedence over the desire to achieve a formal leadership position or to attain power and control over others.

- *Listen first to affirm others.* The servant leader does not have answers; he asks questions.

  The servant leader tries to figure out the will of the group and they further it however he can.

- *Inspire trust by being trustworthy.* Servant leaders build trust by doing what they say they will do, being totally honest with others, and focusing on the well-being of others.

  They share all information, good and bad, and they make decisions to furthers the good of the group rather than their own interests.

- *Nourish others and help them become whole.* Servant leaders care about followers' spirits as well as their minds and bodies, and they believe in the potential of each person to have a positive impact on the world.

  Servant leaders help others find the power of the human spirit and accept their responsibilities.

***In the Lead*:** C. William Pollard, ServiceMaster

ServiceMaster is a successful, dynamic company that cleans and maintains hospitals, schools, and other buildings. ServiceMaster has instilled its employees with a sense of dignity, responsibility, and meaningfulness, thanks to C. William Pollard. Pollard believes it is immoral to take away an employee's right to make decisions and take action. He sees leaders as having a moral responsibility to help employees grow and develop to their full potential, which means giving them the skills, information, tools, and authority they need to act independently.

Q: *How is Pollard a servant leader?*

A: To Pollard, the real leader is not the "person with the most distinguished title, the highest pay, or the longest tenure...but the role model, the risk taker, the servant; not the person who promotes himself, but the promoter of others."

Servant leaders truly value and respect others as human beings, not as objects of labor.

Discussion Question #5: *Should serving others be placed at a higher moral level than serving oneself? Discuss.*

Notes____

To recognize courage in others and unlock your own potential to live and courageously.

Leadership Courage

Leaders sometimes have to reach deep within themselves to find the strength and courage to resist temptations or to stand up for moral principles when others ridicule them.

For leaders, particularly in large organizations, the importance of courage is obscured---the main idea is to get along, fit in, and do whatever brings promotions and pay raises.

What Is Courage?

Courage is the ability to step forward through fear.

Courage does not mean the absence of doubt or fear, but the ability to act in spite of them.

❑ *Living Leadership: Is it Worth the Risk?*

"To try....is to risk failure." "Chained by their own certitude, they are slaves..:"

➢ What does this passage say to you about the courage to take risks?

Courage is not another word for fearless.

It is natural and right for people to feel fear when real risk is involved, whether the risk be loss of job, loss of life, or loss of the acceptance of peers.

- *Courage means accepting responsibility.* Leaders take responsibility for their failures and mistakes.

- *Courage means nonconformity.* Leadership means going against the grain, breaking traditions, reducing boundaries, and initiating change.

  It is easier to stay with the status quo, even if it leads to certain failure, than to initiate change.

In the Lead: Georg Bauer, Mercedes-Benz Credit Corporation

At MBCC, Georg Bauer saw a need to become a faster, leaner, and more customer-focused organization to keep pace with changes in the environment, and he encouraged employees to rebuild the organization from the bottom up. Bauer's "no fear principle assured people that they could take risks and make mistakes without fear of recrimination or job loss. "The future is all about risk-taking," Bauer says.

Q: *Explain how Bauer's courage to take risks helped him as leader.*

A: Bauer 's courage to take risks enabled MBCC to cut costs, diversify into new financing arenas, improve customer service and employee satisfaction, and continue to change to keep pace with shifting market conditions. Going against the status quo is difficult.

- *Courage means pushing beyond the comfort zone.* To take a chance and improve things means leaders have to push beyond the comfort zone.

  When people go beyond the comfort zone, they encounter an invisible "wall of fear." Facing the invisible wall of fear is when courage is needed the most.

- *Courage means asking for what you want and saying what you think.* Leaders have to speak out to influence others.

  It is the ability to say no to unreasonable demands from others. The desire to please others—especially the boss—can sometimes block the truth.

- *Courage means fighting for what you believe.* Courage means fighting for valued outcomes that benefit the whole.

  Leaders take risks, but do so for a higher purpose.

Discussion Question #6: *If you find yourself avoiding a situation or activity, what can you do to find the courage to move forward? Explain.*

Notes____

____

____

How Does Courage Apply to Moral Leadership?

Many in organizations have the courage to be unconventional, to do what they think is right, to dare to treat employees and customers as human beings who deserve respect.

Balancing profit with people, selfishness with service, and control with stewardship requires individual moral courage.

In the Lead: Lawrence Fish, Citizens Bank

Lawrence Fish, CEO of Citizens Bank, is a man who has known both success and failure as a result of his unconventional approaches and ethical beliefs. Fish's unconventional ideas have led to success at Citizens, which now ranks as one of the 35 largest banks in the U.S. Fish believes that life is more than material success. Unlike most big banks, Citizens courts working-class customers and specializes in the human touch rather than promoting fancy devices and new technology.

Q: *Describe Fish's unconventional banking practices.*

A: He gives local bank executives the freedom to decide how to make loans rather than insisting on approval from the home office. He shows that there are banks that operate with a heart.

- *Acting like a moral leadership requires personal courage.* Leaders have to know themselves, understand their strengths and weaknesses, know what they for, and often be nonconformists.

  Honest self-analysis can be painful, and acknowledging personal limitations takes strength of character.

  Moral leadership requires building relationships, which requires sharing yourself, listening, having personal experiences, and making yourself vulnerable.

- *Opposing unethical conduct requires courage.*

  Whistleblowing is employee disclosure of illegal, immoral, or unethical practices in the organization.

  This is still risky for employees who may suffer financially and emotionally from their willingness to report unethical conduct on the part of bosses or coworkers.

  Choosing to act courageously means having conflicting emotions--whistleblowers may feel and ethical obligation to report wrongdoing, but may also feel disloyal to their boss and coworkers.

Finding Personal Courage

➢ *How does a leader find the courage to step through fear and confusion, to act despite the risks involved?*

All of us have the potential to live and act courageously if we can push through our own fears.

People can unlock their courage by committing to causes they believe in, connecting with others, welcoming failure as a natural and beneficial part of life, and harnessing anger.

Believing in a Higher Purpose

Courage comes easily when we fight for something we really believe in.

Service to a larger vision or purpose gives people the courage to step through fear.

Draw Strength from Others

Caring about others and having support form others is a potent source of courage in a topsy-turvy world.

Having the support of others is a source of courage.

Being part of an organizational team that is supportive and caring, or having a loving family, can reduce the fear of failure and help people take risks.

Welcome Failure

Failure can play a creative role in work and in life; success and failure are two sides of the same coin---one cannot exist without the other.

When people accept failure and are at peace with the worst possible outcome, they find they have the fortitude to move forward.

Every time a person moves beyond his comfort zone, fails and tries again, he builds psychological strength and courage.

Harness Frustration and Anger

Organizations see the power of frustration and anger.

Sometimes outrage over a perceived injustice can give a mild-mannered person the courage to confront the situation.

Getting mad at yourself may be the motivation to change.

Anger, in moderate amounts, is a healthy emotion that provides energy to move forward.

The challenge is to harness anger and use it appropriately.

Discussion Question #8: *Do you have the courage to take a moral stand that your peers and even authority figures will disagree with? Why?*

Notes____

DISCUSSION QUESTIONS

1. *If you were in a position similar to Raoul Wallenberg, what do you think you would do? Why?*

Answers will vary. One personal consideration in this question is an individual's level of moral development. An understanding of the stages of moral development can enhance personal moral growth. Those who operate at higher stages of moral development focus on the needs of followers and universal ethical principles. These individuals are similar to Raoul Wallenberg. He placed his ethical principles of saving innocent civilians above the laws of the Nazi regime, which he considered morally wrong.

2. *What are some pressures you face as a student that challenge your ability to do the right thing? Do you expect to face more or fewer pressures as a leader?*

Students can share their experiences as students with the class. One challenge is certainly that of honesty in the age of internet courses. Because students work from home or office on personal computers, it is difficult to verify if a student does the work and takes the test for a webclass or has someone else do it. This places pressure on students to do the right thing and do the work and take the tests themselves.

3. *If most adults are at a conventional level of moral development, what does this mean for their potential for moral leadership?*

Leaders can use an understanding of these stages to enhance their own their followers moral development and to initiate ethics training programs to move people to higher levels of moral reasoning. When leaders operate at level three of moral development, they focus on higher principles and encourage others to think for themselves and expand their understanding of moral issues.

4. *Do you feel that the difference between authoritarian leadership and stewardship should be interpreted as a moral difference? Discuss.*

Yes. Much of the thinking about leadership today implies that moral leadership encourages change toward developing followers into leaders, thereby developing their potential. In authoritarian leadership, followers are given no voice in creating meaning and purpose for their work and no discretion as to how they perform their jobs.

Stewardship places the spotlight on people actually doing the work.

5. *Should serving others be placed at a higher moral level than serving oneself.? Discuss.*

Yes. According to the concept of servant leadership, leaders help others find the power ot the human spirit and accept their responsibilities. This requires an openness and willingness to share in the pain and difficulties of others. An example would be the servant leadership of Mother Teresa, who spent a lifetime serving the poor and afflicted. Her devotion inspired hundreds of people to follow her and attracted millions of dollars in financial support.

6. *If you find yourself avoiding a situation or activity, what can you do to find the courage to move forward? Explain.*

Sources of Personal Courage refer to ways people unlock the courage within themselves, including committing to a cause they believe in, connecting with others, welcoming failure as a natural and beneflcial part of life, and harnassing anger. Courage comes easily when we fight for something we really believe in. Service to a larger vision or purpose gives people the courage to step through fear.

7. *If it is immoral to prevent those around you from growing to their fullest potential, are you being moral?*

Yes. It is the moral responsibility of leaders to speak out to influence others. If there are barriers ---race, education, lack of access to health care---that keep others from reaching their potential, it is the moral duty of leaders to take action. Courage means asking for what you want and saying what you think. It is the ability to say no to unreasonable demands from others. The desire to please others can sometimes block the truth and preserve the status quo. The Civil Rights movement is an example of leaders' speaking out against immoral behavior that kept minorities from reaching their potential.

8. *Do you have the courage to take a moral stand that your peers and even authority figures will disagree with? Why?*

One way to take a moral stand is to oppose unethical conduct, and this requires courage. Whistleblowing is employee disclosure of illegal, immoral, or unethical practices in the organization. This is still risky for employees who may suffer financially and emotionally from their willingness to report unethical conduct on the part of bosses or coworkers. Choosing to act courageously means conflicting emotions--whistleblowers may feel and ethical obligation to report wrongdoing, but may also feel disloyal to their boss and coworkers.

9. *Do you agree that it is important for leaders to do the right thing even if no one will ever know about it? Why or why not?*

Yes, most leaders articulate and uphold high moral standards, and they do the right thing even if they think no one is looking. Leaders realize that what they do in their personal lives carries over to the professional arena. Leaders are a model for the organization twenty-four hours a day seven days a week.

TEACHING TOOLS AND EXERCISES

1. *Leadership Bookshelf: Managing with the Wisdom of Love: Uncovering Virtue in People and Organizations* by Dorothy Marcic.

This work argues that work, just like life and personal relationships can be enriched by a spiritual foundation. Leaders are responsible for building a foundation that strengthens and enriches the lives of organization members.

Do you think personality characteristics such as ego strength, self-confidence, and a sense of independence may enable leaders to behave morally in the face of opposition?

2. *Small Group Discussion*:

Sayings of Confucius

Master Kong (Confucius) 551479 BC has had profound influence on Chinese ethical and political thought. He is not depicted as striving to analyze ethical terms in the manner of Western moral philosophy. Instead his primary purpose is to assist the individual in the essential process of self- cultivation, making him fit to take part in government. The Way (dao) is a term generally used to refer either to the ideal course of conduct for an individual or to an ideal political organization

The Master said: "Be of sincere faith and love learning. Be steadfast unto death in pursuit of the good Way. One does not enter a state which is in peril, nor reside in one which is rebellious. When the Way prevails in the world, then be seen. When it does not, then hide. When the Way prevails in your own state, to be made poor and obscure by it is a disgrace; but when the Way does not prevail in your own state, to be made rich and honorable by it is a disgrace."

Source: Confucius, *The Analects* (New York: Oxford University Press, 1993), 29.

- Why is it important for an individual to avoid a corrupt state (or organization)?
- What does it mean to be steadfast in the pursuit of the good Way?
- Do you see parallels between confucian thought and the stages of moral development? Explain.

3. *On the web:* Are you biased?

Visit *implicit.harvard.edu or* www.tolerance.org/hidden_bias to examine your unconscious attitudes.

The Implicit Association Tests available at this site reveal unconscious beliefs by asking test takers to make split-second associations between words with positive and negative connotations and images representing different types of people. The various tests on this site expose the differences –or the alignment--- between test takers' conscious and unconscious attitudes toward people of different races, sexual orientation, or physical characteristics.

4. *Out-of-class reading*:

Mahzarin R. Banaji, Max H. Bazerman, and Dolly Chugh, "How (Un) Ethical Are You?, *Harvard Business Review* (December 2003): 56-64.

5. *Discuss the following:* Courage---A Holocaust Personal Experience

Fred Friedman survived the Holocaust thanks to a Nazi border guard who recognized him as a Jew but let him slip out of Hitler's Germany. "Somebody could have observed him," said Friedman, who was 12 at the time of his escape in 1938. "And he would have had the same fate that we would have: death."

Friedman, now a 77-year-old retired lawyer, hopes to reinforce the lesson by participating in a nationwide project to help Austrian children grasp the enormity of the Holocaust by focusing on their individual stories.

Put this story in the context of the discussion on courage in the chapter. Also, discuss the actions of Raoul Wallenberg in the opening vignette.

Source: "Holocaust survivors highlight Nazi atrocities," *Odessa American,* (January 27, 2003), 12A.

LEADERSHIP DEVELOPMENT: CASES FOR ANALYSIS

I. Synopsis: Young Leaders Council

Gehan Rasinghe was thrilled to be appointed to the Young Leaders Council at Werner & Burns, a large consulting and financial firm. The purpose of the Council was to provide a training ground for young executives and help them improve their leadership skills. An appointment was for one year or longer, based on an appraisal process introduced by the CEO. Rasinghe was attending his fifth meeting when several members raised a concern about the rating system. They felt is was forced on the group, controlled by top management, and not used as a fair rating of abilities, but a way to "pat your buddies on the back." One member suggested simply giving every other member the highest rating in each category. Rasinghe's gut feeling is that such a "solution" would be unethical.

Case questions and answers

1. *What personal and organizational factors might influence Rasinghe's decision?*

Rasinghe feels like an outsider because he speaks English with an accent and is very quiet. He realizes that if he disagrees with the group, he may alienate himself even more from the rest of his co-workers on the Council. Promotions come from the Council, and Rasinghe realizes that if he goes against the CEO's rating system, he may be overlooked for a promotion. He has to place the best interest of others above personal gain.

2. *Do you believe it would take courage for Rasinghe to vote against the motion? What sources of courage might he call upon to help him vote his conscience?*

Yes, it would take courage to vote against the motion because it is supported by the group. Courage means pushing beyond the comfort zone. To take a chance and improve things means Rasinghe has to push beyond the comfort zone of agreeing with others. Rasinghe is encountering the invisible "wall of fear." Facing the invisible wall of fear is when courage is needed the most.

Courage means asking for what you want and saying what you think. Rasinghe will have to speak out to influence others. Courage is the ability to say no to unreasonable demands from others and face the consequences.

3. *What would you do if you were in Rasinghe's position? Why?*

I would have the courage to vote against the group and explain that it is not right to give everyone high ratings to sabotage the appraisal system. It is better to voice concerns to upper management with the hope that the system could be changed.

II. Synopsis: The Boy, the Girl, the Ferryboat Captain, and the Hermits

A girl lived on one island, and a boy lived on another. They loved each other. The boy had to go on a journey, and the girl wanted to take a ferryboat to get to his island to see him off. She had no money, but they ferryboat captain agreed to take her on board if she spent the night with him. The girl sought advice from a hermit who told her to weigh the alternatives and make a decision. She accepted the ferryboat captain's offer. The boy met her at the dock and asked how she got there without money. She explained what happened, and the boy said he never wanted to see her again. She told her story to a second hermit who went to town to beg for the money to pay for her fare back home. The girl asked how she could repay him, but the hermit said that she owed him nothing. The girl returned home.

Case questions and answers

1. *List in order the characters in this story that you like, from most to least. What values governed your choices?*

The second hermit because he put the welfare of others before his own. The first hermit because he did not try to control the girl and influenced her to consider the consequences of her behavior. The girl because her she acted out of love. The boy because he was judgmental and punishing. The ferry boat captain because he acted selfishly.

2. *Rate the characters on their level of moral development. Explain.*

The second hermit-level 3 because he followed internalized universal principles of right and wrong. The first hermit ---- level 3 because he acted in an independent manner regardless of the expectations of others. The girl --- level 3 because she disobeyed the rules or laws of society to respond to a higher principle of love. The boy-level 2 because he followed the rules, norms and values of the social system. The ferry boat captain-level 1 because he acted out of self interest.

3. *Evaluate each character's level of courage. Discuss.*

The second hermit shows the most courage because he accepts responsibility and gets the money for the girl. The girl shows much courage because she breaks boundaries and traditions and takes risks out of feelings of love. The first hermit shows some courage because he says what he thinks. The boy and the ferry boat captain show no courage, one is guided by social norms, the other by greed.

CHAPTER SEVEN
FOLLOWERSHIP

CHAPTER SUMMARY

Leadership doesn't happen without followers, and the important role of followership in organizations. People are followers more often than leaders, and effective leaders and followers share similar characteristics. An effective follower is both active and an independent in the organization. Being an effective follower depends on not becoming alienated, conforming, passive, or a pragmatic survivor.

Effective followership is not always easy. Effective followers display the courage to assume responsibility, to serve, to challenge, to participate in transformation, and to leave when necessary. Followers also are aware of their own power and its sources, which include personal and position sources. Strategies for being an effective follower include being a resource, helping the leader be a good leader, building a relationship with the leader, and viewing the leader realistically.

Followers want both their leaders and their colleagues to be honest and competent. However, they want their leaders also to be forward-thinking and inspirational. The two latter traits distinguish the role of leader from follower. Followers want to be led, not controlled. Leaders play an important role by creating an environment that enables people to contribute their best. Leaders can use feedback to develop effective followers by making regular feedback a habit, using elements of storytelling, being generous with positive feedback, and helping followers see feedback as an opportunity. They further expand followers' potential and contributions through self-management leadership, which calls for the leader to share power and responsibility in such a way that anyone can become a leader.

Together, leaders and followers forge a sense on interdependence and community in the organization. Community is characterized by inclusivity, a positive culture, conversation, caring, trust, and shared leadership. Communities of practice are an important tool for building community in the organization. Because they are voluntary by nature, communities of practice are created and sustained primarily by followers rather than leaders.

CHAPTER OPENER

Dawn Marshall, Cashier at Pathmark

At Pathmark supermarket, Dawn Marshall, a cashier, has taken what some would consider a boring low-paying job and imbued it with meaning and value. In a society that is rapidly going self-service Marshall specializes in giving people a little bit of luxury in the mundane chore of grocery shopping. She's a good cashier but her forte is bagging.

Marshall knows how to pack the flimsy plastic bags so that eggs don't get broken. Even though Marshall works on her feet all day and has to put up with rude customers, she handles whatever comes her way with a positive attitude. She accepts responsibility for her own personal fulfillment and finds ways to expand her potential and use her capacities to serve the needs of others and the organization. These are the hallmarks of not only good followers, but of good leaders as well. At Pathmark, leadership and followership are closely intertwined. Dawn Marshall is a follower, but she acts like a leader by setting an example for others and using her positive attitude to uplift others.

LECTURE/OUTLINE

To recognize your followership style and take steps to become a more effective follower.

The Role of Followers

➢ *Why is followership important in the discussion of leadership?*

Leadership and followership are fundamental roles that individuals shift into and out of under various conditions. Everyone—including leaders—is a follower at one time.

The nature of the leader-follower exchange involves reciprocity, the mutual exchange of influence.

The followers' influence upon a leader can enhance the leader or underscore shortcomings.

Many of the qualities that are desirable in a leader are the same qualities possessed by an effective follower.

Both leader and follower roles are proactive; together they can achieve a shared vision.

In an organization, leaders can help develop effective followers, just as effective followers can develop better leaders.

Discussion Question #1: *Discuss the role of the follower. Why do you think so little emphasis is given to followership compared to leadership in organizations?*

Notes____

Styles of Followership *Exhibit 7.1*

Robert E. Kelley described five styles of followership categorized according to two dimensions:

- The first dimension: independent, critical thinking, versus dependent, uncritical thinking.

  Independent thinking recalls the discussion of mindfulness; independent thinkers are mindful of the effects of people's behavior on achieving organizational goals.

  A dependent, uncritical thinker does not consider possibilities, does not contribute to the cultivation of the organization, and accepts the leader's ideas without thinking.

- The second dimension: active versus passive behavior.

  An active individual participates fully in the organization, and a passive individual is characterized by a need for constant supervision and prodding.

The extent to which one is active or passive and is critical, independent thinker versus a dependent, uncritical thinker determines a type of followership style:

- An *alienated follower is* a person in the organization who is passive yet independent, critical thinker.

  Alienated followers are often effective followers who have experienced setbacks and obstacles, perhaps broken promises by superiors.

  They focus exclusively on the shortcomings of the organization and other people.

- A *conformist* is a follower who is an active participant but does not utilize critical thinking skills in task behavior.

  A conformist carries out any and all orders regardless of the nature of the tasks, participating willingly but without considering the consequences.

  The only concern is to avoid conflict.

- A *pragmatic survivor* is one who has qualities of all four extremes --- depending on which style fits with the prevalent situation.

  This type of follower uses whatever style best benefits a personal position and minimizes risk.

  Pragmatic survivors emerge when the organization faces desperate times, and followers do whatever is needed to get themselves through the difficulty.

- A *passive follower* is one who exhibits neither critical, independent thinking nor active participation.

  Being passive and uncritical, this type of follower displays neither initiative nor a sense of responsibility.

  Passive followers leave the thinking to their leaders.

  Passive followers are often the result of leaders who are over controlling and punish mistakes.

- An *effective follower* is one who is both a critical, independent thinker and active in the organization.

  Effective followers behave the same toward everyone, regardless of their position.

  They do not try to avoid risk or conflict.

  They initiate change and put themselves at risk to serve the best interest of the organization; they are characterized by both mindfulness and a willingness to act.

  Effective followers are far from powerless.

❑ *Living Leadership: Our Deepest Fear*

Nelson Mandela, "*As we let our own light shine, we unconsciously give other people permission to do the same.*"

➢ What is the meaning of effective followership according to Nelson Mandela?

Discussion Question #2: *Compare the alienated follower with the passive follower. Can you give an example of each? How would you respond to each if you were a leader?*

Notes____

To apply the principles of courageous followership, including responsibility, service, challenging authority, participating in change, and knowing when to leave.

Demands on the Effective Follower

Courage and integrity applies to both effective leaders and followers.

Effective followers know what they stand for and express their ideas to their leaders, even though this might risk their jobs, demean them, make them feel inadequate.

Effective follower accept responsibility, serve the needs of the organization, challenge authority, participate in change, and leave the organization when necessary.

The Will to Assume Responsibility

By assuming responsibility for their behavior and its impact on the organization, effective followers do not presume that a leader or an organization will provide them with security, permission to act, or personal growth.

Followers initiate opportunities for personal fulfillment, growth, and the fullest use of their capabilities.

In the Lead: Chuck Lucier, Booz, Allen, & Hamilton

Chuck Lucier of Booz, Allen & Hamilton believes effective followers are the linchpins of their organizations. By understanding the needs of the organization and their boss's objectives, he believes, followers can expand their own potential and move the organization forward. Lucier recalls his will to assume responsibility as a junior partner. "I took career risk by standing up and saying, "This firm isn't perfect; there are opportunities we are missing, and I want to be part of the solution." He was put in charge of a study that resulted in a successful strategy for the firm which doubled revenue.

Q: *How did Lucier become an effective follower?*

A: One of Lucier's superiors warned him that no one who had ever been put in charge of such a study "was still around three years later." Lucier was willing to take the risk to make to the study even though criticism of the company could have cost him his job.

The Will to Serve

An effective follower discerns the needs of the organization and actively seeks to serve those needs.

Supporting the leader's decision, providing strength, complementing the leader's position, and serving others display effective followership.

Followers act for the common mission of the organization with a passion that equals that of the leader.

The Will to Challenge

Effective followers do not sacrifice the purpose of the organization or their personal ethics in order to maintain harmony and minimize conflict.

They stand up against leaders and decisions when that behavior contradicts the best interest of the organization, or their own integrity.

Good leaders want followers who are willing to challenge them because leaders are human and make mistakes.

The Will to Participate in Transformation

Effective followers view the struggle of corporate change and transformation as a mutual experience shared by all members of the organization.

They are not afraid to confront changes and work toward reshaping the organization.

The Will to Leave

Often organizational or personal changes create a situation in which a follower must withdraw from a leader-follower relationship.

If followers are faced with a leader or an organization unwilling to make necessary changes, it is time to take their support elsewhere.

Another reason for leaving is a person's desire to move on to another phase of life. Sometimes people know they need new challenges.

Discussion Question #9: *Is the will to leave the ultimate courage of a follower compared to the courage to participate in transformation? Which would be the hardest for you?*

Notes____

To understand the leader's role in developing effective followers.

Developing Personal Potential *Exhibit 7.2*

➢ *How do followers expand their potential to be critical, independent thinkers who make active contributions to their organizations?*

One widely-acclaimed approach to helping people deal courageously with life's challenges is Stephen Covey's *The 7 Habits of Highly Effective People.*

The seven habits are arranged along a maturity continuum from dependence to interdependence.

Each habit builds on the previous one so individuals grow further along the maturity continuum as they develop personal effectiveness habits.

- *Dependent* people expect someone else to take care of them and blame others when things go wrong.

- *Independent* people have developed a sense of self- worth and an attitude of self-reliance.

  Independent people accept personal responsibility and get what they want through their own actions.

- *Interdependent* people realize that it is best to work cooperatively with others, that life and work are better when one experiences the richness of close interpersonal relationships.

From Dependence to Independence.

Covey's first three habits deal with self-reliance and self- mastery.

These are called *private victories* because they only involve the follower becoming independent, not the follower in relationships.

- *Habit 1: Be Proactive***.** This means being responsible and not blaming others. Proactive people recognize that they have the ability to choose and to act with integrity.

- *Habit 2: Begin with the End in Mind.* This means starting with a clear mental image of your own destination.

  Beginning with the end in mind means knowing what you want, what is deeply important to you, so that you can live each day in a way that contributes to your personal vision.

- *Habit 3: Put First Things First.* This habit encourages people to gain control of time and events by relating them to their goals and by managing themselves.

  It means focusing on preserving and enhancing *relationships* and on accomplishing *results.*

Effective Interdependence.

The first three habits build a foundation of independence, from which one can move to interdependence --- caring, productive relationships with others --- which Covey calls *public victories.*

Moving to interdependence involves open communication, effective teamwork, and building positive relationships based on trust, caring, and respect.

When a person moves to interdependence, he steps into a leadership role.

- *Habit 4: Think Win-Win.* This implies an understanding that without cooperation, the organization cannot succeed.

  Win-win is a frame of mind and heart that constantly seeks agreements or solutions that are mutually beneficial and satisfying.

- *Habit 5: Seek First to Understand, Then to Be Understood.* Many people do not listen with intent to understand; they are too busy thinking about what they want to say.

  Seeking first to understand requires a nonjudgmental attitude.

  Empathetic listening gets inside another person's frame of reference to better understand how that person feels.

- *Habit 6: Synergize. Synergy* is the combined action that occurs when people work together to create new alternatives and solutions.

  The essence of synergy is to value and respect differences and take advantage of them to build on strengths and compensate for weaknesses.

- *Habit 7: Sharpen the Saw.* This is the process of using and continuously renewing the physical, mental, spiritual, and social aspects of life.

To be effective followers and effective leaders requires living a balanced life.

Notes____

____

____

Sources of Follower Power

Another issue of concern is how followers gain and use power in organizations.

Formal leaders have more power than followers do.

Effective followers participate fully in organizations by culling power from available sources.

Personal sources of power include knowledge, expertise, effort, and persuasion. Position sources of power include location, information, and access.

Personal Sources.

Knowledge is a source of power.

A follower who has demonstrated a record of performance often develops *expertise* and in this way can influence decisions.

The power to influence is also associated with the *effort* put forth by a follower.

Another source of power is *persuasion,* the direct appeal to leaders in an organization for desired outcomes.

In addition to being direct, speaking truthfully to a leader can be a source of power.

Power does not always come from titles or seniority in the organization. Sometimes it can come from knowledge and contributions.

Position Sources

The location of a follower can make that person *visible.*

A central location provides influence to a follower, who is known to many and contributes to the work of many.

A position that is key to the flow of *information* can establish that position and the follower in it as influential to those who seek the information.

Within a *network of relationships,* a follower has greater opportunity to persuade others and to make powerful contributions to numerous organizational processes.

Discussion Question #4: *Which of the five demands on effective followers do you feel is most important? Least important? How does a follower derive the courage and power to be effective? Discuss.*

Notes____

To implement the strategies for effective followership at school or work.

Strategies for Managing Up

Exhibit 7.3

- *Do you think that how followers manage their leaders is just as important as how their leaders manage them?*

Effective followers transform the leader-follower relationship by striving to improve their leaders rather than just criticize them.

Followers develop a meaningful task-related relationship with their bosses that enables them to add value to the organization despite a disagreement with their bosses' decisions.

Leaders are authority figures and may play too large a role in the mind of the follower; followers may be overcritical of leaders.

Effective followers perceive themselves as the equals of leaders, not inherently subordinate.

Strategies enable followers to overcome authority-based relationships and develop effective, respectful relationships with their leaders.

Be a Resourcefor the Leader

Effective followers align themselves to the purpose and the vision of the organization.

They are a source of strength for the leader; they indicate their personal goals and inform the leader about their ideas, beliefs, needs, and constraints.

The more leaders and followers know the day-to-day activities and problems of one another, the better resources they can be for each other.

Help the Leader be a Good Leader

Good followers seek the leader's counsel and look for ways the leader can help them improve their skills, abilities, and value to the organization.

Effective followers help their leaders by telling what they need to be good followers.

If a leader knows what followers appreciate, the leader is more likely to continue that behavior.

Asking for advice, thanking the leader for helpful behavior and being honest about areas that need improvement are important ways followers can affect the conduct of leaders.

Build a Relationship with the Leader

Effective followers work toward a genuine relationship with their leaders, which includes developing trust and speaking honestly on the basis of trust.

A good relationship with the leader makes every interaction more meaningful to the organization.

The relationship is imbued with mutual respect rather than authority and submission.

***In the Lead*:** Wes Walsh

When Wes Walsh came under an autocratic manager, his predecessor warned him to stay away from the infamously autocratic boss. Walsh ignored the advice and started dropping by his boss's office on a regular basis. Walsh sought approval on very small matters and continued frequent interactions before moving on to matters that are more consequential. When an important project had to be addressed, Walsh took his boss on a plant visit. The boss acknowledged the problem and approved a proposal that he had previously rejected.

Q: *How did Walsh effectively use a follower strategy?*

A: Effective followers work toward a genuine relationship with their leaders, which includes developing trust and speaking honestly based on trust. A good relationship with the leader makes every interaction more meaningful to the organization. Walsh developed a good relationship with the boss and was able to get his proposal approved.

View the Leader Realistically

➢ *Why does viewing the leader realistically mean giving up idealized images?.*

Understanding that leaders are fallible and will make mistakes leads to acceptance and the potential for an equitable relationship.

The way in which a follower perceives the boss is the foundation of their relationship.

Effective followers present realistic images of themselves and do not hide their weaknesses or mistakes, nor do they criticize their leaders to others.

It is an alienated follower who complains without engaging in constructive action.

Instead of criticizing a leader to others, it is far more constructive to disagree with a leader directly on matters relevant to the department's or organization's work.

Discussion Question #6: *Describe the strategy for effective followership that you most prefer. Explain.*

Notes____

____

____

To know what followers want and contribute to building a community among followers.

What Followers Want *Exhibit 7.4*

➢ *What expectations do followers have about what constitutes a desirable leader?*

Research shows that followers expect leaders to be honest, forward- thinking, inspiring, and competent.

They want their colleagues to be honest and competent, but also dependable and cooperative.

The hallmark that distinguishes leadership from is not authority, knowledge, power or other conventional notions; it is the leadership activities of fostering a vision and inspiring others to achieve it.

Leaders and followers act in two different roles, but effective behaviors overlap.

Followers do not want to find themselves subjected to leader-behavior that denies them the opportunity to make values contributions.

Leaders have a responsibility to enable followers to fully contribute their ideas and abilities.

Discussion Question #7: *What do the traits followers want in leaders and in other followers tell us about the roles of each? Discuss.*

Notes____

____

____

Using Feedback to Develop Followers *Exhibit 7.5*

Giving and receiving feedback is often difficult for both leaders and followers.

Feedback should be seen as a route to improvement and development, not something to dread and fear.

Feedback occurs when a leader uses evaluation and communication to help individuals and the organization learn and improve.

The feedback process involves four elements:

- *Observations* are visible occurrences, such as a follower's behavior on a job.

- *Assessment* is the interpretation of observed behaviors, an evaluation of the results in terms of vision and goals.

- *Consequence* is the outcome of what was observed and can include both actual consequences possible if no change takes place.

- *Development* refers to the sustainment or improvement of follower behaviors.

Each element is communicated from the leader to the individual or organization.

The development becomes an observation in the next feedback loop.

Leaders can optimize the use of feedback and minimize conflict and the fear that accompanies it; *empathy* is a powerful tool for leaders during the feedback process.

Tips for using feedback to develop effective followers:

- *Make regular feedback a habit.* Leaders should not save everything up for an annual performance review.

- *Use elements of storytelling.* Followers as well as leaders usually learn a lot more from examining the story of how and why something happened than from evaluations that are punitive.

- *Be generous with positive feedback.* Too many leaders offer feedback only when things go wrong. They should congratulate behaviors that support vision and goals.

- *Train followers to view feedback as an opportunity for development.* When people recognize and acknowledge their emotions in response to criticisms, they can "reframe" the feedback to their own advantage.

Discussion Question #5: *Do you think you would respond better to feedback that is presented using elements of storytelling rather than with a traditional performance review format? Discus. How might using story and metaphor help followers reframe negative feedback?*

Notes____

____

____

Leading Others to Lead Themselves

An important step a leader can take to develop effective followers is to accept and acknowledge his limitations and inability to accomplish anything without followers.

Good leaders strive toward a collaborative relationship with followers.

Charles Manz and Henry Sims propose *self-management leadership,* which means leading others to lead themselves.

Self-management leadership calls for leaders t share power and responsibility in such a way that anyone can become a leader depending on the circumstances of the situation.

Leaders coach employees to think critically, make sure the employees have necessary information, and understand how their jobs are relevant to the organization's vision.

Empowerment of frontline employees, participative manage, and other forms of democratic practice are growing trends in organizations.

Self-management leadership hinges on providing employees with directed autonomy.

In the Lead: U.S. Military Academy, West Point

At West Point, everyone leads and everyone follows. It's a 24-hour leadership laboratory where people learn that leadership and followership are two sides of the same whole. An important lesson is that leaders are nothing without followers. Cadets have to learn to subordinate their self-interest for the good of the whole, because that's what they'll be called upon to do when they graduate. However, there's another side to the story, one that instills creativity and flexibility into students who might someday have to make rapid decisions in the chaos of a battlefield. Cadets learn to rely on the competencies of followers and their own judgment.

Q: *How does West Point emphasize the importance of followership when training leaders?*

A: West Point trains leaders to act in ways that encourage followers to think independently and be willing to take risks, challenge unproductive or unethical norms and initiate change for the benefit of the organization. At West Point, everyone is evaluated all the time, and every action is opportunity to learn, to gain new experience, and to grow in understanding.

Building a Community of Followers

Together, followers and leaders provide the dependability, cooperation, and commitment to build a sense of community and interdependence in the organization.

Community provides a spirit of connection that sustains effective relationships and commitment of purpose.

People in a community know that only through trust and teamwork can they accomplish shared goals.

In a community, people communicate openly with each other, maintain their uniqueness, and are committed to something larger than themselves.

Historically, communities were based on service, informed participation, and individual contributions.

Characteristics of Community

Successful communities share a number of important characteristics: inclusivity, a positive culture, conversation, caring and trust, and shared leadership.

- *Inclusivity* In a community, everyone belongs.

  Diversity, divergent ideas, and different points of view are encouraged.

Community focuses on the whole rather than the parts, and people focus on what binds them together.

- *Positive Culture* Leaders and followers perceive the organization as a community with shared norms and values.

  Members care about newcomers and work to socialize them into the culture.

- *Conversation* Conversation is how people make and share meanings that are the basis of community.

  Dialogue means that each person suspends his attachment to a particular viewpoint so that deeper level of listening, synthesis, and meaning evolves from the whole community.

- *Caring and Trust.* Members of a community genuinely care about one another.

  People consider how their actions affect others and the community as a whole.

  Trust is developed from caring relationships and an emphasis on ethical behavior that serves the interests of the whole.

- *Shared Leadership* In a community, a leader is one among many equals.

  People do not try to control others, and anyone can step forward as a leader.

  There is a spirit of equality, and everyone has an opportunity to make a valued contribution.

Communities of Practice

Communities of practice often form spontaneously in organizations s people gravitate toward others who share their interests and face similar problems.

They are made up of individuals who are informally bound to one another through exposure to a similar set of problems and a common pursuit of solutions.

They are similar to professional societies—people join them and stay in them by choice, because they think they have something to learn and to contribute.

Leaders and followers can encourage and support these groups to help people find meaning and build the relationships needed to move the organization forward.

By facilitating relationship across boundaries, communities of practice move both leadership and followership to new levels.

Discussion Question #8: *How might the characteristics of effective followership contribute to building community? Discuss.*

Notes____

DISCUSSION QUESTIONS

1. *Discuss the role of the follower. Why do you think so little emphasis is given to followership compared to leadership in organizations?*

Leadership and followership are fundamental roles that individuals shift in and out of under various conditions. The followers influence upon a leader can enhance the leader or underscore shortcomings. Many qualities desirable in a leader are desirable in a follower. Followers have received little attention because in a vertical hierarchy they were not empowered.

2. *Compare the alienated follower with the passive follower. Can you give an example of each? How would you respond to each if you were a leader?*

An alienated follower is a passive yet independent, critical thinker (e.g., a disgruntled employee) whereas a passive follower is one who exhibits neither critical, independent thinking nor active ideas would be appropriate for the alienated follower and empowerment and job enrichment for the passive follower.

3. *Do you think self-management leadership should be considered a leadership style? Why or why not?*

Yes. It takes a certain behavioral style to develop leaders who enable the organization to react quickly to threats and opportunities. Leaders who practice self-management leadership do not try to control employee behavior, but coach employees to think critically about their own performance and judge how well they are accomplishing tasks and achieving goals. By linking jobs to goals, self-management leaders teach employees to have a framework within which to act.

4. *Which of the five demands on effective followers do you feel is most important to an effective follower? Least important? How does a follower derive the courage and power to be effective? Discuss.*

Most important: Assuming responsibility. Followers initiate opportunities for personal fulfillment, growth, and the fullest use of their capabilities. Least important: Courage to leave. A follower derives courage and power to be effective by having skills that complement the leader's weaknesses, while both are working together in support of the mission.

5. *Do you think you would respond better to feedback that is presented using elements of storytelling rather than with a traditional performance review format? Discus. How might using story and metaphor help followers reframe negative feedback?*

Yes. Followers as well as leaders usually learn a lot more from examining the story of how and why something happened than from evaluations that "chew them out." Examining the story of what happened and why typically puts the leader and follower on equal footing, with both try to examining their roles and responsibilities in the problem. When people recognize and acknowledge their emotions in response to the story or metaphor, they can then "reframe" the feedback to their own advantage.

6. *Describe the strategy for effective followership that you most prefer. Explain.*

Building a relationship with the leader is preferred because this makes every interaction more meaningful to the organization and imbues the work situation with respect rather than authority and submission. Effective followers align themselves to the purpose and the vision of the organization and serve as a source of strength for the leader. They indicate their personal goals and inform the leader about their ideas, beliefs, needs, and constraints. This alignment involves understanding the leader's position—that is, goals, needs, and constraints.

7. *What do the traits followers want in leaders and in other followers tell us about the roles of each? Discuss.*

Followers want leaders to be honest, forward-thinking, inspiring, and competent. A leader must be worthy of trust, envision the future of the organization, inspire others to contribute, and be capable and effective in matters that will effect the organization. They want their colleagues to be honest and competent, but also dependable and cooperative.

8. *How might the characteristics of effective followership contribute to building community? Discuss.*

Effective followers and effective community members share the same characteristics. The follower who has the courage to serve, who is an active, critical thinker, and who maximizes his contribution encourages a sense of community to develop in the organization. In a community, everyone belongs. Individuality and different points of view are encouraged. Community focuses on the whole rather than the parts, and people focus on what binds them together.

9. *Is the will to leave the ultimate courage of a follower compared to the will to participate in transformation? Which would be the hardest for you?*

It is harder to participate in the transformation because a person is still in the same situation dealing with the same people and the same obstacles. As followers view the struggle of corporate change and transformation, it takes courage to support the leader and the organization. Courageous followers are not afraid to confront changes and work toward reshaping the organization.

TEACHING TOOLS AND EXERCISES

1. *Leader's Bookshelf: Leading Up: How to Lead Your Boss So You Both Win* by Michael Useem.

Useem uses heroic accounts and moments of crisis because he believes they are the best teachers. However he points out that opportunities for leading up come to almost all of us in many different situations. How do effective followers act as upward leaders according to Useem?

2. *On the Web:* The Wharton Leadership Digest is a monthly electronic bulletin on current research and writing related to leadership and change management.

"Making Music and Learning Leadership: Cassatt String Quartet," by Susan Leshnower, May 2001. http://leadership.wharton.upenn.edu

A string quartet is an opportunity to learn both leadership and followership. Members have to share ideas, communicate musical ideas, and trust their fellow "team" members. Each member leads and follows. How do the concepts of effective followership apply to a string quartet? Discuss.

3. *Out-of-class activity:* Whistle-Blowing

Review newspapers, magazines, and internet sites for the last three months and find examples of whistle blowing by followers. Write a short summary and present your findings to the class.

4. *Leader's Self-Insight: The Power of Followership*

After taking the survey, students will assess how they carry out their followership role. Then they can discuss the answers to the following questions or keep them in a notebook to be handed in at the end of the semester.

- How do you feel about your follower style?
- What might you do to be more effective as a follower?

5. *Role Play*: Ethical Followership

This role-play encourages a discussion on ethical behavior for followers. In a government warehouse containing cleaning and office supplies, a warehouse worker overhears the supervisor make a deal with a distributor. The distributor says to the supervisor: "You bypass procurement procedures, and I'll sell you brooms at a lower price and give you a

5 percent commission." The supervisor is tired of paperwork and agrees, but does not realize that the worker heard the conversation. What should the worker do? How can this behavior be prevented?

LEADERSHIP DEVELOPMENT: CASES FOR ANALYSIS

I. Synopsis: General Products Britain

Carl Mitchell was delighted to accept a job in the British branch office of General Products, Inc. a consumer products multinational. Two months later, Mitchell was miserable. The problem was George Garrow, the general manager in charge of the British branch, to whom he reported. Garrow had become general manager by "keeping his nose clean," and not making mistakes. As Mitchell complained, "Any time I ask him to make a decision, he just wants to dig deeper and provide 30 more pages of data. Garrow seemed terrified of departing from the status quo. Market share was slipping and Mitchell's two best product managers quit, burned out by analyzing pointless data without results.

Case questions and answers

1. *How would you evaluate Mitchell as a follower? Evaluate his courage and style.*

He shows the courage to challenge because he speaks his mind and takes the risk of blame from Garrow. His followership style is that of an effective follower because he is a critical, independent thinker who is active in the organization.

2. *If you were Mitchell, what would you do now?*

The organization is undergoing transformation since market share is slipping, and two employees have quit. Mitchell should have the courage to participate in the transformation. As followers view the struggle of corporate change and transformation, it takes courage to support the leader and the organization.

3. *If you were Garrow's boss and Mitchell came to see you, what would you say?*

Hopefully, he would listen to Mitchell and take action to make Garrow act in accordance with the company's vision. Mitchell expects Garrow to be honest, forward- thinking, inspiring, and competent. The hallmark that distinguishes the role of leadership, Garrow, from the role of followership, Mitchell, is not authority, knowledge, power or other conventional notions. The distinction lies in the clearly defined leadership activities of fostering a vision and inspiring others to achieve that vision---which Garrow fails to do.

II Synopsis: Trams Discount Store

"Things are different around here" were the first words Jill heard from her new manager. Mr. Tyler was welcoming back Jill to another summer of working at Trams, a nationwide discount store. Reluctantly, Jill worked the evening shift, folding clothes, fixing the racks, and doing price checks. Jill's stomach tied in knots as she remembered her previous work experience at Trams. With the clientele and the number of price checks, it was almost impossible to finish the work, but each night Jill would race against the clock to finish her section. As Jill talked to Mr. Tyler, she sensed things were different. Mr. Tyler left after six leaving the night shift with no supervision. One of the girls explained that they all worked as a team to get the work done. No one did the job completely and breaks stretched to an hour long. Sales declined. The final straw was came when a co-worker asked her to change a price tag.

Case questions and answers

1. *What types of follower courage does Jill need in this situation?*

Jill needs courage to assume responsibility. By assuming responsibility for her behavior and its impact on the organization, courageous followers do not presume that a leader or an organization will provide security, permission to act, or personal growth. Followers initiate opportunities for personal fulfillment, growth, and the fullest use of their capabilities. Jill knows there is wrongdoing and her boss is unwilling to take action, so she should.

2. *If you were Jill, what actions would you take first? If that didn't produce results, what would you do second? Third?*

First, Jill should help Tyler be a good leader Effective followers help their leaders by telling what they need to be good followers---an honest, productive work environment. If Tyler knows what Jill appreciates, he is more likely to perform better as manager. Second, Jill should be honest when Tyler is behaving in a counterproductive manner and communicate the need for him to change. He could stay after 6:00 p.m. and sales staff would work harder. Third, if there is no change in the situation, Jill should have the courage to find another job.

3. *How might Jill use this experience to develop her personal potential?*

She could work for a company that has a strong code of ethics that is communicated clearly to all employees. She could look for a community in which to work. Characteristics of a community include inclusivity, conversation, realism, and shared leadership. She could encourage these traits in her followership role.

CHAPTER EIGHT
MOTIVATION AND EMPOWERMENT

CHAPTER SUMMARY

The chapter introduces a number of important ideas for motivating people in organizations. Individuals are motivated to act to satisfy a range of needs. The leadership approach to motivation tends to focus on the higher needs of employees. The role of the leader is to create a situation in which followers' higher needs and the needs of the organization can be met simultaneously.

Needs-based theories focus on the underlying needs that motivate how people behave. Maslow's hierarchy of needs proposes that individuals satisfy lower needs before they move on to higher needs. Herzberg's two-factor theory holds that dissatisfiers must be removed, and motivators added to satisfy employees. McClelland asserted that people are motivated differently depending on which needs they have acquired. Other motivation theories, including the reinforcement perspective, expectancy theory, and equity theory, focus primarily on extrinsic rewards and punishments, sometimes called "carrot-and-stick" methods of motivation.

The reinforcement perspective proposes that behavior can be modified by the use of rewards and punishment. Expectancy theory is based on the idea that a person's motivation is contingent upon his or her expectations that a given behavior will result in desired rewards. Equity theory proposes that individuals' motivation is affected not only by rewards but also by their perceptions of how fairly they are treated in relation to others. People are motivated to seek social equity in the rewards they expect for performance.

Although carrot-and-stick methods of motivation are pervasive in North American organizations, many critics argue that extrinsic rewards undermine intrinsic rewards, bring about unintended consequences, are too simple to capture organizational realities, and replace workplace cooperation with unhealthy competition.

An alternative approach to carrot-and-stick motivation is that of empowerment, by which subordinates know the direction of the organization and have the autonomy to act as they see fit to go in that direction. Leaders provide employees with the knowledge to contribute to the organization, the power to make consequential decisions, and the necessary resources to do their jobs. Empowerment typically meets the higher needs of individuals.

Empowerment is tied to the trend toward helping employees find value and meaning in their jobs and creating an environment where people can flourish. When people are fully engaged with their work, satisfaction, performance, and profits increase. Leaders create the environment that determines employee motivation and satisfaction. One way to measure how engaged people are with their work is the Q12, a list of 12 questions about the day-to-day realities of a person's job. Other current organizationwide motivational programs include employee ownership, pay for knowledge, gainsharing, pay for performance, and job enrichment.

CHAPTER OPENER

D. Michael Abrashoff, Commander of the USS Benfold

When D. Michael Abrashoff took command of the U.S. Navy destroyer USS *Benfold,* he came face to face with the biggest leadership challenge of his Navy career. Despite the fact that the *Benfold* was a technological marvel, most of its sailors couldn't wait to leave. People were so unhappy and demoralized that walking aboard ship felt like entering a deep well of despair. Abrashoff improved motivation by creating an environment of trust and empowerment. His emphasis on helping people contribute and grow changed many crew members' personal as well as work lives. Abrahoff started listening to ideas from below, meeting individually in his cabin with every one of the 310 sailors. When sailors saw that Abrashoff sincerely wanted and valued their ideas and input, they responded with energy, enthusiasm, and commitment. Under Abrashoff's leadership, the *Benfold* set all-time records for performance and retention.

LECTURE/OUTLINE

To recognize and apply the difference between intrinsic and extrinsic rewards.

Leadership and Motivation *Exhibit 8.1*

➢ *Why is the study of motivation important for leaders?*

Motivation refers to the forces either internal or external to a person that arouse enthusiasm and persistence to pursue a certain course of action.

Employee motivation affects productivity, so part of a leader's job is to channel followers' motivation towards the accomplishment of the organization's vision and goals.

A simple model of human motivations shows that:

- People have basic needs (e.g., for food) that translate into an internal tension that motivates specific behaviors to fulfill the need.
- To the extent that the behavior is successful, the person is rewarded when the need is satisfied.
- The reward informs the person that the behavior was appropriate and can be used again in the future.

The importance of motivation is that it can lead to behaviors that reflect high job performance.

High employee motivation, organizational performance, and profits go hand-in-hand.

Leaders can use motivation theory to help satisfy followers' needs and simultaneously encourage high work performance.

When workers are not motivated to achieve organizational goals, the fault is often the leader's.

Intrinsic and Extrinsic Rewards *Exhibit 8.2*

Rewards can be intrinsic, extrinsic, system wide, or individual.

Intrinsic rewards are the internal satisfactions a person receives in the process of performing a particular action.

Extrinsic rewards are given by another person, typically a supervisor, and include promotions and pay increases.

System-wide rewards apply to all employees or those within a specific category or department.

Individual rewards may differ among people in the same organization. An extrinsic, system-wide reward is a vacation.

An intrinsic system-wide reward is pride in the organization; an extrinsic, individual reward is a bonus check.; an intrinsic, individual reward is a sense of self fulfillment at work.

Although extrinsic rewards are important, leaders work hard to enable followers to achieve intrinsic rewards—both individually and system-wide.

Employees who get intrinsic satisfaction from their jobs often put forth increased effort.

Leaders can create an environment that brings out the best in people.

They try to match followers with jobs and tasks that provide individual, intrinsic rewards.

They strive to create an environment where people feel valued, helping followers to achieve system wide intrinsic rewards.

Notes____

Higher versus Lower Needs *Exhibit 8.3*

Intrinsic rewards appeal to the "higher" needs of individuals, such as accomplishment, competence, fulfillment, and self-determination.

Extrinsic rewards appeal to "lower" needs of individuals, such as material comfort, basic safety, and security.

Conventional approaches appeal to lower basic needs and rely on extrinsic rewards and punishments ---carrot and stick methods--- to motivate subordinates to behave in desired ways.

These approaches are effective, but they are based on controlling the behavior of people by manipulating their decisions about how to act.

The higher needs of people may be unmet in favor of utilized their labor in exchange for external rewards.

Leaders motivate others by providing the opportunity to satisfy higher needs and receive intrinsic rewards.

What is intrinsically rewarding to one individual may not be so to another.

Ideally, work behaviors should satisfy lower and higher needs and serve the organizational mission.

Discussion Question #2: *What is the relationship among needs, rewards, and motivation?*

Notes____

To apply need-based theories of motivation

Needs-Based Theories of Motivation

Exhibit 8.4

➢ *Explain the term "needs-based" theories of motivation?*

Needs-based theories emphasize the needs that motivate people.

Needs are the source of an internal drive that motivates behavior to fulfill the needs.

A leader who understands worker needs can design the reward system to reinforce employees for directing energies and priorities toward attainment of shared goals.

Hierarchy of Needs Theory

The hierarchy of needs theory, proposed by Abraham Maslow, states that humans are motivated by multiple needs which exist in a hierarchical order.

The higher needs cannot be satisfied until the lower needs are met.

Maslow named five levels of motivating needs:

- *Physiological*—the most basic human needs include food, water, and oxygen.

In an organizational setting, these are reflected in needs for adequate heat, air, and base salary.

- *Safety*---the need for a safe and secure physical and emotional environment and freedom from threats.

  In an organizational workplace, safety needs reflect the needs for safe jobs, fringe benefits, and job security.

- *Belongingness*---a desire to be accepted by peers, have friendships, be part of a group, and be loved.

  In the organization, these needs influence the desire for good relationships with co-workers, participation in a work team, and a good relationship with supervisors.

- *Esteem*---the desires for a positive self-image and for attention, recognition, and appreciation from others.

  Within organizations, esteem needs reflect a motivation for recognition, and increase in responsibility, high status, and credit for contributions.

- *Self-Actualization*---the need for self-fulfillment: developing one's full potential, increasing one's competence, and becoming a better person.

  In the organization, this need is met by providing people with opportunities to grow, be empowered and creative, and acquire training for challenging assignments and advancement.

Physiology, safety, and belonging are *deficiency* needs, low-order needs which take priority and must be satisfied before higher-needs, or growth needs, are activated.

The needs are satisfied in sequence. Once a need has been satisfied, it declines in importance and the next higher need is activated.

Discussion Question #1: *Describe the kinds of needs that people bring to an organization. How might a person's values and attitudes, as described in Chapter 4, influence the needs he or she brings to work?*

Notes____

____

____

To motivate others by meeting the higher level needs

Two-Factor Theory *Exhibit 8.5*

Frederick Herzberg developed the two-factor theory.

Hygiene factors, the first dimension, involves the presence or absence of job dissatisfiers such as working conditions, pay, company policies or interpersonal relationships.

When hygiene factors are poor, work is dissatisfying.

Good hygiene factors remove dissatisfaction but do not cause satisfaction and motivation.

Motivators, the second dimension, fulfills high-level needs and includes achievement, recognition, responsibility, and opportunity for growth.

Hertzberg believed that when motivators are present, workers are highly motivated and satisfied.

The leader's role is to go beyond the removal of dissatisfiers to the use of motivators to meet higher level needs and steer employees toward greater achievement and satisfaction.

***In the Lead*:** Ann Price, Motek

When Ann Price founded Motek, she wanted to create a company whose primary mission was to improve the lives of its employees and customers rather than to reward shareholders or investors. Price incorporates both low-level hygiene factors and high-level motivators at Motek. Pay is satisfactory, but the benefits are amazing. All employees get five weeks of paid vacation and 10 paid holidays, no one is permitted to work past 5 p.m. or on weekends. The working environment is calm, almost serene. Employees are highly motivated and committed because of the challenge, responsibility, and opportunity for personal growth that Motek provides. Employees vote on everything from the office furniture to their own job assignments and pay raises.

Q: *How does Ann Price use the two-factor theory to motivate employees?*

A: Price has successfully applied the two-factor theory to provide both low-level hygiene factors and incorporate high-level motivators. By meeting employees' higher as well as lower-level needs, Price has created happy employees and a successful organization.

Discussion Question #9: *Do you agree that hygiene factors, as defined by Herzberg's two-factor theory, cannot provided increased satisfaction and motivation. Discuss.*

Notes____

Acquired Needs Theory

Acquired needs theory, a needs-based theory developed by David McClelland, proposes that certain types of needs are acquired during an individual's lifetime.

- *Need for achievement*---the desire to accomplish something difficult, attain a high standard for success, master complex tasks, and surpass others.

  People with a high need for achievement tend to enjoy work that is entrepreneurial and innovative.

- *Need for affiliation*---the desire to form close personal relationships, avoid conflict, and establish warm friendships.

  People who have a high need for affiliation are successful "integrators," coordinating the work of others.

- *Need for power* --- the desire to influence or control others, be responsible for others, and have authority over others.

  A high need for power is associated with successful attainment of top level positions in the organizational hierarchy.

Needs theories focus on underlying needs that motivate how people behave.

Leaders can work to meet followers' needs and elicit appropriate and successful work behaviors.

Discussion Question #10: *Would you rather work for a leader who has a high need for achievement, high need for affiliation, or high need for power? Why?*

Notes____

To implement individual and system-wide rewards.

Other Motivational Theories

Three additional motivation theories, the reinforcement perspective, expectancy theory, and equity theory, focus primarily on extrinsic rewards and punishments, sometimes called the "carrot and stick" approach.

Carrot-and-stick approaches tend to focus on lower needs, although higher needs can sometimes also be met.

Reinforcement Perspective on Motivation

The reinforcement approach. sidesteps the deeper issue of employee needs described in the needs-based theories.

Reinforcement theory looks at the relationship between behavior and its consequences by changing or modifying the followers' on-the-job behavior through rewards or punishments.

Behavior modification is a set of techniques by which reinforcement theory is used to modify behavior.

The assumption underlying behavior modification is the *law of effects:* positively reinforced behavior tends to be repeated, and behavior that is not reinforced tends not to be repeated

Reinforcement is anything that causes a certain behavior to be repeated or inhibited.

There are four ways in which leaders use reinforcement to modify or shape employee behavior:

- *Positive reinforcement* is the administration of a pleasant and rewarding consequence following a behavior---praise for an employee who arrives on time.

- *Negative reinforcement* is the withdrawal of an unpleasant consequence once a behavior is improved.

  Referred to as *avoidance learning,* negative reinforcement means that people learn to perform the desired behavior by avoiding unpleasant situations---a boss stops reprimanding an employee for tardiness once the employee arrives on time.

- *Punishment* is the imposition of unpleasant outcomes on an employee---a supervisor berates an employee for performing a task incorrectly.

- *Extinction* is the withdrawal of a positive reward, meaning the behavior is no longer reinforced and is less likely to occur in the future---a tardy employee does not receive pay raises and realizes that lateness is not producing the desired outcome.

Leaders can reinforce behavior after each occurrence, *continuous reinforcement,* or intermittently, *partial reinforcement.*

With partial reinforcement, the desired behavior is reinforced often enough to make the employee believe the behavior is worth repeating, but not every time it is demonstrated.

Research has found that partial reinforcement is more effective.

In the Lead: Kevin Kelly, Emerald Packaging Inc.

Emerald Packaging is a family-owned business that prints plastic bags for prepackaged salads and vegetable. The company employs about 100 people and is the tenth largest manufacturer in Union City, California. Kevin Kelly, vice president of operations, developed a positive reinforcement scheme to motivate and reward workers: 1. Monthly Quality Award, 2. Safety Program, and 3. Profit Sharing Plan. Kelly reports that customer returns for poor quality are down by 75 percent. The quality rewards are enough to get employees' to put increased effort into the job. Safety results are also impressive. Profit sharing has been less effective. Instead, Kelly prefers positive reinforcement tied to specific behaviors.

Q: *How did Kevin Kelly successfully use reinforcement theory to motivate employees?*

A: Kelley instituted a plan for reinforcing correct behaviors. He wanted to improve quality and safety and included profit sharing. Customer returns for poor quality declined by 75 percent and . there was only one minor accident in five months. Profit sharing did not motivate behaviors that are more desirable. Kelly now prefers to use positive reinforcement tied to specific behaviors.

Discussion Question #3: *What do you see as the leader's role in motivating others in an organization?*

Notes____

Expectancy Theory *Exhibit 8.6*

Expectancy theory suggests that motivation depends on individuals' mental expectations about his ability to perform tasks and receive desired rewards.

Expectancy theory is based on the individual's effort, possibility of high performance, and the desirability of outcomes following high performance.

The key factors are the expectancies for the relationships among *effort, performance,* and *outcomes* with the value of the outcomes for the individual.

- The E>P expectancy is the probability that putting effort into a task will lead to high performance.

  For this expectancy to be high, the individual must have the ability, previous experience, and necessary tools, information, and opportunity to perform.

- The P>O expectancy involves whether successful performance will lead to the desired outcome.

  If this expectancy is high, the individual will be more highly motivated.

Valence refers to the value of outcomes to the individual.

If the outcomes are not valued, motivation will be low. If outcomes have a high value, motivation will be higher.

Expectancy theory is personalized to subordinates' needs and goals.

To increase motivation, leaders can increase followers' expectancy by clarifying individual needs, providing desired outcomes, and ensuring that individuals have the ability and support to perform well and attain their desired outcomes.

In the Lead: Steve and Diane Warren, Katzinger's Delicatessen

When Steve and Diane Warren implemented open book management, they taught employees how to read the financial statements and told them if financial performance improved, the owners would share the rewards with employees. Most workers were young and not committed to the long haul, so their E-→P expectancy and E→O expectancy were low. The Warrens knew they needed a simple, short-term goal to energize workers. They proposed that if food costs were reduced to below 35 percent of sales without sacrificing service quality, workers would be rewarded with half the savings.

Q: *How did Expectancy Theory help motivate the Warrens' employees?*

A: The workers knew that if they worked together, they could meet the goal; thus, the E→P expectancy was high. Workers proposed ideas to reduce waste. The P→O expectancy was high because of the level of trust. The workers were highly motivated to cooperate. At the end of the year, savings totaled $30, 000, and $15,000 was distributed among the workers for helping to meet the goal.

Discussion Question #6: *What are the features of the reinforcement and expectancy theories that make them seem like carrot-and-stick methods for motivation? Why do they often work in organizations?*

Notes____

____

____

Equity Theory

➢ *Do you think motivation is affected by the perceptions of how fairly employees are treated in relation to others?*

Equity theory proposes that people are motivated to seek social equity in the rewards they expect for performance.

If they perceive their rewards as equal to what others receive for similar contributions, they believe their treatment is fair and are more highly motivated.

When they believe they are not treated fairly, motivation declines.

People evaluate equity by a ratio of inputs to outputs.

Employees make comparisons of what they put into a job and the rewards received relative to those of others.

Outcomes include pay, recognition, promotions, and other rewards.

Equity exists when the ratio of one person's outcomes to inputs equals the ratio of others' in the work group.

Inequity occurs when the input/outcome ratios are out of balance (e.g., an experienced employee receives the same salary as a new, less educated employee).

Equity theory has been criticized because a number of key issues are unclear.

The important point is that motivation is influenced by relative as well as absolute rewards.

This concept reminds leaders to be cognizant of the effects of perceived inequity on follower motivation and performance.

Discussion Question #7: *Why is it important for leaders to have a basic understanding of equity theory? Can you see ways in which some of today's popular compensation trends, such as gainsharing or pay for performance, might contribute to perceived inequity among employees?*

Notes____

To avoid the disadvantages of "carrot-and-stick" motivation

The Carrot and Stick Controversy

➢ *Why are "carrot-and-stick" practices controversial?*

Reward and punishment practices dominate firms which reward performance or merit with pay.

Many companies regard their incentive programs as successful; financial incentive can be effective, and some researchers argue that money leads to higher performance.

Yet, critics argue that extrinsic rewards are neither adequate nor productive motivators and may work against the best interests of the organization.

Reasons for this criticism include:

- *Extrinsic rewards diminish intrinsic rewards.* The motivation to seek an extrinsic reward such as a bonus or approval leads people to focus on the reward rather than the work.

  Numerous studies have found that giving people extrinsic rewards undermines their interest in the work itself.

  With extrinsic rewards, individuals tend to attribute their behavior to extrinsic rather than intrinsic factors, diminishing their own contributions.

- *Extrinsic rewards are temporary.* Bestowing people with outside incentives might ensure short-term success, but not long-term quality.

  The success of reaching immediate goals is followed by unintended consequences.

  Because people are focused on the reward, the work holds no interest, without which the potential for exploration, innovation, and creativity disappears.

- *Extrinsic rewards assume people are driven by lower needs.* Praise and pay increases tied only to performance presumes that the primary reason people initiate and persist in actions is to satisfy lower needs.

  Research showed that employees at the best 100 companies mentioned intrinsic rather than extrinsic rewards as their motivation; many had passed up other job offers because of motivators such as fun, challenge, flexibility, and the potential to learn.

  Behavior is also based on self-expression, self-esteem, self-worth, feelings, and attitudes.

- *Organizations are too complex for carrot and stick approaches.* The current organizational climate is marked by uncertainty and high interdependence among departments and with other organizations.

  By contrast, the carrot-and-stick approach is quite simple, and the application of an overly simplified incentive plan to a highly complex system creates misdirection.

  Extrinsic motivators often end up rewarding behaviors that are the opposite of what the organization wants; managers want long-term growth but reward quarterly earnings.

- *Carrot and stick approaches destroy people's motivation to work as a group.* Extrinsic rewards and punishments create a culture of competition versus a culture of cooperation.

  In a competitive environment, people see their goal as individual victory, as making others appear inferior.

Without the effort to control behavior individually through rigid rewards, people can see co-workers as part of their success.

When leaders focus on higher needs, they can make everyone feel valued.

In the Lead: Blackmer/Dover Inc.

Bill Fowler is one of the fastest and most accurate workers at the Blackmer/ Dover factory. It's a precision task that requires a high level of skill, but Fowler refuses to share his tricks of the trade even with his closest fellow workers. One reason is that Fowler believes managers could use his ideas and shortcuts to speed production and make his job harder. His knowledge has given him power, increased status, and a bigger paycheck. If other workers gained the same knowledge, Fowler would no longer enjoy a superior status.

Q: *How had the carrot-and-stick approach created a culture of competition at Blackmer?*

A: Difficulty in getting people to share knowledge and cooperate illustrates the problems with the carrot-and-stick approach at Blackmer/Dover. New leaders are looking for motivational tools that will encourage another kind of behavior; greater cooperation, knowledge sharing, and collaboration between workers and management.

Discussion Question #10: *If you were a leader at a company like Blackmer/Dover, discussed in the chapter, what motivational techniques might you use to improve cooperation and teamwork?*

Notes____

____

____

❑ *Living Leadership: On the Folly of Rewarding A While Hoping for B*

Managers who complain about the lack of motivation in workers might do well to examine whether the reward system encourages behavior different from what they are seeking. Students are rewarded for making good grades, not for acquiring knowledge, and may resort to cheating.

➢ Give other examples of unintended behavior as a result of the reward system.

Some incentive programs are successful, especially when people are actually motivated by money and lower needs.

One way for leaders to address the carrot-and-stick controversy is to understand a program's strengths and weaknesses and acknowledge the positive but limited effects of extrinsic motivators.

Rewards can be linked to behavior promoting the higher needs of both the organization and the individual, such as rewarding quality, long-term growth, or a collaborative culture.

Discussion Question #5: *What is the carrot and stick approach? Do you think it should be minimized in organizations? Why?*

Notes____

To implement empowerment by providing the five elements of information, knowledge, discretion, meaning, and rewards.

Empowering People to Meet Higher Needs

➢ *Can leaders can meet higher motivational needs by shifting power from the top of the hierarchy and share it with subordinates?*

Empowerment is power sharing, the delegation of power or authority to subordinates in the organization.

Leaders are shifting from efforts to control through the carrot-and-stick approach to providing employees with power, information, and authority.

Leaders can provide subordinates with the knowledge of how their jobs are relevant to the organization's performance and mission to give them a direction within which to act.

In the Lead: GE/Durham

At General Electric's aircraft-engine factory in Durham, North Carolina, nine teams of workers build some of the world's most powerful jet engines, including the ones that keep Air Force One running. The teams receive a deadline from the plant manager and make all other decisions themselves. The teams write the assembly process, figure out the schedule, order tools and parts, and perform any other jobs necessary, including keeping the plant clean and the machinery and tools in good order. Each team "owns" an engine from beginning to end. The team is responsible for every step of the process. The philosophy is one of continuous improvement.

Q: *How does GE motivate its employees through empowerment?*

A: Each team "owns" an engine from beginning to end. The team is responsible for every step of the process. The philosophy is one of continuous improvement. Employees have a high level of responsibility and strive everyday to produce the perfect jet engine. Some factory workers say that they cannot wait to get to work every day. The autonomy of empowered employees gives GE an enormous advantage.

Empowerment provides strong motivation to meet the higher needs of individuals.

Individuals have a need for *self-efficacy*, the capacity to produce results, to feel they are effective.

Increased responsibility motivates most people to strive to do their best.

The shift to shared power and company-wide participation frees leaders to concentrate on the big picture and frees employees to apply abilities and talents.

Leader benefit from the additional capability employee participation brings to the organization.

Discussion Question #4: *Do you believe it is possible to increase the total amount of power in an organization? Discuss.*

Notes____

____

____

Elements of Empowerment

Increased power and responsibility leads to greater motivation, increased employee satisfaction, and decreased turnover and absenteeism.

The first step is effective hiring and training; however, having a competent team of employees isn't enough.

Five elements must be present before employees can truly be empowered: information, knowledge, discretion, meaning and rewards.

- *Employees receive information about company performance.* Employees must understand company-wide business and have regular information about company performance.

- *Employees receive knowledge and skills to contribute to company goals.* Companies train employees to have the knowledge and skills that lead to competency---the belief that one is capable of accomplishing the job successfully.

- *Employees have the power to make substantive decisions.* Competitive companies give workers the power to influence work procedures and organizational direction through quality circles and self-directed work teams.

- *Employees understand the meaning and impact of their job.* Empowered employees consider their job important and personally meaningful and see themselves as influential in their work roles.

- *Employees are rewarded based on company performance.* Research has revealed the important role of fair reward and recognition systems in supporting empowerment.

  Rewards are just one component of empowerment rather than the sole basis of motivation.

Empowerment Applications *Exhibit 8.7*

Many companies are implementing empowerment programs, but they are empowering workers to various degrees.

Current methods of empowering employees fall along a continuum.

The continuum runs from a situation whereby front line workers have no discretion to full empowerment whereby workers participate in formulating strategy (e.g., self- directed teams given the power to hire, discipline, and dismiss team members and set compensation rates.)

Implementing Empowerment can be difficult in established organizations because it can destroy hierarchies and upset the familiar balance of power.

Those companies that have redistributed power and authority the *least* have been the most successful (e.g., quality circles, job enrichment programs), according to a study.

Workers sometimes balk at the added responsibility freedom brings.

Discussion Question #8: *What are the advantages of an organization with empowered employees? Discuss.*

Notes____

Organization-Wide Motivational Programs

Leaders can motivate employees using other recent programs that are more than the carrot and stick approaches, but less that full empowerment.

One approach is to foster an organizational environment that helps people find true value and meaning in their work.

A second approach is to implement organizationwide programs such as employee ownership, paying for knowledge, gainsharing, pay for performance, and job enrichment.

Giving Meaning to Work

One way people get intrinsic rewards at work is to feel a deep sense of importance and meaningfulness, such as people who work for a social cause or mission.

A Gallup Organization study conducted over 25 years found that the single most important variable in whether employee feel good about their work is the relationship to the supervisor.

Good leaders channel employee motivation by tapping into each person's talents, skills, interests, and needs.

The researchers developed a metric called the Q12, a list of 12 questions that provides a way to evaluate how leaders are doing in creating an environment that meets higher-level needs.

When a majority of employees can answer the Q12 questions positively, the organization enjoys a highly motivated, engaged, and productive workforce.

These organizations have less turnover, are more productive and profitable, and enjoy greater employee and customer loyalty.

In the Lead: St. Lucie Medical Center

In the late 1990s, St. Lucie Medical Center, a for-profit hospital in Florida was serving more patients more profitably than ever before. But leaders knew there was a serious problem brewing just under the surface. Annual turnover of nurses, clinicians, and support staff was a troubling 35 percent. Even more alarming was the growing talk of patients and physicians being put off by the hospital staff's pervasive discontentment. Leaders underwent an in-depth assessment and employees took the Gallup Q12 survey to measure their engagement to their jobs. As a result St. Lucie began building work units around the complementary talents of individual workers.

Q: *How did the Gallup Q12 survey help develop a system to improve hospital conditions?*

A: Creating the work unit so that nurses could work with their strengths rather than struggling to develop traits they didn't have improved both the empathetic care and operational excellence. The results of the revitalization process were astounding. The attrition rate dropped and St. Lucie soared to the 99th percentile in Gallup's database.

Other Approaches *Exhibit 8.8*

There are a number of other approaches to improving organizationwide motivation.

Forms of "at risk" pay are becoming more common than fixed salary in many companies.

- *Employee ownership* is a psychological commitment to the mission of the organization whereby employees act as owners.

  Owning company stock motivates individuals to perform at their best level.

- *Gainsharing* is a motivational approach that encourages people to work together rather than focus on individual achievements and rewards; ties additional pay to improvements in overall employee performance.

  Employees are asked to actively search for ways to make process improvements, with any resulting financial gains divided among employees.

- *Pay for knowledge* programs base an employee's salary based on the number of tasks skills he or she possesses.

Employees are motivated to acquire more skills to increase their salaries.

- *Pay for Performance* links a portion of employees' monetary rewards to results or accomplishments.

- *Job enrichment* is a motivational approach that incorporates high-level motivators into the work, including job responsibility, recognition, and opportunities for growth, learning, and achievement.

  One way to enrich an oversimplified job is to enlarge it, that is to extend the responsibility to cover several tasks instead of only one.

Discussion Question #9: *Discuss whether you believe it is a leader's responsibility to help people find meaning in their work? How might leaders do this for employees at a fast food restaurant? How about for employees who clean restrooms at airports?*

Notes____

____

____

DISCUSSION QUESTIONS

1. *Describe the kinds of needs that people bring to an organization. How might a person's values and attitudes, as described in Chapter 4, influence the needs he or she brings to work?*

Humans are motivated by multiple needs which exist in a hierarchical order wherein higher needs cannot be satisfied until the lower needs are met. Maslow named five categories of needs: physiological, safety, belongingness, esteem, and self-actualization. Physiology, safety, and belonging are *deficiency* needs. Needs are satisfied in sequence. Once a need has been satisfied, it declines in importance and the next higher need is activated.

Individual differences are discussed in Chapter 4. One way in which leaders try to enable all followers to achieve intrinsic rewards is by giving them more control over their own work and the power to affect outcomes.

2. *What is the relationship among needs, rewards, and motivation?*

Good hygiene factors satisfy lower-level needs and remove dissatisfaction but do not cause satisfaction and motivation. Herzberg believed that when motivators are present, workers are highly motivated and satisfied. Thus, hygiene factors and motivators are two distinct factors that influence motivation. High-level motivators such as challenge must be present for employees to be motivated to excel. Intrinsic rewards lead to greater motivation than extrinsic rewards.

3. *What do you see as the leader's role in motivating others in an organization?*

The leader's role is to go beyond the removal of dissatisfiers to the use of motivators to meet higher level needs and steer employees toward greater achievement and satisfaction. Leaders can work to meet followers' needs and elicit appropriate and successful work behaviors.

4. *What is the carrot and stick approach? Do you think it should be minimized in organizations? Why?*

The carrot and stick approach is a reward and punishment motivation practice. Despite numerous successful incentive programs, critics argue that extrinsic rewards are neither adequate nor productive motivators and may work against an organization. Reasons for this criticism include: 1) Extrinsic rewards diminish intrinsic reward; 2) Extrinsic rewards are temporary; 3) Extrinsic rewards assume people are driven by lower needs; 4) Organizations are too complex for carrot and stick approaches; and 5) Carrot and stick approaches destroy people's motivation to work as a group.

5. *What are the features of the reinforcement and expectancy theories that make them seem like carrot and stick methods for motivation? Why do they often work in organizations?*

Reinforcement theory looks at the relationship between behavior and its consequences by changing or modifying the follower's on-the-job behavior through reward or punishment. Expectancy Theory suggests that motivation depends on individuals' mental expectations about their ability to perform tasks and receive desired rewards. Incentive programs are successful when the people are motivated by money and lower needs.

6. *Why is it important for leaders to have a basic understanding of equity theory? Can you see ways in which some of today's popular compensation trends, such as gainsharing or pay for performance, might contribute to perceived inequity among employees?*

Motivation is influenced by relative as well as absolute rewards. Leaders should be cognizant of the effects of perceived inequity on follower motivation and performance. Equity theory suggests that when people believe they are not treated fairly, motivation declines. Employees make comparisons of what they put into a job and the rewards received relative to those of others.

Gainsharing rewards groups for reaching goals, but group members may perceive inequity if some members work harder than others, yet receive the same rewards. Inequity occurs when the input/outcome ratios are out of balance. Likewise, pay for performance links a portion of employees' monetary rewards to results or accomplishments. Some may not feel that the performance warranted a reward because of the level of effort exerted.

7. *What are the advantages of an organization with empowered employees? Discuss.*

The advantages of empowerment include providing strong motivation because it meets the higher needs of individuals. Empowerment increases the total amount of power in the an organization. Freedom from over-control allows subordinates to utilize their talents and abilities. Leaders benefit from the capabilities employee participation brings to the organization. Leaders can devote more time to vision, and subordinates can respond quicker to customers.

8. *Do you agree that hygiene factors, as defined by Herzberg's two-factor theory, cannot provided increased satisfaction and motivation. Discuss.*

Hygiene factors involve the presence or absence of adequate working conditions, pay, company policies or interpersonal relationships. When hygiene factors are poor, work is dissatisfying. Good hygiene factors remove dissatisfaction but do not cause satisfaction and motivation. In fact, research has shown that some incentive programs—using monetary rewards--- are successful, especially when people are actually motivated by money and lower needs. Leaders should understand a program's strengths and weaknesses and acknowledge the positive but limited effects of hygiene factors, i.e., extrinsic motivators, .

9. *Discuss whether you believe it is a leader's responsibility to help people find meaning in their work? How might leaders do this for employees at a fast food restaurant? How about for employees who clean restrooms at airports?*

Yes, One way people get intrinsic rewards at work is to feel a deep sense of importance and meaningfulness, such as people who work for a social cause or mission. A Gallup Organization study conducted over 25 years found that the single most important variable in whether employee feel good about their work is the relationship to the supervisor. Good leaders channel employee motivation by tapping into each person's talents, skills. Leaders can do this for a fast food restaurant by finding out the talents and skills of the employees and putting them in positions which utilize those skills. For example, a friendly, extroverted person makes a good host or hostess to seat customers in fast food chains such as IHOP. Leaders could also offer training in marketing and customer service so that employees could improve their skills and have a good feeling about working at the restaurant. Also, fast-food chains often have a career ladder which appeals to higher needs; a waiter could become a manager.

At the airport, any job is very desirable because of the pay and benefits, so in this case money can be a powerful motivator. These jobs are highly sought after making them even more desirable. However, employees work in teams and on certain shifts and a sense of camaraderie helps them keep the restrooms clean. Many are immigrants who speak the same language, share the same customs, and enjoy the airport atmosphere.

10. *If you were a leader at a company like Blackmer/Dover, discussed in the chapter, what motivational techniques might you use to improve cooperation and teamwork?*

A number of approaches might improve cooperation. Gainsharing is a motivational approach that encourages people to work together rather than focus on individual achievements and rewards; ties additional pay to improvements in overall employee performance. Employees are asked to actively search for ways to make process improvements, with any resulting financial gains divided among employees. Gainsharing could help change the competitive culture at Blackmer/Dover.

TEACHING TOOLS AND EXERCISES

1. *Small Group Activity:* Read *Fortune* magazine's annual list of "100 Best Companies to Work For."

Companies that rank high are ones that show genuine caring for employees, enabling them to feel like important members of a community. Which companies are in the top 10? Why are these companies more than just a place to work? Discuss these companies in small groups.

2. *On the Web:* Motivation

Go to www.swlearning.com/management. Click on Management News, click on Topic Index, click on motivation, and then click on *Perks Help Keep Four Seasons Staff Pampering Guests.* How does the Four Seasons use reinforcement to motivate its employees? Explain Expectancy Theory using the Four Seasons as an example.

3. *Discussion*: Acquired Needs Theory on the Job

After reviewing McClelland's *acquired needs theory,* divide the class into three groups. Each group will present to the class the pros and cons of working for a leader with one of the three needs: need for achievement, need for affiliation, and need for power.

4. *Out-of-class reading:* "Leading by Feel," *Harvard Business Review* (January, 2004): 27-37.

Eighteen leaders and scholars explore how to manage emotional intelligence.
How does a leader's emotional intelligence affect the motivation of followers? Prepare a one-page summary of the article.

5. *Leader's Self-Insight*: Your Approach to Motivating Others

Without greatly expanding your knowledge of motivation theory and techniques, you will not function well as a motivator in today's workplace. After completing the survey, students will answer the following questions and compare their scores with other students or keep them in their notebook.

- Are you surprised by your score? Why?
- Does it reflect how you feel about yourself as a motivator? Explain.

LEADERSHIP DEVELOPMENT: CASES FOR ANALYSIS

I. Synopsis: The Parlor

The Parlor, a local franchise operation located in San Francisco serves sandwiches and small dinners in an atmosphere reminiscent of the "roaring twenties." The business had been so successful that Richard Purvis, owner and manager, decided to hire a manager and devote more time to other business interests. The new manager, Paul McCarthy, decided to initiate an economy program to increase his earnings. He changed the wholesale meat supplier and lowered both his cost and product quality. He increased the working hours of minimum wage employees and reduced the time of those employed at a higher rate. He eliminated the fringe benefits. Customers began to complain about the service and there was a complete turnover in short-order cooks. One cook became involved in a shouting match, and McCarthy fired him on the spot.

Case questions and answers

1. *Contrast the beliefs about motivation held by Purvis and McCarthy.*

Purvis believes that employees are motivated by intrinsic rewards, pride and satisfaction in working for a first-rate establishment. McCarthy believes that employees are motivated by extrinsic rewards, money. McCarthy believes in the carrot and stick method. Employees do what they are told or they are fired.

2. *Do you consider either Purvis or McCarthy a leader? Discuss.*

No. According to Herzberg, the leader's role is to go beyond the removal of dissatisfiers to the use of motivators to meet higher level needs and steer employees toward greater achievement and satisfaction. Purvis and McCarthy should be working to meet the employees' needs and elicit appropriate and successful work behaviors. Neither empowers the employees.

3. *What would you do now if you were in Purvis' position? Why?*

Purvis should put an empowerment plan in place and begin with McCarthy. However, elements of empowerment must be present: 1) Employees receive information about company performance; 2) Employees receive knowledge and skills to contribute to company goals; 3) Employees have the power to make substantive decisions; 4) Employees understand the meaning and impact of the job; and 5) Employees are rewarded based on company performance. Empowerment provides strong motivation because it meets the higher needs of individuals. Empowerment increases the total amount of power in an organization.

II. **Synopsis:** **Cub Scout Pack 81**

Things have changed at Cub Scout Pack 81. Six years ago, the pack was on the verge of disbanding. There were barely enough boys for an effective den, and they had been losing membership for as long as anyone could remember. The cub master was trying to pass his job onto any parent foolish enough to take it. Today, the pack has one of the largest memberships of any in the Lancaster/Lebanon Council. The cub master depends on the parents and the boys to get things done. Everybody understands that we want to have a successful program, and that means we all have to participate to achieve that success. By unleashing the energy the boys have, the Cub Scout Program can accomplish many goals. At the Scout Expo, the pack placed fourth five years ago, but now has received several first place awards.

Case questions and answers

1. *What are some of Mike Murphy's basic assumptions about motivation?*

Murphy realizes that increased power and responsibility leads to greater motivation, increased satisfaction, and decreased turnover and absenteeism. The first step is effective hiring and training. He depends on the parents and the boys to get things done. Everybody understands that to have a successful program, all have to participate to achieve that success.

2. *Why do you think he has been so successful in turning the organization around?*

Murphy did not try to do everything himself. He did not plan and execute all the programs and simply inform the parents and scouts about activities. He involved them in all phases of the pack activities. By unleashing the energy the boys have, Murphy presented the positive vision that is not anything the Cub Scout Program cannot do. The boys and the parents responded to Murphy's visionary leadership.

3. *How would you motivate people in a volunteer organization such as the Cub Scouts?*

I would try to match the interests of the volunteers to the tasks and activities. Then I would allow the volunteers to carry out projects using their own efforts and ideas. As a leader, however, I would make sure the volunteers shared the big picture---why is this activity important. I would emphasize the meaning and significance of the project, such as helping others in the community.

CHAPTER NINE
LEADERSHIP COMMUNICATION

CHAPTER SUMMARY

Effective communication is an essential element of leadership. Leaders are communication champions who inspire and unite people around a common sense of purpose and identity. They lead strategic conversations that get people talking across boundaries about the vision, key strategic themes, and the values that can help the group or organization achieve desired outcomes.

Four elements necessary for strategic conversations are an open communication climate, active listening, discernment, and dialogue. Open communication is essential for building trust, and it paves the way for more opportunities to communicate with followers, thus enabling the organization to gain the benefits of all employees minds. However, leaders must be active listeners and must learn to discern the hidden undercurrents that have yet to emerge. It is through listening and discernment, both with followers and customers, that leaders identify strategic issues and build productive relationships that help the organization succeed. When active listening spreads throughout a group, a type of communication referred to as dialogue can occur. Through dialogue, people discover common ground and together create a shared meaning that enables them to understand each other and share a view of the world.

Leader communication is purpose-directed, and an important element is persuading others to act in ways that achieve goals and accomplish vision. Four steps for practicing the art of persuasion are to establish credibility, build goals on common ground, make your position compelling, and connect with others on an emotional level. Leaders use rich communication channels, communicate through stories and metaphors, and rely on informal as well as formal communication. Electronic channels can be very advantageous if used appropriately, but their use increases the potential for communication errors, and these channels are not very effective for complex or sensitive messages. The final point emphasized in this chapter is that effective communication becomes even more crucial during times of rapid change and crisis. Four critical skills for communicating in a crisis are to remain calm, be visible, "get the awful truth out," and communicate a vision for the future.

CHAPTER OPENER

Martin Luther King, Jr., Communicator with Vision

In December of 1955, Martin Luther King, Jr. was installed as president of the new Montgomery Improvement Association. That same evening, he was called upon to address a crowd of thousands about the bus boycott that had begun a few days earlier. In his impromptu speech, King referred to his audience as people "tired of being pushed out of the glittering sunlight of life's July and left standing amidst the chill of an alpine November. He reminded the audience or Rosa Parks' arrest and conviction for refusing to give up her bus seat to a white person. He commended her integrity. What made King's first public role in a political arena so powerful that it ignited the support of thousands? With his initial words, King created the parameters of a social movement. He discerned that the audience was tired of injustice. His metaphor contrasting summer sunshine with winter winds made the experience of racism tangible, felt upon the skin of each person in the crowd. King communicated with words and actions a vision and possibility of equality.

LECTURE/OUTLINE

To act as a communication champion rather than just as an information processor.

How Leaders Communicate *Exhibit 9.1*

➢ *Can effective leadership occur without effective communication?*

Leadership means communicating with others so they are influenced and motivated to perform actions that further common goals and lead toward desired outcomes.

Comunication is the process by which information and understanding are transferred between a sender and a receiver.

Two common elements in every communication situation are the sender, anyone who wishes to communicate, and the receiver, the person to whom the message is sent.

- The sender initiates a communication by *encoding* a thought or idea.
- The message is the tangible formulation of the thought or idea, and the *channel* is the medium by which the message is sent.

  The channel could be a report, telephone call, or e-mail.

- The receiver *decodes* the symbols to interpret the meaning of message.

  Encoding and decoding are potential sources for communication errors because individual differences, knowledge, values, attitudes, and background act as filters and may create "noise" when translating from symbols to meaning.

- *Feedback* occurs when a receiver responds to the sender's communication with a return message.

Feedback is a powerful aid to communication because it enables the sender to determine whether the receiver correctly interpreted the message.

Management Communication

➢ *Why is the manager's primary role that of "information processor?"*

Managers scan their environments for important written and personal information, gathering facts, ideas, and data which is then sent to subordinates to use them.

A manager receives subordinate messages and feedback to see if "noise" interfered with translation.

Communication effectiveness lies in the accuracy of facts, statistics, and decisions.

Effective managers establish themselves at the center of information to facilitate the completion of tasks.

Leader Communication *Exhibit 9.2*

➢ *How does leader communication serve a different purpose than management communication?*

Leaders communicate the big picture--the vision --- rather than facts and pieces of information.

Whereas a manager acts as an information processor, a leader is a communication champion.

A *communication champion* is a person who is philosophically grounded in the belief that communication is essential to building trust and gaining commitment to the organizational vision.

Leaders use communication to inspire and unite people around a common sense of purpose and identity; people need a vision to motivate them towards the future.

Learning, problem-solving, decision-making, and strategizing are all oriented around and stem from the vision.

Communication champions visibly and symbolically engage in communication-based activities.

Leaders actively communicate through words and actions every day.

Leader communication is *purpose-directed* in that it directs everyone's attention toward vision, values, and desired outcomes of the organization and persuades people to help achieve the vision.

- *Living Leadership: Opening a Window to a Brighter World*

  A blind man was brought to the hospital, both depressed and seriously ill. His roommate described the outdoors to him everyday, and he grew happier by learning about the world around him. The roommate changed to a man who didn't want to be bothered telling stories. The blind man became depressed and seriously ill.

- What does this story tell you about the leader as a communication champion?

Discussion Question #1: *How do you think typical leadership communication differs from conventional management communication?*

Notes____

To use key elements of effective listening and understand why listening is important to leader communication

---

Leading Strategic Conversations

Strategic conversation is communication that takes place across boundaries and hierarchical levels about the group or organization's vision, critical strategic themes, and values that can help achieve desired outcomes.

Leaders facilitate strategic conversations by:

- Actively listening to others to understand their attitudes and values, needs, personal goals, and desires
- Setting the agenda for conversation by underscoring the key strategic themes linked to organizational success
- Selecting the right communication channels and facilitating dialogue.

Four key components necessary for strategic conversations are an open communication climate, active listening, discernment, and dialogue.

Creating an Open Communication Climate *Exhibit 9.3*

Open communication means sharing information throughout the company, especially across functional and hierarchical levels.

This runs counter to the traditional flow of selective information downward from supervisors to subordinates.

People need a clear direction and an understanding of how they can contribute.

Leaders break down conventional hierarchical and departmental boundaries that may be barriers to communication, enabling them to convey a commitment to organizational vision, goals, and values.

In an open climate, a leader's communication of the vision "cascades" through an organization.

Consistent and frequent communication brings follower acceptance and understanding.

Open communication builds trust, an essential element in leader-follower relationships because it inspires collaboration and commitment to common goals.

Leaders also want an open communication climate because it helps employees understand how their actions interact with and affect others.

Communication across traditional boundaries enables leaders to hear what followers have to say.

New voices and continuous conversation involving a broad spectrum of people revitalize and enhance communication.

***In the Lead*:** Ginger Graham, Advanced Cardiovascular Systems

Advanced Cardiovascular Systems (now Guidant Corporation) was the darling of the medical devices industry. The company reached $100 million in sales within five years of launching its first product and revolutionized the field of angioplasty. The new CEO Ginger Graham saw that internal and external relationships were marked by conflict and discord rather than harmony and cooperation. The internal strife was affecting the company's competitiveness. Graham decided to tell the truth by telling employees that she saw deteriorating morale and blaming. She received a standing ovation from employees and began to build a culture based on honesty.

Q: *How does Graham create an open communication climate?*

A: Open communication builds trust because it inspires collaboration and commitment to common goals. Graham reversed top-down communication by assigning each manager with a "coach" from lower ranks of the organization. Coaches were assigned to gather information from everyone in the organization and meet with coaches once a quarter. Managers began sharing information ---both good and bad—with employees. This policy relieved tension and conflict.

Discussion Question #2: *If you were to evaluate an organization based on the degree of open communication climate, what things would you look for? Discuss.*

Notes____

____

____

Listening *Exhibit 9.4*

➢ *Why is listening an important tools for a leader's communication?*

It is only by listening that leaders can identify strategic themes and understand how to influence others to achieve desired outcomes.

Listening also helps to build trust and create an open communication's climate because people are willing to share their ideas, suggestions, and problems when they think someone is listening.

Listening involves the skill of grasping and interpreting a message's genuine meaning.

There are keys to effective listening:

- A good listener's total attention is focused on the message; he is not thinking about an unrelated problem.

- A good listener listens actively, finds areas of interest, is flexible, works hard at listening, and uses thought speed to summarize, weigh, and anticipate what the speaker says.

- Effective listening is engaged listening—asking lots of questions and providing feedback.

- Being a good listener expands the leader's role in the eyes of others.

- Active listening is a daily, ongoing part of a leader's communication.

When leaders fail to listen to employees, it sends the signal, "you don't matter," which decreases employee commitment and motivation.

Discussion Question #3: *A manager in a communication class remarked, "Listening seems like minimal intrusion of oneself into the conversation, yet it also seems like more work." Do you agree or disagree? Discuss.*

Notes____

____

____

Discernment

One of the most rewarding kinds of listening involves discernment.

Discernment involves detecting the unarticulated messages hidden below the surface of spoken interaction, complaints, behavior, and actions.

A discerning leader pays attention to patterns and relationships underlying the organization and those it serves.

Discernment is a critical skill because it enables them to tap into the unarticulated, often deep-seated needs, desires, and hopes of followers and customers.

To recognize and apply the difference between dialogue and discussion.

Dialogue *Exhibit 9.5*

Dialogue occurs when active listening and attention to unspoken undercurrents spread throughout the organization.

Dialogue is active sharing and listening in which people explore common ground and grow to understand each other and share a world view.

There is a distinction between a dialogue and a discussion.

A discussion explores opposition by individuals who advocate their positions and convince others to adopt those positions.

A discussion is resolved by logic or "beating down" opponents.

A dialogue requires that participants suspend their attachments to a particular point of view so that a deeper level of listening, synthesis, and meaning can emerge.

A dialogue reveals feelings and builds common ground, with more emphasis on inquiry than advocacy.

Both forms of communication, dialogue and discussion, can result in organizational change.

However, the result of a discussion is limited to a specific topic, whereas the result of a dialogue is characterized by group unity, shared meaning, and transformed mindsets.

In the Lead: Henry Bertolon, NECX

From the outside, everything looked rosy at NECX, a leading independent distributor of semiconductors and other computer products. CEO Henry Bertolon could see that the company was suffering from the strain of rapid growth and beginning to come apart at the seams. "We'd have meetings that just melted down," he says, "Everyone would scream at each other and then leave." Bertolon hired a psychologist to help solve communication problems. A one-day-a-week program was instituted to get people talking—and listening—to one another on a deeper, authentic level. Bertolon is convinced that the sessions have had a positive impact on communication, interpersonal relationships, and the bottom line.

Q: *How did the use of dialogue improve communication at NECX?*

A: Getting people to communicate in ways that build common understanding and meaning is critical to success. The dialogue sessions at NECX created a safe environment for people to reveal their feelings, explore ideas, and build common ground. It kept employees loose, flexible, and open to new ideas.

Discussion Question #4: *How does dialogue differ from discussion? Give an example of each from your experience.*

Notes____

To use communication to influence and persuade others.

The Leader as Communication Champion

Leaders communicate to persuade and influence others, to sell others on the vision and influence them to behave in ways that achieve goals that help accomplish the vision.

Leaders can follow four steps to practice the art of persuasion:

- *Establish credibility.* A leader's credibility is based on the leader's knowledge, expertise, and relationship with others.

- *Build goals on common ground.* To be persuasive, leaders describe how what they're requesting will benefit others as well as the leader.

- *Make your position compelling to others.* Leaders appeal to others on an emotional level by using symbols, metaphors, and stories to express their messages, rather than relying on facts and figures.

- *Connect emotionally.* Good leaders sense others' emotions and adjust their approach to match the audience's ability to receive their message.

Persuasion is a valuable communication process, not a manipulation, that can lead to a shared solution or commitment.

Acting as a communication champion requires that leaders communicate frequently and easily with others in the organization.

The term *communication apprehension* is defined as "an individual's level of fear or anxiety associated with either real or anticipated communication with another person or persons."

Some individuals may consciously or unconsciously avoid situations where communication is required.

Discussion Question #8: *How do leaders use communication to influence and persuade others? Think of someone you have known who is skilled at persuasion. What makes this person an effective communicator?*

Notes____

To select an appropriate communication channel for your leadership message.

Selecting Rich Communication Channels *Exhibit 9.6*

A *channel* is a medium by which a communication message is carried from sender to receiver.

Leaders can choose among several communication channels--- face-to-face, telephone, memo or letter, e-mail, instant messaging, or newsletter.

Communication media such as Web pages, intranets, and extranets have expanded leaders' options for communicating to followers and customers or clients.

The Continuum of Channel Richness

➢ *How do channels differ in their capacity to convey information?*

Channel richness is the amount of information that can be transmitted during a communication episode.

The richness of an information channel is influenced by three characteristics:

- the ability to handle multiple cues simultaneously
- the ability to facilitate rapid, two-way feedback;
- the ability to establish a personal focus for the communication.

Face-to-face communication is the richest medium because it permits direct experience, multiple information cues, immediate feedback, and personal focus.

Telephone conversations are next in richness. Eye contact, gave, posture, and other body language cues are missing, but the human voice carries a tremendous amount of emotional information.

E-mail, which lacks visual and verbal cues, is now used for communications once handled by telephone because of speed and reduced long-distance telephone costs.

Other forms of electronic communication, such as video conferencing allow for voice and body language cues.

A lower level of richness is offered by the Internet and company intranets, but they have opened avenues for keeping in touch.

The companies most successful in using the Web are those that supplement electronic media with the human touch.

Written media that are personalized, such as notes and letters, can be personally focused, but convey only cues written on paper and are slow to provide feedback.

Written communication is the lowest in richness because it is not focused on a receiver.

Routine messages can be effectively communicated through a channel lower in richness whereas nonroutine messages are characterized by time pressure and surprise

The leader must select a channel to fit the message.

Althoug effective leaders maximize all channels, they don't let anything substitute for the rich face-to-face channel when important issues are at stake.

Discussion Question #5: *Some senior executives believe they should rely on written information and computer reports because these yield more accurate data than face-to-face communications do. Do you agree?*

Notes____

____

____

Effectively Using Electronic Communication Channels *Exhibit 9.7*

➢ *While electronic communication has many advantages, what are its disadvantages?*

People come across as sounding cold, arrogant or insensitive when discussing a sensitive issue via e-mail.

The growing use of technology for communicating has deprived people of "human moments" that energize people, inspire creativity, and support emotional well-being.

Tips for effectively using electronic communication include:

- *Combine high-tech and high-touch* Never allow electronic communication to take the place of human connections.

- *Consider the circumstances.* People who know each other well can communicate about more complex issues via email, but not those who have a new working relationship.

- *Read twice before you hit the "Send" button* You can check grammar and spelling. Never send an email when you are angry.

- *Know what's off limits.* Select rich channels of communication for important, complex, or sensitive messages; layoffs, firings, and reprimands should be done in person.

Stories and Metaphors

Stories enable leaders to connect with people on an emotional as well as an intellectual level.

Leaders have to be conscious of the language they use in all situations.

Just being aware of the terminology and the definitions and text is one way leaders enhance communication with others.

Even simple language choices make a tremendous difference for leadership.

By using language rich in metaphor and storytelling, leaders can create a deep and lasting effect on others.

Telling stories is a powerful way to relay a message because a story evokes both visual imagery and emotion, which helps employees connect with the message and key values.

Stories can bind people together and create a shared sense of purpose and meaning.

A Stanford Business School study used several methods to convince students that a company practiced a policy of avoiding layoffs; of all the approaches, the students presented with a story were the most convinced about the policy.

Discussion Question #9: *Why is storytelling such a powerful means of communication for a leader? Can you give examples from your own experience of leaders who have used metaphor and story? What was the effect of followers?*

Notes____

____

____

Informal Communication

➢ *Do leaders just communicate stories with words?*

They also *embody* the stories in the way that live their lives and what they seek to inspire in others.

Leaders are watched, and their appearance, behavior, actions, and attitudes are symbolic to others.

Symbols are a powerful informal tool for communicating what is important.

Nonverbal communication, messages transmitted through action and behavior, accounts for over one half of the entire message received in a personal encounter.

People interpret leader actions as symbols, just as they attach meaning to words.

In interpreting a leader's nonverbal cues, followers determine whether a leader's actions correspond to verbal messages.

If there is a discrepancy, research suggests that the nonverbal is granted more weight by the interpreter.

Leaders use actions to symbolize their vision and draw attention to values and ideas.

"Management by walking around," means that leaders leave their offices and speak directly to employees as they work.

These impromptu encounters send positive messages to followers.

The communication is richer, therefore likely to make a lasting impression in both direction.

Both leaders and followers benefit from informal channels.

Discussion Question #6: *Why is "management by wandering around" considered effective communication?*

Notes____

To effectively communicate during times of stress or crisis.

Communicating in a Crisis

➢ *Why is a leader's skill at communicating more crucial during change and crisis?*

To be prepared, leaders can develop fur skills for communicating in a crisis:

- *Stay calm; listen harder.* A leader's emotions are contagious, so leaders have to stay calm and focused.

  The leader's job is to absorb people's fears and uncertainties, which means listening is more important than ever.

- *Be visible.* When people's worlds have become ambiguous and uncertain, they need to feel that someone is in control.

  Many leaders underestimate just how important their presence is during a crisis.

- *Tell the truth.* Leaders gather as much information from as many diverse sources as they can, do their best to determine the facts, and then "get the awful truth out."

- *Communicate a vision for the future.* Although leaders should first deal with the physical and emotional needs of people, they also need to get back to work as soon as possible.

  Moments of crisis present excellent opportunities for leaders to communicate a vision for the future that taps into people's emotions and desires for something better.

In the Lead: Ned Barnholt, Agilent Technologies

Agilent Technologies, an $8.3 billion technology spinoff of Hewlett-Packard, has been battered not only by the slumping economy, but also by the downfall of telecom giants that were once big buyers of its chips, electronic components, and testing devices. CEO Ned Barnholt feels that workers will give their best if they are treated honestly and listened to, which means keeping a strict open-door policy and practicing management by wandering around. As job cuts were unavoidable, Barnholt got on the PA system himself and told employees about the bad financial state of the company.

Q: *How did Barnholt manage in a crisis?*

A: Barnholt was visible and told the truth. The leaders did not hide in their offices and send out pink slips. Barnholt sent manager s to training sessions to learn about how to let people go. He insisted that the managers be as honest as possible, keep their doors open as usual, and field every question or challenge sent their way. They used face-to-face communication and kept employees up-to-date.

Discussion Question #7: *If you were to communicate symbolically with your team to create a sense of trust and team work, what would you do?*

Notes____

DISCUSSION QUESTIONS

1. *How do you think typical leadership communication differs from conventional management communication?*

The manager's role is that of "information processor." Managers scan their environments for important written and personal information, gathering facts and data which is sent to subordinates. Communication effectiveness lies in accuracy of formulation, especially for facts, statistics, and decisions. Leaders communicate the big picture --- the vision. Learning, problem, decision-making, and strategizing are all oriented around and stem from the vision. Communicating the vision is about drawing it to the forefront in people's minds during day-today interactions and activities.

2. *If you were to evaluate an organization based on the degree of open communication climate, what things would you look for? Discuss.*

It is important to look for consistent and frequent communication from the leader which would increase follower understanding and acceptance. An open communication climate encompasses the recent trend toward "open book management," in which financial information is shared with and explained to all employees to engender an act of ownership.

3. *A manager in a communication class remarked, "Listening seems like minimal intrusion of oneself into the conversation, yet it also seems like more work." Do you agree or disagree? Discuss.*

It's easier to talk and put forth a business agenda or sales pitch than to listen actively. Still, few things are as frustrating as the sense that nobody is listening. When leaders don't listen, its sends the signal, "you don't matter" to organization members, thus decreasing their commitment and motivation. Listening is a requirement of for leader communication.

4. *How does dialogue differ from discussion? Give an example of each from your experience.*

A dialogue reveals feelings and builds common ground, with more emphasis on inquiry than advocacy. A discussion explores opposition by individuals who advocate their positions and convince others to adopt those positions. Discussion is resolved by logic or "beating down" opponents. Dialogue contains group unity, shared meaning, and transformed mindsets.

For example, in scheduling classes, a discussion about an 8:00 a.m. class is resolved by noting that attendance is poor for early classes. A dialogue centers around the teacher's time preference, classroom availability, and student work schedules.

5. *Some senior executives believe they should rely on written information and computer reports because these yield more accurate data than face-to-face communications do. Do you agree?*

No, face-to-face communication permits direct experience. Written communication is not focused on a receiver, uses limited information cues, and fails to provide feedback.

6. *Why is "management by wandering around" considered effective communication?*

Leaders leave their offices and speak directly to employees as they work. These impromptu encounters send positive messages to followers. In addition, the communication is richer, therefore likely to make a lasting impression in both direction.

7. *If you were to communicate symbolically with your team to create a sense of trust and team work, what would you do?*

A leader could use a story to communicate an idea symbolically. Stories are a very powerful way to communicate a message. Many companies such as IBM have sent managers to workshops to learn about the advantages of stories as a way to transmit cultural values and promote change. Stories can promote trust and teamwork.

8. *How do leaders use communication to influence and persuade others? Think of someone you have known who is skilled at persuasion. What makes this person an effective communicator?*

Leaders communicate to persuade and influence others, to sell others on the vision and influence them to behave in ways that achieve goals that help accomplish the vision. Leaders can follow four steps to practice the art of persuasion:

- *Establish credibility.* A leader's credibility is based on the leader's knowledge, expertise, and relationship with others.

- *Build goals on common ground.* To be persuasive, leaders describe how what they're requesting will benefit others as well as the leader.

- *Make your position compelling to others.* Leaders appeal to others on an emotional level by using symbols, metaphors, and stories to express their messages, rather than relying on facts and figures.

- *Connect emotionally.* Good leaders sense others' emotions and adjust their approach to match the audience's ability to receive their message.

Persuasion is a valuable communication process, not a manipulation, that can lead to a shared solution or commitment.

President Bill Clinton is an excellent communicator because of his friendly, down-to-earth, common-man manner. He has been described as a neighbor, someone familiar, easy to get to know. Listeners can connect emotionally with him and therefore be persuaded by his words.

9. *Why is storytelling such a powerful means of communication for a leader? Can you give examples from your own experience of leaders who have used metaphor and story? What was the effect of followers?*

Telling stories is a powerful way to relay a message because a story evokes both visual imagery and emotion, which helps employees connect with the message and key values. Stories can bind people together and create a shared sense of purpose and meaning.

At a conference given by Women Waging Peace at Harvard's Kennedy School of Government, the speaker told the following true story to call attention to the worldwide slave trade of children.

In Thailand, men came to a village and told a poor village family about a good job at a new hotel in a nearby city. They offered the job to the 12 year-old daughter. The family needed the money and accepted the offer. The girl was raped and photographed at the border, her passport taken, and told that the photographs were sent to her village to disgrace her family. The girl became part of the growing number of young prostitutes taken to foreign countries and never seen again. The women at the conference were from all over the world. They were so visibly shaken by the powerful story that no one spoke a single word. The silence was deafening.

TEACHING TOOLS AND EXERCISES

1. *Leader's Bookshelf: Crucial Conversations: Tools for Talking When Stakes Are High* by Kerry Patterson, Joseph Grenny, Ron McMillan, and Al Switzler.

Crucial Conversations offers ideas for thinking about and preparing for difficult conversations, along with specific tips and tools for talking, listening, and acting together. What is the leader's role in the technique of dialogue?

2. *Reinforcement:* Active Listening Skills.

For one week, practice active listening behaviors during your phone conversations. Keep a journal of whether listening actively was easy or difficult, what distractions there were, how you dealt with those distractions, and your assessment of whether or not active listening allowed you to get more out of the conversation.

3. *On the Web:* Crisis Communication

Go to www.msn.com or www.cnn.com and find a current event about a crisis. How was it handled by the leader? (For example, in Feb. 2003, ricin, a poison, was found in three federal building in Washington D.C. How was this crisis communicated to the country?)

4. *Leader's Self-Insight:* Personal Assessment of Communication Apprehension.

To be an effective communication champion, you should work to overcome communication anxiety. Interpersonal conversations create the least apprehension for most people, followed by group discussions, larger meetings, and then public speaking. This questionnaire is about your feelings toward communication with other people. Compare your scores with another student. What aspect of communication creates the most apprehension for you? How do you plan to improve it?

5. *Out-of-class reading:* Tom Peters and Nancy Austin, *A Passion for Excellence: The Leadership Difference* (New York: Random House, 1985).

LEADERSEHIP DEVELOPMENT: CASES FOR ANALYSIS

I. Synopsis: The Superintendent's Directive

Superintendent Porter sent an e-mail directive to each of his eleven principals stating that every teacher was to develop a set of performance objectives for the each class. These objectives were to be submitted one month after school opened. Porter had hired a management consultant to help the teachers write the objectives. Mr. Weigand, the Principal of Earsworth Elementary, sent the following memo: "Friends, Superintendent Porter has asked me to inform you that written performance objectives for your courses must be handed in …." One teacher sent a note asking if there were anything wrong with the teaching at the school.

Case questions and answers

1. *Evaluate the communications of Porter and Weigand. To what extent do they communicate as leaders? Explain.*

Both Porter and Weigand do not communicate by drawing the vision to the forefront of their teachers' minds during day-to-day interactions and activities. They do not communicate as leaders. A leader is a communication champion, grounded in the belief that communication is essential to pursuing the organzational vision.

2. *How would you have handled this if you were Superintendent Porter?*

It is important for Porter to build a shared vision about education and learning. Then Porter should use a rich communication method such as face-to-face communication and visibly and symbolically engage in communication-based activities. A memo is low in channel richness.

3. *How would you have handled the communication if you were the principal of Earsworth Elementary School? Why?*

It is best to engage in a dialogue with the teachers and the superintendent in order to reveal feelings, explore assumptions, and build common ground. A long-term solution, a unified group, shared meaning, and transformed mind sets will result.

II. **Synopsis:** **Imperial Metal Products**

Imperial Metal Products, a mid-sized manufacturing company located in the Southeast, makes wheel rims for automobiles. Even employees who work in the lab complain of the heat because they have to venture onto the production floor to take metal samples. The top management team agreed that employees deserved recognition for their fine work, so. a questionnaire was sent to 100 employees to get reaction to the newly air-conditioned cafeteria. The response rate was excellent, but the managers were shocked. They had expected a majority of employees to be grateful for the air-conditioning, but many did not even know about the air-conditioning and preferred a pay raise. One manager suggested that before doing something to reward employees, the company should find out what employees want.

Case questions and answers

1. *How would you rate the communication climate at Imperial Metal Products?*

I would rate the communication climate as poor because there is a wide gap between the ideas and the impressions of the managers and those of the employees. As a reward for good work, managers gave air-conditioning, but employees did not realize it was installed for their use in the cafeteria, many did not know it had been installed, and many do not use the cafeteria.

2. *What channels do you think top managers should use to improve communications?*

Top managers should use face-to-face communication, the richest communication channel, and institute management-by-walking-around. Top managers would find out how hot it is on the production floor. Air-conditioning the cafeteria has nothing to do with the heat in the area where workers spend the majority of their time. Active listening would be helpful and would show managers how workers think and feel.

3. *If you were a top manager at Imperial, what is the first step you would take? Why?*

I would institute dialogue with the workers by meeting them face-to-face and talking to them.---learning about their ideas and feelings. There is such a communication void that written communication to include email is simply not rich enough to resolve the issues.

4. *Do you think sending a questionnaire to ask people what they want is a good idea? Why or why not?*

No, the first questionnaire gave top managers the information they needed. They have no idea about the workers ideas and feelings. They are not interested in air-conditioning. They would prefer higher salaries (response c), a more equitable work environment. (response a), and clear, concise communication (response b.)

CHAPTER TEN
LEADING TEAMS

CHAPTER SUMMARY

Teams are a reality in most organizations, and leaders are called upon to facilitate teams rather than manage direct-report subordinates. Functional teams are part of the traditional organization structure. Cross-functional teams, including problem-solving teams, process improvement teams, and special purpose teams, often represent an organization's first move toward greater team participation. Cross-functional teams may evolve into self-directed teams, which are member- rather than leader-centered and directed. Two recent types of teams, virtual teams and global teams, have resulted from advances in technology, changing employee expectations, and the globalization of business. New technology both supports teamwork and increases the pressures on organizations to expand opportunities for employee participation and the widespread sharing of information.

Teams go through stages of development and change over time. Guiding a team through these stages is an important part of team leadership. In addition, leaders have to get the team designed right by considering such factors as size, diversity, and interdependence and ensuring that task and socio-emotional roles are filled. These considerations help to determine team effectiveness. The leader's personal role is also crucial. People typically have to change themselves to become good team leaders. Three principles that provide a foundation for team leadership are to recognize the importance of shared purpose and values, admit your mistakes, and provide support and coaching to team members.

These principles apply to virtual and global teams as well. However, being a team leader is even more challenging when people are scattered in different geographic locations and may be separated by language and cultural differences. To create effective, smoothly functioning virtual teams, leaders build trust by building connections in both physical and virtual space, select team members who have the skills and temperaments to work virtually, agree on ground rules for the team, and ensure that all team members effectively use technology. For global teams, leaders also have to manage language and cultural differences and guide people to stretch their minds and behavior to establish a shared culture for the team.

Virtual and global teams increase the potential for misunderstanding, disagreements, and conflicts. However, all teams experience some conflict because of the scarce resources, faulty communication, goal conflicts, power and status differences, or employ the following techniques to help resolve conflicts: unite people around a shared vision, use bargaining and negotiation, bring in a mediator, and help conflicting parties communicate openly and honestly, particularly through dialogue.

CHAPTER OPENER

The Spirit of Teamwork in Basketball

The coach of the winning Los Angeles Lakers, Phil Jackson, had previously led the Chicago

Bulls to six National Basketball Association championships, but many critics dismissed his coaching ability. Anyone could win, with basketball's greatest player, Michael Jordan, on the team. Jackson bases his leadership approach on Native American and Eastern spiritual principles, stressing awareness, compassion, and the importance of selfless team play to achieve victory. His greatest strength is an ability to get wealthy, pampered, and sometimes conceited young players to pull together mentally and spiritually to achieve a common goal. Larry Bird with the Indiana Pacers showed the same passionate team leadership. Both Jackson and Bird expected each player to bring a sense of commitment and personal responsibility to the game. By focusing on the spirit of teamwork, both coaches cultivated the leadership abilities of everyone on the team.

LECTURE/OUTLINE

To turn a group of individuals into a collaborative team that achieves high performance through shared mission and collective responsibility

---

Teams in Organizations

Exhibit 10.1

➢ *Why does the concept of teamwork in organizations represents a fundamental change in the way work is organized?*

Companies recognize that the best way to meet the challenges of higher quality, faster service, and total customer satisfaction is through a coordinated effort by all employees.

Yet, teams are not right for every organizational situation; some tasks by their very nature, such as creative writing, are best performed by individuals.

Organizations frequently fail to realize the benefits of teams because they have a hard time balancing authority between leaders and teams.

Effective teams have leaders who build a team identity, actively involve all members, act as coaches and facilitators rather than managers, and invest time and resources for team learning.

What is a Team?

A *team* is a unit of two or more people who interact and coordinate their work to accomplish a shared goal or purpose.

Teams usually have fewer than 15 people who work together regularly and share a goal.

A team is a group of people, but the two are not equal.

Only when people sublimate their individual needs and desires and synthesize their knowledge, skills, and efforts toward a common goal do they become a team.

The team concept implies a sense of shared mission and collective responsibility.

In the best teams, there are no individual "stars" and everyone sublimates individual ego to the good of the whole.

- *Living Leadership: Lessons from Geese*

If we have as much sense as geese, we will stand by each other in difficult times as well as when we are strong.

> Explain the lessons learned from geese. Do these apply to teams on which you have served?

Discussion Question #1: *What is the difference between a "team" and a "group"? Describe personal experience with each.*

Notes____

To understand and handle the stages of team development, and design an effective team in terms of size diversity, and levels of interdependence.

How Teams Develop *Exhibit 10.2*

> *Do you think new teams are different from mature teams?*

Research suggests that teams develop over several stages.

Each stage confronts leaders and members with problems and challenges.

Forming

The *forming* stage is a period of orientation and getting acquainted.

Team members find out what behavior is acceptable to others, explore friendship possibilities, and determine task orientation.

Uncertainty is high because no one knows what the ground rules are or what is expected.

The leader's challenge is to facilitate communication and interaction among team members.

Storming

During the *storming* stage, individual personalities emerge more clearly.

People become more assertive in clarifying their roles; this stage is marked by conflict and disagreement.

Team members may disagree over their perception of the team's mission or goals; they may vie for position or form subgroups.

The team is characterized by a lack of cohesiveness, and the leader's role is to encourage participation by each team member and help find their common vision and values.

Members need to debate ideas, surface conflicts, disagree with one another, and work through uncertainties.

Norming

At the *norming* stage, conflict has been resolved and team unity and harmony emerge.

Consensus develops as natural team leaders emerge and members' roles are clear.

Team members come to understand and accept one another as differences are resolved.

The team leader should emphasize openness within the team and continue to facilitate communication and clarify roles, values, and expectations.

Performing

During the *performing* stage, the major emphasis is on accomplishing the team's goals.

Members are committed to the team's mission and interact frequently.

The team leader should focus on facilitating high task performance and help the team self manage to reach goals.

***In the Lead*:** McDevitt Street Bovis

McDevitt Street Bovis creates its team-building process for quickly and effectively unifying teams, circumventing damaging and time-consuming conflicts, and preventing lawsuits related to major construction projects. The goal is to take the team to the performing stage as quickly as possible by giving everyone an opportunity to get to know one another, explore the ground rules, and clarify roles, responsibilities and expectations. Rather than the typical construction project characterized by conflicts, frantic scheduling, and poor communications, Bovis wants its collection of contractors, designers, suppliers, and other partners to function like a true team—putting the success of the project ahead of their own individual interests. By talking about conflicting goals, facilitators help the team build common ground.

Q: *How does Bovis use team development?*

A: After jointly-writing a mission statement for the team, the team members clarify roles and responsibilities. The intensive team-building session helps members move through the forming and storming stages of development, but meetings continue throughout the project to keep relationships strong and to keep people on target toward achieving the team mission.

Discussion Question #7: *What are the stages of team development? How can a team leader best facilitate the team at each stage?*

Notes____

Types and Characteristics *Exhibit 10.3*

➢ *Are all teams traditionally used in organizations the same?.*

There are several types of teams, and several characteristics of teams are important to team dynamics and performance.

Traditional Types of Teams

There are three fundamental types of teams used in today's organizations: functional teams, cross-functional teams, and self-directed teams.

Functional Team.

A *functional team* is part of the traditional vertical hierarchy, composed of a supervisor and subordinates in the formal chain of command.

Sometimes called a *vertical team* or *command team,* the functional team may include three or four levels of hierarchy within a department.

Typically, a functional team makes up a single department in the organization.

Cross-functional teams

Cross-functional teams are composed of members from different departments within the organization.

Employees are from about the same hierarchical level, although they cross vertical as well as horizontal boundaries.

Cross-functional teams typically have a specific team leader and coordinate across boundaries to lead projects.

They facilitate information sharing across functional boundaries, generate suggestions for coordinating departments, develop new ideas and solutions for existing problems.

Cross-functional teams may gradually evolve into self-directed teams, which represent a fundamental change in how work is organized.

Evolution to Self-Directed Teams

There is an evolution of teams and team leadership.

The functional team represents grouping individuals by skill, and leadership is based on the vertical hierarchy.

In a cross-functional team, members have freedom from the hierarchy, but the team is leader-centered and leader-directed, although leaders give up some control and power for the team to function effectively.

In the highest stage of evolution, team members work together without the direction of managers, supervisors, or assigned team leaders.

Self-directed teams consist of 5 to 20 members who rotate jobs to produce an entire product or service or at least one complete aspect or portion of a product or service.

Teams possess three elements:

- workers with varied skills and functions whose combined skills are sufficient to perform a major task, thus eliminating barriers and fostering coordination

- access to resources such as information, financial information, and machinery

- decision-making authority to select members, solve problems, and spend money.

In self-directed teams, members take over duties such as scheduling work or vacations, ordering materials, and evaluating performance.

Teams work with minimum supervision, and members are jointly responsible for conflict resolution and decision making.

Members elect their own leader who may change each year.

Discussion Question #2: *What is the difference between a cross-functional team and a self-directed team?*

Notes____

____

____

Understanding Team Characteristics

One of the leader's most important jobs is to get a team designed correctly by considering size, diversity, and interdependence.

The quality of team design has a significant impact on the success of teams.

Size

The ideal size of a work team is though to seven, although teams from 5 to 12 are associated with high performance.

Teams must be large enough to have diverse skills yet small enough for members to feel like part of a community.

Research shows that small teams show more agreement, ask more questions, and exchange more opinions.

Large teams have more disagreements, form subgroups form, and face conflict. Large teams tend to be less friendly.

Diversity

Since teams require a variety of skills, knowledge, and experience, it seems likely that heterogeneous teams would be more effective because members bring diverse abilities and information to a project or problem.

Research supports this idea, showing that heterogeneous teams produce more innovative solutions.

Diversity can be a source of creativity, and can contribute to a healthy level of conflict, which helps to prevent "groupthink," in which people are so committed to a cohesive team that they are reluctant to voice contrary opinions.

Still, conflict that is too strong can limit team satisfaction and performance.

Diversity provides fertile ground for such disagreements.

Racial and national differences can interfere with team interaction; teams of racially and culturally diverse members tend to have more difficulty learning to work well together.

With effective leadership and conflict resolution, the problems seem to dissipate over a period of time.

Interdependence

Interdependence refers to the extent to which team members depend on each other for information, resources, or ideas to accomplish their tasks.

Three types of interdependence affect teams:

- *Pooled interdependence* is the lowest form of interdependence. Members are fairly independent of one another in completing their work, participating *on* a team, but not as a team (e.g., sharing a machine.)

- *Sequential interdependence* is a serial form wherein the output of one team member becomes the input to another team member (e.g., assembly plant team.).

- *Reciprocal interdependence* exists when team members influence and affect one another in reciprocal fashion (e.g., emergency trauma team).

Leaders are responsible for facilitating the coordination and communication needed, depending on the level of team interdependence.

True team leadership is most important when interdependence is high.

For teams with low interdependence, traditional leadership, individual rewards, and granting authority and power to individuals rather than the team may be appropriate.

Discussion Question #5: *Describe the three levels of interdependence. Is team leadership more difficult under low or high interdependence? Discuss.*

Notes____

____

____

In the Lead: Parkland Memorial Hospital

Parkland delivered four out every thousand babies born in the U.S. in 2001, 40 or 50 babies a day. The hospital's stillbirth and neonatal death rates are lower than the national average despite the fact that 95 percent of the women are indigent, and many have drug or alcohol problems. Parkland achieves these results with limited staff and money because of superb teamwork that provides the intense coordination needed to meet any demand. Decision making is decentralized so that employees can respond on their own initiative as problems arise. Clerks, midwives, nurses, technicians, and doctors smoothly coordinate their activities to provide a variety of services as they are needed, adjusting to each team member's strengths and weaknesses and to the changing demands of the problem at hand.

Q: *How do Parkland's leaders use reciprocal interdependence?*

A: Team members influence and affect one another in a reciprocal fashion. While Parkland's leaders believe that it is important to have defined roles, they make it clear that there are no boundaries. Communication is frequent, face-to-face, and flowing in all directions.

To develop and apply the personal qualities of effective team leadership for traditional, virtual, and global teams.

Leading Effective Teams

Team effectiveness is defined as the achievement of four performance outcomes:

- *Innovation/adaptation*---the degree to which teams impact the organization's ability to rapidly respond to environmental needs and changes

- *Efficiency*---whether the team helps the organization attain goals using fewer resources

- *Quality*---achieving fewer defects and exceeding customer satisfaction

- *Employee satisfaction*---the team's ability to maintain employee commitment and enthusiasm by meeting the personal needs of its members.

Three areas related to understanding team effectiveness are team cohesiveness and performance; team task and socio-emotional roles; and the personal impact of the team leader.

Team Cohesiveness and Effectiveness

Team cohesiveness is defined as the extent to which members stick together and remain united in the pursuit of a common goal.

Members of highly cohesive teams are committed to team goals and activities. Members of less cohesive teams are less concerned about the team's welfare.

Cohesiveness is an attractive feature of teams.

Determinants of Cohesiveness Leaders use several factors to influence cohesiveness:

- *Interaction*---the greater the amount of contact, the more cohesive the team.

- *Shared mission and goals*---agreement on purpose and direction makes the team cohesive.

- *Personal attraction to the team*---members find common ground and have similar values

- *Competition*---cohesiveness increases with moderate competition with other teams

- *Team success*---members feel good and their commitment is higher

Consequences of Cohesiveness

The consequences of team cohesiveness can be examined according to morale and performance.

Morale is higher in cohesive teams because of increased communication, a friendly atmosphere, loyalty, and member participation in decisions and activities.

High team cohesiveness has positive effects on the satisfaction and morale of team members.

Cohesiveness and *performance* are positively correlated; cohesive teams unleash employee energy and creativity because working in a team increases individual motivation.

Social facilitation refers to the tendency for the presence of other people to enhance individual motivation and performance.

One study found that team cohesiveness is related to performance since team interdependence is high, requiring frequent interaction and coordination.

Highly cohesive teams are more productive when supported by organizational leaders and less productive when they sense hostility and negativism from leaders.

The support of leaders contributes to the development of high performance norms, whereas hostility leads to team norms and goals of low performance.

In the lead: Ralston Foods Sparks, Nevada

The Ralston Foods plant is a small segment of Ralcorp Holdings, the largest store-brand manufacturer in the United States. The plant previously produced pet food, but that operation shut down in 1990 and the plant was reoutfitted into a cereal plant. Plant manager, David Kibbe, wanted to start the new plant as a team-based organization. He assembled a small team of leaders who believed in participative management and spent millions of dollars training people how to work in a team environment. The leadership team created a culture of trust, credibility, and openness.

Q: *How did Ralston create cohesiveness?*

A: Cohesiveness is based on a shared mission, common ground among members, and Interaction. Small teams in the warehouse and mill areas function entirely without designated leaders and handle all issues and problems that arise in their areas including hiring, firing, scheduling, quality, budget management, and disciplinary problems. Team members have strong bonds that motivate them to perform well for the sake of the team. Thanks to team cohesiveness and top leadership support, Ralston has produced record-breaking output levels and generated significant cost reductions.

Discussion Question #8: *Discuss the relationship between team cohesiveness and performance.*

Notes____

Meeting Task and Socio-emotional Needs *Exhibit 10.4*

Another important factor in team effectiveness is ensuring that the needs for both task accomplishment and team members' socio-emotional well being are being met.

Task-oriented behavior places primary concern on tasks and production and is associated with higher production whereas people-oriented behavior emphasizes concern for followers.

The *task-specialist role* is associated with initiating new ideas or different ways of considering problems, evaluating team effectiveness, seeking information to clarify tasks and responsibilities, summarizing facts and ideas for others, and stimulating others to action.

The *socio-emotional role* includes facilitating other's participation, smoothing conflicts, showing concern for team members' needs and feelings; serving as a role model, and reminding others of standards for interaction.

Ideally, a team leader plays both task-specialist and socio-emotional roles.

It is the leader's responsibility to make sure both types of needs are met.

Providing Support and Coaching to Team Members

Good team leaders make sure people get the training, development opportunities, and resources they need and that they are adequately rewarded for their contributions to the organization.

Rather than thinking about oneself, effective team leaders spend their time taking care of team members.

Discussion Question #6: *Which is more important to team effectiveness---the task-specialist role or the socio-emotional role? Discuss.*

Notes____

The Leader's New Challenge: Virtual and Global Teams *Exhibit 10.5*

➢ *Why is being a team leader more challenging when people are scattered in different geographical locations?*

The key characteristics of global and virtual teams include:

- spatial distance which limits face-to-face communication
- the use of technological communication as the primary means of connecting team members

The leadership challenge is highest for global teams because of the increased potential for misunderstanding and conflicts.

Virtual teams

A *virtual team* is made up of geographically—or organizationally—dispersed members who are linked primarily through advanced information and telecommunication technologies.

Team members use e-mail, voice mail, videoconferencing, Internet and intranet technologies, and various types of collaboration software to perform their work rather than meeting face-to-face.

Uses of Virtual Teams

Virtual teams, sometimes called *distributed teams,* may be temporary cross-functional teams pulled together to work on specific problems, or long-term or permanent self-directed teams.

Using virtual teams allows organizations to use the best people for a particular job, no matter where they are located, thus enabling a fast response to competitive pressures.

Leading the Virtual Team

Leaders of conventional teams can monitor how team members are doing and if everything is on track.

Virtual team leaders have to trust people to do their jobs without constant supervision, and they learn to focus more on results than on the process of accomplishing them.

Too much control can kill a virtual team; virtual team leaders can master the following skills to be successful:

- *Select the right team members.* Effective virtual team leaders put a lot of thought into getting the right mix of people with technical knowledge, skills and personalities.

- *Build trust by building connections.* Virtual teams leaders work hard to build connections among people, from which trust can grow.

- *Agree on ground rules.* Teams should work together to choose the collaboration software and other communications technologies and practice using the technology together.

- *Effectively use technology.* Communication can be a tremendous problem for virtual teams, and the ideas for using electronic communication channels can be helpful (Chap. 9).

Leaders can schedule can regular times for people to interact online and be sure all team members are trained in how to use electronic communications effectively.

Everything needs to be made more explicit online.

Global Teams

Global teams are composed of culturally diverse members who live and work in different countries and coordinate some part of their activities on a global basis.

The use of global teams is increasing.

Why Global Teams Often Fail

All of the challenges of virtual teamwork are magnified in the case of global teams because of the added problem of language and cultural barriers.

Building trust is an even greater challenge when people bring different norms, values, attitudes, and patterns of behavior to the team.

Members from different cultures have different beliefs about authority, time orientation, decision making, and even teamwork itself (e.g., In teams in Mexico, shared leadership conflicts with the value of status and power differences).

Communication barriers can be formidable; members may speak different languages and have different time zones and schedules. Even dialects and accents in the same language present problems.

Leading the Global Team

If managed correctly, global teams have many advantages because increasingly, the expertise and knowledge needed to complete a project is scattered around the world.

All of the guidelines for leading virtual teams apply, global team leaders can improve their success by incorporating the following ideas:

- *Manage language and culture.* Organizations using global teams need language and cross-cultural education to help overcome linguistic and cultural hurdles.

- *Stretch minds and behavior.* As team members learn to expand their thinking and embrace cultural differences, they also learn to develop a shared team culture.

Leaders can work with team members to set norms and guidelines for acceptable behavior.

***In the Lead*:** STMicroelectronics

Leaders at STMicroelectronics (STM) faced a problem when the company won a coveted order for microchips to power the brains for a navigational mapping system to be installed in new Fiats and Peugeots. Winning the order was a major coup, but filling it wasn't going to be easy. Car makers needed the chips in a hurry---if they couldn't get the new navigational systems installed fast, they would lose sales. The people with the expertise to complete the project lived in five different countries, spanned 14 time zones, and spoke six different native languages. Thanks to extensive training and excellent team leadership, STM's global team was a success.

Q: *How did STMicroelectronics use a global team effectively?*

A: One reason the team worked so well is that everyone united around a common purpose and members subordinated their individual viewpoints and egos to their shared goal. When there were disagreements, team members worked hard to understand different points of view rather than letting their own values and attitudes get in the way.

Discussion Question #3: *Why do you think organizations are increasingly using virtual and global teams? Would you like to be a member or leader of a virtual global team? Why or why not?*

Notes____

To handle conflicts that inevitably arise among members of a team.

Handling Team Conflict *Exhibit 10.6*

As one would expect, there is an increased potential for conflict among members of global and virtual teams because of greater chances for miscommunication and misunderstandings.

One study found that in global virtual teams, people show a greater propensity for shirking their duties or giving less than their full effort, which can also lead to team conflicts.

For all team leaders, though no skill is more important than managing the conflicts that will inevitably arise.

Conflict is the hostile or antagonistic interaction in which one party attempts to thwart the intentions or goals of another.

Conflict occurs in all teams and organizations.

High performing teams typically have lower levels of conflict, and the conflict is more often associated with tasks than with interpersonal relationships.

Teams that reflect healthy patterns of conflict are usually characterized by high levels of trust and mutual respect.

Causes of Conflict

➢ *What causes team conflict?*

When teams compete for scarce resources, information, or supplies, conflict occurs.

It also occurs when responsibilities are unclear, when goals are conflicting, or when there is a personality clash.

Sometimes the only solution is to separate the parties and reassign them to other teams where they can be more productive.

Styles to Handle Conflict.

Teams as well as individuals develop specific styles for dealing with conflict, based on the desire to satisfy their own concerns versus the other party's concerns.

There are five styles of handling conflict, measured along two dimensions: assertiveness versus cooperation.

Effective leaders can vary the style to fit a specific situation, as each style is appropriate in certain cases:

- The *competing style*—reflects assertiveness to get one's own way, used when quick decisive action is vital on important issues or unpopular actions.

- The *avoiding style*----reflects neither assertiveness nor cooperation, used for trivial issues, when there is no chance of winning, when a delay to gather information is needed, or when a disruption would be costly.

- The *compromising style*---reflects moderate assertiveness and cooperation, when goals are equally important.

  It is appropriate when the goals on both sides are equally important, when opponents have equal power and both sides want to split the difference, or when people need to arrive at temporary or expedient solutions under time pressure.

- The *accommodating style*---reflects a high degree of cooperativeness, used when people realize they are wrong, when an issue is more important to others than to oneself, when building social credits for use in large discussions, or when maintaining cohesiveness is especially important.

- The *collaborating style*—reflects a high degree of assertiveness and cooperativeness, used to enable both parties to win.

  This style enables both parties to win, although it may require substantial dialogue and negotiation.

  The collaborating style is important when both sets of concerns are too important to be compromised, when insights from different people need to be merged into an overall solution.

In a study of conflicts in virtual teams, researchers found that the competing and collaborating styles had a positive effect on team performance.

The competing style is effective for electronic communication because team members don't interpret the individual's approach as aggressive and are willing to accept a quick solution.

Other Approaches

Research suggests several other techniques that help resolve conflicts among people or teams.

Vision

A compelling vision can pull people together. A vision is for the whole team and cannot be attained by one person.

Its achievement requires the cooperation of conflicting parties.

If leaders can focus on a larger team or organizational vision, conflict will decrease because the people involved see the big picture and realize that they must work together to achieve it.

Bargaining/negotiating

Bargaining and negotiating mean that the parties engage one another to reach a solution

They attempt logical problem solving to identify and correct the conflict; this approach works if individuals can set aside personal animosities and deal with conflict in a businesslike way.

Mediation

Using a third part to settle a dispute involves mediation.

The mediator can discuss the conflict with each party and work toward a solution.

If a solution cannot be reached, the parties may wish to turn the conflict over to the mediator and abide by the solution offered.

Facilitating Communication

On of the most effective ways to reduce conflict is to help conflicting parties communicate openly and honestly.

As conflicting parties exchange information and learn about one another, suspicions diminish and teamwork becomes possible.

A promising avenue for reducing conflict is through dialogue.

Each approach can help resolve conflicts between individuals or teams.

Discussion Question #9: *What style of handling conflict do you typically use? Can you think of instances where a different style might have been more productive?*

Notes____

____

____

DISCUSSION QUESTIONS

1. *What is the difference between a "team" and a "group"? Describe personal experience with each.*

Teams are made up of two or more people. Teams work together regularly. A team is a group of people, but the two are not equal. A group has individual accountability, an identical purpose for the group and the organization, performance goals set by others, and individual work products. A professor or coach can put together a group of people and never build a *team.*

Teams are characterized by equality and achieve high levels of performance through common goal. Teams had mutual accountability, collective work products, and are not inhibited by organizational boundaries. Teams are characterized by equality whereas a group may have individual "stars." An athletic team is an example of team characteristics as opposed to group characteristics.

2. *What is the difference between a cross-functional team and a self-directed team?*

Cross-functional teams are made up of members from different functional departments from about the same organizational level. Teams are involved in shared leadership, purpose, and responsibility by all members working toward projects that affect several departments.

Self-directed teams rotate jobs to produce an entire product or service or at least one complete aspect or portion of it. Self-directed teams possess three elements: 1) workers with varied skills and functions whose combined skills can perform a major task; 2) access to resources; and 3) decision-making authority problems.

3. *Why do you think organizations are increasingly using virtual and global teams? Would you like to be a member or leader of a virtual global team? Why or why not?*

Using virtual teams allows organizations to use the best people for a particular job, no matter where they are located, thus enabling a fast response to competitive pressures. If managed correctly, global teams have many advantages because increasingly, the expertise and knowledge needed to complete a project is scattered around the world. Yes. I enjoy virtual teams. Being a member of a virtual team is an excellent experience because it allows for flexibility in terms of time, scheduling, and location.

4. *Why might a person need to go through significant personal changes to be an effective team leader? What are some of the changes required?*

Effective team leaders must shift their mindset and behavior from a traditional organization because in a team, leaders do not make the decisions. Leaders have to admit ignorance, take care of team members, communicate by listening and asking questions, share power, and build shared values.

5. *Describe the three levels of interdependence. Is team leadership more difficult under low or high interdependence? Discuss.*

Pooled interdependence exists when members are fairly independent of one another in completing their work, participating on a team, but not as a team.

Sequential interdependence is a serial form wherein the output of one team member becomes the input to another team member.

In **reciprocal interdependence,** team members influence and affect one another in reciprocal fashion. Team leadership is more difficult when interdependence is high because the leader does not have the traditional tools of individual rewards, granting authority, and power. p.

6. *Which is more important to team effectiveness---the task-specialist role or the socio-emotional role? Discuss.*

Both are important. However, members selected for a team are specialists who know how to perform the tasks at hand. The socio-emotional role is more complex, but essential so that the team does not become mired in conflict. The socio-emotional role includes facilitating other's participation, smoothing conflicts, showing concern for team members' needs and feelings; serving as a role model, and reminding others of standards for interaction.

7. *What are the stages of team development? How can a team leader best facilitate the team at each stage?*

- **Forming** is a period of orientation and getting acquainted. The leader's challenge is to facilitate communication and interaction among team members.
- **Storming** is a stage during which individual personalities emerge more clearly. The leader's role is to encourage participation by each team member and help find common vision.
- **Norming** is a stage at which conflict has been resolved and team unity and harmony emerge. The leader should emphasize openness within the team and continue to facilitate communication and clarify roles.

- **Performing** is a stage during which the major emphasis is on accomplishing the team's goals. The team leader should focus on facilitating high task performance and help the team self manage to reach goals.

8. *Discuss the relationship between team cohesiveness and performance.*

Cohesiveness and performance are positively correlated. Cohesive teams unleash enormous amounts of employee energy and creativity. Social facilitation refers to the tendency for the presence of other people to enhance individual motivation and performance.

9. *What style of handling conflict do you typically use? Can you think of instances where a different style might have been more productive?*

I typically use a *collaborating style* because it reflects a high degree of assertiveness and cooperativeness, and both parties can win. Then both parties accept the solution in a more positive manner. Yes, many times I choose an *avoidance style* because it is not worth spending time and energy on a trivial decision.

TEACHING TOOLS AND EXERCISES

1. Invite a member of the psychology department to speak to the class on conflict resolution.

2. *On-the-web:* Effective Teams

Go to www.swlearning.com/management Click on Internet Exercises.
Scroll down to Group/Team Development and click on "*1-2-3: Go-o-o-o Team*"
Click on the websites provided and write the answers to the questions about forming and leading teams.

3. *Activity*: Managing Teams

Students will interview three managers at different organizations. Ask them about their experiences in managing teams. What behaviors have they found that work? What behaviors have not been successful in creating an effective team? Students will share their interviews with the class or prepare a short written report.

4. *Out-of-class reading:*

Sacred Hoops by Phil Jackson is an inside look at the higher wisdom of teamwork from the former Chicago Bulls' head coach Phil Jackson. This thought-provoking book takes you inside the mind of the thinking man's coach as he builds one of the greatest teams of all time. The "me" becomes "we."

P. Jackson, *Sacred Hoops* (New York: Hyperion Press, 1995).

5. *Leader's Self-Insight:* How Do You Handle Conflict

Think of some disagreements you have had with a team member, a student group, manager, friend, or co-worker. Review the five stages for handling conflict beginning on p. 411.

Which of the five strategies do you use the most? Which strategy do you find the most difficult? Are there some situations in which you are weak might be more effective? Explain your scores on the questionnaire to another student.

LEADERSHIP DEVELOPMENT: CASES FOR ANALYSIS

I. Synopsis: Valena Scientific Corporation

Valena Scientific Corporation (VSC) is a large manufacturer of health care products. Senior executives decided to create a biotech research program that was self-managed. Informal leaders emerged among the scientists in gene splicing, recombination, and fermentation. The informal group leaders met and discovered that each group had taken a different direction. Each subgroup believed that its direction was the best. Management decided to appoint a formal leader for the program. The chief biologist took nine scientists on a two-day retreat. He assigned them to discussion tables with a member of each subgroup. After they developed a shared vision, they turned to scientific issues. Dramatic changes were observed after the retreat. Problems were communicated, subgroup leaders coordinated many problems, and lunch gatherings began to appear. Cohesion was strong and morale high.

Case questions and answers

1. *Was the research program a group or a team? What type of team were they (functional, cross-functional, self-directed)? Explain.*

The research program is a team because it a unit of two or more people who interact and coordinate their work to accomplish a specific goal. It was a cross--functional team with scientists taken from larger departments and specific team leaders. Cross-functional teams are made up of members from different functional departments within the organization. Members are generally from about the same hierarchical level in the organization, although cross *functional teams* sometimes cross vertical as well as horizontal boundaries. Teams are involved in shared leadership, purpose, and responsibility by all members working toward projects that affect several departments.

2. *Did the interdependence among subgroups change with the interferon project? What were the group norms before and after the retreat?*

Yes. Before the retreat, there was conflict and disagreement, lack of unity, no sharing of information, and competitiveness. After the retreat, the norms were open *communication,* commitment to team success, interaction, and cooperation.

3. *What factors account for the change in cohesiveness after the chief biologist took over?*

After the biologist took over, the team was cohesive. Cohesive teams are friendly, loyal, and members communicate. *Morale* is high. Cohesiveness and *performance* are positively correlated. Cohesive teams unleash enormous amounts of employee energy and creativity. *Social facilitation* is the tendency for the presence of other people to enhance individual motivation and performance. Members from the different subgroups met for lunch and started to form relationships and understand opposing points of view.

II. **Synopsis: Burgess Industries**

Managers at Burgess Industries are struggling to improve productivity and profits. Top executives directed managers to abandon the traditional assembly system, where workers performed a specific task. In the new team system, teams of 30 to 35 workers coordinate their activities to assemble complete garments. People were given training and a brief team-building seminar. Workers were told that they would get more autonomy, and the pay system was revised. A skilled worker could exceed his quota by 20 percent and receive an increase in pay. People were paid based on the total output of the team. The pay of top performers went down because the productivity of the team was affected by slower, inexperienced, or inefficient team members. Skilled workers were frustrated having to wait for slower colleagues. Supervisors provided little direction. The idea was to empower employees to have more control over their own work.

Case questions and answers

1. *Why do you think the experiment in teamwork at Burgess Industries has been unsuccessful? Consider the definition of teams, team characteristics and team dynamics, and issues of leadership.*

The experiment did not use teams in the true meaning of the word. There was a lack of understanding of teamwork. A team is a unit of two or more people who interact and coordinate their work to accomplish a specific team goal. Teams work together regularly. Teams are characterized by equality and achieve high levels of performance through common goal. Teams in organizations have certain characteristics important to team dynamics and performance. size, diversity, and interdependence. The ideal size of a work team is though to seven, although teams from 5 to 12 are associated with high performance. Leaders are responsible for facilitating coordination and communication needed among team members, depending on the level of team interdependence. True team leadership is most important when interdependence is high----at Burgess, interdependence is high.

2. *If you were a consultant to Burgess, what would you recommend managers do to promote more effective teamwork?*

There has been insufficient training in the formation of teams. The teams need a shared vision that reflects the organizational vision. The teams function as groups with individual monetary goals—not team goals. The reward system needs to foster teamwork, rather than competition. The teams are too large for cohesiveness. Supervisors need training as well. They are unaccustomed to the team system and provide little direction.

3. *How would you alleviate the conflicts that have developed among employees?*

The pay system must be revised and the supervisors must act as facilitators to resolve conflict. The pay system is promoting conflict by pitting workers against each other. The pay of top performers went down because the productivity of the team was affected by slower, inexperienced, or inefficient team members. Skilled workers were frustrated having to wait for slower colleagues.

CHAPTER ELEVEN
LEADERSHIP AND DIVERSITY

CHAPTER SUMMARY

Diversity is a fact of life in today's world, and leaders can create change in organizations to keep up. The U.S. population, the workforce, and customer base are changing. People of different national origins, races, and religions are no longer willing to be assimilated into the mainstream culture. Organizations are also operating in an increasingly global world, which means dealing with diversity on a broader stage than ever before.

Dimensions of diversity are both primary, such as age, gender, and race, and secondary, such as education, marital status, and religion. There are several reasons why organizations are recognizing the need to value and support diversity. Diversity helps organizations build better relationships with diverse customers and helps develop employee potential. Diversity provides a broader and deeper base of experience for creativity and problem solving, which is essential to building learning organizations.

One aspect of diversity of particular interest is women's style of leadership, referred to as interactive leadership. The values associated with interactive leadership, such as inclusion, relationship-building, and caring, are emerging as valuable qualities for both male and female leaders in the twenty-first century.

Another important idea is global diversity. Leaders can be aware of the impact culture may have and consider cultural differences in their dealings with followers. Within organizations, people who do not fit the mainstream white, U.S.-born, male culture face a number of challenges, including unequal expectations, the need to live bi-culturally, the glass ceiling, and the opportunity gap.

Organizations evolve through stages of diversity awareness and action, ranging from minimum efforts to meet affirmative action guidelines to valuing diversity as an integral part of organizational culture. The barriers to successful evolution include ethnocentrism, prejudice, the so-called white male club, the paradox of diversity, and actual cultural differences.

Strong, culturally-sensitive leadership is the only way organizations can move through the stages of diversity awareness. Leaders first change themselves by developing personal characteristics that support diversity. They use these personal characteristics to change the organization. The ultimate goal for leaders in the twenty-first century is to build organizations as integrated communities in which all people feel encouraged, respected, and committed to common purpose and goals.

CHAPTER OPENER

Myrtle Potter, CEO of Genentech

Myrtle Potter still remembers what it felt like to arrive for her first day of college at the University of Chicago. She was an outsider from the start, Potter recalls; rural , African

American, and female." One of six children from a family of modest means, Potter is now the chief operating officer of the biotechnology firm Genentech. Her goal is to be CEO. Although Potter is highly ambitious for her own advancement, she is committed to helping others break through barriers. She has an uncanny knack for cultivating and inspiring people from all backgrounds to achieve beyond their expectations.

LECTURE/OUTLINE

To apply an awareness of the dimensions of diversity and multicultural issues in your everyday life.

Diversity Today *Exhibit 11.1*

➢ *How is the face of organizations in America beginning to change?*

Diversity in terms of race, gender, religion, ethnicity, age, nationality, sexual orientation, physical and mental ability, etc. is a fact of life for today's organizations.

The U.S. population, the workforce, and the customer base are changing dramatically.

In the past, the U.S was seen as a "melting pot" where people blended to resemble one another.

Today, the burden of adaptation rests more on the organization than on the individual.

People are no longer willing to give up or hide their values, beliefs, and ways of doing things to "fit in."

In addition to increasing heterogeneity of the U.S. population, organizations are operating on a global playing field , which means that people of different races and nationalities work together.

Successful leaders in an increasing diverse world have a responsibility to acknowledge and value cultural differences and understand how diversity affects organizational outcomes.

Definition of Diversity

Workforce diversity means a workforce made up of people with different human qualities or who belong to various cultural groups.

From the perspective of individuals, *diversity* refers to differences among people in terms of dimensions ---age, ethnicity, gender, or race.

It is important to remember that diversity includes everyone, not just racial or ethnic minorities.

The *diversity wheel*, the myriad combinations of traits that make up diversity, shows how people shape their self-image and world view :

- Primary or core dimensions include age, race, gender, mental or physical abilities.

- Secondary dimensions can be acquired or changed through one's lifetime---education, language, religion..

Secondary dimensions have less impact than those of the core but affect a person's self-definition and worldview and have an impact on how the person is viewed by others (e.g., Gulf War veterans.)

The challenge for leaders is to recognize that each person can bring value and strengths to the workplace based on a unique combination of diversity characteristics.

Organizations establish workforce diversity programs to promote the hiring, inclusion, and promotion of diverse employees and to insure that differences are accepted and respected in the work place.

Discussion Question #1: *How might a leader's role and responsibility change as a company becomes more diverse?*

Notes____

To encourage and support diversity to meet organizational needs.

The Reality of Diversity

The Bureau of Labor Statistics indicate that the number of immigrant workers continues to grow.

During the first decade of this century, minorities will make up 40 percent of people entering the U.S. workforce, with many as first generation immigrants and almost two-thirds female.

By 2020, women will comprise half of the total full-time U.S. workforce.

White males now make up less than half of the U.S. workforce.

An unprecedented number of foreign-born CEOs now run major companies in the United States, Britain, and several other countries.

Employees with global experience and cultural sensitivity are in high demand in many industries.

Notes____

The Need for Organizational Diversity

Organizations are responding to diversity and new attitudes for a number of reasons beyond the fact that shifting demographics make it necessary to do so.

Recent research supports the idea that diversity adds value to organizations and can contribute to a firm's competitive advantage.

Internal diversity can help meet the needs of diverse customers.

Culture plays an important part in determining the goods, entertainment, social services, and household products that people use and buy.

Since two out of every three people in the U.S. are minority-group members or females or both, companies are recruiting minority employees who understand what diverse people want.

Diverse employees can help an organization build better relationships with customers by making them feel connected to the organization.

Notes____

In the Lead: Allstate Insurance Company

Allstate's concept of diversity is a broad one that goes beyond race and gender to include diversity in terms of age, religion, sexual orientation, disability, and other dimensions. Allstate's diversity initiatives have earned the company a string of awards, such as the "1999 Best Companies for Hispanics to Work For." Allstate's internal measurement systems show a steady increase in the customer base and growing levels of customer satisfaction. Leaders at Allstate want to create an environment where diverse people feel comfortable working.

Q: *How has Allstate used diversity?*

A: Allstate's concept of diversity is a broad one that goes beyond race and gender to include diversity in terms of age, religion, sexual orientation, disability, and other dimensions. Allstate actively recruits, develops, and promotes diverse employees. Its percentage of minority employees, female executives, and minority executives are all well above the national average.

Another need for diversity is to develop employee and organizational potential.

People *who* feel valued for what they can bring to the organization, which leads to better morale.

By seriously recruiting and valuing individuals without regard to race, sexual preference, nationality, age, or physical ability, organizations can attract and retain the best human talent.

Diversity develops greater flexibility and provides for a broader, deeper base of experience for problem solving, creativity, and innovation.

Diversity is essential to today's learning organization.

❑ *Living Leadership: Honoring Our Diversity of Gifts*

The simple act of recognizing diversity in corporate life helps us to connect the great variety of gifts that people bring to work and service in the organization.

➢ What does the story of the millwright tell you about understanding diversity?

Discussion Question #2: *How might diversity within the organization ultimately lead to better problem solving and greater creativity?*

Notes____

____

____

Ways Women Lead *Exhibit 11.2*

Leadership traits qualities traditionally associated with white, American-born males include aggressiveness, rational analysis, and a "take-charge" attitude.

Male leaders tend to be competitive and individualistic and prefer working in vertical hierarchies.

They rely on formal authority and position in their dealings with subordinates.

Women tend to be more concerned with consensus building, inclusiveness, participation, and caring.

Men may become less influential in the workforce than women because a women's approach is more attuned to the needs and values of a multicultural environment.

In *interactive leadership*, the leader favors a consensual and collaborative process, and influence derives from relationships rather than position power and authority.

Women's interactive leadership seems appropriate for the future of diversity and learning organizations.

Research indicates that women leaders are more participative and less autocratic, behaviors that fit the new reality of organizations today.

A survey of followers rated female leaders significantly higher than men on several characteristics that are crucial for developing fast, flexible, learning organizations.

Female leaders were rated higher than men on the following dimensions:

- *Idealized influence* means followers identify with and want to emulate the leader.

- *Inspirational motivation* is derived from the leader who appeals emotionally and symbolically to the desire to do a good job.

- *Individual consideration* means that the follower is treated as an individual, but all persons are treated equitably.

- *Intellectual stimulation* means questioning current methods and challenging employees to think in new ways.

The interactive leadership style is not exclusive to women.

Any leader can learn to adopt a more inclusive style by paying attention to nonverbal behavior and developing skills such as listening.

Discussion Question #3: *What is interactive leadership and why may this approach be increasingly important in the twenty-first century?*

Notes____

To consider the role of cultural values and attitudes in determining how to deal with employees from different cultures or ethnic backgrounds.

Global Diversity *Exhibit 11.3*

Globalization of the most rapidly increasing sources of diversity in North American organizations because companies are hiring employees in many countries.

Leaders can develop cross-cultural understanding, the ability to build networks, and the understanding of geopolitical forces.

Two significant aspects of global diversity are the sociocultural environment and communication differences.

The Sociocultural Environment

For companies operating globally, cultural differences may provide potential for difficulties and conflicts than any other source.

Managers in U.S. companies have run into problems trying to transfer their diversity policies and practices to European divisions.

National cultures are intangible, pervasive, and difficult to comprehend.

Social Value Systems

Research done by Geert Hofstede on IBM employees in 40 countries discovered that mind-set and cultural values on four significant dimensions vary widely.

- *Power distance* High power distance means people accept inequality in power among institutions, organizations, and individuals (e.g., Mexico)

  Low power distance means that people expect equality in power (e.g., Sweden)

- *Uncertainty avoidance* High uncertainty avoidance means that members feel uncomfortable with uncertainty and ambiguity and support beliefs and behavior that promise certainty and conformity (e.g., Greece, Portugal).

  Low uncertainty avoidance indicates tolerance for the unstructured, the unclear, and the unpredictable (e.g., Singapore, Jamaica)

- *Individualism and collectivism* Individualism reflects a value for loosely knit social framework in which individuals take care of themselves (e.g., United States.)

  Collectivism reflects a preference for a tightly knit social framework in which people lookout for one another and organizations protect their members' interests (e.g., Ecuador, Panama).

- *Masculinity and femininity* Masculinity reflects a preference for achievement, heroism, assertiveness, work centrality, and material success (e.g., Mexico, Japan, Germany.)

  Femininity reflects the values of relationships, cooperation, group decision making and quality of life (e.g., Sweden, Norway).

Social value differences can significantly affect leadership, working relationships, and organizational functioning.

How leaders handle these and other cultural differences has tremendous impact on the satisfaction and effectiveness of diverse employees.

Discussion Question #4: *Discuss ways in which low uncertainty avoidance as a social value among followers could affect their interaction with leaders who display high uncertainty avoidance.*

Notes____

Other Cultural Characteristics

➢ *Do cultural the characteristics of language, religion, attitudes, social organization, and education affect international leadership? How?*

Some countries, such as India, have several spoken languages; other countries rely heavily on the spoken rather than the written word; and religion includes philosophical attitudes.

Elements of social organization include kinship and families, status systems, and opportunities for social mobility.

Age commands more status and respect in Europe and the Middle East than in the United States.

Leaders working in a global context have found that social and cultural differences cannot be ignored.

Responding to local needs and cultural values can help organizations be competitive and successful.

In the Lead: Denis Hennequin, McDonald's France

In 2002 McDonald's posted its first ever quarterly lost and announced the closing of 175 outlets worldwide. Yet, during the same period, a new McDonald's was opening in France every six days. McDonald's French subsidiary is booming, thanks to leaders who responded to local and national differences rather than trying to transfer the American fast-food concept wholesale. Denis Hennequin, the French CEO, followed a clever strategy for giving McDonald's France its own identity and boosting the chain's attractiveness to customers. Restaurants are adapted to fit the local architecture and the menu includes espresso, brioche, and upscale sandwiches. The average customer spends $9 per visit, compared to an average $4 per visit in the United States.

Q: *How has McDonald's responded to local needs and cultural values?*

A: The French are mistrustful of genetically altered produce and meat, so Denis Hennequin, in a series of humorous ads, addressed these cultural issues and assured the French that McDonald's would give local customers what they liked---local produce and meat. The golden arches are replaced with hardwood floors, beam ceilings, comfortable arm chairs, and music videos. Localizing McDonald's to fit French tastes has made sales soar.

However, blending cultures isn't always easy because cultural differences can create significant barriers to successful communication and collaboration.

Leadership Implications

A study of executives in five countries found that executives differ significantly in their attitudes and managerial values and that this can create leadership problems.

Leaders should be aware of cultural differences in order to lead effectively in a diverse environment.

Culture affects both leadership style and the leadership situation.

How behavior is perceived differs from culture to culture; leaders need to consider cultural values in their dealings with employees.

All leaders need to be aware of the impact that culture may have and consider cultural values in their dealings with employees.

Notes____

To reduce the difficulties faced by minorities in organizations

---

Challenges Minorities Face *Exhibit 11.4*

Valuing diversity and enabling all individuals to develop their talents is difficult to achieve.

Ethnocentrism is the belief that one's own culture and subculture are inherently superior to other groups and cultures.

Many leaders relate to people in the organization as if everyone shares similar values, beliefs, motivations, and attitudes about work and life.

This assumption is false even when dealing with people who share the same cultural background.

Ethnocentric viewpoints combined with a standard set of cultural assumptions and practices create challenges for minority employees and leaders.

Unequal Expectations/Difference as Deficiency

The one-best approach leads to a mind-set that views difference as deficiency or dysfunction.

The perception of most women and minorities is that no matter how many college degrees they earn, how many hours they work, how they dress, or how much effort and enthusiasm they invest, they are never considered as "having the right stuff."

Many men feel uncomfortable with the prevailing attitudes but do not know how to change them.

These attitudes are deeply rooted in our society as well as in our organizations.

Racism and sexism in the workplace often show up in subtle ways--- the disregard by a subordinate for an assigned chore, the ignoring of comments made in a meeting.

Women and minorities generally feel that they are not judged by the same standards as their male counterparts.

Exhibit 11.4 shows the discrepancy between high-achieving men and women in terms of the time they devote to domestic duties.

Living Biculturally

Biculturalism can be defined as the sociocultural skills and attitudes used by racial minorities as they move back and forth between the dominant culture and their own ethnic and racial culture.

Research on differences between whites and blacks focused on issues of biculturalism and how it affects employee's access to information, level of respect and appreciation, and relation to superiors and subordinates.

Minority groups struggle to adopt behaviors and attitudes that will help them succeed in the white-dominated corporate world while maintaining ties to their racial or ethnic community.

***In the Lead*:** J.D. Hokoyama, Leadership Education for Asian Pacifics, Inc.

Asian Americans who aspire to leadership positions are often frustrated by the stereotype that they are hard workers but not executive material. Many times Asian Americans are perceived as too quiet or not assertive enough. Once Chinese American woman says her boss claimed she was not strong enough for an executive-level job because she did not raise her voice in discussions as he did. J.D. Hokoyama started a nonprofit organization to try to change these perceptions. Participants in workshops are taught to use eye contact, start more sentences with "I," and use more assertive body language.

Q: *How are Asian Americans taught to use biculturalism?*

A: Biculturalism is the set of sociocultural skills and attitudes used by racial minorities as they move back and forth between the dominant culture and their own culture. Asian Americans who aspire to leadership positions are viewed as hard workers but not executive material. By understanding the difference between Asian and American values, Asians can more into leadership positions.

Culturally sensitive leadership can help to remove these barriers.

Notes____

The Glass Ceiling

The *glass ceiling* is an invisible barrier that separates women and minorities from top leadership positions.

Prevailing attitudes are invisible obstacles to advancement.

Evidence is that the glass ceiling still exists.

Only 7.3 percent of managers in line positions and 12.5 percent of corporate officers in *Fortune* 500 companies are female.

About 65 percent of women of color plan to leave their management positions because of subtle bias in the workplace.

Women and minorities earn considerably less than their male peers , with women of color earning the least.

As women move up the career ladder, the wage gap widens; the gap between male and female managers grew between the years 1995 and 2000.

The glass ceiling persists because top-level corporate culture in most organizations still revolves around traditional management thinking, a vertical hierarchy populated by white males.

Women are more likely to be promoted if they demonstrate traits associated with masculinity, such as assertiveness, achievement-orientation, and focus on material success.

In general, women and minorities feel that they must work harder and perform at higher levels than white males in order to be noticed, recognized, fully accepted, and promoted.

Discussion Question #5: *What is the glass ceiling and why does it persist in organizations?*

Notes____

____

____

The Opportunity Gap

People may fail to advance to high levels in the organization because they do not have the necessary education and skills.

A final challenge is the lack of opportunities for many minorities to obtain the same level of education as white, American-born individuals.

There is not yet a level playing field in schools and society, which is in turn reflected in unequal opportunities for diverse employees.

Some companies are taking the lead to ensure that minorities get the education, skills, and opportunities they need to participate fully in today's economy.

In the Lead: Ernst & Young LLP

Ernst & Young has long had a sterling reputation in the field of accounting and consulting services, but the firm is striving to become a leader in diversity as well. Leaders launched two diversity initiatives aimed at increasing the recruitment and retention of women and minorities and have invested significant resources in training and mentoring programs. These programs have had a positive impact with the number of minorities recruited each year rising from around 10 percent to around 24 percent.

Q: *Why did E&Y adopt diversity initiatives?*

A: These initiatives give young minority individuals opportunities for career advancement that they might not otherwise have—and they give E & Y access to high-quality minority employees.

Notes____

To break down your personal barriers that may stand in the way of enhancing your level of diversity awareness and appreciation.

Leadership Initiatives toward Organizational Diversity *Exhibit 11.5*

Strong culturally-sensitive leadership can move organizations toward diversity, whereby people are valued for the abilities they bring to the workplace.

Organizational Stages of Diversity Awareness.

➢ *How do organizations as well as individuals vary in their sensitivity and openness to other cultures, attitudes, values, and ways of doing things?*

There are five stages of diversity awareness and action.

The continuum ranges from meeting the minimum legal requirements regarding affirmative action and sexual harassment to valuing diversity as an inherent part of the firm's culture.

- *Stage1*: Leaders meet legal requirements but view women and minorities as a problem.
- *Stage 2*: Leaders recognize the barriers minorities face and that there is high absenteeism and turnover. Awareness is not translated into action.
- *Stage 3*: Leaders become proactive, recruiting and retaining minorities and women to be

competitive.

- *Stage 4*: Top-level leadership commits to valuing diversity as the right thing to do morally.

- *Stage5*: Organizations are gender- and color-blind, judging employees on competence, and erasing stereotypes.

Discussion Question #8: *Recall a company you worked for. At what stage of diversity awareness (Exhibit 11.5) was it? Explain.*

Notes____

____

____

Barriers to Evolution

Leaders face barriers to achieving a high level of diversity awareness, acceptance, and appreciation.

- *Ethnocentrism* Viewing one's culture as the best makes it difficult to value diversity because it tends to produce a monoculture that accepts one way of doing things.

  The goal is to develop *ethnorelativism,* the belief that all groups, cultures, and subcultures are inherently equal.

- *Stereotypes and prejudice* Carried to an extreme, ethnocentrism becomes outright prejudice, the single biggest obstacle to equal opportunity.

  Prejudice is the assumption, without evidence, that minorities are inherently inferior, less competent at their jobs, and less suitable for leadership positions.

- *The "White Male" Club* The work environment for many minorities is lonely, unfriendly, and stressful which is partly attributed to the white male club---exclusion from functions, luncheons, and even regular office banter.

  Minorities feel that they have no one to talk to about their fears, mistakes, and even their ideas for the organization.

- *The Paradox of Diversity* Leaders face the paradox of promoting diversity while maintaining a strong, unified culture.

  People feel more comfortable dealing with others like themselves.

  Some ethnic groups do not interact socially and can be competitive and antagonistic.

  Leaders have to work hard to unite employees, yet allow for individual differences.

- *Actual Cultural differences* Real cultural differences can cause problems in the workplace.

  Most organizations will not accept routine tardiness or absenteeism because their time orientation is culturally different.

  The potential for communication difficulties is much greater in heterogeneous groups, leading to misunderstandings, conflict, and anxiety for leaders as well as employees.

Discussion Question #6: *What is the paradox of diversity and how could it be a barrier to valuing and supporting diversity within organizations?*

Notes____

____

____

Leadership Solutions

The pressure is on the organization to change, and strong leadership is needed.

Without strong leadership, increased cultural diversity can lead to decreased work effort and lower organizational performance.

Personal Qualities for Leading Diverse Organizations

Leaders must develop personal characteristics that support diversity. Leaders should express vision through symbols and rituals that reinforce the value of a diverse workforce:

- A personal, long-range vision that recognizes and supports a diverse organizational community.

- A broad knowledge of the dimensions of diversity and awareness of multicultural issues.

- An openness to change themselves.

- Mentoring and empowerment of diverse employees.

Changing corporate culture

Corporate culture implies creating and communicating a shared vision and values for the organization.

This becomes more critical in an organization made up of diverse individuals with differing beliefs, ideas, and ways of thinking and behaving.

Leaders can begin by actively using symbols for new values, such as encouraging and celebrating the promotion of minorities.

Today's organizational cultures for the most part reflect the white male model of doing business.

When the organizational environment reflects one limited perspective, diverse employees are not going to feel comfortable, not matter how much leaders tout diversity initiatives.

Leaders should develop a culture that supports inclusion and full participation of all individuals, regardless of race, gender, age, cultural or ethnic group, physical ability, or other characteristics.

Leaders have to examine everything from formal policies and practices, to informal patterns of social interaction, to the basic mind-sets of managers throughout the organization.

The most important element in changing the corporate culture to one that values diversity is leadership.

Diversity Awareness Training *Exhibit 11.6*

Leaders understand that their competitiveness may depend on how well they handle diversity issues.

Diversity awareness training helps employees become aware of their own cultural boundaries, their prejudices and stereotypes, so they can work together successfully.

The model shows the five stages of individual diversity awareness which are roughly comparable to the organizational stages shown in Exhibit 11.5.

The continuum ranges from a defensive, ethnocentric attitude to a complete understanding and acceptance of people's attitudes.

- Defense---negative stereotyping, ethnocentric attitude
- Minimizing differences----hides or trivializes cultural differences
- Acceptance---accepts behavioral differences
- Adaptation---empathy with those of other cultures
- Integration----multicultural attitude

The model can help leaders assess their own and employees' openness to change.

People at different levels may require different kinds of training.

A primary aim of diversity awareness training is to help people recognize that their own hidden and overt biases direct their thinking about specific individuals and groups.

One important aspect of diversity training is to bring together people of differing perspectives so that they can engage in learning new interpersonal communication skills.

In the Lead: Denny's Restaurants (Advantica)

Advantica, the parent of Denny's Restaurants, recently closed down its minority mentoring program. Diversity has become such an integral, everyday part of the way the company does business that the special program is no longer needed. However, leaders remain firmly committed to fostering an inclusive environment where everyone feels respected and valued. Things have changed since the early 1990s when Denny's became the icon for racism in the U.S. when six black Secret Service officers accused servers and managers at an Annapolis restaurant of humiliating and discriminating against them while their white colleagues were welcomed.

Q: *How did Denny's change its culture to value diversity?*

A: Advantica spends several million dollars a year on compliance and training, and its diversity training system is one of the most comprehensive in the industry. Results of the training have been so strong that the company was released from the oversight of the Office of Civil Rights Monitor.

Discussion Question #7: *In preparing organizations to accept and value diversity, do you think leaders should focus primarily on changing the underlying culture or on diversity awareness training? Discuss.*

Notes____

DISCUSSION QUESTIONS

1. *How might a leader's role and responsibility change as a company becomes more diverse?*

Successful leaders in an increasingly diverse world have a responsibility to acknowledge and value cultural differences and understand how diversity affects organizational operations and outcomes. Strong culturally-sensitive leadership can move organizations toward diversity, whereby people are valued for the abilities they bring to the workplace. Leaders should develop a culture that supports inclusion and full participation of all individuals, regardless of race, gender, age, cultural or ethnic group, physical ability, or other characteristics.

2. *How might diversity within the organization ultimately lead to better problem solving and greater creativity?*

Organizations use internal diversity to meet the needs of diverse customers. Many companies are developing targeted marketing initiatives aimed at fast-growing minority groups. Another need for diversity is to develop employee and organizational potential. Diversity within the organization provides a broader and deeper base of experience for problem solving, creativity, and innovation. Diversity of thought is essential to the learning organization.

3. *What is interactive leadership and why may this approach be increasingly important in the twenty-first century?*

In interactive leadership, the leader favors a consensual and collaborative process, and influence derives from relationships rather than position power and authority. Women's interactive leadership seems appropriate for the future of diversity and learning organizations. Research indicates that women leaders are more participative and less autocratic, behaviors that fit the new reality of organizations today.

4. *Discuss ways in which low uncertainty avoidance as a social value among followers could affect their interaction with leaders who display high uncertainty avoidance.*

High uncertainty avoidance means that members feel uncomfortable with uncertainty and ambiguity and support beliefs and behavior that promise certainty and conformity (e.g., Precise meeting times and punctuality would be expected). Low uncertainty avoidance indicates tolerance for the unstructured and the unclear (e.g.,. Arriving late would be acceptable.) These conflicting values could present problems for leaders and followers working together.

5. *What is the glass ceiling and why does it persist in organizations?*

The glass ceiling is an invisible barrier that separates women and minorities from top leadership positions. Prevailing attitudes are invisible obstacles to advancement. Evidence is that the glass ceiling still exists. In technology, only 7 percent of top officers in *Fortune* 500 technology companies are female. About 65 percent of women of color plan to leave their management positions because of subtle bias in the workplace. Women and minorities feel that they must work harder and perform at higher levels that their white male counterparts in order to be noticed, recognized, fully accepted, and promoted.

6. *What is the paradox of diversity and how could it be a barrier to valuing and supporting diversity within organizations?*

Leaders face the paradox of promoting diversity and at the same time maintaining a strong, unified corporate culture. Homogenous organizations provide a firmer base is for building a strong culture, where is considered critical to success. People feel more comfortable and satisfied dealing with others like themselves. Culture influences attitudes towards such basic issues as tardiness or absenteeism. Leaders have to work hard to unite employees while allowing individual differences to flourish.

7. *In preparing organizations to accept and value diversity, do you think leaders should focus primarily on changing the underlying culture or on diversity awareness training? Discuss.*

Both. Changing the corporate culture implies creating and communicating a shared vision and values for the organization. This is critical in an organization made up of diverse individuals. Diversity awareness training helps employees become aware of their own cultural boundaries, their prejudices and stereotypes, so they can work together successfully.

8. *Recall a company you worked for. At what stage of diversity awareness (Exhibit 11) was it? Explain.*

I worked for a local bank in the marketing department. It was at Stage 2. There were few minorities and women in leadership positions, but the vast majority of women were not bank officers; they held the traditional jobs of teller, administrative assistant, and secretary. The executive dining room was only for bank officers. The lenders dealt in substantial oil and gas loans and were almost all white males.

TEACHING TOOLS AND EXERCISES

1. *Interview:* Assessing Cross-Cultural Differences

Interview three foreign students at your university. The registrar's office could put you in touch with the students. Ask the following questions: What country are your from and what is your first language? Describe your country's culture in terms of the role of women in the workforce, the benefits provided to employees, how managers treat their employees, and management practices. What problems did you encounter in adapting to this culture? What advice would you give a foreign manager in your home country?

2. *Out-of-class reading.*

Review six recent issues of a business periodical (such as *Business Week, Fortune, Forbes, Fast Company,* or *Wall Street Journal*) Find two articles on international business and evaluate them by asking: What types of cross-cultural differences might arise in these situations? How might managers deal with those cross-cultural differences?

3. *On the Web:* Diversity

Click on www.swlearning.com/management/ Click on internet exercises. Scroll down to Human Resources Management. Scroll down to diversity and click on Managing Diversity. Click on SHRM, The Society of Human Resource Management and review the Workplace Diversity Toolkit.

After reviewing the information, summarize your perceptions based on the information and your personal experiences; then assume the role of a senior company leader and develop a strategy for managing diversity in your organization.

4. *Leader's Self Development:* A Passive Bias Quiz

This quiz is helpful to assess personal bias. The appropriate score for today's world is "0." A score of 40 or more could get you into trouble. You should definitely consider ways to become more diversity aware and culturally sensitive. Students can answer the following questions:

1. Were you surprised by your score? Why?
2. How could this information help you on the job?
3. What steps could you take to become more diversity aware and culturally sensitive?

LEADERSHIP DEVELOPMENT: CASES FOR ANALYSIS

I. Synopsis: Northern Industries

Northern Industries asked you to help resolved some racial issues that according to president Jim Fisher, are "festering" in their manufacturing plant in Springfield, Massachusetts. Northern Industries is a family-owned enterprise that manufactures greeting cards, paper, and plastic holiday decorations. About 80 percent of the full-time workforce is female. A second shift of 50 part-time workers are women and minorities. Each of the minority groups---blacks and Asians-- sticks together. There has been a problem with theft and a Thai worker was fired. There is an angry debate between the shipping/receiving department and sales. The shipping manager who is African American argues that he needs more workers while the other managers remain silent and seem uncomfortable.

Case questions and answers

1. *What recommendations would you make to Northern's leaders to help them move toward successfully managing diversity issues?*

Changing corporate culture is important at Northern. This implies creating and communicating a shared vision and values for the organization. This is critical in an organization made up of diverse individuals with differing beliefs, ideas, and ways of thinking and behaving. Leaders can begin by actively using symbols for new values, such as encouraging and celebrating the promotion of minorities. Top leadership support is essential to changing t he corporate culture. Diversity awareness training would be very helpful.

2. *If you were the shipping and receiving or personnel manager, how do you think you would feel about your job? Discuss some of the challenges you might face at Northern.*

Most of the shipping department is black (eight out of ten are black males) and the department seems like a ghetto. The shipping manager is black but when he complains, the other managers remain silent and seem uncomfortable. The experience of most women and minorities is that no matter how many college degrees they earn, how many hours they work, how they dress, or how much effort and enthusiasm they invest, they are never perceived as "having the right stuff." Women and minorities generally feel that they are not judged by the same standards as their male counterparts.

3. *Refer to Exhibit 11.5. Based on the information in the case, at what stage of personal diversity awareness do leaders at Northern seem to be? Discuss.*

The leaders are barely into stage two. There are blacks and women in managerial positions and legal requirements are met. However, cultural differences and conflicts among ethnic groups are minimized. A joke about the leader's wife is made instead of resolving an argument. The managers remain silent because they are afraid to speak up. Communication is poor.

II. **Synopsis:** **The Trouble with Bangles**

Leela Patel was standing by her machine as she had fore eight hours of each working day for the past six years. Leela was happy; she had many friends amongst the 400 or so women at the food processing plant. Most of them were of Indian origin like herself, although Asian women formed less than a fifth of the female workforce. Leela was a member of a five-girl team that reported to supervisor Bill Evans. Evans explained that a girl caught a bangle in the machine and cut her wrist and the Safety Committee decided that no one will be allowed to wear jewelry other than wedding rings, wristwatches, and pierced earrings. Leela was wearing three bangles. All married Asian women wore bangles. Leela explained that as a Hindu wife, the bangles were important to her religion. Evans was angry, so Leela removed the bangles and replaced it when he left. Within a few days, all the Asian women were wearing their bangles again.

Case questions and answers

1. *What is your reaction to this story? Why do you think you had this reaction?*

My reaction is that Evans did not have the correct training in the culture, religion, and traditions of Asian workers to handle the situation. He was genuinely unaware and as a result, he imposed his ethnocentric point of view: wearing bangles is just like wearing any other kind of jewelry. I had this reaction because it is easy to see a symbol (bangles) without knowing its significance. This is especially true if the symbol does not exist in American culture. Evans did not suggest removing the wedding ring because he understands this powerful symbol as one in his own culture.

2. *Based on this limited information, how would you rate this organization in terms of developing leadership diversity?*

The organization is between Stage1 and Stage 2. There is a grievance system in place whereby workers can voice their opinions, and there is a regional race relations employment advisor. The advisor did confirm that the ban on bangles did not violate any religious observance, so technically the organization was within both the secular and religious law. The company was trying to keep the employees safe and keep the plant clean.

3. *If you were a top manager at this company, what would you do?*

It is not an option to disregard the custom. There must be a communication campaign to try to explain the safety and hygiene issues. Creative solutions should be sought and the Asian women at the plant should be encouraged to help solve the problem. Could the bangles be covered with a cap or smock? Unmarried Asian women, widows, or men could be hired. The married women could be retrained and relocated to jobs that did not require machinery. Of course, their salaries must not be cut. Since the Asian women make up only 20 percent of the workforce, they may have to be replaced by workers with different customs, unless the plant owner is so committed to diversity that newer, safer machinery is installed. That long-term solution would send a very powerful message to the entire workforce.

CHAPTER TWELVE
LEADERSHIP, POWER, AND INFLUENCE

CHAPTER SUMMARY

Leaders use various frames of reference to view the organization and its needs. Frames of reference determine how people gather information, make decisions, and exercise power. There are four frames of reference leaders may use: structural, human resource, political, and symbolic. Most leaders rely heavily on one or the other, but they can learn to use multiple frames of reference to expand their influence and better meet the needs of the organization.

This chapter focuses largely on the political frame of reference. Power and politics are an important, though often hidden, part of all organizations. Power is the ability to influence others to reach desired outcomes. The best-known sources of power are legitimate, reward, expert, referent, and coercive, which are associated with a leader's position and personal qualities. Three distinct outcomes may result from the use of power to influence others: compliance, resistance, and commitment. The effective use of position power generally leads to follower compliance, whereas the excessive use of position power—particularly coercive power—may result in resistance. The follower response most often generated by personal power is commitment.

A key aspect of power is that it is a function of dependency, which is related to a person's control over resources. Dependency is greatest for resources that are highly important, scarce, and have no readily available substitutes. Leaders may gain power by contributing to the organization's purpose via interdepartmental dependencies, centrality, control over information, and coping with uncertainty.

Power is acquired, developed, and exercised through political activities. Political tactics for asserting influence include using rational persuasion, appealing to ideals, values and emotions, using symbolic action, building coalitions, expanding networks, and using assertiveness. Leadership action depends on forming effective social relationships and achieving the desired future through agreements and cooperation in today's complex world. One important consideration for leaders is how to use power and politics ethically and responsibly. Ethical leaders use power to serve the organization's goals, respect the rights of individuals and groups, and strive to be fair in their dealings with others.

CHAPTER OPENER

Six Sigma Initiative

As tired as he was after a long day of meetings, Jim Goetz headed to the lobby of the hotel to do some politicking about ServiceMaster's Six Sigma project to improve customer service. Sigma Six required gathering information on what customers wanted and compiling statistics on service representatives' performance in the field. Geotz created a database along with Web-enabled reporting tools, but some of the branch employees and managers were resistant to using the new system. Goetz saw the opportunity to build a coalition of people to support the use of the Internet as a way to deliver improvements. He knew that for the IT project to be successful, he needed to understand his colleagues' needs and goals as well as his own. Thanks to his informal talks, he knew which people were his alies.

LECTURE/OUTLINE

To recognize your natural leadership frame of reference and how you can expand your perspective.

Leadership Frames of Reference

Exhibit 12.1

A *frame* is a perspective from which a leader views the world.

The concept of frames calls attention to the way people gather information, make decisions, and exercise power.

There are four frames of reference --- structural, human, political, and symbolic.

These frames of reference determine how situations are defined and what actions are taken.

Leaders often begin with a limited structural perspective and develop the other frames based on their own personal development of experiences.

Each frame has strengths and weaknesses, and effective leaders strive for a balanced perspective so that all the needs of the organization are met.

By becoming aware of all four frames, the importance of each, and how using multiple frames, leaders can better understand organizational needs and problems.

Notes____

____

____

The Structural Frame

The organization as a machine is the dominant image in the structural frame; leaders strive for machine-like efficiency and make decisions based on economic efficiency.

Plans and goals are the primary tools of management, and leaders rely heavily on power and authority granted through their position to influence others.

A *structural frame* places emphasis on goal setting and clarifying job expectations as a way to provide order, efficiency, and continuity.

Leaders emphasize job descriptions, hard data, specific polices, accepted standards, and the bottom line.

Acceptance to rules brings order and logic to organizations.

Task-oriented leadership styles, some of the contingency approaches, and transactional leadership rely on this frame.

Carried to an extreme, the structural frame leads to rigidity and even tyranny among leaders.

Notes____

____

____

The Human Resource Frame

According to the *human resource frame*, people are the organization's most valuable resource.

This frame defines problems and issues in interpersonal terms and adjusts the organization to meet human needs.

Leaders focus on relationships and feelings, lead through empowerment and support and encourage open communication.

Effective leaders use the human resource perspective to involve others and give them opportunities for personal and professional development.

They value people, are visible and accessible, and serve others.

This frame can be ineffective if the leader bends to the whims of others, using caring and participation to avoid leadership responsibility.

Notes____

____

____

The Political Frame

The *political frame* of reference views organizations as arenas of ongoing conflict or tension over the allocation of scarce resources.

Leaders spend their time networking and building alliances and coalitions to influence decisions.

These leaders strive to build a power base and frequently exercise both personal and organizational power to achieve their desired results.

Carried to an extreme, this frame can lead to deception, dishonesty, and power plays for the purpose of self-interest.

Yet, effective political leaders use their negotiating, bargaining, and coalition-building skills to serve organizational needs.

Power and politics are an important, although often hidden, part of all organizations.

Power is a reality, and political schemes are a natural part of organizational life.

Notes____

____

____

The Symbolic Frame

To use full leadership potential requires that leaders also develop the ***symbolic frame*****,** in which leaders perceive the organization as a system of shared meaning and values.

The symbolic leader focuses on shared vision, culture, and values to influence others and lead the organization.

Charismatic and transformational leadership rely on this frame.

Leaders use rituals, ceremonies, stories, and symbols to create and reinforce a corporate culture.

Symbolic leaders inspire people to higher levels of performance and commitment; however, this frame can lead to the "messiah" complex by relying too heavily on symbols.

Symbols can be used for dishonest, unethical, and self-serving purposes.

Symbolic leaders are effective when they articulate a vision that is widely shared and understood, and when they support the deepest concerns and values of followers.

Discussion Question #2: *Discuss why symbolic leadership needs to be balanced by other* *leadership perspectives in order to meet organizational needs.*

Notes____

Each frame provides possibilities for enhancing leadership effectiveness, but each is incomplete.

Leaders can learn to integrate multiple frames to use their leadership potential fully.

Effective leaders "understand their own strengths, work to expand them, and build teams that can provide leadership in all four modes.

Discussion Question #1: *Which organizational frame of reference do you most identify with? How do you think this frame of reference could be beneficial or detrimental to your leadership capability?*

Notes____

To use power and politics to help accomplish important organizational goals.

Power, Influence, and Leadership *Exhibit 12.2*

Power is an intangible force in an organization. It cannot be seen, but its effect can be felt.

Power is the ability of one person or department in an organization to influence other people to bring about desired outcomes.

Potential power is realized through politics and influence.

Influence is the effect a person's actions have on the attitudes, values, beliefs, or actions of others.

Whereas power is the capacity to cause a change in a person, influence is the degree of actual change.

Leaders can improve their effectiveness by understanding the various types and sources of power as well as the influence tactics they or their followers may use.

To identify sources of power in organizations and know how to increase power through political activity.

Five Types of Leader Power

Power is often described as a personal characteristic.

Five types of power are available to leaders. The first three—legitimate, reward, and coercive power--- are types of *position power,* defined by the organization's policies and procedures.

A person's position determines the power to reward, punish, or influence subordinates.

Two sources of *personal power,* expert and referent power, are based in the leader's special knowledge or personal characteristics.

Legitimate power

Legitimate power is the authority granted from a formal position in an organization.

Certain rights, responsibilities, and prerogatives accrue to anyone holding a formal leadership position.

Followers accept the legitimate rights of formal leaders to set goals, make decisions, and direct activities.

Reward power

Reward power stems from the authority to bestow rewards on other people.

Leaders control resources and their distributions.

Leaders can use reward power to influence subordinates' behavior.

Coercive power

Coercive power is the authority to punish or recommend punishment.

Supervisors have the right to fire or demote subordinates, criticize, or withdraw pay increases.

Coercive power I the negative side of legitimate and reward power.

Expert power

Expert power results from a leader's special knowledge or skill regarding tasks performed by followers.

When a leader is a true expert, subordinates go along with recommendations because of his superior knowledge.

Leaders at supervisory levels often earn promotions because of their technical experience; at top management levels, leaders may lack expert power because subordinates know more about technical details.

Referent power

Referent power is authority based on personality characteristics that command followers' attention, respect, and admiration so that they want to emulate the leader.

Referent power depends on the leader's personal characteristics rather than on a formal title or position and is visible in the area of charismatic leadership.

- *Living Leadership: The Ripple Effect*

Do you want to be a positive influence in the world? First, get you own life in order.

- How does your behavior influence others through a ripple effect? Give examples.

In the Lead: Lorraine Monroe, Frederick Douglass Academy

When Lorraine Monroe became principal of Harlem's Frederick Douglass School, the school was known for excessive violence, poor attendance, and low achievement. Only five years later, test scores at the school ranked among the best in New York City, and 96 percent of graduates went on to college. Monroe relied on referent power more than on position power for influencing followers. Her personal energy, fears and longings inspired both teachers and students to imagine greater possibilities for themselves and believe they could achieve them.

Q: *How does Lorraine Monroe use referent power?*

A: Lorraine demands the best from people and helps them achieve it. She has lived her own life by her "Twelve Non-Negotiable Rules and Regulations," rules based on respect for oneself, for one's associates, and for the school, and others soon followed her example.

Notes____

Responses to the Use of Power *Exhibit 12.3*

Leaders use the various types of power to influence others to do what is necessary to accomplish organizational goals.

There are three outcomes from the use of power: compliance, resistance, and commitment.

When people successfully use position power, the response is compliance.

Compliance means people follow the directions of the person with power, whether or not they agree with those directions.

The problem is that followers do just enough to satisfy the leader and may not contribute their full potential.

If the use of position power especially coercion exceeds a level people considerate, people may resist the attempt to influence.

Resistance means that employees will deliberately try to avoid carrying out instructions or they will attempt to disobey orders.

The effectiveness of leaders who rely solely on position power is limited.

The follower response most often generated by personal power is commitment.

Commitment means that followers adopt the leader's viewpoint and enthusiastically carry out instructions.

Commitment is preferred to compliance or resistance. Commitment is especially important when the leader is promoting change.

The Role of Dependency *Exhibit 12.4*

➢ *Give an example from your own experience of a person who has control over you because he or she has something you want.*

One of the key aspects of power is that it is a function of dependence----the greater individual B's dependence on individual A, the greater the power A has over B.

People in organizations, as elsewhere, have power because other people depend on them for information, resources, and cooperation.

The more people depend on an individual, the greater the person's power becomes.

When good jobs are plentiful, people feel less dependent on their supervisors; when good jobs are scarce, organizational leaders have greater power over their employees.

Dependency in organizations is related primarily to a person's control over resources.

Dependency is greatest for resources high on three characteristics---importance, scarcity, and nonsubstitutability.

The resource must be perceived as *important* or it does not create dependency.

Scarcity refers to whether the resource is difficult to obtain; the more difficult or expensive the resource, the more dependency created.

Nonsubstitutability means that leaders or employees with control over resources with no viable substitute have more power.

Discussion Question #5: *Do you think supervisors in discount stores such as Wal-Mart and Kmart gave greater or less power over subordinates than they had ten years ago? Discuss the reasons for your answer.*

Notes____

Sources of Leader Power in Organizations *Exhibit 12.5*

The strategic contingencies theory identifies power sources not linked to the specific person or formal position, but to the role the leader plays in the overall functioning of the organization.

Sources of power include: interdepartmental dependency, control over information, centrality, and coping with uncertainty.

Interdepartmental Dependency

Interdepartmental dependency is a key source of leader power.

Materials, resources, and information may flow between departments in one direction.

Leaders receiving resources have less power than those in the department that provides them

Control over Information

Control over information involves access to information and control over how and to whom it is distributed.

It is an important source of power for leaders.

Access to information is somewhat controlled by position---top leaders have more access than lower-level supervisors.

Lower-level employees can gain power by having information needed by leaders to make decisions.

Some leaders actively seek to increase their power by gaining control over information.

Discussion Question #6: *Explain how control over information gives power to a person. Have you ever used control over information to influence a decision with friends or co-workers? Explain.*

Notes____

____

____

Organized Centrality

Centrality reflects a leader's or a department's role in the primary activity of an organization.

One measure of centrality is the extent to which the work of the leader's department affects the final output of the organization.

Centrality is associated with more power because it reflects the contribution made to the organization.

Coping with Uncertainty

The environment can change swiftly and create both uncertainty and complexity for leaders.

In the face of uncertainty, little information is available to leaders on appropriate courses of action.

Leaders in departments that cope well with uncertainty will increase their power.

In the Lead: PepsiCo

It has been more than a decade, but PepsiCo's handling of a crisis that occurred when a couple claimed to have found a hypodermic syringe in an unopened can of Pepsi is a classic for how to handle a crisis. The couple's lawyer contacted the county health department, the bottler and distributor, and the media. Within days, the story was splashed across every front page in the country, and copycats emerged by the dozens.
PR leaders worked with top executives to respond quickly to consumer fears with a massive public relations and education campaign. Company leaders took to the airwaves to express deep concern, recalled their product, and aggressively inspected their bottling plants—despite the certainty the there was nothing wrong. Before long, the supposed victims confessed that it was a hoax.

Q: *How did the leaders at PepsiCo effectively cope with uncertainty?*

A: They didn't hide in their offices. Leaders in the public relations department at PepsiCo took action to help the company cope with a critical uncertainty after it appeared, giving them and their department increased power. Pepsi's market standing was temporarily damaged, but its reputation as an ethical company was still intact.

Discussion Question #4: *What types and sources of power would be available to a leader of a student government organization? To a head nurse in a small hospital?*

Notes____
____
____

Increasing Power through Political Activity

➢ *Why do people who want to increase their power make sure their activities are visible and appreciated by others?*

Acquiring and using power is largely a political process.

Politics involves activities to acquire, develop, and use power and other resources to obtain desired future outcomes when there is uncertainty or disagreement about choices.

Individuals and departments within organizations also engage in political activity; political behavior can either be a positive or negative force.

Uncertainty and conflict are natural in organizations, and politics is the mechanism for accomplishing what cannot be handled through formal policies or position power.

Leaders use politics to increase their personal power.

They find ways to be helpful to others, seek out greater responsibility through committee or volunteer work, and cultivate subordinates' feelings of friendship and loyalty.

Another political approach is called *impression management,* in which leaders seek to control how others perceive them.

They create an impression of greater power; impression management includes tactics such as subtle name-dropping and flattery.

Discussion Question #3: *Do you agree that politics is a natural and healthy part of organizational life? Discuss.*

Notes____

To use the influence tactics of rational persuasion, emotional appeal, symbolic action, building coalitions, expanding networks, and being assertive.

Tactics for Asserting Leader Influence *Exhibit 12.6*

Leaders use power to influence others, which requires both skill and willingness.

Much influence is interpersonal and one-on-one; this is social influence, which involves coalitions, rewards, and inspiration.

Within organizations, leaders use a variety of influence strategies and people who are perceived as having greater power and influence use a wider variety of tactics.

One survey identified more than 4,000 different techniques by which people were able to influence others to do what they wanted.

Exhibit 12.6 lists seven principles for asserting leader influence; most involve the use of personal power or the use of rewards and punishments.

- *Use rational persuasion* This frequently used influence tactic uses facts, data, and logical arguments to persuade others that a proposed idea or request is the best way to complete a task or accomplish a desired goal.

- *Make people like you.* People would rather say yes to someone they like than to someone they don't like.

When a leader shows concern for others, demonstrates trust and respect, and treats people fairly, people are more likely to want to help and support the leader.

- *Rely on the rule of reciprocity.* Leaders gain power by having something that others value.

  A primary way to turn that power into influence is to share what you have---whether it be time, resources, services, or emotional support.

  Leaders who do favors for others can expect favors in return.

- *Develop allies* Reciprocity also plays an important role in developing networks of allies, people who can help the leader accomplish goals.

  A leader's network of contacts can be expanded by reaching out to establish contact with additional people.

  Some leaders expand their alliances through the hiring, transfer, and promotion process.

In the lead: Philip Purcell, Morgan Stanley Dean Witter

During negotiations for the merger of Morgan Stanley and Dean Witter, Philip Purcell argued that since his firm—Dean Witter—was technically the acquirer of the deal, it was only right that the first CEO come from Dean Witter. Morgan's John Mack, agreed to the terms, saying the merger was too important to make an issue over the top job. When the dust settled at Morgan Stanley Dean Witter, Phillip Purcell had gained complete control of the firm, with all core operations reporting directly to him. Mack was gone.

Q: *How did Purcell use the principles for asserting leadership influence?*

A: By surrounding himself with trusted allies within the firm and on the board, Purcell gained the influence he needed to push his rival for the top job out of the firm.

- *Ask for what you want.* Another way to have influence is to make a direct appeal by being clear about what you want and asking for it.

  Political activity is effective only when the leader's vision, goals, and desired changes are made explicit so the organization can respond.

- *Remember the principle of scarcity.* This principle means that people usually want more of what they can't have.

When things are available, they become more desirable.

Leaders can learn to frame their requests or offers in such a way as to highlight the unique benefits and exclusive information being provided.

- *Extend formal authority with expertise and credibility.* The final principle for asserting authority is the leader's legitimate authority in the organization.

  Research has found that the key to successful use of formal authority is to be knowledgeable, credible, and trustworthy.

  Effective leaders keep the six previous influence principles in mind, realizing that influence depends primarily on personal rather than position power.

Discussion Question #7: *Describe the ways in which you might increase your personal power.*

Notes____

____

____

Ethical Considerations in Using Power and Politics *Exhibit 12.7*

Leadership can be an opportunity to use power to accomplish organizational goals, but power can also be abused.

Personalized, as opposed to socialized, leaders are typically selfish, impulsive, and exercise power for their own self-centered needs and interests rather than for the good of the organization.

Socialized leaders exercise power in the service of higher goals that will benefit others and the organization as a whole.

The unethical use of power has been an increasing concern in the area of sexual harassment.

When access to resources depends on granting sexual favors or tolerating sexually intimidating or threatening comments, the person in a dependent position is being personally violated, where or not the leader actually withholds the resources.

Many organizations are developing policies and procedures that protect individuals from sexual harassment on the job and offer mechanisms for reporting complaints.

Sexual harassment is not only unethical, but also illegal and a clear abuse of power.

Leaders may have difficulty differentiating ethical from unethical uses of power and influence.

First is the question of whether the action is motivated by self-interest or whether it is consistent with the organization's goals.

Once this primary question is answered, there are other questions that can help determine whether a potential influence action is ethical, including whether it meets the standard of fairness.

Would the leader want others to behave in the same way?

These questions can serve as a guide to whether an intended act is ethical.

The most important point is for leaders to be aware of the ethical responsibilities of possessing power and take care to use their power to help rather than harm others.

Leaders should not think of getting their own way, but rather, in terms of building long-term productive relationships that can achieve goals and benefit the entire organization.

Notes____

DISCUSSION QUESTIONS

1. *Which organizational frame of reference do you most identify with? How do you think this frame of reference could be beneficial or detrimental to your leadership capability?*

I identify with the symbolic frame, in which leaders perceive the organization as a system of shared meaning and values. The symbolic leader focuses on shared vision, culture, and values to influence others and lead the organization. Charismatic and transformational leadership rely heavily on this frame. The communication chapter discussed how leaders use rituals, ceremonies, stories, and symbols to create and reinforce a corporate culture.

This frame is beneficial to my leadership capability because it involves followers in the organizational vision around which every action revolves. This frame inspires teamwork and a common work ethic.

2. *Discuss why symbolic leadership needs to be balanced by other leadership perspectives in order to meet organizational needs.*

One danger of relying too heavily on the symbolic frame is that leaders develop a "messiah" complex. The focus shifts to the leader rather than the organization and its members. Symbols can be used for dishonest, unethical, self-serving purposes. Each frame is incomplete and should be integrated with the other three so that leaders can develop their full leadership potential. Effective leaders "understand their own strengths, work to expand them, and build teams that together can provide leadership in all four modes.

3. *Do you agree that politics is a natural and healthy part of organizational life? Discuss.*

Yes, The political frame of reference views organizations as arenas of ongoing conflict or tension over the allocation of scarce resources. Leaders spend their time networking and building alliances and coalitions to influence decisions. These leaders strive to build a power base and they frequently exercise both personal and organizational power to achieve their desired results.

4. *What types and sources of power would be available to a leader of a student government organization? To a head nurse in a small hospital?*

Both a student leader and a head nurse have legitimate power, the authority granted from a formal position in an organization. Certain rights, responsibilities, and prerogatives accrue to anyone holding a formal leadership position. A head nurse also has expert power because of nursing training and experience.

As a source of power, the student government leader has control of information because the faculty transmits information to the student body through the student government leader. The leader decides what and when to communicate information to other students. The head nurse has organized centrality as a source of power. Centrality reflects a leader's or a department's role in the primary activity of an organization. Centrality reflects the contribution made to the organization. A head nurse is in charge of all the nurses in a department without whom hospital activities cannot be carried out---e.g., a head nurse in an intensive care unit.

5. *Do you think supervisors in discount stores such as Wal-Mart and Target have greater or less power over subordinates than they had ten years ago? Discuss the reasons for your answer.*

Leaders have less power over subordinates today because of empowerment and because the nature of dependency has changed. Employees are less willing to tolerate overbearing or incompetent bosses because they feel they can find a job somewhere else.
Leaders must gain and exercise personal power. People remain in a job if they admire and respect the leader

6. *How does control over information gives power to a person? Have you ever used control over information to influence a decision with friends or co-workers? Explain.*

Control over Information involves access to information and control over how and to whom it is distributed. It is an important source of power for leaders. Access to information is somewhat controlled by position---top leaders have more access than lower-level supervisors. Lower-level employees can gain power by having information needed by leaders to make decisions.

I am teaching an online course and will control the submission of homework and tests by lowering students' grades on assignments and tests if emailed after a given date.

7. *Describe the ways in which you might increase your personal power.*

There are six tactics which can be used to increase personal power:

- *Use Rational Persuasion* This tactic uses facts, data, and logical arguments to persuade others.

- *Make people like you* People say yes to someone they like.

- *Rely on the rule of reciprocity.* Leaders who do favors can expect favors in return.

- *Develop allies.* Reciprocity also plays an important role in developing allies.

- *Ask for what you want.* Make a direct appeal by being clear abut what you want and asking for it.

- *Remember the principle of scarcity.* People usually want more of something they can't have.

TEACHING TOOLS AND EXERCISES

1. *Ethical leadership:* Creating an Ethical Climate at Tyco

In the aftermath of what *Business Week* called "one of the most spectacular governance failures in history," the new management team at Tyco is creating an ethical climate. Their publication, a *Guide to Ethical Conduct,* has been translated in 14 languages for their employees. Describe the new ethical guidelines.

Source: Eric M. Pillmore, "How We're Fixing Up Tyco," *Harvard Business Review,* (December 2003): 96-103.

2. *Role Play:* In pairs or small groups, role play the following scenario using Exhibit 12.6., *Seven Principles for Asserting Leader Influence.*

You are a member of a committee that wishes to build a replica of a bridge designed by Leonardo DaVinci over 500 years ago. One such bridge has been built in Oslo, Norway, and the plan is to build similar bridges all over the world. None has been built in the United States. Your community, a small town in West Texas wants to be the first to build this bridge. It will bring tourists to the area and increase revenue for the town. The leader of the committee tries to influence the city council members, played by the other students, to go forth with the project. What elements of personal power can the leader use to make the case?

3. *On the Web:* Political Power

Explore The James MacGregor Burns Academy of Leadership at www.academy.umd.org What offerings does this academy have for political leaders who want to hone their leadership skills?

4. *Out-of-class reading:* Power

Students will read the classic work on power Machiavelli's *The Prince.*

5. *Leader's Self-Insight*: Personal Power Profile

After completing the power profile on p. 484, students will compare results in pairs or small groups. A high score (16 or more) on any of the five dimensions (reward, coercive, legitimate, referent, and expert) implies that you prefer to influence others by employing that particular form of power. A low score (8 and less) implies that you prefer not to employ this particular form of power to influence others.

Were you surprised by the results?
How can this profile help you in your career?

LEADERSHIP DEVELOPMENT: CASES FOR ANALYSIS

Synopsis: The Unhealthy Hospital

When Bruce Reid was hired as Blake Memorial Hospital's new CEO, the mandate had been clear: Improve the quality of care, and set the financial house in order. Reid considered the future of six off-site clinics. The clinics served the poorer neighborhoods but diverted funds away from in-house services. Cutting personnel and freezing salaries could affect Blake's quality of care, which was slipping. There would be political consequences. The commissioner of health services felt that the clinics were essential for the poor. The chief of surgery argued for closing the clinics and bussing patients to the hospital. The director of the clinics argued fro increased funding for the clinics and creating a network of neighborhood centers. Reid felt that whatever he decided would make enemies.

Case questions and answers

1. *What sources of power does Reid have in this situation? Do you believe using legitimate power to implement a decision would have a positive effect at Blake Memorial? Discuss.*

Reid had interdepartmental dependency as a source of power. Materials, resources, and information flow from Reid in one directions to the departments in one direction. He also has control over information, access to information and control over how and to which departments it is distributed. Legitimate power would be a poor way to implement a decision. Reid has the formal authority to close or not close the clinic, but he would disenfranchise many of the department heads and not receive support for his decision. Imposing his will might lead to the department heads leaving the hospital for other hospitals.

2. *What political tactics might you use to resolve this dilemma?*

Appeal to Ideals, Values, and Emotions Reid should attempt to gain enthusiasm and commitment for the clinics by arousing strong emotions about giving poor people good health care and linking his budget to the department heads' needs, hopes, ideals, and dreams---saving lives.

Use Symbolic Action The use of rituals, stories, symbols, and metaphors about other clinics in poor neighborhoods would enable Reid to tap into emotions and generate enthusiasm and commitment for the clinics. Reid could use physical symbols, slogans, and ceremonies to persuade. Symbolic leadership touches the heart rather than the mind.

Build Coalitions Coalition building means taking the time to talk to followers and other leaders to explain problems and describe their point of view. The most important tactic here is coalition building by consulting with the commissioner of health services, chief of surgery, and the director of the clinics.

3. How might Reid's predominant frame of reference influence his actions? Consider how he might act based on each of the four frames.

Reid's predominant frame of reference is the political frame, which views organizations as arenas of ongoing conflict or tension over the allocation of scarce resources. Reid realizes that all departments are in conflict over funding, and he knows he is going to make enemies as soon as he makes a decision. Using the political frame, Reid might decide who is most powerful and side with that group .

Reid could use the structural frame, places emphasis on goal setting and clarifying job expectations as a way to provide order, efficiency, and continuity. In this case, he would decide based on the best financial situation.(developing a network of clinics or transporting the poor to the hospital.)

Using the human resource frame, Reid would define problems and issues in interpersonal terms and adjusts the organization to meet human needs. He would consider the needs of the poor first and the financial issues second.

If Reid used the symbolic frame, he would promote the clinics based on the views that the hospital is a system of shared meaning and values—offering high quality health care to everyone, independent of the ability to pay.

2. **Synopsis:** Waite Pharmaceuticals

Amelia Lassiter is chief information officer at Waite Pharmaceuticals, a large California-based company. Lassiter suggested to president James Hsu that Waite implement a new global knowledge sharing application that promises to cut development time and costs in half. Hsu asked Lassister to identify three major firms who could handle the IT development for a presentation to the Board of Directors. At Hsu's office, Lassiter was greeted by the attractive, executive assistant Lucy Lee, a women whose lack of talent and experience made her a liability. Lee was deferential to Hsu and condescending to everyone else. Lassiter was asked to consider Standard Systems, a small consulting firm owned by Lee's uncle. Following evaluations, Lassiter selected three companies placing Standard last. Lassiter offered to present her findings to the Board, but Hsu refused . Following the board meeting, Lassiter was shocked to find out that the board selected Standard Systems as the consulting firm for the knowledge sharing application.

Case questions and answers

1. *How would you explain the Board's selection of Standard Systems?*

The Board deferred to Hsu's recommendation because as president, he has legitimate power, the authority granted from a formal position at Waite. Certain rights, responsibilities, and prerogatives accrue to anyone holding this formal leadership position. Hsu's source of power also comes from control over information, access to information and control over how and to whom it is distributed. Hsu had the ability to withhold Lassiter's rating of last place for Standard Systems. The Board has no way of knowing the ratings unless Hsu chooses to disclose them. He also has the ability to exclude Lassiter from the meetings so she cannot inform the Board.

2. *Discuss the types, sources, and relative amount of power for the three main characters in this story.*

Hsu's has legitimate power because he is the president and his sources of power include control over information (see question 1) and organized centrality. Centrality reflects Hsu's role in the primary activity of Waite. Centrality is associated with more power because it reflects the contribution made to the organization.

Lassiter has expert power. She is the chief information officer and the knowledge sharing application was her idea. She has done the research on the three firms and knows their consulting capabilities. Her source of power stems from coping with uncertainty The pharmaceutical environment changes swiftly, creating both uncertainty and complexity. Lassiter understands the importance of increasing productivity and speeding up the process of bringing drugs to the marketplace to remain competitive. She also has control over information as a source of power. She knows which companies are more qualified than Standard and can distribute her research to others, although she risks making an enemy out of her boss.

Lee has reward power and coercive power. She rewards her boss with deferential treatment and makes him feel important while condescending to other organizational members. A quid pro quo arrangement is implied because Standard Systems is owned by her uncle. If Hsu does not comply, she can punish him by withholding her favors or exposing his behavior to the Board. Her source of power is dependency. The more Hsu depends on her, the greater her power becomes. Lee has the most power because she is controlling Hsu to the point of having him breach his ethical commitment to Waite and the Board of Directors.

3. *How might Lassiter have increased her power and influence over this decision? If you were in her position, what would you do now?*

Lassiter could increase her power by using the following tactics. She could build a coalition, taking time to talk to other department heads within Waite to explain problems and describe their point of view. She could use assertiveness by being clear about which firm should be selected and why. Lassiter needs courage to be assertive, saying what she believes to persuade others. I would contact other department heads and the board to investigate the Hsu's unethical behavior, pointing out that this situation falls under sexual harassment even though it is consensual. The Board is ultimately responsible for the company's behavior.

CHAPTER THIRTEEN
CREATING VISION AND STRATEGIC DIRECTION

CHAPTER SUMMARY

Leaders establish organizational direction through vision and strategy. They are responsible for studying the organization's environment, considering how it may be different in the future, and setting a direction everyone can believe in. The shared vision is an attractive, ideal future for the organization that is credible yet not readily attainable.

A clear, powerful vision links the present and future by showing how present actions and decisions can move the organization toward its long-range goals. Vision energizes employees and gives them an inspiring picture of the future to which they are eager to commit themselves. The vision can also give meaning to work and establish a standard of excellence by presenting a challenge that asks all workers to give their best.

The mission includes the company's core values and its core purpose or reason for existence. Visions for the future change, whereas the mission should persist, as does the enduring character of the organization.

Strategy is the serious work of figuring out how to translate vision and mission into action. Strategy is a general plan of action that describes resource allocation and other activities for dealing with the environment and helping the organization reach its goals. Like vision, strategy changes, but successful companies develop strategies that focus on core competence, develop synergy, and create value for customers. Strategy is implemented through the systems and structures that are the basic architecture for how things get done in the organization.

Leaders decide on direction through rational analysis as well as intuition, personal experience, and hopes and dreams. Leaders make a real difference for their organization only when they link vision to strategic action, so that vision is more than just a dream. Superior organizational performance is not a matter of luck. It is determined by the decisions leaders make.

CHAPTER OPENER

Dr. Irwin Redlener, Creating a Children's Hospital

Dr. Irwin Redlener jumped at the chance to shape a new kind of children's hospital at the Montefiore Medical Center in the Bronx, New York. Redlener had a personal vision that health care could be used as a lever to address the myriad problems of the world's most disenfranchised children and families. His vision was that people broaden the mind-set about the role of doctors, the nature of medical institutions, and the standard approach to health care. He urged the facility to be the center of a comprehensive children's health system throughout the Bronx, involving a dynamic relationship between the hospital and the community. The ideas and imagination of the late astronomer and author Carl Sagan served as a roadmap. "He (Sagan) believed that the process of finding where you fit into the universe and the inspiration that comes from learning something about your world can be a gateway to a whole set of possibilities for children who have been otherwise contained in a very limited world view."

LECTURE/OUTLINE

To explain the relationship among vision, mission, strategy, and implementation mechanisms.

Strategic Leadership *Exhibit 13.1*

➢ *Do you think superior organizational performance is a matter of luck?*

Superior organizational performance is largely determined by choices leaders make.

Top leaders are responsible for knowing the organization's environment, considering the situation in 5 to 10 years, and setting the direction for the future that everyone can believe in.

Strategic leadership is one of the most critical issues facing organizations.

Strategic leadership is the ability to anticipate and envision the future, maintain flexibility, think strategically, and initiate changes that will create a competitive advantage for the organization in the future.

The complexity of the environment and the uncertainty of the future can overwhelm an executive; thus, many focus on internal organizational issues where they have more control.

It is easier for leaders to handle routine operational issues and see instant results.

Most leaders have difficulty finding the quiet time needed for "big-picture" thinking.

The first step to remaining competitive is to develop an understanding of the trends and discontinuities to gain an edge.

Leaders need quiet time and mental space to think creatively about all the information they are absorbing and how to put it to use.

Globalization, deregulation, advancing technology, and changing demographics and lifestyles are profoundly altering the way businesses are perceived and operate.

No organization can thrive for long without a clear viewpoint and framework for the future.

Several levels make up the domain of strategic leadership.

Strategic leadership is responsible for the relationship of the external environment to choices about vision, mission---its core values, purpose, and reason for existence.

Strategy provides the direction for translating the vision into action and is the basis for the development of specific mechanisms to help the organization achieve goals.

Each level of the hierarchy supports the levels above it.

Notes____

To create your personal leadership vision.

Leadership Vision

Exhibit 13.2

A *vision* is an attractive, ideal future that is credible yet not readily attainable.

A vision is not just a dream --- it is a view of the future that everyone in the firm can believe in, that can realistically be achieved yet offers a future that is better than what now exists.

Many successful organizations do not have easily-communicated slogans, but their visions are powerful because leaders paint a compelling picture of where the organization wants to go.

A vision is an important aspect of transformational leadership.

Notes____

In the Lead: Brian Gallagher, United Way of America

The nation's largest charity, United Way of America, may be on the verge of a transformation if CEO Brian Gallagher can inspire people with his vision of a new approach to fighting hunger, homelessness, or crime. Gallagher hopes to trans form United Way from an organization that just raises money to a community partner that works actively to solve specific social problems. Gallagher began testing his vision in Ohio; he formed a community coalition that devised specific strategies for fighting homelessness. The group created the Family Housing Collaborative which assists in housing, job training, and day care services.

Q: *How does Gallagher use vision to further United Way?*

A: A vision is an attractive, ideal future that is credible yet not readily attainable. It is an ambitious view that everyone in the organization can believe in. A vision can realistically be achieved. Selling his vision on a national scale will be a challenge for Gallagher, but some people believe a new approach is needed. Gallagher wants to transform United Way into a community problem solver.

Exhibit 13.3

A vision is shown as a guiding star, drawing everyone in the organization along the same path toward the future.

Vision is based in the current reality but is concerned with a future that is substantially different that the status quo; taking the organization on this path requires leadership.

Compare this to rational management which leads to the status quo.

What Vision Does

Vision provides a link between today and tomorrow, to energize and motivate employees toward the future, to provide meaning for people's work, and to set a standard of excellence in the organization.

Vision Links the Present to the Future

A vision is always about the future, but it begins in the present.

The problem for today's organizations is that managers spend most of their time dealing with current problems and little time contemplating and visualizing the future.

Some have suggested that leaders need "bifocal vision," the ability to care for today's needs and meet current obligations while aiming towards dreams of the future.

Discussion Question #1: . *A management consultant said that strategic leaders are concerned with vision and mission, while strategic managers are concerned with strategy. Do you agree? Discuss.*

Notes____

____

____

Vision Energizes People and Garners Commitment

People want to feel enthusiasm about their work; a powerful vision frees people from the mundane by providing them with a challenge worthy of their best efforts.

Vision needs to transcend the bottom line because people commit to something truly worthwhile, something that makes life better better for others, or improves their communities.

Vision Gives Meaning to Work

People need to find dignity and meaning in their work.

Even people performing routine tasks can find pride in their work when they have a larger purpose for what they do.

A clerk who thinks of his job as "processing insurance claims" will feel differently that one who thinks of the same job as helping fire victims put their lives in order.

People are drawn to companies that offer them a chance to do something meaningful.

Discussion Question #2: *A vision can apply to an individual, a family, a college course, a career, or decorating your apartment. Think of something you care about for which you want the future to be different from the present and write a vision statement for it.*

Notes____

____

____

Vision Establishes a Standard of Excellence and Integrity

Vision provides a measure by which employees can gauge their contributions to the organization.

Most workers welcome the chance to see how their work fits into the whole.

A vision is like a focus button; it clarifies an image of the future and lets people see how they can contribute.

Vision clarifies and connects to the core values and ideals of the organization and sets a standard of integrity for employees.

To make a difference a vision must be widely shared and is often created with the participation of others.

A good organizational vision is a shared vision.

In the Lead: Walt Disney

Walt Disney created a clear picture of what he wanted Disneyland to be. His vision translated hopes and dreams into words and allowed employees to help create the future. Notice how the vision says nothing about making money--- the emphasis is on a greater purpose that all employees could believe in. " The idea of Disneyland is a simple one. It will be a place for people to find happiness and knowledge. ….And it (Disneyland) will remind us and show us how to make these wonders part of our lives."

Q: *How did Walt Disney develop a vision that communicated the core values of his company?*

A: Disney painted a clear, inspiring picture of Disneyland, which had a powerful impact on people. His vision gave meaning and value to workers' activities. His vision was widely shared by workers.

Notes____

____

____

____

To use the common themes of powerful visions and apply what good visions can do.

Common Themes of Vision

Vision has broad appeal, helps deal with change, encourages faith in the future, reflects high ideals, and defines the organization's destination and how to get there.

- *Living Leadership:* *Vision's Offspring*

A compelling vision inspires and nurtures three qualities, here personified as individuals—clarity, commitment, and imagination.

➢ Do you think followers would benefit from contact with the following "people" in an organization? Explain.

Vision Has Broad Appeal

Although a vision can only be achieved through people, many visions fail to involve employees adequately; a vision cannot be the sole property of the leader.

.

The ideal vision "grabs people in the gut" and motivates them. It is identified with the organization as a whole and allows each individual to act independently but in the same direction.

Discussion Question #3: *If you worked for a company like Microsoft that has a strong vision for the future, how would that affect you compared to working for a company that did not have a vision?*

Notes____

____

____

Vision Deals with Change

Vision helps the organization achieve bold change. It involves action and challenges people to make important changes toward a better future.

Change can be frightening, but a clear sense of direction helps people face uncertainties.

Vision Encourages Faith and Hope

Vision exists only in the imagination----it is a picture of the world that cannot be observed or verified in advance.

Vision is an emotional appeal to our fundamental human needs and desires --- to feel useful important and useful, to believe we can make a real difference in the world.

Vision Reflects High Ideals

Good visions are idealistic.

Vision has the power to inspire and energize people only when it paints an uplifting future.

When John F. Kennedy announced the "man on the moon" vision, NASA had only a small amount of the knowledge needed to accomplish the feat.

Vision Defines the Destination and the Journey

A good vision includes the specific outcomes that the organization wants to achieve.

It also incorporates the underlying values that will help the organization get there.

A powerful vision can have a significant impact on an organization and its employees, but only if it is clearly communicated to everyone throughout the organization.

In the Lead: **Merix Corp.**

Most of us have heard the saying that a picture is worth a thousand words. Leaders at Merix Corp. in Oregon took the saying to heart and used graphics as a tool to articulate the company's strategic vision. Chair and CEO Debi Coleman held a company retreat where employees talked about their feelings about Merix and where it should be headed. A consultant from a strategic visioning and process-consulting firm then mapped out the themes that emerged. The resulting graphic vision statement conveys the image of a futuristic company, going where no one has gone before, on the leading edge of technology.

Q: *How did Coleman use a vision statement for the Merix Corp.?*

A: As Coleman explains, "Each of these images means something to us. If you could put this drawing on a computer and double-click on each image, underneath each one you would find serious plans, strategies with time lines, and performance measures. If you look around Merix, this picture is on people's wall, on workbenches, even on T-shirts.

Discussion Question #5: *What does it mean to say that the vision can include a description of both the journey and the destination?*

Notes____

____

____

Discussion Question #6: *Many visions are written and hung on a wall. Do you thing this type of vision has value? What would be required to imprint the vision within each person?*

Notes____

____

____

A Vision Works at Multiple Levels

➢ *Is a vision is only for the company as a whole, or also for divisions, departments, and individuals?*

Successful individuals, just like successful leaders, have developed a clear mental picture of their vision and how to achieve it.

People who do not have this clear vision of the future have less chance of success.

Top leaders of an effective organization develop a vision for the organization, and a project team leader five levels beneath the CEO develops a vision with team members for a new project.

When every person understands and embraces the vision , the organization becomes self-adapting.

Self-reference is a principle stating that each element in a system will serve the goals of the whole system when the elements are imprinted with an understanding of the whole.

Thus, the vision serves to direct and control people for the good of themselves and the organization.

To develop a shared vision, leaders share their personal visions with others and encourage others to express their dreams for the future.

Good leaders give up the idea that vision emanates from the top.

One successful leader refers to leadership as "discovering the company's destiny and having the courage to follow it."

Discussion Question #4: *Do you agree with the principle of self-reference? In other words, do you believe if people know where the organization is trying to go, they will make decisions that support the desired organizational outcome?*

Notes____

____

____

Mission

Exhibit 13.5

Mission is not the same as its vision.

The *mission* is the organization's broad purpose and reason for existence.

It defines the company's core values and provides a basis for creating the vision.

Whereas vision is a desire for the future, mission is what the firm "stands for."

Whereas visions continue to grows and change, the mission persists in the face of changing technologies, economic conditions, or other environmental shifts.

The mission defines the enduring character—the spiritual DNA----of the organization and can be a leadership tool to help employees find genuine meaning in their work.

The mission has two parts:

- *Core values* which guide and define the organization.

  The core values guide the organization "no matter what."

- *A core purpose* which describes why the company exists.

  An effective purpose statement does not just describe products or services, it captures people's idealistic motivations for why the organization exists.

Exhibit 13.6

The core values and core purpose are frequently expressed in a *mission statement.*

Some companies include the specific vision for the future as a part of their mission statements.

The mission serves as the glue that holds the organization together in times of change and guides strategic choices and decisions about the future.

Discussion Question #7: *What is the difference between mission and vision? Can you give an example of each?*

Notes____

To understand how leaders formulate and implement strategy.

Strategy Formulation

➢ *Do you think that strong missions and guiding visions are enough to make strong, powerful organizations?*

For organizations to succeed, they need to translate vision, values, and purpose into action. Formulating strategy a specific step toward the future.

Strategic management is the set of decisions and actions used to formulate and implement strategies to achieve a competitively superior fit between the firm and its environment so as to achieve organizational goals.

The leader's job is to find this fit and translate it into action.

Strategy is the general plan of action that describes resource allocation and other activities for dealing with the environment and helping the organization attain its goals.

In formulating strategy, leaders ask questions such as:

- "Where is the organization now?
- Where does the organization want to be?
- What changes and trends are occurring in the competitive environment?
- What courses of action can help us achieve our vision?"

Developing strategy requires actively listening to people both inside and outside the organization, as well as examining trends and discontinuities in the environment.

Innovative thinking carries a lot of risk; sometimes leaders have to shift their strategy several times before they get it right.

To improve the chances for success, leaders develop strategies that focus on three qualities: core competence, developing synergy, and creating value for consumers.

Core Competence

Core competence is something the organization does extremely well in comparison to competitors.

Leaders try to identify the organization's unique strengths----what makes their organization different from others in the industry (e.g., Amgen is superior in research).

In the Lead: Rodney England, England Inc.

One of the few advantages U.S. manufacturers have is offering an array of fabric choices and building a sofa to match the customer's décor. The only problem is that delivery time stretches to months. England, Inc., now owned by La-Z-Boy has managed to cut delivery time to three weeks. The company under the leadership of Rodney England builds about 11,000 sofas and chairs a week, all made to order. Another key to speed is that England runs its own trucks and England has the discipline to keep costs—and therefore prices---comparatively low.

Q: *How Rodney England's use of strategy helped England Inc.?*

A: Some retailers think England has the best speed and discipline in the industry. The bottom line for leaders is that the strategy is working. Although sales fro the entire domestic upholstery-manufacturing industry have been failing, England's sales have jumped 8.3 percent in one year.

Notes____

Synergy

Synergy occurs when organizational parts interact to produce an effect greater than the sum of the parts acting alone.

As a result, the organization may attain a special advantage with respect to cost, market power, technology, and employee skills.

Alliances between companies can be a source of synergy.

Value creation

Focusing on core competencies and attaining synergy helps companies create value for the customer.

Value can be defined as the combination of benefits received and the costs paid by the customer.

A product that is low cost but does not provide benefits is not a good value.

Delivering value is at the heart of strategy.

In the Lead: Steve Sanger, General Mills, Inc.

Steve Sanger's first question when a new product is being developed or an old product needs a boost is, " Can we make it 'one-handed'?" Growth has stalled for most food companies, but General Mills has fared better than most, largely because of chairman and CEO's Sanger's strategy of designing everyday, reasonably priced foods for people who like to keep one hand free for typing or driving while they eat.

Q: *How is value the key to strategy at General Mills?*

A: With the way people are eating today, convenience is the byword. Few companies have adapted to the American pursuit of mobility as we as General Mills. Though not quite one-handed, the Bowl Appetit line of single-serving rice- and –pasta-based meals is making lunch at the office easier than ever.

Discussion Question #8: *What is the difference between synergy and value creation with respect to strategy?*

Notes____

To apply the elements of an effective strategy

Strategy in Action *Exhibit 13.7*

Strategy formulation integrates knowledge of the environment, vision, and mission with the company's core competence to achieve synergy and create value for customers.

Strategy implementation puts strategy into action by adjusting various parts of the organization and directing resources to accomplish strategic goals.

This is the basic architecture for how things get done in the organization.

Strategy implementation is the most important as well as the most difficult part of strategic management, and strong leadership is an important tools for strategy implementation.

Leaders are responsible for making decisions about changes in structure, systems, policies, to support the company's strategic direction.

Leaders make decisions every day that support company strategy.

A simplified model shows how leaders make strategic decisions.

The two dimensions considered are whether a particular choice will have a high or low strategic impact on the business and whether implementation of the decision will be easy or difficult.

- A change, which produces a high strategic impact and is easy to implement would be a leader's first choice for putting strategy into action.

- Leaders also pursue activities that have a low strategic impact but which are relatively *easy* to implement (e.g., incremental improvements in products, processes, and techniques).

  Small changes can be needed to symbolize improvement and success to people within the organization.

- The final category relates to changes that are both difficult to implement and have a low strategic impact.

  Effective leaders strive to avoid decisions that fall into this category.

Discussion Question #9: *Strategic vision and strategic action are both needed for an effective leader. Which do you think you are better at doing? Why?*

Notes____

The Leader's Contribution

Exhibit 13.8

Leaders are ultimately responsible for establishing organizational direction through vision and strategy.

When leadership fails to provide direction, organizations flounder.

When McDonald's franchisees saw profits sink in the 1990s, they criticized leaders for their failure to provide vision and strategy.

Strategic management is one of the most critical jobs of a leader, but leaders may exhibit different strategy styles that can be effective.

Stimulating Vision and Action

There are four possibilities of leadership in providing direction----four types of leaders based on their attention to vision and attention to action.

- The person who is low on both dimensions is uninvolved and not a leader at all.
- The leader who is all action and little vision is a Doer.
- The Dreamer provides a big idea but is weak on implementation.
- The Effective Leader dreams big *and* transforms those dreams into significant strategic action either through personal activities or by hiring other leaders who can effectively implement the vision and strategy.

How Leaders Decide

To determine strategic direction for the future, leaders look inward, outward, and forward.

Leaders scan both the internal and external organizational environment to identify trends threats and opportunities for the organization.

In the Lead: Andrea Jung, Avon Products Inc.

Andrea Jung recently stood before thousands of Avon representatives and vowed that Avon Products Inc. can be as big in the beauty business as Walt Disney Co. is in entertainment. Jung landed the top job in 1999 and began formulating a new vision and strategy by looking at where Avon is now and where it needs to go in the future. Most women in the U.S. work outside the home, making the company's traditional direct-sales approach seem destined to fade into history. Another trend is the explosion of the internet as a place of doing business. Jung intends to rebuild Avon from the ground up giving women a choice of buying through a traditional representative, from a store, or online.

Q: *How did Andrea Jung use environmental changes and trends to develop Avon's strategy?*

A: Most women in the U.S. work outside the home, making the company's traditional direct-sales approach seem destined to fade into history. Another trend is the explosion of the internet as a place of doing business. Jung's strategy is to rebuild Avon from the ground up giving women a choice of buying through a traditional representative, from a store, or online. Leaders like Andrea Jung recognize that organizations need both a broad and inspiring vision and underlying plan for how to achieve it.

One approach leaders take in setting a course for the future is through hard analysis.

Situation analysis includes a search for SWOT ---strengths, weaknesses, opportunities, and threats that affect organizational performance.

Another formula is a five-force analysis developed by Michael Porter to include: potential entrants in an industry, the bargaining power of suppliers ; the threat of substitutes; the bargaining power of buyers; and rivalry among competitors.

Relying too heavily on rational analysis can kill a vision.

Overly rational people have a hard time letting go and dreaming.

To connect with people's yearning for something great, visions can transcend the rational.

Although it is based on reality, it comes from the heart rather than the head.

Notes____

____

____

The Leader's Impact

➢ *How can a leader's link between vision and strategy can make a significant difference for the organization's future?*

A leader's greatest discretion is over strategic vision and strategic action.

Research shows that strategic thinking and planning for the future can positively affect a company's performance and financial success.

One way leader impact has been evaluated is to examine whether top executive turnover makes a difference; top leader succession explains from 20 to 30 percent variance in a firm's outcomes.

Recent research has explored the notion of leadership teams; many researchers believe that the configuration of the top leadership team is more important than the characteristics of the CEO.

The emerging focus on leadership teams is more realistic than focusing on individual leadership.

An effective can identify and implement strategy, discern an accurate interpretation of the environment, and of develop capability based on empowered employees and a shared vision.

Without a capable and effectively interacting top leadership team, a company may not adapt readily in a shifting environment.

Discussion Question #10: *If a new top leader is hired for a corporation, and performance improves, to what extent do you think the new top leader was responsible compared to other factors? To what extent do you think a new coach is responsible if her basketball team did better after she took over?*

Notes____

____

____

DISCUSSION QUESTIONS

1. *A management consultant said that strategic leaders are concerned with vision and mission, while strategic managers are concerned with strategy. Do you agree? Discuss.*

Leaders are concerned with vision, mission, and strategy. When leaders rely solely on formal strategic planning, competitor analysis, or market research, they miss opportunities. Too much rational analysis can kill vision. Still, leaders need a broad and inspiring vision and an underlying plan for how to achieve it. To decide and map a strategic direction, leaders strive to develop industry foresight based on trends in technology, demographics, government regulation, and lifestyles that with help them identify new competitive advantages.

2. *A vision can apply to an individual, a family, a college course, a career, or decorating your*

apartment. Think of something you care about for which you want the future to be different from the present and write a vision statement for it.

A vision statement lets people know where the organization wants to go in the future. A vision illustrates a challenge --- it is an ambitious view of the future that requires people to do their best. See Exhibit 13.2. A medical researcher might write—wipe out the disease of AIDS. A teacher might write----teach character in the classroom.

3. *If you worked for a company like Microsoft that has a strong vision for the future, how would that affect you compared to working for a company that did not have a vision?*

Microsoft has a shared vision. When a vision is shared among individuals and employees, it has real impact. As Peter Senge said in *The Fifth Discipline,* a shared vision changes people's relationship with the organization. It creates a common identity and allows each employee to look at a manager and think of "our company" rather than "their company." Without a company vision, employees are not willing to make an emotional commitment just for the sake of increasing profits.

4. *Do you agree with the principle of self-reference? In other words, do you believe if people know where the organization is trying to go, they will make decisions that support the desired organizational outcome?*

Yes, According to the principle of self-reference, each element in a system will serve the mission of the whole system when the elements are imprinted with an understanding of the mission of the whole. One successful leader refers to leadership as "discovering the company's destiny and having the courage to follow it." A vision serves to direct and control people for the good of themselves and the organization.

5. *What does it mean to say that the vision can include a description of both the journey and the destination?*

A good vision includes the specific outcomes that the organization wants to achieve. It also incorporates the underlying values that set the rules for achievement. A powerful vision can have a significant impact on an organization and its employees, but only if it is clearly communicated to everyone.

6. *Many visions are written and hung on a wall. Do you thing this type of vision has value? What would be required to imprint the vision within each person?*

Writing the vision on the wall serves as a constant reminder to everyone in the organization; however, activities supporting the vision are needed to imprint it within each person. People need the reinforcement of the vision when engaging in everyday work activities. It is easy to slip into a routine, focus on a specific task, and lose sight of the big picture. A vision that is written and hung on the wall serves as a continuous reinforcement.

7. *What is the difference between mission and vision? Can you give an example of each?*

The mission is the organization's core broad purpose and reason for existence. It defines the company's core values and provides a basis for creating the vision. Whereas vision is an ambitious desire for the future, mission is what the organization the organization; and the *core purpose* which describes why the company exists. For example, Hallmark's values include "Excellence in all we do." Discovery Toys' purpose to help parents experience the joys and benefits of playing with their children.

8. *What is the difference between synergy and value creation with respect to strategy?*

Core competence is something the organization does extremely well in comparison to competitors, its unique strengths (e.g., Amgen is superior in research). Synergy occurs when organizational parts interact to produce an effect greater than the sum of the parts. Core competence and synergy create value for the customer, the combination of benefits received and the costs paid by the customer.

9. *Strategic vision and strategic action are both needed for an effective leader. Which do you think you are better at doing? Why?*

Answers will vary. I am better at strategic vision because I am able to see the big picture, dream idealistically of the world as a better place, and look at the challenges presented for the future. Putting my ideas into action is far more difficult and requires strategic planning.

10. *If a new top leader is hired for a corporation, and performance improves, to what extent do you think the new top leader was responsible compared to other factors? To what extent do you think a new coach is responsible if her basketball team did better after she took over?*

If a new leader or coach shares a personal vision and encourages others to express their dreams for the future, synergy can occur and corporate and team performance can improve. Still, external environmental factors negatively or positively influence outcomes, not just a new leader.

TEACHING TOOLS AND EXERCISES

1. *Small Group Exercise:* Vision Statements

In small groups, evaluate the vision statements in Exhibit 13.2 on p. 514. Also consider Microsoft's slogan, "Your potential inspires us to create products that help you reach it."

How do vision statements connect the present to what the organization's aspirations? After discussing these vision statements, each group will select an organization and write a vision statement. These vision statements will be presented to the class for comment and evaluation.

2. *Out-of-class assignment:* Michael Porter's Five-Force Analysis Model

Students will research and review Michael Porter's well-known Five-Force Analysis Model. Porter proposed that strategy is the result of five competitive forces: potential new entrants into an industry; the bargaining power of buyers; the bargaining power of suppliers; the threat of substitute products; and rivalry among competitors. After carefully examining these forces, students can discuss how leaders can develop effective strategies to remain competitive. Students should select industries or businesses as examples.

3. *On the Web:* Visionary Leaders

Go to www.msn.com. Look at the business news and find an example of a visionary leader who has had dramatic effects on the performance of an organization or work group. Students will prepare a description of this leader.

4. *Role Play:* Environmental Scanning

Select an organization with which you are familiar, either as an employee or as a customer. One person is the top manager in the organization. The other is a first-line supervisor in the organization.

Top manager: Discuss the types of information from environmental scanning you think would be important. Discuss where you would find this information.

First-line supervisor: Would the types of information from environmental scanning that you would want be different? Explain.

6. *Leader's Self-Insight*: Visionary Leadership

The questionnaire pertains to two dimensions of visionary leadership. Creating the vision is whether you think about the future, whether you are excited about the future. Implementing the vision is about the extent to which you communicate, allocate the work, and provide rewards for activities that achieve the vision. After scoring your questionnaire, discuss the following questions with another student.

- Are your scores consistent with your understanding of your own strengths and weaknesses?
- What might you do to improve your scores?

LEADERSHIP DEVELOPMENT: CASES FOR ANALYSIS

I. Synopsis: Metropolis Police Department

You are in a hotel room watching the evening news as a local reporter interviews people who complain about abuse and mistreatment by police officers. Some believe the problem is the police department's authoritarian style. Police managers encourage paramilitary values and a them-against–us attitude. Training emphasizes police techniques, the appropriate use of guns, and new technology, with no training on how to handle people. The chief of police is considered insensitive towards minorities and makes racist remarks. You have been invited to interview for the job of police chief.

Case questions and answers

1. *Identify themes that you would like to make part of your vision for the police department.*

    - Vision links the present to the future: citizens in Metropolis will feel safe.

    - Vision energizes people and garners commitment: The entire police force will work as a team as partners against crime on behalf of the community.

    - Vision gives meaning to work: Police offices will feel a sense of pride in protecting the families of Metropolis.

    - Vision Establishes a Standard of Excellence: Metropolis will have the safest streets and lowest crime rate in the state.

    - Vision has broad appeal: our police force will make Metropolis a safe community

2. *If you get the job, how will you gain acceptance for your vision? How will you gain acceptance for your vision? How will you implement changes that will support the new vision and values?*

It would be important to share the vision to create a common identity and allow each officer to look at the chief of police and think of "our police force" not "his police force. The vision has to become a common thread connecting all member, involving them personally and emotionally. Implementation should include training, reward and pay incentives, a review of policies and procedures to move in the direction of a more people-oriented less autocratic style. The Hersey and Blanchard model should be used to determine the readiness of the police officers before changing leadership style.

3. *Would you relish the challenge of becoming police chief of Metropolis? Why or why not?*

The task is challenging and certainly has value in the larger sense. Crime and violence in America are on the rise; anyone who could successfully attack these social problems would provide a valuable service.

II. **Synopsis: The Visionary Leader**

When Frank Coleman first began his job as president of Hi-Tech Aerostructures, most managers and employees felt a surge of excitement. Hi-Tech Aerostructures is a 50-year old family-owned manufacturing company that produces parts for the aircraft industry. Coleman had a vision for transforming Hi-Tech into a world-class manufacturing facility. In addition to implementing cutting-edge technology, the vision included transforming the sleepy paternalistic culture to a more dynamic, adaptive one and empowering employees to take a more active, responsible role in the organization. Vice president David Deacon was on the transformation team. Coleman and Deacon crafted a vision statement. Coleman laid out broad ideas for the vision statement. When team submitted specific plans and goals months later, Coleman suggested revisions. Nearly a year later, the team waited for Coleman's response to the revised proposal. Once again Coleman suggested a different approach. Deacon felt that Coleman would lay out his vision and ask the team to start over.

Case questions and answers

1. *How effective would you rate Coleman as a visionary leader? Discuss.*

A visionary leader effectively communicates the vision to followers. If Deacon and his team keep laying out unacceptable plans and goals, then Coleman has not explained the vision clearly. Leaders must link vision and strategy to make a real difference for the organization's future. Coleman is not doing this at Hi-Tech. In addition, Coleman is out of touch because the emerging focus on leadership teams is more realistic than focusing on individual leadership.

2. *Where would you place Coleman on the types of leaders illustrated in Exhibit 13.8. Where would you place Deacon?*

Coleman is the Dreamer; he is good at providing a big idea with meaning for self and others. He can effectively inspire others with a vision, yet he is weak on implementing a strategic vision. The vision is only a dream, a fantasy, because it has little chance of ever becoming a reality. Vision has to be translated into specific goals, objectives, and plans.

Deacon is the Doer because he is all action and little vision. Deacon is a hard worker and dedicated to the job and the organization, but he is working blind. Without a sense of purpose and direction, activities have no real meaning and do not truly serve the organization. Deacon is trying to please Coleman.

3. *If you were Deacon, what would you do?*

I would suggest hard analysis. Situation analysis using SWOT—strengths, weaknesses, opportunities, and threats that affect organizational performance. Deacon could obtain information from a variety of sources, such as customers, government reports, suppliers, consultants, or associations. He could gather information about internal strengths and weaknesses from sources such as budgets, financial ratios, profit and loss statements, and employee surveys. Vision and strategy have to be based on a solid factual foundation coupled with the dream. There has to be a balance between formal strategic planning, competitor analysis, and market research with the hopes and dreams of Coleman.

CHAPTER FOURTEEN
SHAPING CULTURE AND VALUES

CHAPTER SUMMARY

Leaders influence organizational culture and ethical values. Culture is the set of key values, norms, and assumptions that is shared by members of an organization and taught to new members as correct. Culture serves two critically important functions----to integrate organizational members so they know how to relate one another and to help the organization adapt to the environment.

Strong, adaptive cultures have a positive impact on organizational outcomes. A culture gap exists when an organization's culture is not in alignment with the needs of the external environment or company strategy. Leaders use ceremonies, stories, symbols, specialized language, selection, and socialization to influence cultural values. In addition, leaders shape cultural values most strongly through their daily actions.

Leaders consider the external environment and the company's vision and strategy in determining which values are important for the organization. Four types of culture may exist in organizations: Adaptability, Achievement, Clan, and Bureaucratic. Each type emphasizes different values, although organizations may have values that fall into more than one category.

Of the values that make up an organization's culture, ethical values are among the most important. Ethics is the code of moral principles and values that govern the behavior of a person or group with respect to what is right or wrong. Leaders' personal beliefs and level of moral development influence their personal ethics. For organizations to be ethical, leaders have to be openly and strongly committed to ethical conduct in their daily actions.

Leaders can also influence ethical values in the organization through codes of ethics, ethics committees or ombudspersons, training programs, and disclosure mechanisms to support employees who voice concerns about ethical practices.

CHAPTER OPENER

Culture at Commerce Bank

Commerce Bank is one of the fastest growing banks in the United States—but it's also one of the goofiest places of business you're likely to find. Commerce's two costumed mascots regularly visit branches and mingle with customers at special events. Mr. C. a jolly, oversized, red letter serves as the bank's walking logo. People love getting their picture taken with Mr. C says the vice president of the Wow Department. All this silliness has a very serious purpose. Whereas most banks try to steer their customers from branches to ATMs and online banking, Commerce looks for ways to lure more customers in. Buildings are designed to attract visitors with floor to ceiling windows and historic murals. President and CEO Vernon Hill says, " Culture, culture, culture...Without the Wow, Commerce would be just another bank."

LECTURE/OUTLINE

To understand why shaping culture is a critical function of leadership.

Organizational Culture *Exhibit 14.1*

Leaders emphasize specific cultural values depending on the organization's situation.

Organizational culture became a topic of interest in the 1980s when Japanese companies were outperforming their American counterparts.

Researchers thought that national culture and corporate culture could explain differences in performance.

Leaders now understand when a company's culture fits the needs of its external environment and company strategy, employees can create a competitive organization.

What is Culture?

Some refer to culture as the character or personality of an organization; how an organization "feels" is a manifestation of the organizational culture.

One company might have a sense of formality with employees in business attire, while another company might allow employees to wear jeans.

Culture can be defined as the set of key values, assumptions, understandings, and norms, ways shared by members of an organization and taught to new members as correct.

Culture is a pattern of shared assumptions about how things get done in an organization.

Culture can be conceptualized as three levels with each level less obvious:

- At the surface level are visible artifacts such as dress, patterns of behavior, physical symbols, ceremonies, and office layout.

- At a deeper level are the expressed values and beliefs, which are not observable but can be discerned from how people explain and justify what they do.

  These are values that members hold at a conscious level.

- Some values are so deeply embedded in a culture that organizational members may not be consciously aware of them.

  These basic underlying assumptions are the deepest essence of the culture.

  Assumptions start out as expressed values, but over time they become more deeply embedded and less open to question.

  Organization members take them for granted and are not aware of the assumptions that guide their behavior, language, and patterns of social interaction.

Importance of Culture

Culture gives employees a sense of organizational identity and generates a commitment to particular values and ways of doing things.

Culture serves two important functions:

- It integrates members so that they know hoe to relate to one another.
- It helps the organization adapt to the external environment.

Internal Integration

Culture helps members develop a collective identity and know how to work together effectively.

Culture can imprint a set of unwritten rules inside employees' minds, which can be very powerful in determining behavior, thus affecting organizational performance.

Organizations are putting increased emphasis on developing strong cultures that encourage teamwork, collaboration, and mutual trust

In an atmosphere of trust, people are more likely to share ideas, be creative, and be generous with their knowledge and talents.

External Adaptation

Culture determines how the organization meets goals and deals with outsiders.

The right cultural values can help the organization respond rapidly to customer needs and to competitors.

Culture can encourage employee commitment to the core purpose of the organization, its specific goals, and the basic means used to accomplish goals.

Culture should embody the values and assumptions needed by the organization to succeed in the environment

In the Lead: Pat Kelly, PSS World Medical

PSS World Medical, a specialty marketer and distributor of medical products and supplies, has thrived in a fiercely competitive industry by offering superior service and responsiveness to customers. Company practices such as same-day delivery, no minimum order sizes, and a no-hassles return policy have earned PSS a loyal following. Kelly attributes success to a corporate culture based on the idea of personal responsibility and values of honesty, trust, and mutual respect.

Q: *Describe the culture at PSS World Medical*

A: The company practices open book management, sharing all financial and operating information with employees, and managers encourage employees to ask questions without fear of punishment. PSS creates an atmosphere in which employees want to excel. The culture unleashes all employees' energy and enthusiasm.

Culture is important for binding employees together, making the organization a community rather than just a collection of individuals.

Discussion Question #1: *Describe the culture for an organization you are familiar with. Identify the physical artifacts and underlying values and assumptions. What did you learn?*

Notes____

To know characteristics of an adaptive as opposed to an unadaptive culture.

Culture Strength and Adaptation *Exhibit 14.2*

Culture strength refers to the degree of agreement among employees about the importance of specific values and ways of doing things.

If widespread consensus exists, the culture is strong and cohesive; if little agreement exists, the culture is weak.

The effect of a strong culture is not always a positive one. Sometimes a strong culture can encourage the wrong values and cause harm to the organization and its members (Enron).

A strong culture increases cohesion and commitment to the firm's values, goals, and strategies, but firms may have unethical, unhealthy values that don't fit the environment.

Research found that a strong culture does not ensure success unless it also encourages a healthy adaptation to the external environment.

❑ *Living Leadership: Flexible or Rigid*

The ability to embrace change is characteristic of growth and vibrancy

➢ How does this concept apply to adaptive cultures?

Adaptive corporate cultures have different values than unadaptive cultures:

- In adaptive cultures, leaders are concerned with customers and those internal people, processes, and procedures that bring about useful change.
- In unadaptive cultures, leaders are concerned with themselves or their own special projects, and their values tend to discourage risk- taking and change.

A strong culture is not enough, because an unhealthy culture may encourage the organization to move in the wrong direction.

Discussion Question #2: *Discuss how a culture could have either positive or negative consequences for an organization.*

Notes____

____

____

When the organization is not in alignment with the needs of the external environment, a *culture gap* occurs, the difference between desired and actual values and behaviors.

Culture gaps can be immense particularly in the case of mergers.

Organizations can be much more effective when the culture fits the external environment.

An important step toward more adaptive values is to recognize when people are adhering to the wrong values or when important values are not held strongly enough.

Organizational leaders should remember that human systems---in particular the habits and values of corporate culture---are what make any change initiative successful.

The problem of integrating cultures increase in scope and complexity with global companies and cross-cultural acquisitions.

Discussion Question #3: *What is a culture gap? What are some techniques leaders might use to influence and change cultural values when necessary?*

Notes____

To understand and apply how leaders shape culture and values through ceremonies, stories, symbols, language, selection and socialization, and daily actions.

Shaping Culture

An organization exists only because of the people who are a part of it, and those people both shape and interpret the character and culture of the organization.

Leaders formulate a viewpoint about an organization and the values that help people achieve the organization's mission, vision, and goals.

An organization's culture is often a reflection of the values advocated by a strong top leader.

In the Lead: David Sun and John Tu, Kingston Technology Co.

"Business is not about money," says David Sun, vice president and chief operating officer of Kingston Technology Co, which manufactures memory products for personal computers, laser printers, digital cameras, and other products. "It's about relationships," Sun and his co-founder, John Tu, have instilled values of caring, trust, collaboration, and sharing in their company. Employees feel that the owners are part of the team. When Sun and Tu sold the 80 percent of the company, they set aside $100 million of the proceeds for employee bonuses.

Q: *How is Kingston's culture a reflection of the founders?*

A: There are many stories of the leaders quietly offering money, time, and other resources---or just genuine concern---to employees who were dealing with family or personal troubles. Because employees are treated with kindness, care, and respect, they pass that on in their relationships with each other, with customers, suppliers, and other outsiders. Employees are highly motivated to meet organizational goals and keep the company's reputation fore doing the right thing.

Leaders use several techniques to maintain healthy cultures, provide smooth internal integration, and enable the organization to adapt to the needs of the external environment.

To enact cultural values, leaders uses rites and ceremonies, stories, symbols, and specialized language.

They emphasize the selection and socialization of new employees to keep the culture strong.

Perhaps most importantly, leaders signal the cultural values they want to instill in the organization through their day-to-day actions.

Ceremonies

A *ceremony* is a planned activity that makes up a special event and is generally conducted for the benefit of an audience.

Leaders can schedule ceremonies to provide dramatic examples of what the company values.

Ceremonies reinforce specific values, create a bond among employees, and celebrate employees who symbolize important achievements.

A ceremony often includes the presentation of an award.

Stories

A *story* is a narrative based on true events, repeated frequently and shared among employees.

Stories are told to new employees to illustrate the company's primary values, used to keep values alive, and provide a shared understanding among workers.

Storytelling is a powerful way to connect with others on an emotional level, helping to convey and transmit important cultural values.

Symbols

A *symbol* is an object, act, or event that conveys meaning to others.

In a sense, stories and ceremonies are symbols, but leaders use physical artifacts to symbolize particular values.

A nearly life-size wooden heifer at Mitel Corp. symbolizes the importance of destroying sacred cows, "the barriers that everyone *knows* about but nobody talks about."

Specialized Language

Leaders often use slogans to express corporate values, and employees repeat them.

Leaders express and reinforce cultural values through written public statements, such as corporate mission statements that express the values of the organization.

Selection and socialization

Selection and socialization of new employees helps maintain specific cultural values.

Companies with strong, healthy cultures have careful and rigorous hiring practices.

For example, Starbucks Coffee emphasizes socialization as the key to its strong culture.

Daily Actions

Leaders must signal and support important culture values through their daily actions.

Employees learn what is valued most by watching attitudes and behaviors leaders reward, how leaders react to crises, and whether the leader's behavior matches the values.

In the Lead: Bob Kierlin, Fastenal Co.

Inc. magazine once referred to Bob Kierlin, the top leader of Fastenal Co. as "the cheapest leader in America." Kierlin runs a national powerhouse that operates 800 branch sites which sell and manufactures nuts and bolts, fasteners, and safety supply tools. Bob Kierlin is the kind of guy who just loves a bargain. He clips coupons, eats McDonald's extra value meals, and has taken the same paycheck for the last decade. Workers respect Kierlin—he treats everyone the same, whether you're a janitor or vice president. Employees share the cultural values that Kierlin models everyday—not just the value of the buck, but the importance of being fair.

Q: *How do employees at Fastenal learn what is valued most by their leader?*

A: Kierlin models the values and attitudes he espouses---a culture of frugality and fairness. Because of a profit-sharing plan, employees know that cutting costs fattens everyone's paycheck, but the quality of their relationships is just as important. Fastenal is a growing company, because it invests wisely in new equipment, technology, and people.

Leaders can change unadaptive cultures by their actions.

Through ceremonies, stories, symbols, language, hiring and training practices, and their own behavior, leaders influence culture.

When culture change is needed to adapt to the environment or bring about smoother internal integration, leaders are responsible for instilling new cultural values.

Discussion Question #8: *What is meant by the idea that culture helps a group or organization solve the problem of internal integration?*

Notes____

To identify the cultural values associated with adaptability, achievement, clan, and bureaucratic cultures, and the environmental conditions associated with each.

The Competing Values Approach to Shaping Values *Exhibit 14.3*

Leaders today recognize the importance of shred values and invest time in thinking about and discussing them.

Organizational values are the enduring beliefs that have worth, merit and importance for the organization.

Changes in the nature of work and increasing diversity in the workforce have made values a topic of concern.

In considering what values are important for the organization, leaders consider the external environment and the company's vision and strategy.

Although cultures vary widely, companies within the same industry often reveal similar values because they are operating in similar environments.

Key values should embody what the organization needs to be effective.

The correct relationship among cultural values, organizational strategy, and the external environment can enhance a company's performance.

Organizational cultures are assessed along many dimensions, but this model focuses on:

- the extent to which the external environment requires flexibility or stability
- the extent to which the strategic focus is internal or external.

Together the dimensions form four quadrants, each representing a cultural category with emphasis on specific values.

The four cultures include: Adaptability, Achievement, Clan, and Bureaucratic.

An organization may have cultural values that fall into more than one category, or even into all categories; however, successful organizations lean toward one cultural category.

Adaptability Culture

The *adaptability culture* is characterized by values that support the organization's ability to interpret and translate signals from the environment into new behavior responses.

Employees have the autonomy to make decisions.

Leaders encourage and reward creativity, experimentation, and risk-taking.

Achievement Culture

The *achievement culture* is characterized by a clear vision of the organization's goals, and leaders focus on the achievement by specific targets.

This is a results-oriented culture that values competitiveness, aggressiveness, personal initiative, and the willingness to work long and hard to achieve results.

An emphasis placed on winning is the glue that holds the organization together.

Clan Culture

The *clan culture* has an internal focus on the involvement and participation of employees to meet changing expectations from the external environment rapidly.

This culture places value on meeting the needs of employees.

These organizations are friendly places to work and employees seem almost like a family.

Leaders emphasize fairness, consideration, and avoiding status differences.

Discussion Question #4: *Compare and contrast the achievement culture with the clan culture. What are some possible disadvantages of having a strong clan culture? A strong achievement culture?*

Notes____

Bureaucratic Culture

The *bureaucratic culture* has an internal focus and consistency orientation for a stable environment.

This culture supports a methodical, rational, orderly way of doing business.

Following the rules and being thrifty are valued.

The organization succeeds by being highly integrated and efficient.

In today's world, few organizations operate in a stable environment, and most leaders are shifting away from bureaucratic cultures because of the need for flexibility.

Each of the four cultures can be successful.

The emphasis on various cultural values depends on the organization's strategic focus and on the needs of the external environment.

***In the Lead*:** Dick Brown, Electronic Data System

Electronic Data Systems (EDS) was a pioneer in the information technology services industry, but as the environment changed and became more competitive, EDS failed to shift its cultural values. Faster, nimbler start-ups were beating EDS at its own game. When Dick Brown became CEO, he discovered that the old culture of isolationism, information hoarding, rampant individualism, slow response times, and separation of managers and employees on the front line had worked in the 1980s, but the 21st century demanded new values. Brown implemented new initiatives designed to foster a companywide culture based on individual autonomy and responsibility, quick feedback, open communication, and rapid response.

Q: *How did the Brown redefine the culture at EDS?*

A: EDS had a bureaucratic culture, but Brown wanted an adaptability culture that was focused on collaborating to better serve clients. Shifting to an adaptability culture has helped EDS reap increases in sales, profits, and market share.

Discussion Question #6: *In which of the four types of culture (adaptability, achievement, clan, bureaucratic) might you expect to find the greatest emphasis on ethical issues? Why?*

Notes____

____

____

Ethical Values in Organizations

Of the values in an organization's culture, ethical values are considered highly important and have gained renewed emphasis in today's era of financial scandals and moral lapses.

Most organization's with long-term success have leaders who include ethics as part of the formal policies and informal cultures of their companies.

Ethics is the code of moral principles and values that governs the behavior of a person or group with respect to what is right or wrong.

Ethics sets standards as to what is good or bad in conduct and decision making.

Many people believe that if you are not breaking the law, then you are behaving. in an ethical manner, but ethics often go far beyond the law.

The law arises from a set of codified principles and regulations.

Ethical standards apply to behavior not covered by law.

The standards for ethical conduct are embodied within each employee and the organization itself.

A recent survey about unethical conduct showed that over half of the respondents cited poor leadership as a faction.

Leaders can create a climate that emphasizes ethical behavior.

To use the concept of value-based leadership

Values-Based Leadership

Ethical values in organizations are developed through *value-based leadership,* a relationship between leaders and followers based on shared, strongly internalized values that are advocated and acted upon by the leader.

Leaders influence ethical values through personal behavior and through the organization's systems and politics.

Personal Ethics

Value-based leaders generate trust and respect from employees, based not on stated values but on the courage, determination, and self-sacrifice in upholding those values.

For organizations to be ethical, leaders need to be openly and strongly committed to ethical conduct.

The family backgrounds and spiritual beliefs of leaders often provide principles by which they conduct business.

Personality characteristics such as ego strength, self-confidence, and independence may enable leaders to make ethical decisions even if those decisions are unpopular.

One important personal factor is the leader's stage of moral development, which affects an individual's ability to translate values into behavior.

At the highest level of moral development are people guided by high internal standards.

When faced with difficult decisions, values-based leaders know what they stand for, and they have the courage to act on their principles.

Discussion Question #7: *If a leader directs her healthcare company to reward hospital managers strictly on hospital profits, is the leader being ethically responsible? Discuss.*

Notes____

____

____

Organizational Structure and Systems

Leaders influence ethical values through formal systems, programs, and policies.

Formal systems that effectively influence ethics are codes of ethics, ethical structures, training programs, and disclosure mechanisms.

Code of Ethics

A *code of ethics* is a formal statement of the company's ethical values.

It communicates to workers what the company stands for.

Codes of ethics state the values and behavior that are expected and those that are not tolerated.

Some companies include ethics as a part of the statements that include their mission.

These statements define ethical values as well as corporate culture and contain language about company responsibility, quality of product, and treatment of employees.

Structure

Ethical structure represents the various positions an organization uses to encourage ethical behavior.

One example is the ethics committee---a group of employees appointed to oversee the company's ethics and provide rulings on questionable ethical issues.

Many organizations are setting up ethics departments that manage and coordinate all corporate ethics activities.

There departments are run by a *chief ethics officer,* a high-level company executive who oversees all aspects of ethics.

Most ethics offices are also counseling centers to help employees resolve ethical dilemmas; the focus is on helping employees make the right decisions and disciplining wrongdoers.

Training

To make sure ethical issues are considered in daily actions, leaders often implement training programs to supplement a written code of ethics.

Disclosure Mechanisms

Leaders can support employees who do the right thing and voice concern about unethical practices.

One important step is to develop policies about *whistle-blowing,* employee disclosure of wrong-doing in the organization.

Leaders set the standard for how whistleblowers will be treated, and create a climate where people feel free to point out problems without fear of punishment.

Leaders instill and encourage ethical values most clearly through their own personal values.

Discussion Question #5: *Which do you think is more important for improving ethical values in an organization: a code of ethics, leader behavior, or employee training? Discuss.*

Notes____

____

____

DISCUSSION QUESTIONS

1. *Describe the culture for an organization you are familiar with. Identify the physical artifacts and underlying values and assumptions. What did you learn?*

At Medical Center Hospital in Odessa, Texas, the physicians make hospital rounds wearing cowboy boots and blue jeans under their white hospital clinic coats. They generally do not wear ties. The underlying assumptions include the following: Odessa is a friendly, small town where patients can get personalized medical treatment and really trust their physicians, who are members of their community. The white coat connotes professionalism and a high standard of care, but the lack of a tie connotes a level of informality to put patients and their families at ease. There is nothing more Texan than cowboy boots.

2. *Discuss how a culture could have either positive or negative consequences for an organization.*

In adaptive cultures, leaders are concerned with customers and those internal people, processes, and procedures that bring about useful change. In unadaptive cultures, leaders are concerned with themselves or their own special projects, and their values tend to discourage risk-taking and change. A strong culture is not enough, because an unhealthy culture may encourage the organization to move in the wrong direction.

3. *What is a culture gap? What are some techniques leaders might use to influence and change cultural values when necessary?*

The difference between desired and actual values and behaviors is called a culture gap. To change cultural values, a leader can listen to employees and build trust by accepting employee ideas and initiatives. Culture can be shaped through ceremonies, stories, symbols, and careful selection and socialization of new employees.

4. *Compare and contrast the achievement culture with the clan culture. What are some possible disadvantages of having a strong clan culture? A strong achievement culture?*

An achievement culture shows a clear vision of the organization's goals. Leaders focus on the achievement by specific targets such as sales growth. This culture values competitiveness, aggressiveness, personal initiative, and the willingness to work.. Emphasis is placed on winning. A clan culture has an internal focus on the involvement and participation of employees, and places value on meeting their needs, and being fhendly. Employees are like family. The clan culture might not be aggressive enough to outperform the competition, and an achievement culture might have high turnover because of little regard for individual needs.

5. *Which do you think is more important for improving ethical values in an organization: a code of ethics, leader behavior, or employee training? Discuss.*

Leader behavior is more important because leaders can create and sustain a climate that emphasizes ethical behavior for all employees. Ethical values are developed and strengthened through value- based leadership.

6. *In which of the four types of culture (adaptability, achievement, clan, bureaucratic) might you expect to find the greatest emphasis on ethical issues? Why?*

Ethical behavior would be prevalent in the clan culture because of the values of fairness, social equality, consideration, and cooperation. The clan culture has an internal focus on the involvement and participation of employees to meet changing expectations from the external environment rapidly. This culture places value on meeting the needs of employees. These organizations are friendly places to work and employees seem almost like a family.

7. *If a leader directs her healthcare company to reward hospital managers strictly on hospital profits, is the leader being ethically responsible? Discuss.*

No, to be ethically responsible, rewards should be based on following a code of ethics, a formal statement of the company's ethical values. A profit-driven rewards system could encourage employees to ignore ethical values such as honesty, fairness, and personal integrity.

8. *What is meant by the idea that culture helps a group or organization solve the problem of internal integration?*

Leaders recognize the complex interrelationship of parts of the organization. All parts, such as strategies, reward systems, and training programs, are interlinked so that change in one area requires change in others. For example, Southwest Airlines has a clan culture based on human needs, caring, and consideration. All facets of Southwest are linked through these cultural values.

TEACHING TOOLS AND EXERCISES

1. *Class activity:* Culture

If you are taking more than one course, assess the culture of the various classrooms in which you are enrolled. How do the cultures differ? Which culture(s) do you prefer? Why?

2. *Out-of-class assignment.* Organizational Culture

Using Exhibit 14.2 on p. 562, Adaptive Versus Unadaptive Cultures, you will give examples of companies from your own experience or from your research that have adaptive or unadaptive organizational cultures. Present your examples to the class.

3. *Discuss the following:* Flap Over Gas Additive Lingers

The Bush administration quietly shelved a proposal to ban a gasoline additive that contaminates drinking water in many communities, helping an industry that has donated more than $1 million to Republicans. The Environmental Protection Agency's decision had its origin in the early days of President Bush's tenure when his administration decided not to move ahead with a Clinton-era regulatory effort to ban the additive. The proposed regulation said the environmental harm of the additive leaching into ground water overshadowed its beneficial effects to the air. The producers of the additive told the Clinton administration that limiting its use "would inflict grave economic harm on member companies."

Discuss the culture of the administration that might lead to the decision to ban the additive. Discuss the ethical issues involved.

Source: "Flap over gas additive MTBE lingers," *Odessa American* (February 16, 2004): 3A.

4. *On the Web:* A Good Corporate Citizen? This Scanner Can Tell.

Go to www.swlearning.com/management/ Click on Management News. Click on Topic Index: Ethics and Social Responsibility. Click on A Good Corporate Citizen

A new digital tool uses a bar code reader to reveal whether a product has been made by a company with pollution complaints or ethics violations. The device could be used by consumers to make more informed buying decisions. Read about this product and write the answer to the questions for this internet exercise.

5. *Leader's Self-Insight* Culture Preference Inventory

The scores represent preferences for achievement, bureaucratic, adaptability, and clan cultures. Your personal values are consistent with the culture for which you achieved the highest score although all four sets of values exist within you just as they exist within an organization. Compare you scores with other students and discuss their meaning.

1. Are you pleased with your preferences?
2. Do you think your scores accurately described you?
3. How could this information help you in your career?

LEADERSHIP DEVELOPMENT: CASES FOR ANALYSIS

1. **Synopsis: Lisa Benavides, Forest International**

Lisa Benavides has just been hired as the vice president of human resources for Forest International. The new CEO recruited Benavides because he has ideas about empowerment, shared leadership, and teamwork that he hopes to implement in the company. Forest International operates in a dangerous industry; paper mills, sawmills, and plywood factories are filled with noise, saw blades, chemicals, and chutes loaded with tons of lumber. Forest has a poor safety record, productivity has been declining, and competitors are gaining market share. The CEO wants Benavides to help improve the safety record and increase productivity.

At Forest, taking chances proves you're a true "Forest-man." Workers brag about their "close calls" and share stories about dangerous encounters. Benavides believes that both worker and manager attitudes pose a problem. Workers believe that managers care more about profits than their well-being.

Case questions and answers

1. *How would you relate the culture of Forest International as it relates to internal integration and external adaptation?*

Forest International has an achievement culture, characterized by a clear vision of the organization's goals, and leaders focus on the achievement by specific targets such as sales growth. This is a results-oriented culture that values competitiveness, aggressiveness, personal initiative, and the willingness to work long and hard to achieve results. An emphasis is placed on winning.

Production managers emphasize the importance of keeping the line moving, getting the product out no matter what. Rather than finding a supervisor and asking that the production line be shut down, most line employees take changes on sticking their hands into moving equipment whenever there is a minor problem. Workers believe that mangers care more about productivity and profits than they do about the well-being of people at the plant.

2. *Would you expect that changing the culture at Forest would be easily accomplished now that a new CEO is committed to change?*

No, there will have to be small changes to enact the CEO's ideas about empowerment, shared leadership, and teamwork. However, the leader is important in shaping values, and the new CEO seems earnest in changing the safety and production record. New safety measures can be put in place followed by a communication campaign. The new president must show the workers that management values their well-being. The president's attitude and actions will signal a change. An organization's culture is often a reflection of the values advocated by a strong top leader.

3. *If you were Lisa Benavides, what suggestions would you make to Forest's new CEO?*

Lisa should try to shift Forest to a clan culture; this is what the new CEO values so he will be an important part of changing the culture. A clan culture has an internal focus on the involvement and participation of employees to meet changing expectations from the external environment rapidly. This culture places value on meeting the needs of employees. These organizations are friendly places to work and employees seem almost like a family. Leaders emphasize fairness, consideration, and avoiding status differences. New rituals, stories, and symbols can help change the culture at Forest to show that management cares about the workers.

2. **Synopsis:** **Acme and Omega**

Acme Electronics and Omega Electronics both manufacture integrated circuits and other electronic parts as subcontractors for large manufacturers. Both Acme and Omega are located in Ohio and often bid on contracts as competitors. Acme has sales of $100 million and employs 950 people. Omega has annual sales of $80 million and employs 800 people. The president of Acme believes that Acme is a far superior company, attributing its effectiveness to management's ability to run a tight ship. Acme had detailed charts and job descriptions. Tyler believed that everyone should have clear responsibilities and narrowly defined jobs. Omega's president does not believe in organizational charts, which put artificial barriers between specialists who should be working together. Employees rotate among departments to be familiar with activities throughout the organization. Acme announced the acquisition of Omega. The Omega managers resisted the merger, but the Acme president is determined to unify the companies quickly.

Case questions and answers.

1. *Using the competing values model, what type of culture (adaptability, achievement, clan, bureaucratic) would you say dominant at Acme? At Omega? What is your evidence?*

The bureaucratic culture is dominant at Acme with its focus on formality, order, obedience and rationality. Acme runs according to an organizational chart, which delineates clear responsibilities and narrowly defined jobs. The clan culture is dominant at Omega with its emphasis on consideration, agreement, social equality, and fairness. There is no organizational chart because it puts artificial barriers between people who should be working together. Employees at Omega are rotated among departments to be familiar with activities throughout the organization.

2. *Is there a culture gap? Which type of culture do you think is most appropriate for the newly merged company? Why?*

Yes. The difference between desired and actual values and behaviors is called a culture gap. There is a difference between the values and behaviors at Acme and Omega. Acme has a formal, structured culture whereas Omega has an informal, less structured culture.

The Adaptability Culture would be most appropriate because of the rapidly changing external environment. The bureaucratic culture functions in a stable environment, and the clan culture is not generating the profit level that would be acceptable to the new owners, Acme. The adaptability culture allows for creativity experimentation and risk-taking, but is very responsive to customers.

3. *If you were John Tyler, what techniques would you use to integrate and shape the cultures to overcome the culture gap?*

To change cultural values, Tyler can listen to employees and build trust by accepting employee ideas and initiative. Culture can be shaped through ceremonies, stories, symbols, language, and the selection and socialization of new employees. It is Tyler's responsibility to instill the new cultural values on a daily basis, namely through his own behavior. Social events can help integrate the workers of both companies. Listening to the ideas of Omega's workers will help them feel valued. Tyler will have to change his personal attitude toward Omega's culture or the merger will be a flop.

CHAPTER FIFTEEN
DESIGNING AND LEADING A LEARNING ORGANIZATION

CHAPTER SUMMARY

This chapter traced the evolution of leadership though and action, which reflects a shift from stable to chaotic environments. Early leadership perspectives emphasized great men and the traits that enabled them to succeed in government, commerce, the military, or social movements. The next era was rational management that fit the organizational context of vertical hierarchies and bureaucracies. Because of the world's transition to a more chaotic environment in recent years, team leadership became important, with its potential for enabling horizontal organizations and open communication. Finally, the most recent era is about learning leadership, in which leaders use the skills of vision, alignment, and relationships to unlock personal qualities of followers in adaptive, learning organizations.

Leaders can use an understanding of the adaptive learning cycle to encourage ongoing learning. The cycle of action, feedback, and synthesis means that people sense the environment and act on what they observe, then evaluate feedback to see whether actions led to the desired effect. Learning leaders encourage experimentation, taking risks, making mistakes, and reflecting because these activities lead to learning and change. To design learning organizations, leaders look at the five elements of structure, tasks, systems, strategy, and culture.

For many of today's companies, these elements developed during a time when environments were stable and organizations were based primarily on mass-production technology. Characteristics such as a strong vertical hierarchy, specialized routine jobs, formal information and control systems, a directed competitive strategy, and strong internal culture helped organizations perform efficiently and consistently. However, these organizations may no longer work in today's chaotic world.

Many leaders are transforming their organizations into something called the learning organization, a fluid, flexible system almost like a biological entity, capable of continuous learning and adaptability. Boundaries between organizations are also becoming permeable, as even competitors collaborate to share resources and exploit new opportunities. In a learning organization, responsibility and authority are pushed down to the lowest level. Strategy, rather than being directed top-down as in a traditional organization, can emerge from anywhere in the learning organization. In addition, learning organizations develop cultural values that emphasize adaptation and change.

Today's leaders face a dual challenge to maintain efficient performance and become a learning organization at the same time. Leaders meet the challenge by building ambidextrous organizations that incorporate structures and processes appropriate to innovation and learning as well as to the efficient implementation of ideas. Other ways to support both efficiency and learning are to embrace new technology and use after-action reviews. Both of these approaches facilitate the adaptive learning cycle, and provide ways for leaders to support learning and change at the same time they enhance the organization's efficiency and productivity.

CHAPTER OPENER

Lorenzo Zambrano, CEO of Cemex

Cementos Mexicanos (Cemex) specializes in developing areas of the world—specializes in developing areas of the world---places where anything can, and usually does, go wrong. To cope with the extreme complexity of their business, CEO Lorenzo Zambrano and other leaders developed a new approach to delivering cement, which they call "living with chaos." Rather than trying to change the customers, the weather, the traffic, or the labor conditions, Cemex designed a company in which last-minute changes and unexpected problems are routine. A core element of the new approach is the company's complex information technology infrastructure, which includes a global positioning satellite system and on-board computers in all delivery trucks that are continuously fed with streams of day-to-day data on customer orders, production schedules, traffic problems, and weather conditions. Cemex trucks now operate as self-organizing business units. Cemex has transformed the industry by combining extensive networking technology with a new leadership approach that taps the mind power of everyone in the company.

LECTURE/OUTLINE

To trace the evolution of leadership through four eras to the learning leadership required in many organizations today..

The Evolution of Leadership *Exhibit 15.1*

Many concepts of leadership emerged during times of stability, when people believed the world was stable and could be predictable and controlled with logic and rationality.

The concepts and organizational forms created during this stable era still shape the design of many organizations and the training of managers.

Leaders in today's fast-shifting world stand at the threshold of a new era, and they are learning to free themselves from outdated practices and patterns to meet new challenges.

Discussion Question #1: *Do you agree that the world of organizations is shifting to a new era? How do you feel about being a leader during this time of transition?*

Notes____

____

____

Context of Organizational Leadership

Leadership is directly related to the leader's way of thinking about self, followers, organizations, and the environment.

The evolution of leadership thought and action has unfolded in four eras discussed according to two dimensions:

- whether leadership works on a *micro* level or a *macro* level
- whether environmental conditions are *stable* or *chaotic.*

The micro side of leadership concerns specific situations, tasks, and individuals.

The focus is on one person and one task at a time, and on the processes and behaviors needed to reach certain goals.

This is a logical objective approach to leadership.

The macro side transcends individuals, groups, and specific situations to focus on whole communities, whole organizations, and deeply fundamental ideals, values, and strategies.

It is concerned with purpose, strategy, meaning, and culture.

The stable versus chaotic dimensions refers to whether elements in the environment are dynamic.

An environment is stable if it remains the same over months or years.

Under chaotic conditions, environmental elements shift abruptly.

Leaders learn to support risk learning.

Framework

Each cell in the Leadership Evolution model summarizes an era of leadership thinking, which may have been correct once, but inappropriate for today's fast-changing world.

Macro Leadership in a Stable World

Era I may be conceptualized as pre-industrial and pre- bureaucratic.

Most organizations were small and run by a single individual who hired workers because they were friends or relatives not because of their skills or qualifications.

This is the era of "Great Man" leadership and the emphasis on personal traits of leaders.

A leader was conceptualized as a single hero who saw the big picture and how everything fit into a whole.

Micro Leadership in a Stable World

Era 2 sees the emergence of hierarchy and bureaucracy.

Although the world remains stable, organizations have begun to grow so large that they require rules and standard procedures to ensure that activities are performed efficiency and effectively.

Hierarchy of authority provides a sensible mechanism for supervision and control of workers, and decisions based on tradition are replaced with precise procedures.

This era sees the rise of the "rational manager" who directs and controls others using an impersonal approach.

The focus is on details rather than the big picture; the rational manager was well-suited to a stable environment.

The idea that leaders could analyze their situation, develop plans, and control the results was quite compelling----but rational management is no longer sufficient in today's world.

Micro Leadership in a Chaotic World

Era 3 represented a shock to managers in North America and Europe.

The world was no longer stable, and prized techniques of rational management were no longer successful.

Beginning with the OPEC oil embargo of 1972-73 and continuing with severe global competition in the 1980s and early 1990s, managers saw environmental conditions become chaotic.

This became an era for confusion for leaders as the Japanese began to dominate commerce with their ideas of team leadership and superb quality.

Managers tried team-based approaches, downsizing, quality programs and empowerment as ways to improve performance and get more motivation and commitment from employees.

This is the era of the team leader.

Many of today's leaders are comfortable with teams, diversity, and open communication while others are still trapped in the old ways of rational management for a stable world.

Macro Leadership in a Chaotic World

Enter the digital information age.

Era 4 represents the *learning leader* who has given up control in the traditional sense and uses vision, values, and relationships rather than position to influence others.

Leaders constantly experimenting, learning, and changing both in their personal and professional lives, and they encourage the development and growth of others.

Leaders need resilience to flourish in an environment of chaos and uncertainty.

Leaders strive to create the *learning organization,* in which each person is intimately involved in identifying and solving problems.

Leaders stop managing details and focus on creating a vision and shaping the culture and values to achieve it.

Implications

The implication is that leadership reflects the era or context of the organization and society.

Many organizations and leaders are struggling with a transition form a stable to a chaotic environment and the qualities needed.

To recognize how leaders build learning organizations through changes in structure, tasks, systems, strategy, and culture.

The Adaptive Learning Cycle *Exhibit 15.2*

- *What is learning?*
- *Why do some individuals and organizations learn faster and better than others?*

Learning is a change in behavior or performance that occurs as a result of experience.

Today's leaders look for ways to build and enhance learning capabilities in individuals and the entire organization.

The model illustrates the *adaptive learning cycle*, a cycle of action, feedback, and synthesis that all living organisms share.

Every living thing survives by sensing the environment around it, responding with action, and correcting itself if feedback and synthesis indicate that previous actions were inappropriate.

A person sensing the environment might include observing others, reading, or listening to sources of information; then the individual acts; feedback can be positive or negative.

By evaluating feedback, the individual determines if the actions achieved the desired effect.

Learning organizations "live" the adaptive learning cycle every day.

Leaders encourage experimentation, taking risks, making mistakes, and changing.

Adaptive learning leads to new products, services, and better ways of doing business.

Research indicated that the average life span of *Fortune 500* companies is 50 years because they focus on profit and shut down the feedback that encourages learning and change.

Learning organizations keep feedback mechanisms open to evolve, adapt, learn, and grow.

Discussion Question #2: *Think of a recent personal experience that illustrates the adaptive learning cycle. Do you think adaptive learning might affect some parts of an organization more than others? Discuss.*

Notes____

____

____

From Efficient Performance to the Learning Organization *Exhibit 15.3*

When the environment was stable, leaders could effectively use rational management to maintain control and stability within the organization.

Today, designing organizations strictly for efficient performance is generally not effective.

Knowledge and information are more important than production machinery.

Many leaders are redesigning their companies toward the *learning organization*, one in which everyone is engaged in identifying and solving problems.

The learning organization is skilled in acquiring, transferring, and building knowledge that enables the organization to continuously experiment, improve, and increase its capability.

The learning organization is based on equality, shared information, little hierarchy, and a shared culture that encourages adaptability and enables the organization to seize opportunities and handle crises.

Two Models of Organization comparee organizations designed for efficient performance with those designed for continuous learning by looking at five elements of organizational design: structure, tasks, systems, strategy, and culture.

- The efficient performance organization is based on a hard, rational model, characterized by a vertical structure, formalized systems, routine tasks, competitive strategy, and a rigid culture.

- The learning organization emerges from a soft, intuitive perspective of organizations.

  Structures are more horizontal and employees are empowered to act independently and creatively.

  Strategy emerges from collaborative links within and among organizations, and the culture encourages experimentation and adaptability.

❑ *Living Leadership: Five Beliefs for Learning Leaders*

Learning leaders encourage adaptation through their beliefs: Failure is an opportunity.

➢ What are the five beliefs that leaders who want to encourage adaptive learning live by?

Discussion Question #3: *What are the primary differences between a traditional, functionally-organized company and the horizontally-organized learning organization?*

Notes____

To know when and how horizontally-oriented structures provide advantages over vertical, functionally organized ones.

Organization Structure *Exhibit 15.4*

➢ *Describe the traditional organizational structure.*

The traditional organizational structure, shaped like a pyramid with the CEO at the top, and everyone else in layers down below, is a legacy that dates back nearly a century.

These vertical structures are effective in stable times.

However, they become a liability in a fast- changing environment.

Hierarchical, vertical structures create distance between managers and workers and build walls between departments; they do not allow for the fast coordinated response needed in today's world.

Many organizations are shifting toward horizontal structures based on work processes rather than departmental functions.

Most companies are in the middle of the evolutionary scale.

Vertical Structure

Activities are grouped together by function from the bottom to the top of the organization as shown in part A.

Little collaboration occurs across departments, and employees are committed to achieving the goals of their own functional units.

The whole organization is coordinated and controlled through the vertical hierarchy, with decision-making authority residing with upper-level managers.

This structure promotes efficient production and indepth skill development of employees. Hierarchy of authority provides a sensible mechanism of control.

However, in a rapidly changing environment, the vertical hierarchy becomes overloaded.

Top executives cannot respond quickly enough to threats or opportunities.

Poor coordination among departments inhibits innovation.

Most companies maintain elements of a traditional structure but have found ways to increase horizontal communication and collaboration across departments.

Notes____

____

____

Horizontal Structure

Horizontal structure is created around work flows or processes rather than departmental functions.

The people who work on a particular process have access to each other to communicate and coordinate their efforts, share knowledge, and provide value directly to customers.

Self-directed teams are the fundamental unit of the horizontal structure; they are made up of employees with different skills who rotate jobs to produce a product or service.

Boundaries between departments are reduced or eliminated.

The vertical hierarchy is flattened, with only a few executives in traditional support functions such as finance or human resources.

Team members are given the skills, information, tools, motivation, and authority to make decisions and are empowered to respond creatively and flexibly to the challenges that arise.

In a horizontal learning organization, effectiveness is measured by end-of-process performance objectives---based on bringing value to the customer---as well as customer satisfaction, employee satisfaction, and financial contribution.

In the Lead: GE Salisbury

General Electric's plant in North Carolina, which manufactures lighting panel boards for industrial and commercial purposes, used to be organized functionally and vertically. By the early 1990s, GE Salisbury had made the transition to a horizontal structure that links sets of multiskilled teams who are responsible for the entire build-to-order process. The key to success of the horizontal structure is that all the operating teams work in concert with each other and have access to the information they need to meet team and process goals.

Q: *How has GE Salisbury restructured to become a learning organization?*

A: Learning organizations strive to break down boundaries GE leaders reorganized the plants into a number of horizontal groups based on work flows rather than functions. Teams are linked and assume responsibility for setting their own production targets, determining production schedules, assigning duties, and identifying and solving problems.

Companies collaborate in new ways to share resources and exploit opportunities.

Emerging forms such as the network organization and the virtual organization are horizontal teams of companies rather than teams of individuals.

A network structure keeps key activities at home and out-sources otherfanctions such as sales to partner organizations or individuals.

Discussion Question #4: *Discuss the primary reasons so many of today's organizations are empowering lower level workers.*

Notes____

To distinguish between tasks and roles and how each impacts employee satisfaction and organizational performance.

Task versus Roles

A *task* is a narrowly defined piece of work assigned to a person.

In a stable environment, tasks tend to be rigidly defined, and employees have little to say about performing their jobs.

A *role* is a part in a social system with discretion and responsibility (e.g., the role of a mother in a family or a manager on an organization).

An organizational role is an opportunity to use one's ability to achieve an outcome.

In chaotic environments, employees need freedom and responsibility to make decisions and react quickly to changing conditions.

Mechanistic and Organic Processes

Burns and Stalker use the terms *mechanistic* and *organic* to explain organizational responses to the external environment.

When the external environment is stable, tasks tend to be mechanistic with rigid rules and a clear hierarchy.

Knowledge and control are centralized at the top, and employees are told what to do and how to do it.

Mechanistic tasks characterize the efficient performance organization (e.g., the mass-production assembly line.)

Workers perform routinized, structured tasks.

In rapidly changing environments, tasks are much looser, free flowing, and adaptive; Burns and Stalker call the organization *organic.*

Leaders push authority and responsibility down to lower level employees, encouraging them to experiment, learn, and solve problems.

Teamwork is highly valued, and there are few strict rules and procedures.

The organization is more fluid and can adapt to environmental changes.

From Routine Task to Empowered Roles

Learning organizations use an organic form.

Employees play a role in the department or team, and roles are adjusted or redefined through employee interaction within and among teams.

Empowerment means sharing power with everyone in the organization so each person can act more freely to accomplish a job.

Knowledge work relies on project teams and cross-functional collaboration that is inherently resistant to formal authority.

In the learning organization, the leader's role is to give workers information and the right to act on it.

In the Lead: **Lynn Mercer, Lucent Technologies**

Philip Dailey strings cable inside a steel box the size of a refrigerator---a digital transmitting station for cellular phone systems. Studying a bottleneck along the assembly line, Dailey realized a way to increase output by 33 percent. He did not have to talk to his bosses about his insight; he simply recruited temporary workers from other teams and made it happen. Lynn Mercer, plant manager at Lucent Technologies' factory, distributes authority three levels down because she believes those people know the job better than she does. Teams elect their own leaders to oversee quality, training, scheduling, and coordination with other teams. The factory is flooded with information because Mercer believes that is how any complex system balances it. Every procedure is written down, but procedures are constantly changing---any worker can propose changed any procedure in the plant.

Q: *How does Lynn Mercer use empowerment at Lucent?*

A: Empowerment means sharing power so that everyone in the organization can act more freely to perform a job. Lynn Mercer distributes authority three levels down because she believes those people know the job better than she does. Teams elect their own leaders to oversee quality, training, scheduling, and coordination with other teams.

Discussion Question #7: *What is the difference between a task and a role? Between formal systems and personal networks? Discuss.*

Notes____

To meet the dual challenge of supporting both efficiency and learning by using ambidextrous organization design elements, embracing technology, and using after-action reviews.

Systems versus Networks *Exhibit 15.5*

In small, young organizations, communication is generally informal and face-to-face.

There are few formal control and information systems because leaders work closely with employees.

As companies grow, they establish formal systems to manage the growing amount of complex information.

The danger is that formal systems become so entrenched that information no longer filters down to the people on the front lines who need it for their jobs and customer service.

The grapevine is a remnant of the time of freely shared information.

People who thrive in learning organizations are those who build extensive networks of personal and organizational relationships.

Leaders not only spend time networking with others inside and outside the company but understand and nourish the personal networks of others throughout the organization.

Knowledge is shared rather than hoarded, and ideas may be implemented anywhere in the country to improve the organization.

Learning organizations encourage open lines of communication with customers, suppliers, and even competitors.

Bringing outside organizations into communication networks enhances learning capability as well as potential to serve customers better.

Learning organizations practice *open-book management,* which means sharing data about budgets, profits, expenses, and other financial matters with everyone in the organization.

Competitive versus Linked Strategy

Top managers in traditional organizations formulate and implement strategy and engage in strategic planning.

In learning organizations, strategy emerges bottom up as well as top down.

When all employees are linked with the vision, their collective actions contribute to strategy development.

Strategy can also emerge from partnership linkages with suppliers, customers, and even competitors.

Learning organizations have permeable boundaries and are linked with other companies, giving each greater access to information about new strategic needs and direction.

Some learning organizations openly share information with competitors or allow competitors to observe their "best practices"; they believe that sharing keeps their company competitive.

Discussion Question #5: *Discuss how bringing other organizations into a company's information network might contribute to strategy.*

Notes____

Rigid versus Adaptive Culture

Many organizations become victims of their own success, clinging to outdated values and behaviors because of rigid cultures that do not encourage adaptability and change.

A learning organization has a strong, adaptive culture to include the following values:

- *The whole is more important than the part, and boundaries between parts are minimized.* People are aware of the whole system, how everything fits together, and the relationships among various organizational parts.

  Everyone considers how his actions affect other elements of the organization.

- *Equality is a primary value.* The culture of a learning organization creates a sense of community, compassion, and caring for one another.

  Each person is valued, and the organization becomes a place for creating a web of relationships that allow people to develop their full potential.

- *The culture encourages change, risk-taking, and improvement.* A basic value is to question the status quo, the current way of doing things.

  Constant questioning of assumptions opens the gates to creativity and improvement.

In the Lead: Bill George, Medtronic, Inc.

When Bill George took over as CEO of Medtronic, Inc. in 1989, it was a $1 billion company that primarily made and sold pacemakers. Twelve years later, it had grown to a value of $63 million. Part of the reason is that George and his top leadership team focused everyone on the company's mission and created a structure, culture, and management system that encourage learning, innovation, and adaptability. Rather than focusing of shareholder value, leaders at Medtronic align everyone's actions toward the mission of "restoring people to full life and health." To fulfill the mission, they have built an adaptable organization based on teamwork rather than a rigid hierarchy.

Q: *How has Medtronic s created a learning environment?"*

A: People at Medtronics are encouraged to tap into their passions for ideas that may lead to new products or administrative innovations. Risk-taking is rewarded, and failure is seen as a route to learning and adaptability. Even though George left in 2001, the learning environment he helped to create at Medtronic has remained strong and continues to help the company adapt in a volatile industry.

Discussion Question #6: *Why are cultural values of minimal boundaries and equality important in a learning organization compared to an efficient performance organization?*

Notes____

____

____

The Leader's Dual Challenge

Leaders face the challenge to maintain efficient performance and become a learning organization at the same time.

This is achieved by balancing the hard and soft aspects of organizational design.

Three leader approaches are to embrace both efficiency and learning in organization design elements, to embrace new technology, and to use a mechanism called the *after-action review.*

Embracing Efficiency and Learning

Ambidextrous organizations are flexible organizations in which leaders incorporate structures and management processes that are appropriate to innovation and learning, as well as to the efficient implementation of ideas.

The organization behaves in an organic, flexible way when the situation calls for creativity and the initiation of new ideas and a more mechanistic way to put those ideas to use.

One type of department is a *skunkworks*, a separate small, informal group where talented people have the time and freedom to be creative and developing breakthrough ideas.

A *venture teams* is like a small company with a separate location so it is not constrained by traditional organizational procedures as they work on a project or idea.

The problem for traditional organizations is that rigid boundaries limit learning and change.

Notes____

Embracing New Technology

➤ *Now that the economic bubble of the 1990s has burst, what is the status of the information technology revolution?*

The number of Internet users and online sales continue to grow.

Leaders in traditional companies are using e-business to improve internal coordination, collaborate with partners, cut costs, increase productivity, and serve customers better.

Technology can keep people all across the organization in touch through networks of computers and the use of *intranets*---internal communication systems that use the Internet.

Knowledge management refers to the efforts to systematically gather knowledge, make it widely available throughout the organization, and foster a culture of collaboration and learning.

Another way in which information technology contributes to learning is by creating a sense of community of customers among far-flung people in today's global economy.

There are two main reasons that embracing technology spurs adaptive learning.

For one thing, share information shares power. New technology enables leaders to share all information, so that people have access whatever they need, whenever they need it.

Technology breaks down the rigid boundaries of a hierarchical pyramid to create a web of relationships---the organization becomes a form that links partners, employees, external contractors, suppliers and customers.

Open, web-like systems allow for ideas, decisions, and strategies to emerge from anywhere within or outside the organization.

Discussion question #8: *How can the use of new technology support and accelerate the adaptive learning cycle?*

Notes____

____

____

Using After-Action Reviews

➢ *Why are reviews of past events useful?*

An essential element of the learning process is that people have time to reflect on what happened or did not happen in response to a particular action and why.

When people review the experiences of the past, they learn valuable lessons for how to do things better in the future.

After-action review (AAR) is a disciplined procedure whereby leaders invest time to help people review their events and activities on a regular basis and continually learn from them.

An AAR for a small event might only last a few minutes, while the AAR of a major project might last a day or so.

The key is that leaders invest the time on a regular daily basis and instill a spirit of inquiry, openness and learning.

***In the Lead*:** U.S. Army

At the National Training Center, U.S. Army troops engage in simulated battle; the "enemy" has sent unmanned aerial vehicles to gather data. After the exercise, unit members and their superiors hold an after-action review to review battle plans, discuss what worked and what didn't, and talk about how to do things better. In the U.S. Army, after-action reviews, take just 15 minutes, and they occur after every event---large or small, simulated or real. The review involves asking four questions: What was supposed to happen? What actually happened? What accounts for the difference? What can we learn?

Q: *How did AAR help the U.S. as a learning institution?*

A: AAR is a process of identifying mistakes, of innovating, and of continuous learning from experience. The lessons learned are stockpiled, and compile intelligence reports.

The organization is learning by applying feedback and synthesis to understand and learn from consequences.

Compiling what is learned creates an improved organization.

As an organizational learning method, AARs are an ongoing practice rather than a special procedure.

After-action reviews can spur greater learning when they are integrated into the daily life of the organization and part of the culture that encourages people to ask questions.

Discussion question #9: *Do you think it is reasonable for a leader to conduct an after-action review for every identifiable event, large or small? Have you participated on a work, school, or sports team that used a process similar to that of the after-action review? How did it affect your learning?*

Notes____

____

____

DISCUSSION QUESTIONS

1. *Do you agree that the world of organizations is shifting to a new era? How do you feel about being a leader during this time of transition?*

Yes, this is the digital information age. *Era 4* represents the *learning leader* who has given up control in the traditional sense and uses vision, values, and relationships rather than position to influence others. Leaders constantly experimenting, learning, and changing both in their personal and professional lives, and they encourage the development and growth of others. This is an exciting time because technology has permitted people from all over the world to work together of projects.

2. *Think of a recent personal experience that illustrates the adaptive learning cycle. Do you think adaptive learning might affect some parts of an organization more than others? Discuss.*

A surgeon at the local hospital has excellent skills and training but could not get along with the referring doctors. When he went to the supervisor to see if his contract would be renewed, he was told that it would not be renewed because his referrals were low. He realized that his own behavior towards the other doctors had cost him his referrals and his job. Adaptive learning affects all parts of the organization. Feedback causes a person or an organization to change behavior or suffer adverse consequences. Learning takes place.

3. *What are the primary differences between a traditional, functionally-organized company and the horizontally-organized learning organization?*

In a Vertical Structure, activities are grouped together by ftmction from the bottom to the top of the organization. Little collaboration occurs across departments, and employees are committed to achieving the goals of their own functional units. The whole organization is coordinated and controlled through the vertical hierarchy, with decision-making authority residing with upperlevel managers. A Horizontal Structure is created around work flows or processes rather than departmental fitrictions; processes are based on meeting customer needs. Self-directed teams are made up of employees with different skills who rotate jobs to produce a product or service. They deal directly with customers, making changes, and improvements. Team members have the authority to make decisions.

4. *Discuss the primary reasons so many of today's organizations are empowering lower level workers.*

Fully empowered employees are given larger roles with decision-making authority and control over how job performance and power to influence and change organizational goals, structures, and reward systems. A company can then respond rapidly to changing environmental conditions. Knowledge work relies on project teams and cross-functional collaboration that is inherently resistant to formal authority. In the learning organization, the leader's role is to give workers information and the right to act on it.

5. *Discuss how bringing other organizations into a company's information network might contribute to strategy.*

By linking with suppliers, customers, and even competitors, organizations become collaborators more than competitors, experimenting to find the best way to learn and adapt. As a result, each organization has greater access to information about new strategic needs and directions.

6. *Why are cultural values of minimal boundaries and equality important in a learning organization compared to an efficient performance organization?*

People are aware of the whole system, how everything fits together, and the relationships among various organizational parts. Everyone considers how his actions affect others. This reduces boundaries. Equality creates a sense of community, compassion, and caring for one another. In an efficient performance organization, workers identify only with their function or department and not the whole organization.

7. *What is the difference between a task and a role? Between formal systems and personal networks? Discuss.*

A task is a narrowly defined piece of work assigned to a person. In a stable environment, tasks are rigidly defined, and employees have little to say about performing their jobs. A role is a part in a social system with discretion and responsibility. Companies establish formal systems to manage the growing amount of information. However, formal systems become so entrenched that information no long filters down to the people who need it. With personal networks, people serve on teams and talk to whoever has the information.

8. *How can the use of new technology support and accelerate the adaptive learning cycle?*

Technology can keep people all across the organization in touch through networks of computers and the use of *intranets*---internal communication systems that use the Internet.

Knowledge management refers to the efforts to systematically gather knowledge, make it widely available throughout the organization, and foster a culture of collaboration and learning. Another way in which information technology contributes to learning is by creating a sense of community of customers among far-flung people in today's global economy.

There are two main reasons that embracing technology spurs adaptive learning.
For one thing, share information shares power. New technology enables leaders to share all information, so that people have access whatever they need, whenever they need it. Technology breaks down the rigid boundaries of a hierarchical pyramid to create a web of relationships---the organization becomes a form that links partners, employees, external contractors, suppliers and customers.

9. *Do you think it is reasonable for a leader to conduct an after-action review for every identifiable event, large or small? Have you participated on a work, school, or sports team that used a process similar to that of the after-action review? How did it affect your learning?*

Yes, the ARR can be very short, 15 minutes or less. I have participated in planning and implementing many special events, and following the event, an evaluation pointed to the strengths and weakness of the outcome. The ARR allowed for better future planning. Here is a simple example. A local medical group has a flower sale to benefit children's charities. We took phone orders from our members, and hoped they would send in their payment. It became an accounting nightmare because people forgot to send in checks. The volunteers had to keep calling and sending bills. The next year, we used credit cards and the process was far smoother.

TEACHING TOOLS AND EXERCISES

1. *Leader's Bookshelf: Good to Great: Why Some Companies Make the Leap...And Others Don't* by Jim Collins

Collins identifies 11 great companies and identifies a number of characteristics that distinguish them. See p. 608. What are some of the key factors? Discuss them in small groups.

2. *On the Web:* Medtronic

Find out what makes Medtronic, Inc., featured on p. 615, a learning organization. Go to www.vault.com, Vault, a health care career web site and then go to the Medtronic website at www.medtronic.com What is Medtronic doing to remain competitive?

3. *Leader's Self Insight*: Am I Networked?

Networking is the active process of building and managing productive relationships—a vast web of personal and organizational relationships. Networking builds social, work, and career relationships that facilitate mutual understanding and mutual benefit. Learning organizations Accomplish much of their work through networks rather than formal hierarchies. People with active networks tend to be more effective change managers and have a broader impact on the organization. Discuss the results of your questionnaire with another student.

4. *Out-of-class assignment:* The Learning Organization

Many organizations are striving to be learning organizations and encourage learning to take place on a continual basis throughout the organization. Review several business publications such as *Fortune* or *Business Week* or find the website of such a company. How does this company encourage organizational learning? Why does this organization view learning as a critical ingredient for organizational effectiveness?

5. *Interview:* Interview three managers from three different companies. Find out if these companies have elements of a learning organization. If not, what would you recommend if you were the leader of these organizations.

LEADERSHIP DEVELOPMENT: CASES FOR ANALYSIS

Synopsis: The Fairfax County Social Welfare Agency

The Fairfax County Social Welfare Agency was created in 1965 to administer services under six federally funded social service grants. The agency's organizational structure evolved as new grants were received and as new programs were created. Staff members---generally the individuals who had written the original grants---were assigned to coordinate the activities required to implement the programs. All program directors reported to the agency's executive director, Wendy Eckstein, and had a strong commitment to the success and growth of their respective programs. The organizational structure was simple, with a comprehensive administrative department handling client records, and personnel matters. The sense of program ownership was intense. There was a great deal of conflict among program directors and their subordinates. Client complaints increased and Eckstein discovered the following: staff members tended not to refer clients to other programs; a total absence of integration prevailed; and programs showed duplication. A major reorganization is being considered.

Case questions and answers

1. *Refer back to Exhibit 15.3. What elements of the agency could be causing the problems?*

The elements causing problems are the rigid culture, the formal structure, and the competitive strategy. Hierarchical structures create distance between managers and workers and build walls between departments; they do not allow for the fast, coordinated response needed in today's world.

At the agency, all program directors reported to the agency's executive director, Wendy Eckstein, and had a strong commitment to the success and growth of their respective programs without coordination with other departments. The organizational structure was simple, with a comprehensive administrative department handling client records, and personnel matters. There is a lack of coordination between staff members and program directors. Staff members tended not to refer clients to other programs; a total absence of integration prevailed; and programs showed duplication.

2. *In what era (Exhibit 15.1) do the program directors seem to be. Explain.*

The program directors seem to be in *Era 2,* the hierarchy and bureaucracy. Hierarchy of authority provides a sensible mechanism for supervision and control of workers, and decisions based on tradition are replaced with precise procedures. This era sees the rise of the "rational manager" who directs and controls others using an impersonal approach. The focus is on details rather than the big picture; the rational manager was well-suited to a stable environment.

There is a clear hierarchy at the agency because all program directors report to the agency's executive director. Knowledge and control are centralized at the top, in the office of Wendy Eckstein, and employees are told what to do. Mechanistic tasks characterize the efficient performance organization. At the agency, the organizational structure is simple, with a comprehensive administrative department handling client records, and personnel matters. The sense of program ownership is intense.

3. *If you were Eckstein, how would you lead the agency toward becoming more of a leaming organization? Discuss.*

Eckstein should dismantle the vertical hierarchy and adopt more of a horizontal structure, created around work flows or processes rather than departmental functions. The people who work on a particular process have access to each other to communicate and coordinate their efforts, share knowledge, and provide value directly to clients. She should empower staff members and allow them to make decisions.

Eckstein should lead the organization towards a symbolic frame; the organization is perceived a system of shared meanings and values--- helping individuals by availing them of all the services at the welfare department. Eckstein should use rituals, ceremonies, stories, and symbols to create and reinforce a more open corporate culture that is needed for the learning organization. As a leader of a learning organization, Eckstein needs to emphasize shared vision, culture, and values and inspire the employees to higher levels of performance and commitment. Workers need to see the big picture, creating a better life for the citizens of Fairfax County, not their individual program.

2. **Synopsis: Acworth Systems**

Richard Acworth feels his company slipping away. Acworth Systems helps companies design, install, and implement complex back-office software systems. Richard and his brother Tom started the company and made a conscious choice to run the company with as few formal rules and procedures as possible. Acworth had no formal organization chart, no job titles or descriptions, and very few rules. Acworth employees were a close-knit group. However, all that was before the growth explosion. Within a year, sales grew from $5 million to nearly $20 million and the staff grew from 20 to 75. Consultants who were constantly on the go working out of their homes and keeping in touch with headquarters via phone and e-mail. Teams rarely called on one another for help anymore. Everyone was so busy handling their own projects that had little interest in anyone else's problems. Acworth scheduled a few "all-hands" meetings to try to keep everyone focused on common goals. Richard and Tom spend most of their time trying to find out where the teams are and whether projects are on schedule. A management consultant suggested that Acworth get some structure.

Case questions and answers

1. *What do you think is the primary problem at Acworth Systems?*

   The primary problem is insufficient communication. In a horizontal structure, sharing information and knowledge is critical so that everyone is working in accordance with the shared vision and does not lose touch with core values. This is harder as an organization grows and becomes more decentralized. People throughout the organization need to have access to whatever information they need whenever they need it—and they often won't know what they need until the very moment it's needed. Today, organizations share astonishing amounts of information with customers, partners, and even competitors.

2. *What elements of a learning organization are evident at Acworth? What elements seem to be missing?*

The elements of a learning organization evident at Acworth are a decentralized horizontal structure with authority and decision making given to teams. Acworth empowers its employees, sharing power with employees. In a learning organization, people serve on teams, and Acworth has divided employees into self-directed teams.

What is missing at Acworth is a shared vision for the organization. In a learning organization, the whole is more important than the part, and boundaries between parts are minimized. People are aware of the whole system, how everything fits together, and the relationships among various organizational parts. Everyone considers how their actions affect other elements of the organization.

Also missing is a system of personal networks. Open-book management and open communication are accepted methods. New information technology plays a significant role in keeping people in large, complex organizations in touch. Networks of computers, Internet technology, and the use of intranets and extranets can change the locus of knowledge by getting information to people who really need it.

3. *Do you agree that Acworth needs to create "some structure" for the organization? Discuss how they might do so.*

Yes. Acworth leaders face the challenge of balancing the hard and soft aspects of organizational design. Organizations need mechanisms for controlling and directing resources, but Tom and Richard can build mechanisms that are based on shared purpose, common assumptions, and trust. The Acworth brothers can build a shared vision, help employees see the whole system, and expand the opportunity for employees to shape the future. Acworth Systems can use symbols, rituals, and stories to reinforce the culture's core values and reestablish a feeling among employees of being close-knit despite company growth.

CHAPTER SIXTEEN
LEADING CHANGE

CHAPTER SUMMARY

The important point of this chapter is that tools and approaches are available to help leaders manage and create change. Change is inevitable in organizations, and the increased pace of change in today's global environment has created even greater problems for leaders struggling to help their organizations adapt. A major factor in the failure of organizations to adapt to changes in the global environment is the lack of effective change leadership. Leaders who can successfully accomplish change typically define themselves as change leaders, describe a vision for the future in vivid terms, and articulate values that promote change and adaptability. Change leaders are courageous, are capable of managing complexity and uncertainty, believe in followers' capacity to assume responsibility for change, and learn from their own mistakes.

Major changes can be particularly difficult to implement, but leaders can help to ensure a successful change effort by following the eight-stage model of planned change --- establish a sense of urgency; create a powerful coalition; develop a compelling vision and strategy; communicate the vision; empower employees to act; generate short-term wins; consolidate gains and tackle bigger problems; and institutionalize the change in the. organizational culture. Leaders also facilitate change on a daily basis by using everyday change strategies , including disruptive self-expression, verbal jujitsu, variable-term opportunism, and strategic alliance building.

A critical aspect of leading change is understanding why people resist change and how to overcome resistance. Leaders can use communication and training, participation and involvement, and ---as a last resort---coercion to overcome resistance. Leaders can use communication and training, participation and involvement, and ---as last resort— coercion to overcome resistance. Leaders should recognize that change could have negative as well as positive consequences. One of the most difficult situations leaders may face is downsizing. Leaders should use techniques to help ease the stress and hardship for employees who leave as well as maintain the morale and trust of those who remain.

Leaders are also responsible for moving the organization forward by leading for innovation. One way is by creating an environment that nourishes creativity in particular organizations or the entire organization. Five elements of innovative organizations are alignment, self-initiated activity, unofficial activity, diverse stimuli, and within-company communication. These correspond to characteristics of creative individuals. Creative people are less resistant to change.

Although some people demonstrate more creativity than others, research suggests that everyone has roughly equal creative potential. Understanding the stages of the creative process can help people be more creative. These stages---recognition of a problem or opportunity, information gathering, incubation, insight, and evaluation and implementation---do not always occur in the same order and may overlap. Leaders can encourage and support creativity to help followers and organizations be more responsive and change-ready.

CHAPTER OPENER

Bill Zollars, Yellow Freight System

Bill Zollars saw the chance to create a new company at Yellow Freight System. Zollars signed on as CEO with a mandate—not just to revive the company's image, but to transform Yellow Freight into a completely different company. Today, Yellow is still in the business of hauling big, heavy freight, but how shipments are delivered and the mind-sets of the people doing the work have been totally altered. For years, Yellow was obsessively focused on internal efficiency, but it practically ignored the needs of customers. The company now offers one-stop shopping for a broad range of transportation needs. Customers, not Yellow Freight employees, decide when freight will be delivered—in a week, in two days, or in four hours—Yellow makes sure it is delivered on time. Sophisticated and highly integrated information technology systems speed up order processing, manage customer relationships, monitor thousands of trucks and shipping orders, and facilitate rapid loading and unloading. "You have to keep reinventing the company, because the market keeps changing, " Zollars says. "If you don't, you end up coasting."

LECTURE/OUTLINE

To recognize social and economic pressure for change in today's organizations.

Leaders have had to reconceptualize every aspect of their business to meet the needs of customers, keep employees motivated, and be competitive in a global economy.

Social, economic, and technological changes in the environment have affected every organization.

Leaders are responsible for guiding people through the discomfort and dislocation brought about by major change.

Change or Perish *Exhibit 16.1*

Organizations must poise themselves to change, not only to prosper but to survive in today's world.

Rapid technological changes, a globalized economy, and changing markets and the rise of e-commerce are creating more threats and more opportunities for leaders.

Many changes are driven by advances in computer and information technology.

A problem for today's organizations is the failure to adapt to changes in the environment.

Leaders serve as role models for change and provide the motivation and communication for change.

Research has identified some key characteristics of leaders who accomplish successful change projects:

- They define themselves as change leaders.
- They demonstrate courage.
- The believe employees can assume responsibility
- They can assimilate and articulate values that promote adaptability.
- The recognize and learn from their mistakes
- They can manage complexity, uncertainty, and ambiguity.
- They have vision, and can describe it in vivid terms.

In the Lead: Barbara Waugh, Hewlett-Packard

Barbara Waugh began her career at Hewlett-Packard in a mid-level personnel position at HP labs---not the place one would think of for instituting massive change. Yet Waugh always identified herself as an agent for change and looked at opportunities to make things better. Waugh developed a reputation for getting things done, and many people came to her with problems. Waugh helped each individual assume responsibility and take steps toward accomplishing his change goals. During her time in personnel, Waugh contributed directly or indirectly to numerous change projects, including new products, new mentoring relationships, and a 20 percent reduction in development life cycles.

Q: *Describe the change at Hewlett-Packard.*

A: Change did not happen easily, but as a good leader, Waugh facilitated change and helped HP adapt to external threats and new opportunities. Waugh's passion and ability as a change leader led her to a position as worldwide changed manager at HP Labs.

Discussion Question #8: *Is the world really changing faster today, or do people just* *assume so?*

Notes____

To implement the eight-stage model of planned major change and use everyday strategies for gradual change.

Leading Major Change

Exhibit 16.2

Major change does not happen easily.

Leaders are responsible for guiding employees and the organization through the change process.

To implement the eight-stage model of planned change successfully, leaders must pay careful attention to each stage.

- Stage 1: leaders *establish a sense o urgency* that change is needed.

  Crises or threats will thaw a resistance to change.

- Stage 2: leaders *establish a coalition* with enough power to guide the change process and then developing a sense of teamwork.

  For the change process to succeed, there must be a shared commitment to the need and possibilities for organizational transformation.

- Stage 3: leaders *develop a vision and strategy.* Leaders are responsible for formulating and articulating a compelling vision that will guide the change effort and develop the strategies for achieving that vision.

- Stage 4: leaders use every possible means to *communicate the vision and strategy.*

  At this stage, the coalition of change agents should set an example by modeling the new behaviors needed from employees.

- Stage 5: leaders *empower employees throughout the organization to act on the vision.*

This means getting rid of obstacles to change, which may require revising systems, structures, or procedures that hinder or undermine the change effort.

- Stage 6: leaders *generate short-term wins.* Leaders plan for visible performance improvements, enable them to happen, and celebrate employees who were involved in the improvements.

- Stage 7: this stage builds on the credibility achieved by short-term wins to *consolidate improvements, tackle bigger problems, and create greater change.*

  A highly-visible and successful short-term accomplishment boosts the credibility of the change process and renews the commitment and enthusiasm of employees.

- Stage 8: this stage *institutionalizes the new approaches in the organizational culture.* This is the follow-though stage that makes the changes stick.

Stages overlap, but skipping stages can cause the change process to fail.

Transformational change involves profound changes in all parts of the organization simultaneously.

Discussion Question #1: *Of the eight stages of planned change, which one do you think leaders are most likely to skip? Why?*

Notes____

____

____

Strategies for Everyday Change *Exhibit 16.3*

➢ *How can leaders work on a daily basis to gradually shift attitudes, assumptions, and behaviors toward a desired future?*

Leaders can learn strategies for everyday change that will have a constructive impact as everyday conversations and small actions throughout the organization.

There are four types of incremental changes which range from the leader working alone to working directly with others in a more directed and extensive change effort.

- *Disruption self-expression.* The leader acts in a way that others will notice and that reflects the values or behaviors that he wishes to instill in followers.

  Disruptive self-expression quietly unsettles others' expectations and routines—e.g., the leader wears casual pants and sweaters when others wear suits.

- *Verbal jujitsu* A leader turns an opponent's negative attitudes, expressions, or behaviors into opportunities for change that others in the organization will notice.

- *Variable-term opportunism.* A more public approach is for leaders to look for, crate, and capitalize on opportunities for motivating others to change.

- *Strategic alliance building* The leader works closely with others to move issues to the forefront more quickly and directly that would be possible working alone.

In the Lead: Paul Wielgus, Allied Domecq

Paul Wielgus doesn't consider himself a revolutionary, but he sparked a transformation at the global company Allied Domecq, whose brands include Courvoisier and Beefeater, by effectively persuading people who were originally opposed to his plans. Wieglus headed a new learning and training department designed to help people throughout the company break out of outdated thinking and be more creative and adaptable. The problem was, even though the department had the support of top management, many executives thought it was a waste of time and money. One senior executive from the audit department. soundly berated Wieglus and criticized the department's activities. Rather than becoming defensive, Wieglus used the meeting as an opportunity to sell him on the benefits of the program. His strategy was to treat the opposition as a friend and potential ally.

Q: *How did Wieglus use strategies for effective change?*

A: Wieglus enthusiastically explained how the training workshops functioned and the dramatic changes he had seen in employees. Before long, the senior executive was scheduling training for the internal audit department. Wieglus understood the importance of building strategic alliances by reaching out to the opposition as well as to those who already agreed with and supported his ideas.

Discussion Question #2: *Which of the everyday change strategies would you be most comfortable using and why? What are some situations when a passive, private strategy such as disruptive self-expression might be more effective than an active, public strategy such as strategic alliance building.*

Notes____

To use techniques of communication, training, and participation to overcome resistance to change.

Dealing with Resistance

Leaders see change as a way to strengthen the organization, but many people view change as painful and disruptive.

A critical aspect of leading people through change is understanding that resistance to change is natural---and there are legitimate reasons for it.

Why Do People Resist Change?

Employees resist change because it violates *personal compacts,* the reciprocal obligations and commitments that define the relationship between employees and the organization.

They include such things as job tasks, performance requirements, evaluation procedures, and compensation packages.

The personal compact incorporates elements such as mutual trust and dependence, as well as shared values.

Employees perceive that change violates the personal compact for several reasons:

- *Self-interest* Employees typically resist a change they believe will take away something of value.

  Changes in job design, structure, or technology may lead to a perceived loss of power.

  Fear of personal loss may be the biggest obstacle to change.

- *Uncertainty* is the lack of information about future events; it represents a fear of the unknown.

  Employees many not understand how a proposed change will affect them and fear whether they can meet the demands of the new task.

- *Different Assessments and Goals* People affected by the innovation may assess the situation differently from those who propose the change.

  Sometimes critics voice legitimate disagreements over the proposed benefits of a change.

Leaders cannot ignore resistance to change, but can diagnose the reasons and come up with ways to gain acceptance of the change by employees.

- *Living Leadership: Dealing with a Dead Horse*

Ancient wisdom says that when you discover that you are astride a dead horse, the best strategy is to dismount. In government and many other overly bureaucratic organizations are tried.

- What are the strategies for dealing with the "dead horse" scenario?

Overcoming Resistance

Leaders can improve the chances for a successful outcome by following the eight-stage model.

Leaders can use elements such as storytelling, metaphor, humor, and a personal touch to reach employees on an emotional level and sell them on proposed changes.

Leaders may use specific implementation techniques to smooth the change process:

- *Communication and Training* Open and honest communication is the best way to overcome resistance to change.

  It reduces uncertainty, gives people a sense of control, clarifies the benefits of the change, and builds trust.

  Employees frequently need training to acquire skills for their role in the change process or their new responsibilities.

- *Participation and involvement* Participation involves followers in designing the change and gives them a sense of control over change activity.

- *Coercion* As a last resort, leaders overcome resistance by threatening employees with job loss, promotion, firing or transfer.

  Coercion may be necessary in crisis situations when a rapid response is needed or when there are administrative changes that flow from the top down.

Discussion Question #5: *Why do employees resist change? What are some ways leaders can overcome this resistance?*

Notes____

____

____

To address effectively and humanely the negative impact of change

The Negative Impact of Change

Leaders are responsible for smoothly implementing changes that can help the organization survive and prosper.

It is essential for leaders to recognize that change can have negative as well as positive consequences.

The Two Faces of Change

Effectively and humanely leading change is one of the greatest challenges for leaders.

The nature and pace of change in today's environment can be exhilarating but also inconvenient, painful, and scary.

Changes can cause real, negative consequences for individual employees, who may experience high levels of stress, be compelled to learn new tasks, or lose their jobs.

Some difficult changes are related to structure, such as redefining positions, reengineering, and redesigning jobs.

Leadership and downsizing

Downsizing, which refers to reducing the size of a company's workforce, is not as widespread as in the 1980s and 1990s but is still part of many change initiatives.

Reengineering projects, mergers and acquisitions, global competition, the trend toward outsourcing, and transition from an industrial to an information economy have led to job reductions.

Some mergers mean that some functions are redundant or that less profitable facilities are closed leading to job loss.

If downsizing is not carefully handled, it can have a detrimental impact.

When job cuts are necessary, leaders should be prepared for increased conflict and stress, even greater resistance to change, and a decrease in morale, trust, and commitment.

Several techniques can help leaders smooth downsizing and ease tensions for employees who leave as well as those who remain:

- *Involve employees* One important way to cut jobs and keep morale high among remaining employees is to let lower-level employees assist with shaping the criteria for which jobs will be cut or which employees will leave the company.

Leaders can offer options such as job-sharing and part-time work, which may suit some employees well, enabling them to remain employed part-time and allowing the company to retain their talents.

- *Communicate more, not less* Some leaders seem to think the less that is said about a pending layoff, the better. Not so.

  Leaders should provide advance notice with as much information as possible.

  Remaining employees need to know what is expected of them, whether future layoffs are a possibility, and what the organization is doing to help co-workers who have lost their jobs.

- *Provide assistance to displaced workers* Leaders have a responsibility to help disabled workers cope with the loss of their jobs and get reestablished in the job market.

  The organization can provide training, severance packages, extended benefits, and outplacement assistance.

- *Help the survivors thrive* Leaders should remember the emotional needs of survivors.

  Many people experience guilt, anger, confusion, and sadness after the loss of colleagues and these feelings should be acknowledged.

  People may feel concerned about their own jobs and have difficulty adapting to changes in job duties.

Notes____

To expand your own and others' creativity and facilitate organizational innovation..

Leading for Innovation *Exhibit 16.4*

In response to the question, "What must one do to survive in the 21st century?" the top answer among 500 CEOs surveyed by the American Management Association was "practice creativity and innovation."

Effective leaders find ways to promote creativity in the departments where it is most needed.

The best way to facilitate change is to create an environment that nourishes creativity.

Creativity is the generation of new ideas that result in improved efficiency and effectiveness of the organization.

Creativity is a process rather than an outcome, a journey rather than a destination.

One of the most important leadership tasks is to harness the creative energy of all employees to further the interests of the organization.

Discussion Question #7: *Planned change is often considered ideal. Do you think unplanned change could be effective? Discuss. Can you think of an example?*

Notes____

____

____

The Innovative Organization

Six elements of creative organizations are listed in the lefthand column; these elements correspond to the characteristics of creative people, listed in the right-hand column.

Alignment

The interests and actions of all employees should be aligned with the company's purpose, vision, and goals.

Leaders make clear what the company stands for, consistently promote the vision, and clearly specify goals.

In addition, they make a commitment of time, energy, and resources to activities that focus people on innovation.

An *idea incubator* is a safe harbor where ideas from employees throughout the organization can be developed without interference from company bureaucracy or politics.

Self-initiated activity

Most people have a natural desire to explore and create, which leads them to want to initiate creative activity on their own.

Leaders are responsible for unleashing deep-seated employee motivation for creativity.

Leaders encourage an entrepreneurial spirit by instilling values of risk-taking and exploration and providing the structures that encourage people to explore new ideas.

Corporate entrepreneurship is an internal entrepreneurial spirit that includes values of exploration, experimentation, and risk taking.

One important outcome is to facilitate *idea champions,* people who passionately believe in a new idea and actively work to overcome obstacles and resistance.

In the Lead: Erkki Kuisma and Yrjö Neuvo, Nokia

Erkki Kuisma was conducting radio frequency research at Nokia when he came up with what seemed like a crazy idea—why not hide a cell phone's antenna inside the phone? Kuisma tinkered around with his idea and eventually cut the antenna off from an existing phone model, patched the hole, and devised an antenna from copper tape. It worked. The idea hit resistance among Nokia executives who were afraid that customer would doubt the phone's power. Kuisma's boss, Yrjö Neuvo waged daily warfare against the hierarchy to champion the new idea. The Nokia 8800 became one of the most profitable products in the company's history.

Q: *How did Nokia profit from idea champions?*

A: Yrjö Neuvo, head of research and development at Nokia, fosters an entrepreneurial spirit by encouraging people to try crazy things and never shrink from making mistakes. Leaders at Nokia encourage "uninhibited dabbling," allowing employees to develop new technologies without company approval. User-changeable batteries and chat rooms are among the ideas developed at Nokia.

Discussion question #6: *Why are idea champions considered to be essential to innovation? Do you think these people would be more important in a large organization or a small one? Discuss.*

Notes____

Unofficial activity

Employees need to be able to experiment and dream outside of their regular job description.

Leaders can give employees free time for activities not officially sanctioned.

Diverse Stimuli

It is impossible to know what stimulus will lead any particular person to come up with a creative idea.

Leaders can provide the sparks that set off creative ideas.

Leaders can rotate employees through different jobs to provide diverse stimuli, let them engage in volunteer activities, and give them opportunities to mix with people different from themselves.

Internal Communication

Creativity flourishes when there is frequent contact with interdisciplinary networks of people at all levels of the organization.

Leaders can provide opportunities for employees to communicate across boundaries.

They can make collaboration and sharing of information an integral part of the culture and facilitate coordination for the implementation of change and innovation projects.

In the Lead: Carlos Ghosn, Nissan

When Carlos Ghosn arrived as the new CEO of Nissan, the company had been struggling to turn a profit for eight years. Ghosn knew he was facing a do-or-die situation—it was either to turn things around or the business would cease to exist. However, he also knew that simply mandating a series of dramatic top-down changes would create resistance, damage morale, and ultimately put the company in even more trouble. Ghosn decided to mobilize Nissan's line managers through a series of cross-functional teams that would identify and lead the radical changes that needed to be made.

Q: *How did Ghosn make collaboration and sharing an instrument for change?*

A: Ghosen used cross-functional teams to help mastermind a transformation that saved the company. By improving internal communication and coordination, Ghosen has put Nissan back on the right road. The cross-functional teams continue to operate as an integral part of Nissan's management structure.

Leaders can use the five characteristics of innovative organizations to ignite creativity in specific departments or the entire organization.

Creative people are known for open-mindedness, curiosity, independence, self-confidence, persistence, and a focused approach to problem solving.

Leaders can help both individuals and organizations be more creative.

Discussion Question #3: *Do you think creative individuals and creative organizations have characteristics in common? Discuss.*

Notes____

Stages in the Personal Creative Process *Exhibit 16.5*

An important part of becoming more creative process is understanding the stages of the creative process.

In one model of creativity, stages do not always appear in order and may overlap.

A person who encounters a block may revert to an earlier stage.

- *Stage 1*: *Recognition of Problem/Opportunity* Creativity often begins with the recognition of a problem that needs to be solved or an opportunity to explore.

- *Stage 2*: *Information Gathering* The next step is to search for background information and knowledge.

  This may involve reading in a variety of fields, attending professional meetings and seminars, travel, talking to new people, and scanning magazines.

- *Stage 3*: *Incubation* In this stage, a person allows the subconscious to mull things over.

  This stage takes place when a person is involved in activities totally unrelated to the subject—even during sleep.

- *Stage 4*: *Insight* A person hits upon an idea. In most cases, the idea does not come as a bolt out of the blue, but in gradual increments.

- *Stage 5*: *Evaluation and Implementation* Creative people may fail before they succeed and cycle back through information gathering and incubation stages.

  Others may think the "brilliant" idea is crazy, but creative people do not give up when they run into obstacles.

Leaders of today's organizations have powerful reasons to encourage creativity because they need employees to contribute to new ideas.

Creative people are less resistant to change because they are open-minded, curious, and willing to take risks.

Discussion Question #4: *What advice would you give a leader who wants to increase creativity in her department?*

Notes____

____

____

DISCUSSION QUESTIONS

1. *Of the eight stages of planned change, which one do you think leaders are most likely to skip? Why?*

I think leaders are most likely to skip stage eight---institutionalizing the new approaches into the organizational culture. This is the follow-through stage that makes the changes stick. Leaders may skip this stage because old habits, values, traditions, and mind-sets die hard. It is easy to slip back into the old ways. It is difficult for the new values and beliefs to be instilled into the culture so that employees view the changes as normal and as an integral part of how the organization operates. This stage also requires leadership development and succession or else the new values are not carried forward.

2. *Which of the everyday change strategies would you be most comfortable using and why? What are some situations when a passive, private strategy such as disruptive self-expression might be more effective than an active, public strategy such as strategic alliance building.*

Answers will vary. I prefer disruptive self-expression because the leader is a role model, and the followers closely observe the behavior of the leader. If the manager clears his tray in the lunchroom, for example, the employees will take note and start clearing away their own dishes. This is more powerful than a memo from the boss in a command-and-control style informing the employees of a new policy. Top-down rules cause hostility among employees and resistance. Disruptive self-expression is non-threatening yet effective.

3. *Do you think creative individuals and creative organizations have characteristics in common? Discuss.*

Yes, creative organizations and creative people share the following characteristics:

- *Alignment* The interests and actions of employees aligned with the company's purpose, vision, and goals.
- *Self-initiated activity*--- a natural desire to explore and create, which leads to creative activity.
- *Unofficial activity*---experimentation and dreaming outside of the regular job.

- *Serendipity*---combining a fortunate accident with sagacity.
- *Diverse Stimuli*--- stimuli that leads to a creative idea.
- *Internal Communication* Creativity flourishes when there is contact with interdisciplinary networks.

The creative individual and creative organization are open-minded, willing to take risks, and explore opportunities for creativity.

4. *What advice would you give a leader who wants to increase innovation in her department?*

Leaders promote the company vision. Leaders are responsible for unleashing deep-seated employee motivation for creative acts. Leaders can give employees free time and encourage "fortunate accidents" by creating a culture that values risk. They can provide the sparks that set off creative ideas. Finally, leaders can provide opportunities for employees to interact.

5. *Why do employees resist change? What are some ways leaders can overcome this resistance?*

Employees resist change because it violates personal compacts, the reciprocal obligations and commitments that define the relationship between employees and the organization. Leaders can overcome this resistance through communication and training, employee participation and involvement, and coercion (i.e., threats of job loss, promotion, or transfer.)

6. *Why are idea champions considered to be essential to innovation? Do you think these people would be more important in a large organization or a small one? Discuss.*

Idea champions are essential to innovation for companies of all sizes. The global marketplace is so competitive that companies must provide innovative products and services at competitive prices to survive.

7. *Planned change is often considered ideal. Do you think unplanned change could be effective? Discuss. Can you think of an example?*

Unplanned change is effective because it is essentially the result of creativity. Successful leaders find ways to encourage the development and sharing of new ideas, which start often start out as unplanned change. In response to the question, "What must one do to survive in the 21st century?" the top answer among 500 CEOs surveyed by the American Management Association was "practice creativity and innovation." On of the best ways to facilitate continuous change is to create an environment that nourishes creativity.

An example of unplanned change is 3M's Post It "sticky" notes. This innovation started out as the result of a market-driven need----a bookmark that would not fall out of the book when opened. The Post It note was to stick to the page without leaving a mark or tearing the page. From this unplanned idea for change grew a communication tool that has become a basic office supply item for businesses, schools, and homes. It should be noted that once an unplanned change takes hold, it is incorporated into the planning process. The latest innovation is the poster-size version used for presentations at meetings.

8. *Is the world really changing faster today, or do people just assume so?*

The world is changing faster today as a result of technology. Rapid technological changes, a globalized economy, changing markets, and e-commerce create more threats as well as more opportunities. Advanced information technology improves productivity, customer service, and competitiveness, but because technology changes so rapidly, leaders must adopt new ways of doing business. The Internet and e-commerce have increased domestic and international competition and challenged organizations to deliver goods and services rapidly.

TEACHING TOOLS AND EXERCISES

1. *Small Group Exercise:* Resistance to Change

In small groups, students will share experiences at home, at school, or at work in which they encountered resistance to change. How were these situations handled? Referring to the models and strategies presented in the chapter, how could these situations have been better handled?

2. *On the Web.* Nokia, An Innovative Company

Go to the Nokia website at www.nokia.com and see how the company remains innovative. What is Nokia doing to keep its competitive edge in the cellular phone market. What other innovations are on the horizon at Nokia. Report your findings to the class.

3. *Interview:* Interview three managers at different organizations about changes they have implemented. What was their experience in implementing the change? How did they manage resistance to change.

4. *Leader's Self-Insight:* Do You Have a Creative Personality?

After checking each adjective that accurately describes your personality and scoring your responses, answer the following question. To what extent do you think your score reflects your true creativity. Compare your score to others in your class. Can you think of types of creativity this test might not measure?

5. *Out-of-class reading:* Breakthrough Ideas for 2004

From the fields of biology, neuroscience, economics, positive psychology, network science, marketing, management theory, and more—here are the emergent ideas that are changing the way business is done.

The HBR Breakthrough Ideas for 2004, *Harvard Business Review* (February 2004)13-37.

LEADERSHIP DEVELOPMENT: CASES FOR ANALYSIS

1. **Synopsis: Southern Discomfort**

Jim Malesckowski remembers the call from his boss, CEO Jack Ripon: "I just read your analysis and I want you to get down to Mexico right away. We cannot make the plant in Oconomo work anymore ---the costs are too high. Check out the costs to move." Instead of the $16 an hour average wage paid at the Oconomo, Wisconsin plant, the wages paid to Mexican workers would amount to about $1.60 an hour. That is a savings of $15 million a year. The apparel plant in Oconomo had been in operation since 1921, but competitors had already edged past the company in terms of price and were close to overtaking it in quality. Union leaders resisted the idea of lower wages and the idea of cross-training individuals. Jim realized that the costs were too high, unions were unwilling to cooperate, and the company needed to make a better return on its investment. It all sounds right but feels wrong, said Jim to himself.

Case questions and answers

1. *If you were Jim Malesckowski, would you fight to save the plant? Why?*

The financials are not given in the case and that makes a decision difficult. However, from a humanitarian point of view, the plant should be saved because so many lives depend upon it. The plant can only be saved if costs can be lowered, unions cooperate, and the return-on-investment improved. There will have to be downsizing of the work force to save money, job sharing, and programs to assist displaced workers. Leaders have a responsibility to help disabled workers cope with the loss of their jobs and get reestablished in the job market. The organization can provide training, severance packages, extended benefits, and outplacement assistance.

2. *Assume you want to lead the change to save the plant. Describe how you would enact the eight stages outlined in Exhibit 16.2.*

- *Stage 1:* Explain that the plant is ready to close if drastic measures are not taken.
- *Stage 2:* Form a group of union leaders and managers.
- *Stage 3:* Develop a vision for the changed plant and a strategy for change.
- *Stage 4:* Have the union leaders communicate the vision to the workers.
- *Stage 5:* Let the plant workers become involved in the change strategy and empower them.
- *Stage 6:* Communicate about any cost reductions and product improvements immediately.

- *Stage 7:* Assess improvements and add total quality management.
- *Stage 8*: Make TQM a permanent. part of the plant.

3. *How would you overcome union leader resistance?*

The methods for overcoming employee or union leader resistance include: communication and training, participation and involvement to provide a sense of control over change activity, and coercion, threats of job loss or firing. The best way is to involve the current employees and their union leaders in change activities. The union is gripped by fear and must be included in the planning.

The purpose of the union is to protect jobs for its members; if the union refuses to compromise, the jobs will moved to Mexico. The Union will lose ground locally and nationally. It is in the Union's best interest to give up resistance to change and be involved in keeping the plant open.. Communication is very important. Union leaders must understand the economic issues faced by the company; the plant is not profitable and will have to move to Mexico if nothing is changed.

2. **Synopsis: Mediscribe Corporation**

MediScribe provides medical transcriptions, insurance claims, and billing and collection services for doctors, clinics, and hospitals. As production supervisor, Ramona Fossett is responsible for the work of nearly 40 employees. Fossett agreed to have a team of outside consultants conduct a study to improve efficiency and output. The consultants spent three days studying job descriptions, observing daily tasks, and recording the work of the data entry clerks.. After three days, they were ready to begin more detailed studies. The next morning, four data entry clerks in the study were absent; the following day, 10 were absent. The leader of the systems analysis team explained that if there were continued absences, his team world have to drop the study or move onto another department. Fossett knew that she would be held responsible for the failure of the study. She began to consider alternative actions that would provide the necessary conditions for the study. She was concerned about implementing procedural changes that he knew would be mandated after the study was completed.

Case questions and answers

1. *Why do you think employees are reacting in this way to the study?*

The employees were not properly prepared for the study through effective leadership communication. Fossett failed to explain the value of the study to the company to accomplish the organizational vision. It is important to involve the employees in a change effort. Fossett has not done this and has created resistance to chance. The employees only see themselves and "guinea pigs," not as part of the big picture to keep the company competitive.

Resistance to change results from violation of personal compacts. These perceptions stem from: *Self-interest* Employees resist a change they believe will take away something of value and out of fear. *Uncertainty* is the lack of information about future events. *Different Assessments and Goals* The employees affected by the study may assess the situation differently from Hale and the CEO.

2. *How could leaders have handled this situation to get greater cooperation from employees?*

Fossett could have used the techniques for overcoming resistance to change.

Communication and Training Communication informs employees about the need for change and the consequences of change which prevents false rumors and misunderstandings.

Participation and involvement Participation involves employees in designing the change and gives them a sense of control over change activity. Fossett could have explained the purpose of the study and stressed the benefit to the company in terms of more efficiency. Greater efficiency makes a company more able to respond to today's fast-pace economic climate. This in turn makes the company more competitive.

3. *If you were Ramona Fossett, what would you do now? What would you do to implement any changes recommended by the study?*

I would use the techniques of communication and employee involvement. I would try to avoid the third technique of coercion----threats to fire employees. I would also consider a reward for those who participated in the study to encourage them to participate willingly. It is important for the employees to take part in the study because they will be more ready to accept the study's recommendations. I would use the eight step model outlined in Exhibit 16.2. and carefully implement each step. Fossett is responsible for guiding employees and the organization through the change process.

TEST BANK
Daft, The Leadership Experience, 3rd Edition

CHAPTER ONE: WHAT DOES IT MEAN TO BE A LEADER?

TRUE-FALSE QUESTIONS

1. Leadership is defined an influence relationship among leaders and followers who intend real changes that reflect their shared purposes. T, p. 5

2. Leaders of today must maintain strict control of work processes to assure that the organization functions efficiently. F, p. 9

3. Leaders of today must become comfortable with change and uncertainty. T, p. 9

4. Many organizations were built on assumptions of uniformity and specialization. T, p.12

5. A study showed that leaders who failed were described as having good people. skills. F, p. 26

6. The move to empowerment is an integral part of the old paradigm. F, p. 8

7. Management and leadership are the same thing. F, p. 16

8. Knowledge management, which relies on a culture of sharing rather than hoarding information, has taken firm hold in many companies. T, p. 11

9. Leadership is considered an art because of a growing body of objective facts and knowledge that describe the leadership process. F, p. 29

10. Leadership focuses on motivating and inspiring people. T, p. 19

11. To adapt to a chaotic world , leaders strive to create learning organizations. T, p. 25

12. The Behavior Theories studied « larger-than-life » leaders. F, p. 23

13. The Great Man Theories are emerging leadership theories F, p. 23

14. Situational Theories are based on the idea that the leaders should analyze their situation and tailor their behavior to improve leadership effectiveness T, p. 23

15. Since the 1970s, leadership ideas may focused on how leaders and followers interact and influence one another. T, p. 24

MULTIPLE CHOICE QUESTIONS

1. Empowerment implies:

a. structured jobs and work processes.
*b. workers using their own power effectively and responsibly. p. 9
c. strict control.
d. decision-making by the leader

2. Leadership involves all EXCEPT:

a. creating change
b. influencing followers
*c. maintaining stability p. 5
d. shared purpose

3. Attempts to achieve teamwork, empowerment, and diversity can succeed only if:

a. leaders follow the principles and practices of the industrial era.
b. managers want to treat people the way they treat machines or the bottom line.
*c. leaders value change over stability, control, competition, and uniformity. p. 9
d. leaders hire people who think and work alike.

4. Reasons for executive derailment include:

a. insensitive, abrasive, intimidating, bullying style.
b. good people skills.
c. overmanaging: unable to delegate or build a team.
*d. both a & c p. 26

5. Managers and leaders are different because:

a. Managers learn a set of skills for planning, organizing directing, and controlling.
b. Leaders must find the capacity to help create a vision of what the organization can be.
c. Leadership calls for caring about and engaging the whole employee.
*d. Managers maintain stability while leaders promote change. p. 18

6. Leadership is an art because of all EXCEPT:

*a. Leadership is a growing body of objective facts and knowledge. p. 29
b. Leadership has skills that cannot be learned from a textbook.
c. Leadership takes practice.
d. Leadership takes hands-on experience.

7. Leadership is a science because of all EXCEPT:

a. Leadership research is a growing scientific field.
b. Leadership is a growing body of objective facts.
* c. Leadership depends upon an individual's personality traits and people skills. p. 29
d. Training in leadership skills can help achieve organizational goals.

8. Strong leadership is needed because:

a. the environment of the 21st century is predictable.
b. planning, leading, organizing, and controlling are the required skills for the future.
c. giving workers clear job assignments is the main task of a business executive.
* d. of globalization, e-commerce, telecommuting, virtual teams, and outsourcing. p. 7

9. In the new reality for leadership, the new paradigm does NOT include:

*a. Uniformity p. 8
b. Collaboration
c. Diversity
d. Information

10. The concept of knowledge management relies on:

*a. a culture of sharing information p. 11
b. a culture of hoarding information.
c. a culture of competition within the organization.
d. a culture of aggressiveness.

11. Charismatic leadership is NOT :

a. an influence theory
*b. a relational theory p. 24
c. based on the leader's personality.
d. based on the leader's qualities.

12. The theory of a leader who puts others' needs and interests above his own is called :

*a. servant leadership p. 24
b. transformational leadership
c. charismatic leadership
d. transactional leadership

13. ________________ considered if a leader acted in an autocratic or democratic manner toward followers and how this correlated to leadership effectiveness.

a. Trait Theories
b. Situational Theories
c. Great Man Theories
*d. Behavior Theories p. 23

14. In a turbulent world, a key aspect of being a leader is ________________.

a. creating a learning organization
b. facilitating change
*c. both a & b p. 25
d. having an extroverted personality

15. Leadership vision is

a. a picture of the future
b. a desired future
c. an ambitious view of the future
*d. all of the above p. 16

SHORT ANSWER

1. __________ is an influence relationship among leaders and followers who intend real changes and outcomes than reflect their shared purpose.

   Answer : Leadership

2. An picture of an ambitious desirable future for the organization or team is a ________.

   Answer : vision

3. ____________ is a written, spoken or implied contract wherein people accept either a superior or subodinate role and sees the use of coercive as well as noncoercieve behavior as an acceptable way of achieving desirable results.

   Answer : Position power

4. ____________ are studies of « larger-than-life » leaders to define a leader.

   Answer : Trait Theories

5. The theories that consider the contextual and situational variables that influence what leadership behaviors will be effective are called________________

   Answer : Situational Theories

6. Leadership based on the qualities and personality of the leader is called __________.

   Answer : Charismatic Leadership

7. A relational theory that develops followers into leaders and brings about significant change by elevating leaders and followers to higher levels of motivation and morality

   ____

   Answer : Transformational leadership

8. Leaders strive to create_______________organizations in which each person is intimately involved in identifying and solving problems to make the organization grow and meet challenges.

Answer : learning

9. ___________is the attainment of organizational goals in an effective and efficient manner through planning, organizing, staffing, directing, and controlling organizational resources.

Answer : Management

10. Good leadership brings about_____________

Answer : change.

SHORT ESSAY QUESTIONS

1. Describe the new reality for leadership.

The world of organizations is changing rapidly. Globalization. Deregulation. E-commerce. Telecommuting. Virtual teams. Outsourcing. It takes strong leaders to effect the changes needed for survival and to guide people and organizations through the uncertainty and confusion of rapid change. Although many leaders are still operating from an old-paradigm mind-set, they are increasingly ineffective. As more work becomes knowledge and information-based, leaders have to take a new approach. Effective and successful leaders will respond to the new reality. p. 7.

2. What does empowerment mean?

Empowerment does not mean that those from on high are graciously handing down power, but that power belongs to all workers. Empowerment emphasizes collaboration over competition and conflict. Self-directed teams and other forms of horizontal collaboration are eliminating boundaries among departments. Leaders will need to create an environment of teamwork and community that fosters collaboration and mutual support. p. 9.

3. Why do some managers reach a plateau, get fired, or become forced to take early retirement?

Attempts to achieve teamwork, empowerment, and diversity may fail because leaders' and workers' beliefs are stuck in the old paradigm that values control, stability and homogeneity. A study at the Center for Creative Leadership in Greensboro, NC showed that 75% of the managers who arrived at the top had people skills. As Exhibit 1.5 shows, unsuccessful managers were insensitive to others, abrasive, cold, arrogant, untrustworthy, overly ambitious and selfish, unable to delegate or build teams, and unable to acquire appropriate staff to work for them. p. 26

4. Management and leadership are not the same. Explain.

Management can be defined as the attainment of organizational goals in an effective and efficient manner through planning organizing, staffing, directing, and controlling organizational resources. Management focuses on establishing detailed plans and schedules for achieving specific results, then allocating resources to accomplish the plan.

Leadership calls for creating a compelling vision of the future and developing farsighted strategies for producing the changes needed to achieve that vision. Leadership is concerned with communicating the vision and developing a shared culture and set of core values that can lead to the desired future state. This involves others as thinkers, doers, and leaders themselves. Leaders encourage people to expand their minds and abilities and to assume responsibility for their own actions. p.15

5. Management is both an art and a science. Explain.

Leadership is an art because many leadership skills and qualities cannot be learned from a textbook. Leadership takes practice and hands-on experience. Learning about leadership research helps people analyze situations from a variety of perspectives and learn how to be effective as leaders. Leadership is a science because a growing body of knowledge and objective facts. p. 29.

ESSAY QUESTIONS

1. Give an overview of the various leadership theories.

p.p. 23-25

2. What does leadership involve?

pp. 4-6

3. Explain the leadership shift from hero to humble.

p. 13.

CHAPTER TWO: TRAITS, BEHAVIORS, AND RELATIONSHIPS

TRUE-FALSE QUESTIONS

1. The Great Man approach sought to identify the traits leaders possessed that distinguished them from people who were not leaders. T, p. 47

2. Researchers contend that some traits are essential to leadership: self- confidence, honesty, integrity, and drive. T, p. 48

3. The trait approach says that anyone with the appropriate behavior can be a good leader. F, p. 54

4. The leadership continuum model implies that a participative leadership can be used when subordinates are able to learn decision-making readily. T, p. 55

5. Directing tasks, planning, and ruling with an iron hand is a "consideration" style. F, p. 56

6. The University of Michigan studies showed that goal emphasis, work facilitation, support, and interaction facilitation can be performed by subordinates. T, p. 59

7. The *Leadership Grid* shows that team management is the least effective style. F, p. 60

8. Dyadic theory examines why leaders have greater impact on some followers than on others. T, p. 63

9. Leader-member exchange research emphasizes that all employees should be managed in the same manner. F, p. 66

10. Leader dyads can be expanded to systems and cut across work units, functional, divisional, and organizational boundaries. T, p. 68

11. A characteristic considered essential for effective leadership is drive. T, p. 52

12. A democratic leader is one who tries to centralize authority and derive power from position. F, p. 54

13. Consideration is the extent to which a leaser is sensitive to subordinates. T, p 56

14. The Leadership Continuum is a theory based on the notion that a leader develops a unique relationship with each subordinate or group. F, p. 64

15. Critics of early LMX theory felt that distinguishing between and in-group

and out-group would lead to resentments or even hostility. T, p. 67

MULTIPLE CHOICE QUESTIONS

1. Trait research does NOT consider the following personal characteristics of leaders:

   a. physical characteristics such as energy.
   b. personality characteristics such as creativity and self-confidence.
   c. social characteristics such as popularity and interpersonal skills.
   *d. educational characteristics such as an advanced academic degree. p. 48

2. Possessing the traits of honesty and integrity are essential for leaders in order to:

   a. build productive relationships
   b. minimize skepticism and build trust
   *c. both a & b p. 50
   d. seek achievement and have high energy.

3. Autocratic versus democratic leadership research showed all EXCEPT:

   a. groups with autocratic leaders only performed well under leader supervision.
   *b. groups with democratic leaders only performed will when the leader supervised. p. 54
   c. groups with autocratic leaders had feelings of hostility.
   d. groups with democratic leaders had positive feelings.

4. The Leadership Continuum by Tannenbaum and Schmidt suggested that leaders should be boss-centered or subordinate-centered depending on:

   a. organizational circumstances
   b. the skill level of the employees
   c. the self-confidence, creativity, and energy of the leader
   *d. both a & b p. 54

5. Initiating structure describes the following leadership behavior:

   *a. A leader who is task-oriented and directs subordinates' work. p. 56
   b. A leader who is sensitive to subordinates and respects their ideas, and feelings.
   c. A leader who seeks input from subordinates regarding important decisions.
   d. A leader who listens carefully to problems.

6. The University of Michigan research reached all the following conclusions EXCEPT:

a. Goal emphasis, work facilitation, and support can be performed by subordinates.
*b. Only the leader can supply the job-centered and employee-centered behaviors. p. 59
c. A leader is identified by one or the other behavior style, not both.
d. Leadership behavior affected the performance and satisfaction of subordinates.

7. "High-high" leadership behavior is generally considered desirable because:

a. leaders display concern for both people and production.
b. leaders will meet people-oriented and task-oriented needs simultaneously.
*c. both a & b p. 61
d. task-oriented behavior was associated with higher productivity.

8. The Vertical Dyad Linkage model argues for all EXCEPT:

*a. Subordinates provide the same descriptions about the same leader. p. 64
b. Subordinates exist in a "in-group" or an "out-group" in relation to the leader.
c. Subordinates provide very different descriptions of the same leader.
d. Subordinates who rated the leader highly had a close relationship with the leader.

9. The leader-member exchange explores all EXCEPT:

a. communication frequency
b. value agreement
*c. traits p. 66
d. job satisfaction

10. During the Partnership Building stage of the dyadic approach,

a. leader dyads are created across levels and boundaries
*b. leaders can reach out to create a positive exchange with every subordinate. p. 67
c. leaders' behaviors and traits have different impacts on individuals.
d. leadership is not individualized for each subordinate.

11. Even if leader dyads extend to larger systems and across organizational boundaries, the theory suggests :

*a. that leaders need to build networks on one-to-one relationships. p. 68
b. that leaders no longer need to build networks on one-to-one relationships.
c. that leaders can use teams
d. that leaders can use self-directed teams to replace one-on-one relationships.

12. In the Leadership Grid, the term « Country Club Management » refers to :

a. the exertion of minimum effort to get required work done.
b. efficiency in operations from arranging work conditions.
*c. thoughtful attention to the needs of people for satisfying relationships. p. 60
d. work accomplishment from committed people and interdependence.

13. Active leaders need self-confidence because :

a. followers will not cooperate if the leader is does not have this characteristic.
b. they initiate changes and must make decisions without adequate information.
c. leaders could be paralyzed into inaction without confidence.
*d. both a & c. p. 50

14. Trait research has identified all of the following categories as essential to leadership EXCEPT :

a. work-related characteristics
b. social background
c. personality
*d. culture p. 48

15. Drive is considered essential to effective leadership because :

a. leaders with drive seek achievement
b. leaders with drive actively pursue goals
c. leaders with drive have stamina
*d. all of the above p. 52

SHORT ANSWER

1. __________the distinguishing personal characteristics of a leader, such as intelligence, honesty, self-confidence, and appearance.

   Answer : Traits

2. _________a leadership perspective that sought to identify the inherited traits leaders possessed that distinguished them from people who were not leaders.

   Answer : Great Man approach

3. The Behavior approach recognized_________ and ______________leadership styles.

   Answer : autocratic / democratic

4. The extent to which a leader is task oriented and directs subordinates' work activities toward goal achievement is called____________________

   Answer : initiating structure.

5. A leadership behavior that displays a focus on the human needs of subordinates is called __________.

   Answer : employee-centered.

6. In the Leadership Grid, __________________is considered the most effective style.

   Answer : team management

7. The _______________leader displays a concern for both people and production.

   Answer : « high-high »

8. The ___________examines why leaders have more influence ad greater impact on some members than others

   Answer : dyadic theory

9. _______________is a theory based on the notion that a leader develops a unique relationship with each subordinate which determines how the leader behaves toward the member.

Answer : Individualized leadership

10. The Leader-Member Exchange (LMX) is n individualized leadership model that explores _______________.

Answer : leader-member relationships

SHORT ESSAY QUESTIONS

1. Describe trait approach research.

The traits and their respective categories comprise trait approach research (physical characteristics, intelligence and ability, personality, work-related characteristics, an social characteristics). Effective leaders were often identified by exceptional follower performance, or a high status position within an organization and a salary that exceed that of one's peers. p. 46.

2. Describe the Leadership Continuum by Tannenbaum and Schmidt.

Tannenbaum and Schmidt indicated that leadership behavior could exist on a continuum reflecting different amounts of employee participation. One leader might be autocratic (boss-centered) another democratic (subordinate-centered), and a third a mix of the two styles. Boss-centered or subordinate-centered leadership depended on circumstance. p. 54.

3. What are the characteristics of a "high-high" leader?

The research into the behavior approach culminated in two predominate types of leadership behaviors people-oriented and task-oriented. A "high-high leader, one who displays concern for both people and production. There is a general belief that "high-high" leadership is a desirable quality, because the leader will meet both needs simultaneously. p. 61.

4. Describe the Vertical Linkage Model.

   The Vertical Linkage Model argues for the importance of the dyad formed by a leader with each member of the subordinate group. Subordinates were found to exist in an "in-group" and "outgroup" in relation the leader. In-group members had high access to the leader, expressed greater mutual influence, and had higher satisfaction and performance. p. 64.

5. Describe the leader-member exchange relationship.

   Stage two in the development of the dyad theory explored the leader-member exchange, discovering that the impact on outcomes depends on how the process develops over time. Studies evaluated: communication frequency, value agreement, characteristics of followers, job satisfaction, job climate, and commitment. The theory proposes that this higher-quality relationship will lead to higher performance and more interesting assignments, greater responsibility, and rewards such as pay increases and bonuses. p. 66.

ESSAY QUESTIONS

1. When might an autocratic leader might be more effective ? When might a democratic leader be more effective ?

   p. 54.

2. Is the « Great Man » perspective on leadership alive today ? Discuss.

   p. 46

3. What leadership style best describes you ? Explain.

CHAPTER THREE: CONTINGENCY APPROACHES

TRUE-FALSE QUESTIONS

1. There is not one best way of leadership. Contingency means "it depends." T, p. 81

2. A task-oriented leader performs better in situations of intermediate favorability because human relations skills are important for high group performance. F, p. 88

3. To use Fiedler's contingency theory, a leader should know if he has a relationship- or task-oriented style. T, p. 88

4. The major impact of Fiedler's model may have been to stir other researchers to to consider situational factors more seriously. T, p. 90

5. According to the Hersey and Blanchard model, subordinates vary in readiness level. T. p. 91

6. In the Hersey and Blanchard model, the *telling style* is based on high concern for both relationships and tasks. F, p. 91

7. Path clarification means that the leader works with subordinates to identify the behaviors needed to accomplish tasks. T, p. 95

8. According to the path-goal theory, the follower increases leader motivation by clarifying the path to rewards and increasing values and desires. F, p. 95

9. The four leadership classifications of the Fiedler model include supportive, directive, participative, and achievement-oriented. F, p. 96

10. If a subordinate is unchallenged by the task, an achievement-oriented behavior is used to set higher goals, according to path-goal theory. T, p. 96

11. The Vroom-Jago Contingency Model has five levels of subordinate participation in decision making, ranging from highly autocratic to highly democratic. T. p. 100

12. Further development of the Vroom-Jago model added concern for time constraints and concern for follower development. T, p. 102

13. A substitute counteracts the leadership style and prevents the leader from displaying certain behaviors. F. p. 108

14. Physical separation of leader and subordinate neutralizes leadership styles. T, p.108

15. Recent research has shown that substitutes for leadership can be designed in organizations. T, p. 109

MULTIPLE CHOICE QUESTIONS

1. Contingency approaches can best be described as:

   a. leadership styles that seek to delineate the characteristics of situations
   b. leadership styles appropriate for one situation which may not work in another.
   c. leadership traits or behaviors that can improve performance in all situations.
   *d. both a& b

   p. 80

2. In the contingency approaches, all the situational variables are important to leadership style EXCEPT :

   a. task
   b. structure
   *c. culture
   d. environment

   p. 81

3. To use Fiedler's Contingency Theory, a leader needs to know:

   a. whether his leadership style is relationship oriented.
   b. whether his leadership style is task-oriented.
   c. whether the situation is favorable or unfavorable to the leader.
   *d. all of the above

   p. 82

4. In Fiedler's model, leadership style was measured with a questionnaire known as :

   *a. the least preferred coworker (LPC) scale.
   b. leader participation styles
   c. neutralizers
   d. the leadership grid

   p. 84

5. Hersey and Blanchard's Situational Theory focuses on:

   *a. the characteristics of followers as an important element of the situation
   b. the readiness of the leader
   c. the characteristics of the leader
   d. whether the situation is favorable or unfavorable to the leader

   p. 91

6. A leader who shared ideas with followers and facilitates decision making is using Hersey and Blanchard's__________________

a. telling style
b. selling style
*c. participating style p. 91
d. delegating style

7. Hersey and Blanchard's model, the delegating style can be effective :

*a. when followers have very high levels of education, experience, and readiness. p. 92
b. when followers lack experience and education
c. when followers have poor ability and skills
d. when followers are at a moderate readiness level.

8. The path-goal theory includes all EXCEPT:

a. clarifying the follower's path to the rewards that are available.
*b. determining whether the situation is favorable or unfavorable to the leader p. 95
c. increasing the rewards that follower values and desires.
d. working with subordinates to identify behaviors for task accomplishment.

9. According to the path-goal model, a subordinate who lacks self-confidence would respond best to:

a. directive leadership behavior to clarify the path to reward.
*b. supportive leadership behavior to increase confidence. p. 96
c. achievement-oriented leadership to set high goals.
d. participative leadership to clarify the follower's needs

10. Two important situational contingencies in the path-goal theory are :

a. the personal characteristics of the group members and the work environment.
b. ability, skills, needs, and motivations and the degree of task structure
c. substitutes for leadership and readiness level of the leader
*d. both a & b p. 97

11. The degree of participation in the Vroom-Jago model depends on responses to eight questions which include all EXCEPT:

a. How important is the quality of the decision?
b. Do I have sufficient information to make a high-quality decision?
*c. How will the shareholders view this decision? p. 100
d. How important is the subordinate commitment to the decision?

12. In the Vroom-Jago model, the Leader Decision Styles do NOT include :

a. Decide
b. Facilitate
c. Delegate
*d. Empower p. 101

13. Highly educated, profession subordinates who know their tasks do not need a leader. This is an example of:

a. path-goal theory
b. the readiness level of subordinates
*c. a substitute for leadership p. 108
d. participative leadership

14. Kinko's, a nationwide copy center, has numerous locations and managers have limited personal interaction. This is an example of

a. achievement-oriented leadership
b. path-goal theory
c. a substitute for leadership
*d. a neutralizer p. 108

15. If group cohesiveness meets employee social needs, the leader can concentrate on task-oriented behaviors. This shows all EXCEPT:

a. the leader should adopt a style to complement the organization.
*b. the character traits of the leader are very important p. 109
c. a leader can evaluate the situation and avoid leadership overkill
d. the leader can ensure that both task and people needs are being met.

SHORT ANSWER

1. _____________ is a theory meaning one thing depends on another.

Answer : Contingency

2. _____________________ is a model to diagnose whether a leader is task-oriented or relationship oriented and help leaders match their styles to the organizational situation.

Answer : Fiedler's Contingency model

3. Hersey and Blanchard's ___________________________ is an extension of the Leadership Grid focusing on the characteristics of followers as the important element of the situation, and of determining effective leader behavior.

   Answer : situational theory

4. ________________ is a contingency approach to leadership in which the leader's responsibility is to increase subordinates' motivation by clarifying the behaviors necessary for task accomplishment and rewards.

   Answer : Path-goal theory

5. ______________ is a contingency models that focuses on varying degrees of participative leadership, and how each level of participation influences quality and accountability of decisions.

   Answer : Vroom-Jago contingency model

6. A_____________ is a situational variable that makes leadership unnecessary or redundant.

   Answer : substitute

7. A _________________ is a situational characteristic that counteracts the leadership style and Prevents the leader from displaying certain behaviors.

   Answer : neutralizer

8. In Fiedler's theory, a ________________is concerned with people.

   Answer : relationship-oriented leader

9. The Vroom-Jago model focuses specifically on varying degrees of____________ leadership.

   Answer : participative

10. The essence of the Hersey and Blanchard's situational theory is to select a style that is appropriate for the ____________ level of each subordinate.

    Answer : readiness

SHORT ESSAY QUESTIONS

1. Describe Fiedler's theory

   The cornerstone of Fiedler's theory is the extent to which the leader's style is relationship oriented or task-oriented. A *relationship-oriented leader* is concerned with people; a task *oriented leader* is motivated by task accomplishment. Fiedler's model presents the leadership situation in terms of three elements that can be favorable or unfavorable to a leader: the quality of *leader-member relations, task structure,* and *position power.* pp. 83-88.

2. Describe the path-goal theory.

   Path-Goal Theory states that the leader's responsibility is to increase subordinates' motivation to attain personal and organizational goals. The leader increases follower motivation by either (1) clarifying the follower's path to the rewards that are available or (2) increasing the rewards that the follower values and desires. p. 95

3. How does a leader tailor rewards to the situation?

   Situational Contingencies include (1) the personal characteristics of group members and (2) the work environment. The leader increases the amount of rewards to enhance satisfaction and job performance. The leader works with subordinates to help them acquire the skills and confidence need to perform tasks or develops new rewards to meet a subordinate's specific needs. Leadership behavior is tailored to the situation. p. 97

4. Describe the Vroom-Jago Contingency Model.

   The Vroom-Jago Contingency Model focuses on varying degrees of participative leadership, and how each level of participation influences quality and accountability of decisions. The model tells the leader precisely the correct amount of participation by subordinates to use in making a particular decision. This helps the leader gauge the appropriate amount of participation for subordinates. There are three components: leader participation styles, a set of diagnostic questions with which to analyze a decision situation, and a series of decision rules. p. 100

5. When can leadership be substituted?

   Situational variables can be so powerful as to substitute or neutralize the need for leadership. Highly educated, professional subordinates who know how to do their tasks do not need a leader who initiates structure for them and tells them what to do. Long-term education often develops autonomous, self-motivated individuals. Thus, task-oriented and people-oriented leadership is substituted by professional education and socialization. pp. 108.

ESSAY QUESTIONS

1. New research has continued to improve Fiedler's model, and it is still considered an important contribution to leadership studies. However, it's major impact may have been to stir other researchers to consider situational factors more seriously. Discuss.

   pp. 83-90

2. Leaders should adopt a style with which to complement the organizational situation. Discuss.

   pp. 91-94

3. The ability to use substitutes to fill leadership « gaps » is often advantageous to organizations.

   pp. 108-111

CHAPTER FOUR: THE LEADER AS AN INDIVIDUAL

TRUE-FALSE QUESTIONS

1. The Big Five personality dimensions include extroversion, agreeableness, conscientiousness, emotional stability, and openness to experience. T, p. 125

2. Most leaders score consistently high on all of the Big Five dimensions. F, p. 128

3. A person with an external locus of control believes he is the "master of his own fate." F, p.129

4. Knowledge of individual differences gives leaders valuable insights into their own behavior as well as followers and offers a framework to diagnose a situation. T, p. 132

5. Instrumental values are beliefs about the types of behavior appropriate for reaching goals T, p. 133

6. A persons values cannot change throughout life. F, p. 134

7. The collection of attitudes a leader has about himself is called self-concept. T, p. 137

8. A Theory Y leaders believes subordinates are lazy and dislike work. F, p. 139

9. Hermann believes people can learn to use their "whole brain" not just one or two quadrants. T, p. 142

10. The Myers-Briggs Type Indicator uses four different pairs of attributes such as introversion versus extroversion. T, p. 146

11. Charismatic leaders have the ability to inspire and motivate people to do more. T, p.149

12. Socialized charismatic leaders are self-aggrandizing, nonegalitarian, and exploitive. F, p. 152

13. Transformational leadership is a transaction or exchange process between leaders and followers. F, p. 153

14. Transformational leadership inspires followers to go beyond their own self-interests for the good of the group. T, p. 153

15. Effective leaders do not exhibit both transactional and transformational leaders. F, p. 155

MULTIPLE CHOICE

1. The Big Five personality dimensions do NOT include:

   a. extroversion
   b. emotional stability
   c. openness to experience
   *d. education p.125

2. The degree to which a person has a broad range of interests and is imaginative, creative, and willing to consider new ideas is called :

   a. emotional stability
   b. extroversion
   c. agreeableness
   *d. openness to experience p. 127

3. A person with an internal locus of control:

   a. believes that luck is the key to success.
   b. feels that there is little control over events.
   c. places primary responsibility on outside forces.
   *d. believes they are "masters of their own fate." p. 129

4. Security, a comfortable life, and good health are examples of:

   *a. end values or terminal values p. 133
   b. feelings
   c. attitudes
   d. instrumental values

5. A Theory X leader believes all EXCEPT:

   a. subordinates enjoy work
   *b. subordinates are lazy and dislike work p. 139
   c. subordinates seek responsibility
   d. subordinates will exercise creativity and imagination

6. Four quadrants of the brain are related to different thinking styles. This model is called:

*a. the whole brain concept — p. 142
b. Theory X and Theory Y
c. The path-goal theory
d. The Myers-Briggs Type Indicator

7. According to the Hermann's "whole brain" concept:

a. leaders cannot learn to rely on all four quadrants of the brain.
*b. leaders can learn to rely on all four quadrants of the brain. — p. 144
c. the situation is the most important factor in decision making.
d. self-concept is the most important factor in decision making.

8. The Myers-Briggs Type Indicator (MBTI):

a. expresses the belief that workers dislike their jobs.
b. suggests that leaders have specific traits.
*c. is a personality test that measures how individuals solve problems. — p. 146
d. determines whether a situation is favorable or unfavorable.

9. Based on limited MBTI research, the two preferences in that seem to be most strongly associated with leadership are :

*a. thinking and judging — p. 147
b. extroversion and feeling
c. intuition and perceiving
d. sensing and thinking

10. Charismatic leaders are known for all EXCEPT:

a. having an emotional impact on people
b. appealing to both the heart and mind.
*c. having excellent planning and organizing skills. — p. 148
d. inspiring and motivating people

11. Charisma can be potentially dangerous because:

a. it can be used to exploit, manipulate, and deceive others.
b. it is based on emotion rather than logic or reason.
*c. both a & b p. 152
d. it is effective in a stable, unchanging environment.

12. Charismatic leaders often emerge in troubled times because :

a. they offer solutions
b. they reduce stress and anxiety among followers
c. they have inspiring personalities
*d. both b & c p. 149

13. Transformational leaders do all EXEPT:

a. develop followers into leaders.
*b. promote stability p. 153
c. inspire followers to go beyond their own self-interest for the good of the group.
d. paint a vision of a desired future.

14. Transactional leaders are important for all the following reasons EXCEPT :

a. they recognize followers' needs
b. they keep the organization running smoothly
*c. they promote change p. 153
d. they are good at traditional management functions.

15. Values affect leadership because of all the following reasons EXCEPT;

a. values affect a leader's perception of situations and problems
b. values guide a leader's choices and actions.
c. values affect how a leader relates to others
*d. values are a snapshot of the future for the organization p. 134

SHORT ANSWER

1. _____________________ is the set of unseen characteristics and processes that underlie a relatively stable pattern of behavior in response to ideas, objects, and people in the environment.

   Answer: Personality

2. _________________defines whether a person places primary responsibility for what happens to him within himself or on outside forces.

   Answer: Locus of control

3. The belief that power and status differences should exist in an organization is called

   ___________________ .

   Answer: authoritarianism

4. _______________ are fundamental beliefs that an individual considers to be important, that are relatively stable over time, and that have an impact on attitudes and behavior.

   Answer: Values

5. _____________________are beliefs about the kind of goals or outcomes that are worth trying to pursue.

   Answer: End values

6. _______________________ is the collection of attitudes we have about ourselves, includes self-esteem and whether a person generally has a positive or negative feeling about himself.

   Answer: Self-concept

7. The assumption that people are basically laze and motivated to work and that they have a natural tendency to avoid responsibility is called _____________.

   Answer: Theory X

8. ___________ is an approach that considers not only a person's preference for right-brained versus left-brained thinking, but also conceptual versus experiential thinking; identifies four quadrants of the brain related to different thinking styles.

   Answer: Whole brain concept

9. This personality test measures how individuals differ in gathering and evaluating information for solving problems and making decisions. _________________

   Answer: Myers-Briggs Types Indication (MBTI)

10. _____________ are leaders who have the ability to inspire and motivate people to do more than they would normally do, despite obstacles and personal sacrifice.

    Answer: Charismatic leaders

SHORT ESSAY QUESTIONS

1. How do values affect leadership?

   Values affect leaders in several ways. A leader's personal values affect perception of situations and problems. How a person makes sense out of the environment and interprets information results from values. A leader who values ambition and career success may view a problem as an impediment to personal success. Values affect how leaders relate to others. A leader who values conformity may have a difficult time with a follower who is self-reliant.

   Values guide a leader's choices and actions. A leader who values courage is likely make decisions that may be unpopular. Values concerning goals help determine a leader's actions as well. p. 134

2. Distinguish between Theory X and Theory Y leaders.

   Theory X reflects the assumption that people are basically laze and not motivated to work and that they have a natural tendency to avoid responsibility. A Theory X leader believes that people must be coerced, controlled, directed, or threatened to get them to put forth their best effort. Theory Y is based on the assumption that people do not inherently dislike work and will commit themselves willingly to work that they care about. Theory Y assumes that under the conditions, people will seek out greater responsibility and will exercise imagination and creativity in the pursuit of solutions to organizational problems. A Theory Y leader does not believe people have to be coerced and controlled to perform effectively. p. 139.

3. What is the importance of the "whole brain" concept?

   The area of individual differences is cognitive style, how a person, perceives, processes, interprets, and uses information. Cognitive approaches are preferences that are not necessarily rigid. The "whole brain" concept broadens the idea that individuals prefer right- or left-brain thinking and includes conceptual versus experiential thinking. Herman identifies for quadrants of the brain related to different styles. The importance lies in the belief that individuals can learn to use all four quadrants and developed a balanced thinking style, rather than relying on one or two preferred quadrants. pp. 141-145.

4. What is meant by "The Black Hat of Charisma?

   Charisma is not always used to benefit the group, organization, or society. It can also be used for self-serving purposes, which leads to deception, manipulation, and exploitation of others. Because the basis of charisma is emotional rather than logical or rational, it is risky and potentially dangerous. One explanation relates to the differences between personalized and socialized leaders. Personalized charismatic leaders react to organizational problems in terms of their own needs whereas socialized leaders respond to the needs of the whole organization. Personalized charismatic leaders are self-aggrandizing and nonegalitarian. This is what is meant by the "black hat" or dark side of charisma. p. 152

5. How do transactional and transformational leaders differ?

   Transformational leaders develop followers into leaders. Transformational leaders elevate followers' concerns from lower-level physical needs (e.g., safety and security) to higher-level needs (e.g., self-esteem and self-actualization). Transformational leaders inspire followers to go beyond their own self-interests for the good of the group. Transformational leaders paint a vision of a desired future state and communicates it in a way that makes the pain of change worth the effort. Transactional leaders promote stability. p. 153-155.

ESSAY QUESTIONS

1. Many top leaders of e-commerce and high-tech organizations exhibit a high internal locus of control. Explain why this is so.

   p. 130

2. Why do think that understanding how personality traits and dimensions affect behavior can be a valuable asset for leaders?

   p. 131

3. Studies have shown that personalized charismatic leaders can have a significant detrimental impact on long-term organization performance. Yet, leaders who have been consistently successful in improving organizational performance exhibit a pattern of socialized behavior. Explain these findings.

   p. 151-153

CHAPTER FIVE: LEADERSHIP MIND AND HEART

TRUE-FALSE QUESTIONS

1. Mental models are deep-seated assumptions, values, attitudes, and beliefs that help leaders make sense of the world. T, p. 179

2. Leaders have many mental models that tend to govern how they interpret experiences and how they act in response to people and situations. T, p. 179

3. Whereas competence is limited and quantifiable, capacity is unlimited. T, p. 177

4. Leaders cannot change their assumptions. F. p. 180

5. Perceptions are not part of a person's mental model, determining how a leader views people, situations, and events. F, p. 182

6. Mindfulness can be defined as questioning assumptions and interpreting data according to one's own beliefs, ideas, and thinking. F, p. 184

7. The Pike Syndrome refers to the power of conditioning that guides behavior. T, p. 185

8. Leaders have to put aside preconceptions, suspend beliefs ; this can be referred to as « beginner's mind. » T, p. 185

9. Systems thinking means seeing patterns in the organizational whole instead of just the parts, and learning to reinforce or change systems-patterns. T, p. 188

10. An important element of systems thinking is to discern circles of causality. T, p. 189

11. The first step to "emotional intelligence" is to be aware of the kinds of emotions. T, p. 191

12. Anger and enjoyment are components of emotional intelligence. F, p. 192

13. An unspoken notion among many senior-level executives is that fear is good. T, p. 199

14. Fear-based motivation makes an employee feel valued as a person. F, p. 202

15. A leader's emotional abilities and understandings do not play a role in charismatic and transformational leadership behavior. F, p. 196

MULTIPLE CHOICE QUESTIONS

1. Human emotion is the most basic in the organization because:

   a. people cannot be separated from their emotions.
   b. leaders generate employee commitment to shared vision through emotion.
   *c. both a & b — p. 192
   d. relationships are far less important than formal rules.

2. Competence is:

   a. the most important dimension of leadership.
   b. all that is needed for a leader to succeed.
   *c. less important for leadership than personal capabilities. — p. 177
   d. adequate for a leader in a time of uncertainty and organizational change.

3. Deep-seated assumptions, values, attitudes, beliefs, biases, and prejudices that determine how leaders make sense of the world are called:

   a. the Pike Syndrome
   *b. mental models — p. 179
   c. the "whole brain" concept
   d. mindfulness

4. The leader's mind can be developed beyond the nonleader's in critical areas:

   a. open mindedness and systems thinking
   b. mental models, and personal mastery.
   *c. both a & b — p. 184
   d. competency in skills

5. Leaders should be aware of how their mental models affect thinking because :

   *a. blind spots can limit understanding and effectiveness. — p. 179
   b. the leader's perceptions do not affect the employees.
   c. mental models are independent of organizational needs.
   d. the leader's assumptions are personal and do not affect employees.

6. Independent thinking means:

a. seeing patterns in the organizational whole instead of just the parts.
b. deep-seated assumptions, beliefs, blind spots, biases, and prejudices.
c. personal vision, facing reality, and holding creative ten.
*d. questioning assumptions and interpreting data according to one's own beliefs. p. 184

7. An important element of systems thinking is to discern circles of causality because:

*a. managers can guide the system when they understand it conceptually. p. 189
b. problems are solved by breaking down into discrete pieces.
c. each piece adds to the success of the whole.
d. relationships between the parts of the system are unimportant.

8. Assumptions are :

a. not part of a leader's mental model.
*b. part of a leader's mental model. p. 180
c. an expression of the organizational mission
d. a personality trait

9. Stereotyping is :

a. a perceptual distortion
b. a tendency to assign a person to a group or broad category
c. a way to attribute widely held generalizations about a group or individual
*d. all of the above p. 183

10. The eight families of emotion refers to:

a. the fears that individuals experience.
*b. categories recognized worldwide based on photos of facial expressions. p. 192
c. the joys that individuals experience.
d. emotional intelligence

11. Some researchers suggest that ___________ more than intellectual ability drives our thinking and decision making, as well as out interpersonal relationships.

a. vision
b. neutralizers
c. education
*d, emotion p. 191

12. Self-awareness refers to:

a. the ability to connect to others.
b. the ability to put oneself in some else's shoes.
*c. being conscious of the emotions within. p. 194
d. the ability to be hopeful and optimistic.

13. Emotional intelligence is related to effective leadership because :

a. emotional abilities play a key role in charismatic leadership.
b. emotional abilities play a key role in transformational leadership.
*c. both a & b p. 196
d. emotional abilities play a key role in technical expertise.

14 Fear in the workplace results in all EXCEPT:

*a. employees feeling valued. p. 199
b. employees not doing their best.
c. employees not taking risks or changing the status quo.
d. employees not speaking up.

15. In the workplace, love:

a. energizes employees in their jobs.
b. involves attraction, fascination, and caring for people and work.
c. means more than feelings, it is translated into behavior.
*d. all of the above. p. 202

SHORT ANSWER

1. ___________ are theories people hold about specific systems in the world and their expected behavior

   Answer: Mental Models

2. During the ________________we observe information (sensory data) from the environment, screen and select stimuli, and organize selected date into patterns for interpretation and response.

   Answer: perception process

3. _____________ is the process of continuously reevaluating previously learned ways of doing things in the context of evolving information and shifting circumstances.

   Answer: Mindfulness

4. _____________is the ability to see the synergy of the whole rather than separate elements of a system and to learn to reinforce whole system patterns.

   Answer: Systems thinking

5. ________________ is a person's abilities to perceive, identify, understand, and successfully manage emotions in self and others.

   Answer: Emotional intelligence

6. ________________ is the discipline of personal growth and learning and mastering yourself; it embodies personal visions, faking reality, and holding creative tension.

   Answer: Personal mastery

7. The components of emotional intelligence include ________________, self-awareness, self-management, and social awareness.

   Answer: relationship management

8. ________________ is the ability to put yourself in someone else's shoes.

Answer: Empathy

9. According to the author, ______________ can prevent people from doing their best, from taking risks, and challenging and changing the status quo.

Answer: fear

10. ________________ is motivation based on feeling valued in the job.

Answer: Love-based motivation

SHORT ESSAY

1. What are mental models? What is their importance?

   Mental models are deep-seated assumptions, values, attitudes, beliefs, biases, and prejudices that determine how leaders make sense of the world. Leaders should be aware of how these elements affect their thinking and may cause "blind spots" that limit their understanding. Mental models are important because they govern how leaders interpret their experiences and the action they take in response to people and situations. Two important components of mental models are assumptions and perception. p. 179

2. Describe the Pike Syndrome. How does this pertain to leadership?

   The power of conditioning is called the Pike Syndrome. A hungry pike in an aquarium with a glass divider makes repeated attempts to attack minnows but only hits the glass. The divider is removed, but the pike makes no attempt to attack the minnows because conditioning has made the task seem futile. Leaders have to forget many conditioned ideas and remain open minded to be effective. p. 185

3. What are the implications of emotional intelligence for leaders?

   A leader's emotional abilities play a key role in charismatic leadership behavior. A high level of self- awareness, combined with managing one's own emotions, allows a leader to display self confidence and earn respect. Emotional restraint allows a leader to consider the needs of others. The emotional state of the leader affects the entire group, department, or organization. Leaders who maintain balance are positive role models. Emotional intelligence enables leaders to respect followers as whole human beings with feelings, ideas, and opinions. p. 191.

4. What is the result of fear in the workplace?

   Fear in the workplace can diminish trot and communication. Employees feel threatened by repercussions if they speak up about work-related concerns. Fears center around lack of career advancement, damaged relations with the supervisor, or job loss. Employees are afraid to talk about a wide range of issues, but mainly the interpersonal and relationship skills of executives. When fear is high, managers destroy the opportunity for feedback, blinding them to reality and denying them the chance to alter their decisions and behaviors. p. 199

5. How can love be used positively in the workplace?

   Love is more than feelings; it is translated into behavior. Feelings of unity and cooperation in organizations by leaders or followers translate into acts of helping, cooperation, sharing, and understanding. Sentiments emerge as action. When leaders address emotional needs, people respond by loving their work and becoming emotionally engaged in solving problems and serving customers. p. 202.

ESSAY QUESTIONS

1. *Emotional contagion* means that leaders who are able to maintain balance and motivation positive role models to help motivate and inspire those around them. Discuss and give examples.

   p. 196

2. How can leaders expand the capacities of their minds and hearts through development and practice ?

   pp. 176-177

3. What are the basic assumptions behind systems thinking ?

   p. 188

CHAPTER SIX: COURAGE AND MORAL LEADERSHIP

TRUE-FALSE QUESTIONS

1. Stewardship is the belief that leaders are deeply accountable to others as well as to the organization, without trying to control others. F, p. 228

2. Research has indicated that most people think CEOs are honest, and hard-working F, p. 216

3. Moral leadership is about distinguishing right from wrong and doing right, seeking the just, the honest, and the good. T, p. 222

4. Standing up for what is right is a primary way in which leaders create an environment of integrity. T, p. 219

5. At the preconventional level, people learn to conform to the expectations of others. F, p. 224

6. A leader who is visionary, empowering and committed to serving others is operating at the postconventional or principle level. T, p. 224

7. Participation management encourages managers to direct and control employees. F, p. 228

8. The success of Japanese firms that emphasize employee involvement encouraged many U.S. organizations to try participatory management practices. T, p. 228

9. A principle of stewardship is to localize decisions and power to those closest to the work and the customer. T, p. 228

10. Authoritarian management takes stewardship assumptions about leaders and followers one step further. F, p. 229

11. Ethical leaders put values into action; employees learn about values that are important to the organization by watching leaders. T, p. 220

12. Courage is another word for fearlessness. F, p. 234

13. To take a chance and improve things means leaders have to step through fear and confusion and act despite the risks involved. T, p. 241

14. Anger and frustration cannot be used for positive outcomes. F, p. 243

15. Stewardship leaders guide the organization without dominating it and facilitate followers without controlling them. T, p. 229

MULTIPLE CHOICE QUESTIONS

1. The public feels that:

   a. business practices are basically unethical and socially irresponsible.
   b. the most desired qualities in a leader are honesty and integrity.
   c. most business leaders stand up for what is right.
   *d. both a & b — p. 216

2. The ethical pressures that challenge leaders include:

   *a. doing the right thing despite pressure to increase profits — p. 217
   b. finding new products and services to remain competitive
   c. carrying out the leadership vision.
   d. selecting employees with the right technical skills.

3. The actions that make leaders go wrong include all EXCEPT :

   a. breaching agreements
   b. neglecting follower development
   c. excessively promoting self-interest
   *d. taking responsibility — p. 219

4. Moral leadership is about all EXCEPT:

   a. distinguishing right from wrong.
   *b. taking away from others to enhance oneself. — p. 221
   c. reward ethical conduct
   d. seeking the just and the honest in practice.

5. Raoul Wallenberg is an example of the principled level of moral development because:

   *a. he was guided by an internalized set of principles recognized as right or wrong. — p. 216
   b. he lived up to the expectations of others.
   c. he followed the rules to avoid punishment.
   d. he acted in his own interest.

6. Leaders can create organizational systems that support ethical behavior by:

a. creating open-door policies
b. establishing ethics codes
c. rewarding ethical conduct
*d. all of the above p. 220

7. The continuum of leadership thinking includes all EXCEPT:

a. authoritarian management
b. servant leadership
c. stewardship-empowering leadership
*d. charismatic leadership p. 227

8. Servant leadership can best be described as the belief that:

a. leaders are deeply accountable to others.
b. employee participation should be increased through teams.
*c. self-interest should be replaced by serving the needs of others. p. 230
d. power, purpose, and privilege reside with those at the top of the organization.

9. Robert Greenleaf defined _____________ through a character in a novel who performs the lowliest, most menial tasks for the group.

*a. a servant leader. p. 229
b. an authoritarian leader
c. a participative leader
d. a stewardship leader

10. ServiceMaster sets high ethical standards as part of the organizational culture because:

a. the leader's behavior is an important tool for shaping ethical values.
b. of the belief that organizations have an obligation to benefit society.
c. organizations are only responsible to their shareholders.
*d. both a & b p. 233

11. The conventional level of personal moral development is characterized by:

a. following rules
b. following internalized principles of justice
c. follows authority with blind obedience.
*d. fulfilling duties and obligations of the social system p. 225

12. Pushing beyond the comfort zone is an act of:

*a. courage p. 237
b. vision
c. goal setting
d. ethics

13. Aspects of courage include all EXCEPT:

a. fighting for what you believe
b. asking for what you want and saying what you think
c. nonconformity
*d. being fearless p. 235

14. Colleen Rowley, an FBI staff member called attention to agency shortcomings that may have contributed to the September 11, 2001 tragedy. This behavior is best described as:

a. ethical behavior
b. courage
c. stewardship
*d. whistleblowing

15. Most adults operate at level______________ of moral development.

a. one
*b. two p. 226
c. three
d. four

SHORT ANSWER

1. ________ is a belief that leaders are deeply accountable to others as well as to the organization, without trying to control others, define meaning, and purpose for others, or take care of others.

   Answer : Stewardship

2. Distinguishing right from wrong and doing right ; seeking the just, honest, and good in the practice of leadership. _____________

   Answer : Moral leadership

3. ______________________ is the level of personal moral development in which leaders are guided by an internalized set of principles universally recognized as right or wrong.

   Answer : Principled level

4. ___________________ is leadership in which the leader transcends self-interest to serve the needs of others, help others grow, and provide opportunities for others to gain materially and emotionally.

   Answer : Servant leadership

5. ___________________ is employee disclosure of illegal, immoral, or unethical practices in the organization.

   Answer : Whistleblowing

6. ________________ is the ability to step forward through fear.

   Answer : Courage

7. This leadership mind-set emphasizes tight top-down control, standardization and specialization, and management by impersonal measurement and analysis.

____

Answer : Authoritarian Management

8. Leaders are responsible for outcomes, but they may act as mentors and coaches. They have given up some of their control, but they are still responsible for the morale and performance of employees.

____

Answer : Participative Management

9. At the preconventional level of personal moral development, employees

_________________________________,

Answer : follow rules, act in their interest, obey authority

10. An ________________ leader possesses humility, maintains concern for the greater good, fulfills commitments, strives for fairness, serves others, and shows courage.

Answer : ethical

SHORT ESSAY QUESTIONS

1. What is ethical leadership?

Ethical leadership does not mean ignoring profit and loss or production costs. It combines a concern for rational measures of performance with a recognition of the importance of treating people right every day. Rational leadership focuses on self, whereas ethical leadership is about others. p. 218

2. Why is the study of moral leadership important.

   Moral leadership uplifts people, enabling them to be better than they were without the leaders. Specific personality characteristics such as ego strength, self-confidence, and a sense of independence may enable leaders to behave morally in the face of opposition. Leaders can develop these characteristics through hard work. A leader's capacity to make moral choices is related to the level of moral development. p. 219

3. What is the concept of servant leadership described by Robert Greenleaf.?

   According to Greenleaf, servant leaders: 1) put service before self-interest; 2) listen first to affirm others; 3) inspire trust by being trustworthy; and 4) nourish others and help them become whole. Servant leaders truly value and respect others as human beings, not as objects of labor. pp. 229-233

4. What is courage?

   Courage is the ability to step forward through fear. Courage does not mean the absence of doubt or fear, but the ability to act in spite of them. Courage is not another word for fearless. It is natural and right for people to feel fear when real risk is involved, whether the risk be loss ofjob, loss of life, or loss of the acceptance of peers. pp. 234-242.

5. Why is whistleblowing an act of courage?

   Whistleblowing is employee disclosure of illegal, immoral, or unethical practices in the organization. This is still risky for employees who can lose their jobs. Choosing to act courageously means conflicting emotions-whistleblowers may feel disloyal to their boss and coworkers. p. 240-241

ESSAY QUESTIONS

1. What aspect of courage do you find the most difficult? What aspect is the easiest?

   p. 234

2. Describe the ethical climate in U.S. business today. What could be done to change it?

   p. 217

3. How can anger and frustration turn into courage?

   p. 243

CHAPTER SEVEN: FOLLOWERSHIP

TRUE-FALSE QUESTIONS

1. The nature of leader-follower relationships involves reciprocity, the mutual exchange of influence. T, p. 256

2. Characterized by both mindfulness and a willingness to act, effective followers are essential for the organization to be effective. T, p. 259

3. The alienated follower is both a critical, independent thinker who is active in the organization. F, p. 258

4. Covey's work shows a maturity continuum that leads from independence to dependence. F, p. 265

5. Followers cannot initiate opportunities for personal fulfillment and the use of their capabilities. F, p. 263

6. Effective followers have to know what they stand for and be willing to express their own ideas to their leaders even this might mean risking their jobs. T, p. 260

6. Interdependent people realize that it is best to work cooperatively with others. T, p. 266

8. A dependent person has developed a sense of self-worth and an attitude of self-reliance. F, p. 265

9. Followers obtain power through personal sources and position sources. T, p. 268

10. Only top mangers have personal and position sources of power to generate influence. F, p. 268

11. One of the strategies for managing up is to be a resource for the leader. T, p. 269

12. According to the author, building a relationship with the leader implies submission and authority. F, p. 272

13. Feedback should be seen as a route to improvement not something to be feared. T, p. 276

14. Leaders who practice self-management leadership do not share power. F, p. 278

15. A community of followers have the traits of inclusivity, realism, and shared leadership. T, p. 279

MULTIPLE CHOICE QUESTIONS

1. Studying followership, is important for all reasons EXCEPT:

*a. Followers do not become leaders. p. 256
b. Followers have an influence on the leader.
c. Desirable qualities in a leader are also desirable in a follower.
d. Leaders and followers are roles that individuals shift in and out of in various conditions.

2. Dependent, uncritical thinkers:

a. are aware of the significance of their actions.
b. are aware of the actions of others.
*c. accept the leader's ideas without thinking. p. 257
e. weigh the impact of decisions on the company vision.

3. Effective followers:

a. assume responsibility for their own behavior and its impact on the organization.
b. do not presume that a leader will provide them with security or permission to act.
c. exercise their potential and initiate opportunities.
*d. all of the above p. 259

4. If a leader's actions and decisions contradict the best interests of the organization, effective followers

*a. take a stand p. 263
b. follow the leader
c.. sacrifice their personal integrity
d. follow passively

5. According to Covey, moving from dependence to independence includes:

a. being proactive
b. starting with a clear mental image of your destination.
*c. both a & b p. 266
d. taking neither initiative nor personal responsibility.

6. Moving to interdependence involves all EXCEPT:

*a. blaming others when things go wrong p. 266
b. open communication
c. teamwork
d. building positive relationships

7. Personal sources of power include:

a. central location
*b. knowledge and effort p. 268
c. network of relationships
d. flow of information

8. Followers can influence their leaders by:

a. being a resource for the leader.
b. building a relationship
c. helping the leader be a good leader.
*d. all of the above p . 269

9. A follower can be a resource for the leader by:

*a. informing the leader about their own ideas, beliefs, needs, and constraints. p. 269
b. giving up idealized leader images.
c. thanking the leader
d. building a relationship.

10. According to the author, tips for using feedback to develop followers do NOT include:

a. Make regular feedback a habit.
*b. Use elements of organizational objectives. p. 276
c. Be generous with positive feedback
d. Train followers to view feedback as an opportunity.

11. The feedback process includes all EXCEPT :

a. observation
b. development
*c. noise p. 277
d. assessment

12. Using elements of storytelling for feedback

a. helps followers and leaders learn how and why something happened.
b. puts the leader and follower on equal footing
c. helps the leader and follower examine their roles in the problem.
*d. all of the above p. 276

13. ____________________ calls for leaders to share power and responsibility in such a way that anyone can become a leader, depending on the situation.

a. Authoritarian management
b. Mentoring
*c. Self-management leadership p. 278
d. Charismatic leadership

14. Characteristics of community include:

a. inclusivity
b. shared leadership
c. dependency
*d. both a & b p. 280

15. ______________________ are made up of individuals who are informally bound to one another through exposure to a similar set of problems and a common pursuit of solutions.

*a. Communities of Practice p. 281
b. Skunkworks
c. Vertical Hierarchies
d. Substitutes for leadership

SHORT ANSWER

1. ______________________________ is failing to consider possibilities beyond what one is told; accepting the leader's ideas without thinking.

   Answer: Uncritical thinking

2. In the four followership styles, the ________________________________ is a person in the organization who is passive, yet independent, critical thinker.

   Answer: alienated follower

3. The ________________________________ is a critical, independent thinker who actively participates in the organization.

   Answer: effective follower

4. _______________ occurs when a leader uses evaluation and communication to help individuals and the organization learn and improve.

   Answer: Feedback

5. _______________________________ is leading others to lead themselves.

   Answer: Self-management leadership

6. ____________________ is a type of communication in which each person suspends his attachment to a particular viewpoint so that a deeper level of listening, synthesis, and meaning evolves from the whole community.

   Answer: Dialogue

7. Sources of follower power include personal sources and ______________________________.

Answer: position sources

8. One way to influence your leader include______________________________________

Answer: (any one of the following) Be a resource, Build a relationship, Help the leader be a good leader, View the leader realistically

9. The feedback process includes observation, assessment, _________________________ and development.

Answer: consequences.

10. According to the Maturity Continuum, the move toward________________________________ is the realization that the best things happen by working cooperatively with others.

Answer: interdependence

SHORT ESSAY QUESTIONS

1. Describe the model of followership styles.

Robert E. Kelley described five styles of followership categorized according to two dimensions, the quality of independent, critical thinking, versus dependent, uncritical thinking. The extent to which one is active or passive, and is a critical or a dependent, uncritical thinker determines whether one is an alienated follower, a conformist, a pragmatic survivor, a passive follower or an effective follower. pp. 258-259.

2. Discuss the demands on effective followers.

Effective followers have to know what they stand for and be willing to express their own Ideas and opinions to their leaders, even though this might mean risking their jobs, being demeaned, or feeling inadequate. p. 260.

3. Describe Covey's model for developing and applying personal leadership qualities.

   Developing Personal Potential can be accomplished through Stephen Covey's approach, which defines a habit as the intersection of knowledge, skill, and desire. Seven habits are arranged along a continuum from dependence to interdependence. Each habit builds on the previous one so individuals grow further along the maturity continuum as they develop personal effectiveness habits. pp. 264-267.

4. What are position sources of power?

   A *central location* provides influence to a follower, because the follower is known to many and contributes to the work of many. A position that is key to theflow *of information* can establish that position and the follower in it as critical-thus, influential-to those who seek the information. Within a *network ofrelationships,* a follower has greater opportunity to persuade others. p. 268.

5. Why is it important for a follower to view the leader realistically?

   Understanding that leaders are fallible and will make mistakes leads to acceptance. Effective followers present realistic images of themselves and do not cover their weaknesses or mistakes. Instead of criticizing a leader to others, it is far more constructive to disagree with a leader directly on occasions relevant to the operation of the organization. p. 273.

ESSAY QUESTIONS

1. How can leaders optimize the use of feedback and minimize the conflict and fear that often accompanies it ?

   pp. 276-278

2. Describe a community of practice.

   p. 281

3. What do followers want from their leaders ? Discuss

   pp. 273-275

CHAPTER EIGHT: MOTIVATION AND EMPOWERMENT

TRUE-FALSE QUESTIONS

1. Motivation refers to the forces that arouse enthusiasm and persistence to pursue a certain course of action. T, p. 294

2. A leader who understands worker needs can design the reward system and direct energies toward shared goals. T, p. 295

3. Hygiene factors fulfill high-level needs and include achievement, recognition, responsibility, and opportunity for growth. F, p. 300

4. People with a high need for achievement tend to enjoy work that is entrepreneurial and innovative. T, p. 302

5. Extinction is the administration of a pleasant and rewarding consequence following a behavior. F, p. 305

6. Expectancy Theory suggests that motivation depends on individuals' mental expectations about their ability to perform tasks and receive rewards. T, p. 306

7. Incentive programs are unsuccessful because people are not motivated by money and lower needs. F, p. 308

8. Equity theory proposes that people are motivated to seek social equity in the rewards they expect for performance. T, p. 309

9. Critics of « carrot-and –stick » methods argue that intrinsic rewards diminish extrinsic rewards. F, p. 311

10. Critics of « carrot-and-stick » methods argue that carrot-and-stick approaches destroy people's motivation to work as a group. T, p. 313

11. Empowerment is power sharing, the delegation of power or authority to subordinates in the organization. T, p. 315

12. Job enrichment is a program that links at least a portion of employees pay on the number of skills he or she possesses. F, p. 326

13. Five elements must be in place before employees can be empowered to perform their jobs: information, knowledge, discretion, meaning, and rewards T, p. 317

14. One way people get extrinsic rewards at work is to feel a sense of meaningfulness and importance about their jobs. F, p. 321

15. Pay-for-knowledge is a motivational approach that encourages people to work together rather than focus on individual achievements and rewards. F, p. 325

MULTIPLE CHOICE QUESTIONS

1. The importance of motivation is:

   a. it can lead to behaviors that reflect high performance within organizations.
   b. that high employee motivation and high organizational performance go hand-in-hand.
   c. high employee motivation can lead to company profits
   *d. all of the above p. 294

2. Intrinsic rewards:

   *a. are the internal satisfaction a person receives by performing a particular action. p. 295
   b. are given by another person, typically a supervisor
   c. include pay raises and promotions
   d. are given to all people within an organization or a specific department.

3. Insurance benefits or vacation time would be examples of

   a. intrinsic, individual rewards
   b. extrinsic, individual rewards
   *c. extrinsic, system-wide rewards p. 295
   d. intrinsic, individual rewards

4. When a union wins good pay, members want social and esteem needs met because:

   a. low-order needs take priority
   b. social and self-esteem needs take priority
   c. once a need is satisfied, it declines in importance and the next need is activated.
   *d. both a & c p. 298

5. According to Hertzberg's two-factor theory, the leader's role is to:

*a. use motivators to meet higher level needs of employees. p. 300
b. provide only hygiene factors to employees
c. remove dissatisfiers
d. use system-wide rewards

6. According to the acquired needs theory, a need for power indicates:

a. the desire to accomplish something difficult, attain a high standard for success
b. the desire to form close personal relationships and avoid conflict.
*c. the desire to influence or control others and have authority over others. p. 302
d. the desire to master complex tasks

7. Immediate praise for an employee who arrives on time increases the likelihood of promptness. This is an example of

a. extinction
b. punishment
*c. positive reinforcement p. 305
d. expectancy theory

8. Wages are based on ratings of skill, effort, and responsibility. This system is an example of :

a. carrot and stick methods
b. the two-factor theory
c. Maslow's hierarchy of needs
*d. expectancy theory p. 306

9. Equity theory proposes that :

a. people are motivated to seek social equity in rewards they expect for performance.
b. if people perceive that their rewards are equal to others, they will be motivated
c. when people perceive they are treated fairly, motivation will decline.
*d. all of the above p. 309

10. Carrot-and-stick approaches destroy motivation to work as group because of all EXCEPT:

a. extrinsic rewards create a culture of competition not collaboration.
*b. each person's success is mutually enjoyed because it benefits the organization. P. 311
c. employees who are mistrustful and threatened will not perform at their highest level.
d. coworkers may seize upon weaknesses to undermine each other and not share solutions.

11. How can leaders address the carrot and stick controversy?

a. leaders can understand a program's strengths and weaknesses.
b. leaders can acknowledge the positive but limited effects of extrinsic motivators.
c. leaders can assure that subordinates' work offers self-satisfaction and a yearly raise.
*d. all of the above p. 315

12. Reasons for empowerment do not include:

a. strong motivation because it meets the higher needs of individuals.
*b. a longer response time because employees are not used to making decisions p. 315
c. employees use more of themselves to do their jobs.
d. the employee reward is intrinsic-a sense of personal mastery and competence.

13. The elements of empowerment include all EXCEPT:

a. information about company performance.
b. knowledge and skills.
*c. individual rewards p. 317
d. rewards based on company performance.

14. One way to enrich a job is to:

*a. enlarge it, to extend the responsibility to cover several tasks. p. 326
b. use reward and punishment.
c. use the carrot and stick method.
d. focus on an employees lower needs.

15. Organizations can give meaning to work through all EXCEPT :

a. making employees feel that they're a part of something
b. engendering a culture of mutual trust
*c. creating a horizontal structure p. 322
d. treating people with care and respect

SHORT ANSWER

1. ________________________ refers to the forces either internal or external to a person that arouse enthusiasm and persistence to pursue a certain course of action

Answer : Motivation

2. ____________________ are internal satisfactions a person receives in the process of performing a particular action.

Answer : Intrinsic rewards

3. ______________________ is a motivational approach that encourages people to work together rather than focus on individual achievements and rewards and ties additional pay to improvements in overall employee performance.

Answer : Gainsharing

4. ______________________ are rewards that apply the same to all people within an organization or within a specific category or department.

Answer : Systemwide rewards

5. ___________________________________ is Maslow's theory that proposes that humans are motivated by multiple needs and those needs exist in a hierarchical order.

Answer : Hierarchy of needs theory

6. ______________________________ are the first dimension of Herzberg's two-factor theory which involves working conditions, pay, company policies, and interpersonal relationships.

Answer : Hygiene factors

7. __________________________ are the second dimension of Herzberg's two-factor theory which involves job satisfaction and meeting higher-level needs such as achievement, recognition, responsibility, and opportunity for growth.

Answer : Motivators

8. ___________________________ : McClelland's theory that proposes that certain types of needs (achievement, affiliation, power) are acquired during an individual's lifetime.

Answer : Acquired needs theory

9. ___________________________ states that positively reinforced behavior tends to be repeated and behavior that is not reinforced tends not to be repeated.

Answer : Law of effects

10. __________________________is a theory that suggests that motivation depends on individuals' mental expectation about their ability to perform tasks and receive desired rewards.

Answer : Expectancy theory

SHORT ESSAY QUESTIONS

1. What is motivation? Why is it important for leaders to understand motivation?

   People have basic needs (e.g., for food) that translate into an internal tension that motivates specific behaviors to fulfill the need. To the extent that the behavior is successful, the person is rewarded when the need is satisfied. Motivation can lead to behaviors that reflect high job performance. High employee motivation, organizational performance, and profits go hand-in-hand. p. 284.

2. Describe the Two-Factor Theory

   The first dimension, called **hygiene factors,** involves the presence or absence of job dissatisfiers such as working conditions, pay, company policies or interpersonal relationships. When hygiene factors are poor, work is dissatisfying. Good hygiene factors remove dissatisfaction but do not cause satisfaction and motivation. The second dimension, called **motivators,** fulfill high-level needs and include achievement, recognition, responsibility, and opportunity for growth. Hertzberg believed that when motivators are present, workers are highly motivated and satisfied. p. 300

3. Describe the reinforcement approach to motivation.

   Reinforcement theory looks at the relationship between behavior and consequences by changing or modifying the follower's on-the-job behavior through reward or punishment. Behavior modification is the name given to a set of techniques by which reinforcement theory is used to modify behavior. Reinforcement is defined as anything that causes a certain behavior to be repeated or inhibited to include positive reinforcement. punishment, and extinction. p. 304

4. How can leaders address the carrot and stick controversy?

   Some incentive programs are successful when employees are motivated by money and lower needs. One way for leaders to address the carrot and stick controversy is to understand a program's strengths and weaknesses and acknowledge the positive but limited effects of extrinsic motivators. Rewards can be linked to behavior promoting the higher needs of both the organization and the individual, such as rewarding quality, long-term growth, or a collaborative culture. p. 311.

5. Why is empowerment difficult to implement?

   Implementing Empowerment can be difficult in established organizations because it can destroy hierarchies and upset the familiar balance of power. Those companies that have redistributed power and authority the least have been the most successful (e.g., quality circles, job enrichment programs), according to a study. Workers sometimes balk at the added responsibility freedom brings. pp. 317-319.

6. Describe Equity Theory.

   Equity theory proposes that people are motivated to seek social equity in the rewards they expect for performance. If they perceive their rewards as equal to what others receive for similar contributions, they believe their treatment is fair and are more highly motivated. When they believe they are not treated fairly, motivation declines.

   People evaluate equity by a ratio of inputs to outputs. Employees make comparisons of what they put into a job and the rewards received relative to those of others. Equity exists when the ratio of one person's outcomes to inputs equals the ratio of others' in the work group. Inequity occurs when the input/outcome ratios are out of balance. p. 309.

ESSAY QUESTIONS

1. Describe the needs-based theories of motivation.

   pp. 298-304

2. Describe the ways to give meaning to work.

   pp. 321-326

3. You are the owner of a small business with 10 employees. What methods would you use to motivate them ?

   Answers will vary.

CHAPTER NINE: LEADERSHIP COMMUNICATION

TRUE-FALSE QUESTIONS

1. Leaders communicate the big picture --- the vision-not just facts and statistics. T, p. 342

2. The key elements of the communication process include encoding, transmitting the message through a channel, and decoding. T, p. 342

3. Managers spend 10% of each working day in communication with others. F, p. 344

4. Leaders facilitate strategic conversations by actively listening, setting the agenda, for conversation, and selecting the right communication channels for dialogue. T, p. 346

5. An open communication climate runs according to the traditional flow of selective information downward from the supervisor to the subordinate. F, p. 347

6. By listening and responding to customer needs, a leader can strengthen trust and build long term relationships. T, p. 352

7. A discussion reveals feelings and builds common ground, with more emphasis on inquiry than advocacy. F, p. 354

8. A discerning leader detects the unarticulated messages hidden below the surface of spoken interaction, complaints, behavior, and actions. T, p. 352

9. Written communication has high channel richness because it permits feed-back. F, p. 361

10. It is up to leaders to select the communication channel to fit the message. T, p. 362

11. Nonverbal communication may be defined as a message transmitted through action and behavior. T, p. 367

12. "Management by wandering around" means that employees speak directly to leaders in their offices. F, p. 368

13. When using email, it is best to consider the circumstances, know what's off-limits, and read the email twice before sending it. T, p. 364

14. Stories do note enable leaders to connect with people on an emotional level. F, p. 365

15. Communicating in a crisis is not the leader's job if there is a public relations department in the company. F, p. 368

MULTIPLE CHOICE QUESTIONS

1. A manager's role is that of "information processor," whereas a leader's role is:

   a. to communicate the big picture --- the vision
   b. to serve as a communication champion
   c. to communicate written information, facts, and data.
   *d. both a & b
   p. 344

2. An open communication climate is essential because:

   a. A vision must be shared and practiced by leaders at every opportunity.
   b. The climate of an organization reflects the leader, who should embody the vision.
   c. Communicating the vision must be built into daily interaction with followers.
   *d. all of the above
   p. 347

3. Being a good listener expands a leader's role in the eyes of others because of all EXCEPT:

   a. active listening is an ongoing part of a leader's communication.
   b. a leader builds long-term relationships with clients by not interrupting and selling.
   *c. a leader concentrates on what to say next rather than on what is being said. p. 351
   d. a good listener finds areas of interest, affirms others, and builds trust.

4. A dialogue is marked by:

   a. opposition by individuals who advocate their positions and convince others.
   *b. group unity, shared meaning, and transformed mindsets. p. 353
   c. logic
   d. "beating down" opponents

5. Discernment involves all EXCEPT:

   a. detecting unarticulated messages hidden below the surface
   b. paying attention to patterns and relationships
   c. listening carefully for undercurrents that have yet to emerge.
   *d. trying to convince others to agree with a point of view. p. 352

6. Influences on channel richness include all EXCEPT:

a. the ability to handle multiple cues simultaneously.
*b. the ability to handle one-way, slow, impersonal feedback. p. 360
c. the ability to facilitate rapid, two-way feedback.
d. the ability to establish a personal focus for the communication.

7. By using language rich in metaphor and storytelling, leaders can:

a. make sense of situations in ways that will be understood in the organization.
b. frame activity with discrete meaning.
c. replace rules and regulations or the policy manual.
*d. all of the above p. 364

8. Messages transmitted through action and behavior are called:

*a. nonverbal communication p. 367
b. channel richness
c. discernment
d. communication champion

9. The person who enables followers to « live » the vision in their day-to-day activities is called a :

a. manager
b. CEO
*c. communication champion p. 344
d. decoder

10. One example of informal communication is:

a. an annual report
*b. management by wandering around p. 368
c. a letter
d. a job description

11. Stories are very powerful communication tools because of all EXCEPT :

a. stories bind people together.
b. stories are very persuasive
c. stories inspire action
*d. stories put noise in the communication process p. 364

12. Email should be used for all EXCEPT:

a. setting up meetings.
b. transmitting standard reports
*c. writing potentially sensitive material p. 365
d. preparing a group of people for a meeting

13. The growing use of email has:

a. increased the potential for communication errors
b. deprived people of "human moments"
c. helped leaders get responses faster
*d. all of the above p. 363

14. To communicate in a crisis, leaders should NOT:

a. be visible
b. tell the truth
*c. avoid visibility p. 369
d. communicate a vision for the future

15. Face-to-face communication can be described as:

*a. the richest form of communication p. 361
b. the poorest form of communication
c. impersonal one-way communication
d. none of the above

SHORT ANSWER

1. ________________ is a process by which information and understanding are transferred between a sender and a receiver.

   Answer: Communication

2. A ____________________________ is a person who is philosophically grounded in the belief that communication is essential to building trust and gaining commitment to a vision.

   Answer: Communication champion

3. ______________________________ refers to communication that takes place across boundaries and hierarchical levels about the group or organization's vision, critical strategic themes, and values that can help achieve desired outcomes.

   Answer: Strategic conversation

4. ____________________________ is communication in which all types of information are shared throughout the company and across all levels.

   Across: Open communication

5. The skill of grasping and interpreting a message's genuine meaning is called__________________

   Answer: Listening

6. ________________________ is listening in which a leader detects unarticulated messages hidden below the surface of spoken interaction.

   Answer: Discernmennt

7. ________________________active sharing and listening in which people explore common ground and grow to understand each other and share a world view.

Answer: Dialogue

8. A____________________ is a medium by which a communication message is carried from sender to receiver.

Answer: channel

9. ____________________________________is the amount of information that can be transmitted during a communication episode.

Answer: Channel richness

10. Messages transmitted through action and behavior are referred to as____________________

Answer: nonverbal communication

SHORT ESSAY QUESTIONS

1. Describe the leader as a communication champion.

   A leader can be a communication champion, philosophically grounded in the belief that communication is essential to pursuing the organizational vision. Leaders use communication to inspire and unite people around a common sense of purpose and identity. A communication champion enables followers to "live" the vision in their day-to-day activities. p. 344

2. Why is listening important?

   The act of listening affirms others, builds trust, and suppresses personal judgments that shape perceptions. Being a good listener expands a leader's role in the eyes of others; it deepens the relationship between a leader and a follower. Active listening is necessary as part of a leader's ongoing daily communication. p. 349.

3. Describe channel richness.

Channel richness is the amount of information that can be transmitted during a communication episode. The richness of an information channel is influenced by three characteristics: the ability to handle multiple cues simultaneously; 2) the ability to facilitate rapid, two-way feedback; and 3) the ability to establish a personal focus for the communication. Face-to-face communication is the richest because it permits direct experience. Written communication is the lowest in richness because it is not focused on a receiver, uses limited information cues, and fails to provide feedback. p. 360.

4. Why is nonverbal communication important?

Nonverbal communication refers messages transmitted through action and behavior. People interpret leader actions as symbols, just as they attach meaning to words. In interpreting a leader's nonverbal cues, followers determine the extent to which a leader's action's correspond with verbal messages. Leaders use actions to symbolize their vision and their commitment to it. For example, by closing the office door, a leader conveys inaccessibility. p. 367.

5. What is a strategic conversation?

Strategic conversation refers to people talking across boundaries and hierarchical levels about the group or organization's vision, critical strategic themes, and the values that can help achieve desired outcomes. Leaders facilitate strategic conversations by actively listening, setting the agenda by underscoring the key strategic themes linked to organizational success, and selecting the right communication channels and facilitating dialogue. p. 346.

ESSAY QUESTIONS

1. Contrast dialogue and discussion.

pp. 353-354

2. How should a leader communicate in a crisis?

pp. 368-371

3. One example of informal communication is "management by wandering around." Describe and evaluate this communication method.

p. 368

CHAPTER TEN: LEADING TEAMS

TRUE-FALSE QUESTIONS

1. Many organizations have reported great success with teams, including increased productivity, quality improvements, and high employee satisfaction. T, p. 386

2. A team is the same as a group. F, p. 387

3. A virtual team is part of a traditional, vertical hierarchy. F, p. 405

4. Leaders of global teams have to coordinate across time, distance, and culture. T, p. 408

5. The first stage of team development is called norming. F, p. 391

6. Small teams have more disagreements, subgroups form, and conflicts occur. F, p. 395

7. Interdependence is the extent to which team members depend on each other for information, resources, or ideas to accomplish their tasks. T, p. 396

8. During the forming stage of team development, the leader facilitates and interaction among team members. T, p. 389

9. Conflict emerges when teams compete for scarce resources, such as money, information, or supplies. T, p. 411

10. Employee morale is higher in cohesive teams. T, p. 398

11. Vision, bargaining/ negotiating,. mediation, and facilitating communication are not methods of handling conflict. F, p. 414

12. Diversity within a team can contribute to a healthy level of conflict that leads to better decision-making. T, p. 395

13. Team effectiveness requires meeting the needs for task accomplishment but not the needs for socio-emotional well-being. F, p. 401

14. Team leaders frequently overlook how important it is for people to feel that their contribution is valued. T, p. 405

15. Effective leaders should use the same conflict resolution style in every situation. F, p. 411

MULTIPLE CHOICE QUESTIONS

1. A team has all the following components EXCEPT:

   a. Teams share a goal.
   *b. Teams have individual "stars." p. 387
   c. Teams are made up of two or more people.
   d. Teams work together regularly

2. Leaders of global teams have to:

   a. coordinate across distance, time, and culture.
   b. be flexible and culturally astute
   c. learn to blend diverse backgrounds
   *d. all of the above p. 408

3. The role associated with facilitating others' participation, smoothing conflicts, showing concern for team members' needs, and reminding others of standards is the:

   a. managerial role.
   b. authoritarian leadership role
   c. task-specialist role
   *d. socio-emotional role p. 401

4. Large groups are less effective because:

   *a. there are more disagreements, subgroups form, and conflicts arise. p. 395
   b. members feel like a part of the group.
   c. there is more agreement
   d. more questions are asked.

5. In an emergency room, trauma team members cover their teammates. This is an example of:

   a. pooled interdependence
   b. sequential interdependence
   *c. reciprocal interdependence p. 396
   d. team leadership

6. The "storming" stage of team development is characterized by:

*a. conflict and disagreement p. 390
b. orientation
c. establishment of order and cohesion
d. cooperation and problem solving

7. Leaders use several factors to influence cohesiveness to include all EXCEPT:

a. interaction
b. shared mission and goals
*c. individual monetary rewards p. 398
d. team success.

8. The main advantage of a virtual team is:

a. the lack of supervision
b. the ability to monitor team members
*c. the ability to use the best people for a particular job p. 406
d. the ability to have control over team members.

9. As a result of cohesiveness, teams have:

a. good morale
b. poor morale
c. high productivity
*d. both a & c p. 398

10. Conflict is not caused by:

a. teams competing for scarce resources, information, or supplies.
*b. mutually accepted goals. p. 410
c. unclear responsibilities.
d. a personality clash.

11. When quick decisive action is vital on important issues, this style is appropriate.

*a. competing style — p. 411
b. avoiding style
c. collaborating style
d. accommodating style

12. Team types do NOT include :

a. functional teams
*b. vertical teams — p. 392
c. cross-functional teams
d. self-directed teams

13. Virtual team leaders should master all the following skills EXCEPT:

a. select the right team members.
b. agree on ground rules
c. build trust by building connections
*d. use email for conflict resolution — p. 408

14. Global teams fail because :

a. communication barriers can be formidable.
b. values, attitudes and beliefs differ.
c. building trust is difficult
*d. all of the above — p. 408

15. The specific changes a leader can make to develop effective team leadership include all EXCEPT :

a. recognize the importance of share purpose and values
b. admit your mistakes
* c. mediation — p. 403
d. provide support and coaching to team members

SHORT ANSWER

1. A ________________________ is a unit of two or more people who interact and coordinate their work to accomplish a shared goal or purpose.

   Answer : team

2. In the ________________ stage of team development, orientation and getting acquainted takes place.

   Answer : forming

3. During the ____________________ stage of team development, individual personalities and conflicts emerge.

   Answer : storming

4. ____________________________ are made up of a supervisor and subordinates in the formal chain of command.

   Answer : Functional teams

5. ___________________ are teams made up of members from different functional departments within an organization.

   Answer : Cross-functional teams

6. ___________________________ are teams made up of 5 to 20 members who work with minimum supervision and rotate jobs to produce a complete product or service.

   Answer : Self-directed teams

7. ____________________________ is the extent to which team members depend on each other for information, resources, or ideas to accomplish their ideas.

Answer : Interdependence

8. ___________________________________ is the extent to which members stick together and remain united in the pursuit of a common goal.

Answer : Team cohesiveness

9. A_____________________________ is a team leadership role associated with facilitating others' participation , smoothing conflicts, showing concern for team members' needs and feelings, serving as a role model, and reminding others of standards for team interaction.

Answer : socio-emotional role

10. A____________________________________ is made up of geographically or organizationally dispersed members who share a common purpose and are linked primarily through advanced information technologies.

Answer : virtual team

SHORT ESSAY QUESTIONS

1. Describe the evolution of team leadership.

   In the functional team, leadership is based on the vertical hierarchy. In a cross-functional team, members have more freedom from the hierarchy, but the team typically is leader-centered and leader-directed, although they give up some control and power for the team to function effectively. In the highest stage of evolution, team members work together without the direction of managers, supervisors, or assigned team leaders. p. 392.

2. Why are small teams more effective than large teams?

   Teams must be large enough to have diverse skills, about seven people, yet small enough for members to feel like part of a community. Research shows that small teams show more agreement, ask more questions, and exchange more opinions. Large teams, 12 or more, have more disagreements, subgroups form, and conflicts occur. Large teams tend to be less friendly. p. 395.

3. Describe the leadership styles for handling conflict.

   Effective leaders and team members vary their style of handling conflict to fit a specific situation, as each style is appropriate in certain cases : the competing style, the avoiding style, the compromising style, the accommodating style, and the collaborating style. p. 411

4. What challenges face leaders of global teams?

   Global teams bring new challenges to the concept of teamwork. Leaders have to coordinate across time, distance, and culture. Global team leaders have to be flexible and culturally astute, able to deal with differences without compromising any team member's integrity. p. 408.

5. Describe a virtual team.

   A virtual team is made up of geographically-or organizationally-dispersed members who are linked primarily through advanced information and telecommunication technologies. Team members use e-mail, voice mail, videoconferencing, Internet and intranet technologies, and various types of collaboration software to perform their work rather than meeting face -to-face. Virtual teams may be temporary cross-functional teams pulled together to work on specific problems, or they may be long-term or permanent self-directed teams. Team leadership is shared or altered, depending on the expertise needed at each stage of the project. p. 405

ESSAY QUESTIONS

1. What is the team leader's personal role in developing an effective team?

   p. 403

2. Why has the use of teams increased dramatically ?

   p. 386

3. An important factor in team effectiveness is ensuring that the needs for both task accomplishment and team members' socio-emotional well-being are met. Discuss

   p. 401

CHAPTER ELEVEN: DEVELOPING LEADERSHIP DIVERSITY

TRUE-FALSE QUESTIONS

1. Today, the U.S. aims to be a "melting pot" where people blend to be the same. F, p. 430

2. Diversity means including those who differ in age, ethnicity, gender, or race. T, p. 431

3. Women leaders tend to be competitive and prefer vertical hierarchies. F, p. 438

4. In interactive leadership, the leader favors a consensual and collaborative process. T, p. 438

5. It is imperative that leaders in international organizations learn to understand local cultures and deal with them effectively. T, p. 440

6. Research showed that male leaders were rated as having more idealized influence, providing more inspirational motivation, and being more considerate. F, p. 439

7. High uncertainty avoidance reflects a value for a loosely knit social framework in which individuals are expected to take care of themselves. F, p. 441

8. The glass ceiling is an invisible barrier that separates white men from top leadership jobs. F, p. 449

9. Barriers to diversity in organizations include ethnocentrism, stereotypes and prejudice and the "white male" club. T, p. 454

10. Without strong leadership, increased cultural diversity can lead to decreased work effort and lower organizational performance. T, p. 420

11. Passive bias is perhaps a bigger problem than blatant discrimination in today's organizations. T, p. 446

12. In some cases, people fail to advance to higher levels in organizations because they don't have the necessary education and skills. This is called diversity. F, p. 450

13. In Hofstede's research, masculinity reflects a preference for achievement, heroism, and assertiveness while femininity reflects the values of relationships and cooperation. T, p. 442

14. All leaders need to be aware of the impact that culture may have and consider cultural values in their dealings with employees. T, p. 445

15. The one-best-way approach does not lead to a mind-set that views differences as deficiency or dysfunction. F, p. 445

MULTIPLE CHOICE QUESTIONS

1. The U.S. workforce is changing to include all EXCEPT:

   a. more women
   *b. more white, American-born men — p. 433
   c. more non-white people
   d. more immigrants

2. Diversity helps organizations:

   a. build better relationships with diverse customers
   b. develop employee potential.
   c. provide a broader base of experience for creativity and problem solving,
   *d. all of the above — p. 433

3. Interactive leaders tend to be:

   a. competitive
   b. individualistic
   *c. consensus builders — p. 438
   d. reluctant to share power

4. A resent survey of followers rate women leaders higher than men on several characteristics:

   a. idealized influence
   b. inspirational motivation
   *c. both a& b — p. 439
   d. individualism

5. High power distance means that:

   *a. people accept inequality in power in institutions, organizations, and individuals. — p. 441
   b. members of a society feel uncomfortable with uncertainty and ambiguity.
   c. a value for loosely knit social framework in which individuals take care of themselves.
   d. values of relationships, cooperation, and group decision making.

6. Cultural characteristics that can affect international leadership include:

a. language
b. education
c. religion
*d. all of the above p. 442

7. Ethnocentrism is the belief that:

*a. one's culture and subculture are inherently superior to other cultures. p. 445
b. all cultures have value.
c. everyone in the organization has the same values, beliefs, and motivations.
d. everyone in the organization has the same attitudes about work and life.

8. The invisible bar that separates women and minorities from top leadership jobs is called:

a. ethnocentrism
b. biculturalism
*c. the glass ceiling p. 449
d. uncertainty avoidance

9. In Stage 1 of organizational diversity awareness and action:

a. diversity is inherent in the culture, and the organization is gender- and color-blind.
*b. legal requirements are met, but diversity is viewed as a problem. p. 452
c. top-level leaders are committed to diversity.
d. diversity is viewed as a competitive weapon.

10. The assumption that minorities are less competent, and less suitable for leadership termed:

a. cultural differences
b. diversity awareness
*c. prejudice p. 453
d. the "white male" club

11. Leaders must develop the following personal characteristics in a multicultural organization.

a. an openness to change themselves.
b. mentoring and empowerment of diverse employees
c. a personal, long-range vision that supports diversity
*d. all of the above

p. 455

12. Diversity awareness training does not include helping employees to:

a. become aware of their own cultural boundaries.
*b. improve technological skills
c. become aware of their prejudices and stereotypes.
d. learn new interpersonal skills.

p. 457

13. In some cases, people fail to advance to higher levels in organizations because they don't have the necessary education and skills. This is termed the :

*a. opportunity gap
b. leadership grid
c. substitutes for leadership
d. ethnocentrism

p. 450

14. To help an organization thrive in today's diverse environment, leaders should :

a. examine formal policies
b. examine informal patterns of social interaction.
c. examine the unwritten rules and assumptions in the organization
*d. all of the above

p. 456

15. Diversity does all EXCEPT :

a. help the organization build better relationships with customers
b. develop employee and organizational potential
*c. perpetuate the glass ceiling
d. provide greater organizational flexibility

p. 436

SHORT ANSWER

1. __________________________________ is a workforce made up of people with different human qualities or who belong to various cultural groups.

   Answer : Workforce diversity

2. The differences among people in terms of age, ethnicity, gender, race, or other dimensions is called_____________________________.

   Answer : diversity

3. ___________________________________ is a leadership style in which people develop relationships with followers, share power and information, empower employees, and strive to enhance others feelings of self-worth.

   Answer : Interactive leadership

4. _________________________refers to how much people accept equality in power.

   Answer : Power distance

5. __________________________refers to the degree to which members of a society feel uncomfortable with uncertainty and ambiguity.

   Answer : Uncertainty avoidance

6. __________________________is the belief that one's own culture and subculture are inherently superior to other cultures.

   Answer: Ethnocentricism

7. ______________________ is the sociocultural skills and attitudes used by racial minorities as they move back and forth between the dominant culture and their own ethnic or racial culture.

Answer : Biculturalism

8. The ________________________ is an invisible barrier that separates women and minorities from top leadership positions.

Answer: glass ceiling

9. ____helps employees become aware of their own cultural boundaries, their prejudices and stereotypes, so they can learn to work together successfully.

Answer: Diversity awareness training

10. ___________________________ refers to the work environment particularly in executive-level positions in which women and minorities are heavily outnumbered.

Answer: The « White Male » club

SHORT ESSAY QUESTIONS

1. Describe the changes in America's workforce.

   The U.S. Department of Labor statistics indicates that the workforce and the customer base are changing dramatically. The workforce will soon be dominated by female and minority workers. In addition, there has been a slow but emphatic shift in our attitudes toward racial, ethnic, cultural, or other « differences.» In the past , the United States was seen as a melting pot where people of different national origins, races, ethnicity, and religions came together and blended to resemble one another. Opportunities for advancement in society favored people who fit in. Today, the burden of adaptation rests more on the organization than on the individual. Organizations are increasingly operating on a global playing field, which means that people of different races and nationalities are living and working together on an unprecedented level. p. 430.

2. Is interactive leadership exclusive to women?

   No, any leader can learn to adopt a more inclusive style by developing the skills and attention to non-verbal behavior, listening, empathy, cooperation, and collaboration. p. 438

3. What are the leadership implications of cultural differences?

   Leaders must be aware of cultural differences in order to lead effectively in a multicultural environment. Culture affects both leadership style and the leadership situation. How behavior is perceived differs from culture to culture. Leaders need to consider cultural values in their dealings with employees. p. 445.

4. What is biculturalism and how does it affect employees?

   Biculturalism can be defined as the sociocultural skills and attitudes used by racial minorities as they move back and forth between the dominant culture and their own ethnic and racial culture. Research on differences between whites and blacks has focused on issues of biculturalism and how it affects employee's access to information, level of respect and appreciation, and relation to superiors and subordinates. Racism is the workplace shows up in subtle ways. p. 446.

5. Explain diversity awareness training.

   Diversity awareness training helps employees become aware of their own cultural boundaries, their prejudices and stereotypes, so they can work together successfully. The five stages of individual diversity awareness include:

   - Defense---negative stereotyping, ethnocentric attitude
   - Minimizing differences----hides or trivializes cultural differences
   - Acceptance---accepts behavioral differences
   - Adaptation---empathy with those of other cultures
   - Integration----multicultural attitude p. 457

ESSAY QUESTIONS

1. Discuss ethnocentrism and its effect on an organization.

   p. 446

2. Discuss the Hofstede studies.

   pp. 440-442

3. Describe the opportunity gap.

   p. 450

CHAPTER TWELVE: LEADERSHIP POWER AND INFLUENCE

TRUE-FALSE QUESTIONS

1. The concept of frames of reference calls attention to the ways people gather information, make decisions and exercise power. — T, p. 474

2. The human resources frame of reference places emphasis on goal setting and clarifying job expectations. — F, p. 476

3. One danger of relying too heavily on the symbolic frame is that leaders develop the "messiah" complex. — T, p. 477

4. Reward power is the authority granted from a formal position in the organization. — F, p. 480

5. The responses to the use of power include compliance, resistance, and commitment. — T, p. 483

6. When unemployment is high, leaders have greater power because people are dependent on the organization for their livelihood. — T, p. 485

7. Dependency is not related primarily to a person's control over resources. — F, p. 485

8. Interdepartmental dependency is a key element underlying leader power. — T, p. 487

9. Control over information is an important source of power for leaders. — T, p. 488

10. Impression management is a political approach which means that leaders seek to control how others perceive them. — T, p. 491

11. Coercive power derives from a leader's special knowledge or skills regarding tasks performed by followers. — F, p. 481

12. Centrality does not include the extent to which a leader's department affects the final output of the organization. — F, p. 488

13. The most frequently used influence tactic is persuasion. — T, p. 493

14. Leaders do not have difficulty distinguishing ethical from unethical uses of power and influence. — F, p. 497

15. Identifying and placing in key positions people who are sympathetic to the desire outcomes of the leader is not a tactic for asserting influence — F, p. 494

MULTIPLE CHOICE QUESTIONS

1. The concept of frames of reference refers to all EXCEPT:

   a. the way people gather information
   b. the way people make decisions
   *c. ethical considerations that leaders face. p. 474
   d. how people exercise power.

2. The symbolic frame:

   *a. refers to the perception of an organization as a system of shared meaning and values. p. 477
   b. views organizations as arenas of ongoing conflict over the allocation of resources.
   c. places emphasis on goal setting and clarifying jobs expectations to provide order.
   d. considers people as the organization's most valuable resource.

3. When workers admire a supervisor because of her personal characteristics, the influence is based on:

   a. legitimate power
   b. reward power
   c. expert power
   *d. referent power p. 481

4. The responses to the use of power include all EXCEPT:

   a. compliance
   b. resistance
   *c. structuralism p. 483
   d. commitment

5. The characteristics that affect dependency in organizations do NOT include:

   *a. experience-whether the leader has allocated resources in the past. p. 485
   b. importance--the resource must be perceived as important
   c. scarcity--whether the resource is easy or difficult to obtain
   d. nonsubstitutability-resources with no viable substitute give leaders more power.

6. Control over information affects leader power because:

a. the leader has control over how and to whom information is distributed
b. leaders providing materials have more power than those who receive them
c. leaders recognize that information is a primary business resource.
*d. both a & c p. 488

7. Political tactics for asserting influence include all EXCEPT:

a. expanding networks
b. using assertiveness
*c. seeking arbitration p. 491
d. using rational persuasion

8. Sexual harassment includes:

a. access to resources and jobs in exchange for sexual favors.
b. access to information in exchange for tolerating sexually intimidating comments.
* c. both a & b p. 496
d. access to expert and legitimate power.

9. A leader who uses stories to build shared values is using:

*a. the symbolic frame p. 477
b. rational persuasion
c. assertiveness
d. networking

10. In an organization, an ethical action must meet the following criteria

*a. The action does not cause harm to others. p. 497
b. The action increases shareholder wealth.
c. The action serves the interest of the CEO?
d. The action promotes the self-interest of the employees?

11. The political frame of reference includes all EXCEPT:

a. mind-set: sees the organization as jungle
b. emphasis: coalition building
c. dangers: power plays for self-interest
*d. focus: empowerment

p. 475

12. Guidelines for ethical action do NOT include the following questions:

a. Is the action consistent with the organization's goals?
*b. Is the action profitable for the organization?
c. Does the action respect the rights of individuals?
d. Does the action meet the standards of fairness?

p. 497

13. The principles for asserting leaders influence include:

a. make people like you
b. remember the principle of scarcity
c. extend formal authority with expertise and credibility
*d. all of the above

p. 493

14. If Paul, a salesman, does not perform as well as expected, his supervisor can put a negative letter in his file. This is an example of:

a. referent power
b. expert power
*c. coercive power
d. legitimate power

p. 481

15. Example: Wal-Mart stops selling point-of-sales research to market researchers, who need purchase information. Wal-Mart uses its position to demand more money. This is the principle of:

a. importance
*b. scarcity
c. legitimate power
d. vertical power

p. 486

SHORT ANSWER

1. A______________________ is a frame of reference that places emphasis on goal setting and clarifying job expectations as a way to provide order, efficiency, and continuity.

   Answer: structural frame

2. A________________________________ is a frame of reference in which people are treated as the organization's most valuable resource.

   Answer: human resources frame

3. __________________ is the ability of one person or department in an organization to influence other people to bring about desired outcomes.

   Answer: Power

4. The effect that a person's actions have on the attitudes, values, beliefs, or actions of others is ______________________.

   Answer: influence

5. __________________________ is authority granted from a formal position.

   Answer: Legitimate power

6. ________________________ is authority based on personality characteristics that command followers' attention, respect, and admiration so that they want to emulate the leader.

   Answer: Referent power

7. Responses to the use of power include compliance, ______________________, and commitment.

Answer: resistance

8. A leader's or department's role in the primary activity of an organization is called

______________________.

Answer: centrality

9. ______________________involves activities to acquire, develop, and use power and other resources to obtain desired future outcomes when there is uncertainty or disagreement about changes.

Answer: Politics

10. The______________________ is a frame of reference in which the organization is perceived as a system of shared meaning and values.

Answer: symbolic frame

SHORT ESSAY QUESTIONS

1. Describe the structural frame of reference.

   The structural frame places emphasis on goal setting and clarifying job expectations as a way to provide order, efficiency, and continuity. Leaders emphasize job descriptions, hard data, specific polices, accepted standards, and the bottom line. Acceptance to rules brings order and logic to organization. Task-oriented leadership styles, some of the contingency approaches, and transactional leadership rely on this frame. Carried to an extreme, the structural frame leads to rigidity and even tyranny. p.475.

2. Describe power in an organization.

   Power is an intangible force in organizations. It cannot be seen, but its effect can be felt. Power is often defined as the potential ability of one person (or department) to influence other persons (or departments) to carry out orders or to do something they otherwise would not have done. Other definitions stress that power is the ability to achieve goals or outcomes that power holders desire. p. 479.

3. What is referent power?

   Referent power comes from leader personality characteristics that command followers' identification, respect, and admiration so they wish to emulate the leader. When workers admire a supervisor because of the way she deals with them, the influence is based on referent power. Referent power depends on the leader's personal characteristics and is visible in the area of charismatic leadership. p. 481.

4. How can a leader increase power through political activity?

   Politics involves activities to acquire, develop, and use power and other resources to obtain desired future outcomes when there is uncertainty about choices. Political activity can be either a positive or negative force. Uncertainty and conflict are natural in organizations, and politics is the mechanism for accomplishing things that cannot be handled through purely formal policies or position power. Leaders can use their personal power by doing things for others that would obligate them. They can cultivate subordinates' feelings of friendship and loyalty. They can also use impression management. p. 490.

5. Why is organizational centrality a source of power?

   Centrality reflects a department's role in the primary activity of the organization. One measure of centrality is the extent to which the work of the leader's department affects the final output of the organization. Centrality is associated with more power because it reflects the contribution made to the organization. p. 488.

ESSAY QUESTIONS

1. Why is power one of the most important concepts in the study of leadership?

   pp. 479-483

2. Discuss the tactics for asserting leader influence.

   pp. 491-496

3. What are the ethical considerations in using power and politics ?

   pp. 496-497

CHAPTER THIRTEEN: LEADERSHIP VISION AND STRATEGIC DIRECTION

TRUE-FALSE QUESTIONS

1. The complex environment can overwhelm executives, and many tend to focus on internal organizational issues. T, p. 511

2. A vision is an attractive, ideal future that is credible, yet not readily attainable. T, p. 513

3. A vision is always about the present, but it begins in the future. F, p. 516

4. Vision gives meaning to work because people want to feel pride in their jobs. T, p. 518

5. A vision statement is appropriate for top management but not for divisions, departments, and individuals. F, p. 513

6. A mission statement has two critical parts: the core values and the core purpose. T, p. 524

7. To remain competitive, leaders develop strategies that focus on core competencies, developing synergy, and creating value. T, p. 526

8. Strategy is not implemented through structural design, pay or reward systems, budget allocations, or organizational rules and policies. F, p. 533

9. For leaders to make a difference, they have to link vision to strategic action. T, p. 535

10. The organization's performance is not impacted by the leader's choices. F, p. 540

11. Martin Luther King Jr.'s speech, "I Have a Dream" is a good example of transformational leadership. T, p. 513

12. Vision is not important for nonprofit agencies like United Way. F, p. 515

13. ServiceMaster helps the housekeepers see their jobs as more than cleaning hospital floors. This example shows how vision links the present to the future. F, p. 518

14. Amgen, a pharmaceutical company, focuses its strategy on high-quality research. This is an example of core competence. T, p. 528

15. The person who is low on providing vision and stimulating action is uninvolved, not really a leader at all. T, p. 535

MULTIPLE CHOICE QUESTIONS

1. Thinking about how to meet future customer needs is more important than ever because of.

   a. globalization
   b. deregulation and advancing technology
   c. changing demographics and lifestyles
   *d. all of the above

   p. 512

2. An effective vision:

   a. provides a link between today and tomorrow.
   b. serves to motivate and energize employees
   *c. both a & b
   d. provides a snapshot of the present

   p. 513

3. Salespeople at Nordstrom have a clear picture of superior customer service so they can serve customers better. This example best shows that:

   *a. vision establishes a standard of excellence
   b. Nordstrom has a good human resources department.
   c. the company is mainly focused on internal organizational issues.
   d. Nordstrom concentrates on short-term results rather than taking the long-view.

   p. 477

4. The common themes of vision include:

   a. a broad appeal
   b. high ideals
   c. an internal communication plan
   *d. both a & b

   p. 520

5. Self-reference means that:

   a. each individual is working in his own direction.
   *b. each element in a system will serve the mission of the whole system
   c. every department can develop its own vision, independent of the company vision.
   d. people who do not have a clear vision of the future have little chance of success.

   p. 524

6. For the New York City Transit, “no graffiti” is the: company's:

*a. vision statement p. 514
b. core values
c. core purpose
d. view of the future.

7. To remain competitive, leaders develop strategies that focus on:

a. core competencies
b. developing synergy
c. creating value
*d. all of the above p. 526

8. The tools of strategy implementation include all EXCEPT:

a. strong leadership
*b. developing a vision for the future. p. 533
c. structural design
d. pay or reward systems

9. According to the model showing four possibilities of leadership, the Effective Leader:

*a. dreams big *and* transforms those dreams into strategic action. p. 535
b. is good at providing a big idea with meaning for self and others.
c. is all action and little vision.
d. is low both on vision and stimulating action.

10. To determine strategic direction for the future, leaders do all EXCEPT:

a. use SWOT analysis
b. consider changes and trends in the environment
c. use resources such as customers, government reports, suppliers, and consultants.
*d. use the Hersey and Blanchard Situational Theory model. p. 539

11. Ken Kutargi, pushed Sony into the risky videogames business in the early 1990s; although profits suffered at first, today Kutargi's division produces huge profits. This is an example of:

*a. strategic leadership
b. management by wandering around
c. substitutes for leadership.
d. referent power

p. 511

12. Henri Ford's original vision for Ford Motor Company stated, "I will build a motor for the great multitude…so low in price that no man making a good salary will be unable to own one…." This example shows how vision:

a. links the present to the future
b. defines the destination and the journey
c. reflects high ideals
*d. all of the above

p. 518

13. Whereas vision continues to grow and change, mission:

a. also continues to grow and change
*b. persists in the face of changing technologies
c. changes with economic conditions
d. reflects environmental shifts

p. 525

14. At Pottery Barn, a thick $24 bath towel is icon of the company's aspiration---design, quality, and price. This is an example of:

a. vision
b. synergy
*c. value creation

p. 531

15. Conventional wisdom said that Amazon.com would join the trash heap of dot.coms, but the vision and ______________________________ of founder Jeff Bezos proved critics wrong.

*a. strategic leadership
b. dreams
c. opportunities
d. experience

p. 538

SHORT ANSWER

1. ______________________________ is the ability to anticipate and envision the future, maintain flexibility, think strategically, and initiate changes that will create a competitive advantage for the organization in the future.

   Advantage: Strategic leadership

2. ______________________ is an attractive ideal future that is credible yet not readily attainable.

   Advantage: Vision

3. ________________________________ is a principle stating that each element in a system will serve the goals of the whole system when the elements are imprinted with an understanding of the whole.

   Answer: Self-reference

4. ______________________ is the organization's core broad purpose and reason for existence.

   Answer: Mission

5. ____ is the set of decisions and actions used to formulate and implement specific strategies that will achieve a competitively superior fit between the organization and its environment so as to achieve organizational goals.

   Answer: Strategic management

6. ______________________ is the general plan of acting that describes resource allocation and other activities for dealing with the environment and helping the organization attain its goals.

   Answer: Strategy

7. ______________________________ is something that the organization does extremely well in comparison to others.

Answer: Core competence

8. ______________________ is the interaction of organizational parts to produce a joint effect that is greater than the sum of the parts.

Answer: Synergy

9. _______________________ is the combination of benefits received and costs paid by the customer.

Answer: Value

10. _______________________________ is integrating knowledge of the environment and with the core competence in such a way as to achieve synergy and create customer value.

Answer: Strategy formulation

SHORT ESSAY QUESTIONS

1. Describe the stages of personal diversity awareness.

   Strategic leadership is responsible for the relationship of the external environment to choices about vision, mission, strategy, and their implementation. At the top of the pyramid is a clear, compelling vision of where the organization wants to be in 5-10 years. The vision reflects the environment and works in concert with the company's mission-its core values, purpose, and reason for existence. Strategy provides direction for translating the vision into action, whereas implementation is through the basic organization architecture (structure, incentives) that make things happen. pp. 512

2. How does vision energize people and create commitment?

   Vision energizes people and garners commitment because people want to feel enthusiasm about their work. A powerful vision frees people from the mundane by providing them with a challenge worthy of their best efforts. People commit their time and energy to causes they believe in, that make life better for others, or improve their communities. p. 516

3. How do leaders formulate strategy?

   Strategy formulation integrates knowledge of the environment, vision, and mission with the company's core competence in a way to achieve synergy and create value. When the elements are brought together, the company has an excellent chance to succeed in a competitive environment. Leaders have to ensure that strategies are implemented --- that actual behavior within the organization reflects the desired direction. p. 522.

4. How do leaders decide?

   Leaders look inward, outward, and forward. They scan both the internal and external organizational environment to identify trends, threats, and opportunities for the organization. One approach leaders take in setting a course for the ' future is through situation analysis: SWOT--strengths, weaknesses, opportunities, and threats. Another formula is a five-force analysis developed by Michael Porter. p. 538.

5. Describe the impact of the leader.

   When leaders link vision and strategy, they can make a real difference for the organization's future. A leader's greatest discretion is over strategic vision and strategic action. Strategic thinking and planning for the future can positively affect a company's performance and financial success. The emerging focus on leadership teams is more realistic than focusing on individual leadership. An effective team may have a better chance of identifying and implementing a successful strategy. p. 540.

ESSAY QUESTIONS

1. What is the difference between a vision and a mission?

   p. 512 p. 524

2. What is meant by core competence and how does the concept fit into strategy formulation?

   pp. 526-531

3. A leader's greatest discretion is often over strategic vision and strategic action. Explain.

   pp. 540-541

CHAPTER FOURTEEN: SHAPING CULTURE

TRUE-FALSE QUESTIONS

1. Culture is defined as the key values, assumptions, understandings, and ways of thinking shared by members of an organization. T, p. 557

7. External adaptation means that culture helps members develop a collective identity and know how to work together effectively. F, p. 559

8. A culture gap is the difference between desired and actual values and behavior. T, p. 562

4. Healthy cultures provide smooth internal integration and enable the organization to adapt to the needs of the external environment. T, p. 565

5. Leaders use slogans to express corporate values but not written public statements. F, p. 567

6. Employees learn what is valued most in a company by watching what attitudes and behaviors leaders reward as well as the leaders own behavior. T, p. 568

7. The adaptability culture is characterized by the values of creativity and risk-taking. T, 571

8. Ethical standards are not part of the formal policies of many organizations. F, p. 580

9. Many people believe that if you are not breaking the law, you are behaving in an ethical manner. T, p. 576

10. Ethical values in a company are strengthened primarily through value-based leadership. T, p. 576

11. In an adaptive organizational culture, managers tend to behave somewhat insularly, politically, and bureaucratically. F, p. 562

12. Eaton Corporation's philosophical statement called, "Excellence Through People" is an example of a symbol. F, p. 567

13. The clan culture is characterized by a clear vision of the organization's goals and leaders' focus on the achievement of people. F, p. 572

14. For organizations to be ethical, leaders need to be openly and strongly committed to ethical conduct. T, p. 576

15. Some companies include ethics as a part of broader statements that define mission. T, p. 580

MULTIPLE CHOICE QUESTIONS

1. The visible level of corporate culture can be best described as:

*a. artifacts such as dress, office layout, symbols, slogans, and ceremonies. p. 557
b. expressed values, underlying assumptions, and beliefs
c. deeper values and shared understandings held by organization members.
d. creativity and risk-taking

2. Culture helps members develop a collective identity and know how to work together efficiently. This is called:

a. external adaptation
*b. internal integration p. 558
c. levels of corporate culture
d. culture gap

3. An adaptive organizational culture is characterized by:

a. managers who care mainly about themselves, their work group, and their own needs.
b. leaders who care deeply about customers, stockholders, and employees.
c. leaders who trust others
*d. both b & c p. 561

4. The difference between actual and desired values and behaviors is called a:

a. ceremony
*b. culture gap p. 562
c. visible behavior
d. clan culture

5. Leaders shape culture because:

a. a culture gap is detrimental to a company and can cause a merger to fail.
b. a healthy culture is needed to adapt to the needs of the external environment.
c. integrating cultures is a simple task.
*d. both a& b p. 564

6. An organization's performance can be enhanced by the correct relationship among:

*a. cultural values, organizational strategy, and the external environment — p. 570
b. cultural values, the leaders behavior, and the leader's personal values
c. an adaptive culture, well-trained workers, and strong leadership behavior.
d. clan culture, bureaucratic culture, and adaptability culture.

7. Cooperation, consideration, fairness are values associated with the:

a. adaptability culture
b. achievement culture
*c. clan culture — p. 572
d. bureaucratic culture

8. The bureaucratic culture has an internal focus and consistency and works well in a(n):

a. dynamic environment
*b. stable environment — p. 573
c. flexible environment
d. external environment

9. A definition of ethics includes all EXCEPT:

a. the code of moral principles
b. the code of values
*c. the law — p. 576
d. the behavior of a person or group with respect to right and wrong.

10. The standards for ethical conduct are:

a. embodied within each employee
b. embodied within the organization itself
*c. both a& b — p. 576
d. covered by the law.

11. Value-based leaders generate respect from employees based on:

a. stated values
b. self-sacrifice leaders' demonstrate.
c. courage and determination seen in a leader's behavior.
*d. all of the above

p. 576

12. Leaders at Baxter International Inc. yanked a product from the market when several people died after undergoing dialysis using a Baxter filter. This is an example of:

a. a company placing emphasis on ethics.
b. a company providing moral leadership
c. a company guilty of a moral lapse.
*d. both a & b.

p. 574

13. The head of quality programs at Mitel Corp placed a nearly life-size wooden heifer outside his office as a _______________of the importance tracking down and destroying sacred cows.

a. paradigm
b. ceremony
*c. symbol
d. model

p. 586

14. Leaders shape values through:

a. stories
b. specialized language
c. selection and socialization
*d. all of the above

p. 564

15. Whistleblowing can be risky because:

a. employees can lose their jobs
b. employees can be transferred
* c. both a & b
d. employees may be promoted

p. 581

SHORT ANSWER

1.________________________is the set of key values, assumptions, understandings, and norms that is shared by members of an organization and taught to new members as correct.

Answer: Culture

2. _____________________refers to the degree of agreement among employees about the importance of specific values and ways of doing things.

Answer: Culture strength

3. _____________________refers to the difference between desired and actual values and behaviors.

Answer: Culture gap

4. _____________________________ are the enduring beliefs that have worth, merit, and importance for the organization.

Answer: Organizational values

5. ______________________________is a culture characterized by values that support the organization's ability to interpret and translate signals from the environment into new behavior responses.

Answer: Adaptability culture

6. _____________________________ is a culture characterized by a clear vision of the organization's goals and leaders' focus on the achievement of specific targets.

Answer: Achievement culture

7. ____________________ is the code of moral principles and values that governs the behavior of a person or group with respect to what is right and wrong.

Answer: Ethics

8. _____________________________ is a relationship between leaders and followers that is based on shared, strongly internalized values that are advocated and acted upon by the leaders.

Answer: Values-based leadership

9. A ____________________________ is a formal statement of the company's ethical values.

Answer: code of ethics

10. ________________________ is employee disclosure of illegal or immoral practices on the part of the organization.

Answer: Whistleblowing

SHORT ESSAY QUESTIONS

1. Describe the three levels of corporate culture.

At the surface level are visible artifacts such as dress, patterns of behavior, physical symbols, ceremonies, and office layout. At a deeper level are the expressed values and beliefs, which are not observable can be discerned from how people explain and justify what they do. These are values that members hold at a conscious level. Some values are so deeply embedded in a culture that members may not be consciously aware of them. These underlying assumptions are the deeper values and shared understandings held by organization members. p. 557

2. Describe culture strength.

Culture strength refers to the degree of agreement among employees about the importance of specific values and ways of doing things. If widespread consensus exists, the culture is strong and cohesive; if little agreement exists, the culture is weak. A strong culture can increase employee cohesion and commitment. p. 560

3. Why are selection and socialization important in shaping culture?

   Selection and socialization of new employees helps maintain specific cultural values. Through training, new recruits hear about a company's values and purpose. Companies with strong, healthy cultures, such as Southwest Airlines, have careful and rigorous hiring practices. Southwest looks for a sense of humor, and only those who fit the culture are hired. p. 565

4. Describe the competing values approach? .

   The correct relationship among cultural values, organizational strategy, and the external environment enhances performance. The fit among environment, strategy, and values is associated with four categories which depend on: 1) if the external environment requires flexibility or stability and 2) if the strategic focus is internal or external. The four quadrants represent cultural categories: Adaptability, Achievement, Clan, and Bureaucratic. p. 570

5. Describe values-based leadership.

   Ethical values in organizations are developed and strengthened through value-based leadership, a relationship based on shared, strongly internalized values that are advocated and acted upon by the leader. For organizations to be ethical, leaders need to be openly and strongly committed to ethical conduct. p. 576

ESSAY QUESTIONS

1. Culture serves two functions---to integrate organizational members so they know how to act and to help the organization adapt to the environment. Explain.

   pp. 557-562

2. How could a strong culture have either positive or negative consequences for an organization ?

   pp. 560-564

3. Why have ethical values gained renewed emphasis today ?

   pp. 574-580

CHAPTER FIFTEEN: DESIGNING AND LEADING A LEARNING ORGANIZATION

TRUE-FALSE QUESTIONS

1. The efficient performance organization uses a horizontal structure and empowers employees. F, p. 600

2. In a vertical structure, activities are grouped together by function from the bottom to the top of the organization. T, p. 602

3. Self-directed teams are made up of employees with different skills who rotate jobs to produce an entire product or service. T, p. 604

4. Bums and Stalker use the terms *mechanistic* and *organic* to explain organizational responses to the external environment. T, p. 606

5. Empowerment programs are easy to implement in established organizations where they upset the familiar balance of power. F, p. 607

6. The learning organization is based on personal networks of information. T, p. 600

7. In a traditional organization, strategy emerges bottom up as well as top down. F, p. 613

8. Adaptation is not necessary for a successful organization; it should cling to its values and behavior. F. p. 614

9. A leader's challenge is to maintain efficient performance and become a learning organization at the same time. T, p. 616

10. A skunkworks has rigid boundaries that limit innovation. F, p. 617

11. An after-action review (AAR) allow leaders to compare the actual outcome with the intended outcome. T, p. 619

12. In an adaptive culture, boundaries between parts are maximized. F, p. 614

13. The leader's dual challenge is to maintain efficient performance and become a learning organization at the same time. T, p. 616

14. A vertical organization allows for open web-like systems that offer ideas, decisions, and strategies to emerge from anywhere within or outside the company. F, p. 618

15. Era II-Rational Management can be described as micro-leadership in a stable world. T, p. 596

MULTIPLE CHOICE QUESTIONS

1. Leadership evolution includes:

    a. Era I-Great Man Leadership
    b. Era II-Rational Management
    c. Era IV-Learning Leadership
    *d. all of the above

    p. 595

2. The learning organization is characterized by all EXCEPT:

    a. horizontal structure
    *b. vertical structure
    c. empowered roles
    d. adaptive culture

    p. 600

3. A vertical structure is characterized by all EXCEPT:

    a. distance between managers and workers
    *b. self-directed teams as thefandamental unit
    c. activities grouped by common function
    d. decision-making authority residing with upper-level managers.

    p. 603

4. A self-directed team:

    a. is made up of employees with different skills who rotate jobs to produce a product/service.
    b. deals with customers, makes changes, and takes responsibility for training.
    *c. both a & b
    d. implements decisions made by top management.

    p. 604

5. One type of horizontal structure is a network structure in which:

    *a. a company keeps key activities in-house and outsources other functions.
    b. decisions are made by top managers.
    c. there are functional departments
    d. there is a hierarchy of authority

    p. 603

6. According to Bums and Stalker, an organic organization:

   a. is governed by formal rules and procedures.
   b. is characterized by a mass-production assembly line.
   *c. is characterized by tasks which are free flowing, looser, and adaptive. p. 606
   d. has jobs structured by standardization and division of labor.

7. Empowerment means emphasis on:

   a. teamwork
   b. leadership at the top of the pyramid.
   c. equality and independent effort
   *d. both a & c p. 607

8. In a learning organization, personal networks of information include:

   a. formal information systems to manage complex information
   b. teams of people who talk to whoever has the information.
   c. open-book management and open communication.
   *d. both b & c p. 610

9. Strategy in a learning organization:

   a. is formulated by top management.
   *b. can emerge from partnership linkages with suppliers, customers, and competitors. p. 613
   c. is part of a formal strategic planning exercise.
   d. is performed by a hired team of strategic planners.

10. The leader's challenge includes all EXCEPT:

   a. supporting order and change.
   b. maintaining efficient performance
   *c. maintaining a set culture p. 616
   d. balancing hard and soft aspects of organizational designs

11. In an adaptive culture,

a. the whole is more important that the part
b. equality is a primary value
c. change, risk-taking, and improvement are encouraged
*d. all of the above p. 614

12. Technology done NOT spur adaptive learning because:

*a. technology fosters the rigid boundaries of a hierarchical pyramid. p. 618
b. sharing information shares power
c. people have access to information whenever needed
d. creates a web-like system that allows for ideas

13. An after-action review (AAR) allows :

a. people to learn valuable lessons on how to do things better
b. leaders to review outcomes of activities and events
*c. both a & c
d. allows leaders to create an atmosphere of rigid control in a company p. 619

14. G. E. Salisbury switched to a horizontal structure to :

a. eliminate bottlenecks in the workflow
b. increate employee and customer satisfaction
c. increase production time
*d. both a & b p. 605

15. A skunkworks can be defined as:

*a. a separate, small, informal group where people can be creative. P. 617
b. an internal communication network that uses the Internet
c. a small company within a large company
d. a communication network

SHORT ANSWER

1. The________________________________is a cycle of action, feedback, and synthesis that all living organisms share.

   Answer: Adaptive learning cycle

2. A ________________________________is one in which everyone is engaged in identifying and solving problems.

   Answer: learning organization

3. A________________________________ is a team made up of employees with different skills who share or rotate jobs to produce an entire product or service.

   Answer: self-directed team

4. A part in a social system is called a ____________________________.

   Answer: role

5. ___________________________is sharing power with everyone in the organization allowing each person to act more freely to accomplish a job.

   Answer: Empowerment

6. ________________________________ are flexible organizations in which leaders incorporate structures and management processes that are appropriate to innovation and learning, as well as to the efficient implementation of ideas.

   Answer: ambidextrous organizations

7. ______________________________ is a change in behavior or performance as a result of experience.

Answer: Learning

8. ____________________________________is a disciplined procedure whereby leaders invest time to help people review their events and activities on a regular basis and continually learn from people.

Answer: After-action review (AAR)

9. A____ is a leader who has given up control in the traditional sense and uses vision, values, and relationships rather than position power to influence others.

Answer: learning leader

10. ______________________________refers to the efforts to systematically gather knowledge, make it widely available throughout the organization, and foster a culture of collaboration and learning.

Answer: Knowledge management

SHORT ESSAY QUESTIONS

1. Why is the efficient performance organization no longer effective?

   When business was stable, leaders emphasized stability. Routine, specialized jobs and standardized control procedures were effective in organizations based on mass production technology. Today, they are often not effective because knowledge and information are more mportant than production machinery. p. 600

2. Describe the horizontal structure.

   Horizontal Structure is created around work flows or processes rather than departmental functions, and processes are based on meeting customer needs. The vertical hierarchy is flattened. **Self- directed teams** are made up of employees with different skills who rotate jobs. They deal directly with customers, making changes, and improvements as they go along. Team members make decisions. p. 602.

3. What is the difference between the mechanistic and organic process?

   Bums and Stalker use the terms *mechanistic* and *organic* to explain organizational responses to the external environment. In a stable environment, tasks are mechanistic with rigid rules and a clear hierarchy. Knowledge and control are centralized. In rapidly changing environments, tasks are much looser and adaptive; the organization is called organic. Leaders push authority to lower level employees, encouraging them to solve problems. Teamwork is highly valued. p. 606

4. Describe the leader's dual challenge in a learning organization.

   Leaders face the challenge to maintain efficient performance and become a learning organization at the same time. This is achieved by balancing the hard and soft aspects of organizational design. Leaders can build mechanisms that are based on shared purpose, common assumptions, and trust. Leaders can support order and change, competition, and collaboration. To keep learning alive, leaders can build a shared vision, help people see the whole system, design horizontal structures, reduce boundaries, initiate change, and expand the opportunity for employees to shape the future. They can challenge assumptions that are no longer appropriate for today's world. p. 616.

5. Describe knowledge management.

Knowledge management refers to the efforts to systematically gather knowledge, make it widely available throughout the organization, and foster a culture of collaboration and learning. Technology can keep people all across the organization in touch. Embracing technology spurs adaptive learning because sharing information shares power. New technology enables leaders to share all information not just part of it, so that people have access to whatever they need whenever they need it. p.617

ESSAY QUESTIONS

1. How do learning organizations use after-action reviews (AAR)?

p. 618

2. Explain how technology plays a key role in a learning organization.

pp. 617-618

3. Describe the evolution of leadership.

pp. 595-597

CHAPTER SIXTEEN: LEADING CHANGE

TRUE-FALSE QUESTIONS

1. Technological changes, a globalized economy, and changing markets are creating more threats as well as more opportunities for organizational leaders. T, p. 635

2. When dealing with a major change effort, leaders can follow the eight-stage change process to provide a strong foundation for success. T, p. 637

3. The eight-stage change model includes empowering employees to act on the vision. T, p. 638

4. Employees resist change because it violates personal compacts. T, p. 644

5. Resistance to change cannot be overcome through communication. F, p. 646

6. Creativity is the generation of new ideas that result in improved efficiency and effectiveness of the organization. T, p. 651

7. Research indicates that most companies successfully harness creativity. F, p. 650

8. Downsizing is a positive change for the organization and does not affect morale and trust.. F, p. 648

9. Leaders can help smooth the downsizing process by involving employees communicating more, and helping the survivors thrive. T, p. 649

10. The desire to initiate creative activity is sometimes squelched early in life by classroom teachers who insist on strict adherence to the rules. T, p. 651

11. Verbal jujitsu is not considered a strategy for change. F, p. 640

12. For leaders, the less said about a pending layoff, the better. F, p. 649

13. Alignment refers to the generation of new ideas that result in improved efficiency. F, p. 651

14. It is impossible to know in advance what stimuli will lead any particular person to come up with a creative idea. T, p. 653

15. During the incubation stage of the creative process, a person allows the subconscious to mull things over. T, p. 656

MULTIPLE CHOICE QUESTIONS

1. Forces driving the need for organizational change include:

   a. globalization
   b. technological change
   c. increased competition
   *d. all of the above p. 634

2. To implement change successfully, leaders:

   a. establish a sense of urgency.
   b. form a guiding coalition
   c. form a venture team.
   *d. both a & b p. 637

3. Employees resist change because:

   a. it violates personal contracts.
   *b. it violates the reciprocal relationship between employees and the organization. p. 644
   c. they believe that change will add something of value to their job.
   d. they have full information about future events.

4. Methods to overcome resistance to change include:

   a. communication and training
   b. participation and training
   c. coercion
   *d. all of the above p. 646

5. Leaders can promote creativity by all EXCEPT:

   a. creating an environment that allows employees to experiment and dream.
   b. giving employees free time for activities not officially sanctioned.
   *c. keeping the communication flow within each department. p. 651
   d. consistently promoting the vision.

6. The innovative organization includes all EXCEPT:

*a. strict rules and regulations p. 651
b. alignment
c. within company communication
d. diverse stimuli.

7. In the incubation stage of the creative process model,

a. a person searches for background information.
*b. a person allows the subconscious to mull things over. p. 656
c. a person recognizes a problem that needs to be solved.
d. a person evaluates and implements the creative idea.

8. The negative impact of change does NOT includet:

a. downsizing and layoffs.
b. increased stress
*c. job enrichment p. 648
d. trust and morale issues

9. Strategies for change include all EXCEPT

*a. increasing the vertical structure p. 640
b. verbal jujitsu
c. strategic alliance building
d. disruptive self-expression

10. Techniques to assist leaders in easing the tensions of downsizing include all EXCEPT :

a. involving employees
b. communicating more, not less
c. providing assistance to displaced workers
*d. using email to communicate layoffs p. 649

11. People who passionately believe in a new idea and actively work to overcome obstacles and resistance are:

*a. idea champions p. 651
b. idea incubators
c. neutralizers
d. communicators

12. Innovation may come from:

a. diverse stimuli
b. unofficial activity
c. internal communication
*d. all of the above p. 653

13. Stages in the creative process do NOT include:

a. information gathering
b. insight
*c. brainstorming p. 656
d. incubation

14. Verbal jujitsu is a strategy for change which involves:

a. building strategic alliances
*b. turning an opponent's negative attitudes into opportunities
c. having the leader act in a way others will notice
d. creating and capitalizing on opportunities for motivating others p. 642

15. Some of the most difficult changes are related to:

a. redefining positions
b. redesigning departments
c. downsizing
*d. all of the above p. 648

SHORT ANSWER

1. A________________________________is the reciprocal obligations and commitments that define the relationship between and the organization.

   Answer: personal compact

2. ______________________ is intentionally reducing the size of a company's workforce.

   Answer: Downsizing

3. ________________________is the generation of new ideas that result in improved efficiency and effectiveness of the organization.

   Answer: Creativity

4. An_________________________________ is a safe harbor where ideas from employees throughout the organization can be developed without interference from company bureaucracy or politics.

   Answer: idea incubator

5. _______________________________ is internal entrepreneurial spirit that includes values of exploration, experimentation, and risk taking.

   Answer: Corporate entrepreneurship

6. _________________________________ are people who passionately believe in a new idea and actively work to overcome obstacles and resistance.

   Answer: Idea champions

7. The first stage in the creative process is ____________________________________

   Answer: recognition of problem/opportunity

8. The forces driving the need for major organizational change include ______________________

   Answer;(any of the following) globalization, technological change, increased competition, changing markets, e-business

9. Implementation techniques for overcoming resistance to change include______________________

   Answer: (any of the following) communication and training, participation and involvement, coercion

10. ____________________________________ is a strategy for everyday change that involves the leader acting in a way that others will notice and that reflects the values to be instilled in others.

    Answer: Disruptive self-expression

SHORT ESSAY QUESTIONS

1. What is the importance of Stage 6, leaders generate short-term wins, in the eight-stage model for change?

   Leaders plan for visible performance improvements, enable them to happen, and celebrate employees who were involved in the improvements. Major change takes time, and a transformation effort loses momentum if there are no short-term accomplishments that employees can recognize and celebrate. p. 656

2. Is creativity a mysterious talent of the select few?

   No. Each of us has the potential to be creative. Some of the myths about creativity suggest that it requires an artistic temperament, that is occurs in quantum leaps, that it can't be planned, that some people are not creative, and that creativity can't be taught. p. 651

3. Why would coercion be used to overcome resistance to change?

   As a last resort, leaders overcome resistance by threatening employees with job loss, promotion, firing or transfer. Coercion may be necessary in crisis situations when a rapid response is needed. Coercion may also be needed for administrative changes that flow from the top down, such as downsizing the workforce. However, as a general rule, this approach to change is not advisable because it leaves employees angry at leaders and the change may be sabotaged. p. 648

4. What is disruptive self-expression?

   This term refers to a strategy for change that is the least conspicuous change method. The leader acts in a way that others will notice and that reflects the values and behaviors that he wishes to instill followers. Disruptive self-expression unsettles others' expectations and routines. For example, the leader wears casual clothes when others wear suits. p. 640

5. What is meant by alignment ?

   For creative acts that benefit the organization to occur consistently, the interests and actions of everyone should be aligned with the organization's purpose, vision, and goals. Leaders make clear what the company stands for, consistently promote the vision, and clarify specific goals. In addition, they make a commitment of time, energy, and resources to activities that focus people on innovation. p. 651.

ESSAY QUESTIONS

1. Today's organizations must change or perish. Explain

   pp. 634-639

2. What is the negative impact of change ?

   pp. 648-650

3. Describe the innovative organization.

   pp. 651-656